SOVIET AND POST-SOVIE

Since the Soviet Union collapsed in 1991, questions of identity have dominated the culture not only of Russia, but of all the countries of the former Soviet bloc. This timely collection examines the ways in which cultural activities such as fiction, TV, cinema, architecture and exhibitions have addressed these questions, and also describes other cultural flashpoints, from attitudes to language to the use of passports. It discusses definitions of political and cultural nationalism, as well as the myths, institutions and practices that moulded and expressed national identity. From post-Soviet recollections of food shortages to the attempts by officials to control popular religion, it analyses a variety of unexpected and compelling topics to offer fresh insights into this key area of world culture. Illustrated with numerous photographs, it presents the results of recent research in an accessible and lively way.

MARK BASSIN is Research Professor in the History of Ideas, Centre for Baltic and East European Studies, Södertörn University, Stockholm.

CATRIONA KELLY is Professor of Russian at the University of Oxford and a Fellow of New College, Oxford.

SOVIET AND POST-SOVIET IDENTITIES

EDITED BY

MARK BASSIN

AND

CATRIONA KELLY

CAMBRIDGE
UNIVERSITY PRESS

CAMBRIDGE
UNIVERSITY PRESS

University Printing House, Cambridge CB2 8BS, United Kingdom

Cambridge University Press is part of the University of Cambridge.

It furthers the University's mission by disseminating knowledge in the pursuit of education, learning and research at the highest international levels of excellence.

www.cambridge.org
Information on this title: www.cambridge.org/9781316631973

© Cambridge University Press 2012

First published 2012
First paperback edition 2016

A catalogue record for this publication is available from the British Library

Library of Congress Cataloguing in Publication data
Soviet and post-Soviet identities / edited by Mark Bassin and Catriona Kelly.
p.   cm.
Includes bibliographical references and index.
ISBN 978-1-107-01117-5
1. Russia (Federation) – Civilization.   2. Popular culture – Russia (Federation)
3. Group identity – Russia (Federation)   4. Nationalism – Russia (Federation)
I. Bassin, Mark.   II. Kelly, Catriona.
DK32.S688 2012
947–dc23
2011040511

ISBN 978-1-107-01117-5 Hardback
ISBN 978-1-316-63197-3 Paperback

Contents

List of illustrations   *page* viii

List of tables   x

List of contributors   xi

Acknowledgements   xiii

PART I   THE STATUS OF NATIONAL IDENTITY   I

Introduction: national subjects
MARK BASSIN AND CATRIONA KELLY   3

1   The contradictions of identity: being Soviet and national
    in the USSR and after
    RONALD GRIGOR SUNY   17

2   Tales told by nationalists
    NANCY CONDEE   37

PART II   INSTITUTIONS OF NATIONAL IDENTITY   53

3   National identity through visions of the past: contemporary
    Russian cinema
    BIRGIT BEUMERS   55

4   Archaizing culture: the Museum of Ethnography
    DMITRY BARANOV   73

5   Rituals of identity: the Soviet passport
    ALBERT BAIBURIN   91

v

PART III   MYTHS OF NATIONAL IDENTITY   111

6 'If the war comes tomorrow': patriotic education in the Soviet
   and post-Soviet primary school
   VITALY BEZROGOV
                                                                          113

7 Conquering space: the cult of Yuri Gagarin
   ANDREW JENKS
                                                                          129

8 Nation-construction in post-Soviet Central Asia
   SERGEI ABASHIN
                                                                          150

PART IV   SPACES OF NATIONAL IDENTITY   169

9 Soviet and post-Soviet Moscow: literary reality
   or nightmare?
   DINA KHAPAEVA
                                                                          171

10 From the USSR to the Orient: national and ethnic symbols in
    the city text of Elista
    ELZA-BAIR GUCHINOVA
                                                                          191

11 The place(s) of Islam in Soviet and post-Soviet
    Russia
    VICTORIA ARNOLD
                                                                          212

PART V   LANGUAGES OF NATIONAL IDENTITY   235

12 Language culture and identity in post-Soviet Russia: the
    economies of *mat*
    MICHAEL GORHAM
                                                                          237

13 Policies and practices of language education in post-Soviet
    Central Asia: between ethnic identity and civic
    consciousness
    OLIVIER FERRANDO
                                                                          254

14 Surviving in the time of deficit: the narrative construction
    of a 'Soviet identity'
    ANNA KUSHKOVA
                                                                          278

PART VI   CREEDS OF NATIONAL IDENTITY   297

15 Competing orthodoxies: identity and religious belief in Soviet
    and post-Soviet Russia
    CATRIONA KELLY   299

16 'Popular Orthodoxy' and identity in Soviet and post-Soviet
    Russia: ideology, consumption and competition
    ALEXANDER PANCHENKO   321

17 Religious affiliation and the politics of post-Soviet identity: the
    case of Belarus
    GALINA MIAZHEVICH   341

Index   362

Illustrations

3.1 A scene from *Hipsters* (*Stiliagi*, Valerii Todorovskii, 2009).
(Courtesy of Red Arrow Production Company.) *page* 64

4.1 'Red Tea-House', from the exhibition 'Uzbeks in the Past
and the Present', 1935. (Courtesy of the Russian
Ethnographical Museum, St Petersburg.) 78

4.2 'Collective Farm Worker's House', from the exhibition
'Russians of the Central Black-Earth Region', 1936.
(Courtesy of the Russian Ethnographical Museum, St
Petersburg.) 78

7.1 One of the many thousands of leaflets dropped from
aeroplanes over Soviet cities after Gagarin's flight.
(Courtesy of the Unified Gagarin Memorial Museum
Complex, city of Gagarin.) 131

7.2 Gagarin as the son and brother so many had lost during the
war. (Courtesy of the Unified Gagarin Memorial Museum
Complex, city of Gagarin.) 138

7.3 Model of a proposed palace to be built on the site where
Gagarin landed just outside Saratov. (Courtesy of the
Gagarin Memorial Museum, Saratov, 2007. Photograph
by Andrew Jenks.) 145

9.1 Yuri Pimenov, *New Moscow* (1937). (Tretyakov Gallery,
Moscow.) 173

9.2 'Glory to You, Invincible Moscow', poster for the 800th
anniversary of the founding of Moscow, 1947. (Dina
Khapaeva.) 175

9.3 Contrasting faces of post-Soviet Moscow. (Photographed
in 2008 by Catriona Kelly.) 180

10.1 Golden Gates, Elista. (Photograph by Elza-Bair
Guchinova.) 195

10.2 The Golden Hermitage of Buddha Shakyamuni, Elista. (Photograph by Elza-Bair Guchinova.) 197

10.3 Great Patriotic War memorial ('To the Fallen Heroes'), Elista. (Photograph by Elza-Bair Guchinova.) 198

11.1 The Blue Cathedral Mosque in Kazan, under restoration. (Photographed in 2010 by Catriona Kelly.) 213

11.2 The Cathedral Mosque in Perm. (Photographed in 2009 by Victoria Arnold.) 220

11.3 The Kul Sharif Cathedral Mosque in Kazan, rebuilt in 2005. (Photographed in 2010 by Catriona Kelly.) 226

14.1 An instant meal of tinned braised meat and tinned peas. *Kniga o vkusnoi i zdorovoi pishche* [The book of tasty and nutritious food], Moscow, 1964. (Catriona Kelly.) 287

14.2 Tins of sprats and pike-perch. *Kniga o vkusnoi i zdorovoi pishche* [The book of tasty and nutritious food], Moscow, 1964. (Catriona Kelly.) 290

15.1 Still life from a closed church: an icon and smashed window-frame in the Smol'nyi Cathedral. (Photographed by the Leningrad State Restoration Workshops, 1924. Courtesy of the Institute of the History of Material Culture, Russian Academy of Sciences, St Petersburg.) 301

15.2 Church of the Trinity. (Photographed *c*.1937. Courtesy of the Central State Archive, St Petersburg.) 302

15.3 Church of St Anna of Kashino, St Petersburg. (Photographed by Catriona Kelly, 2008.) 310

Map 1 The Ferghana Valley 256

Tables

13.1 Ethnic distribution of the population and schoolchildren
and university students per tuition language in Uzbekistan,
Kyrgyzstan and Tajikistan   *page* 259
13.2 Schools and pupils by language of education in Uzbekistan   262
13.3 Schools and pupils of Spitamen district according to
language of education   267
13.4 Population ethnic distribution and school languages in
Andarak (Leylek district) and Uch-Korgon (Kadamzhai
district)   270
17.1 Interview sample   348

Contributors

MARK BASSIN is Research Professor of the History of Ideas at the Centre for Baltic and East European Studies, Södertörn University, Sweden. His co-edited book, *Space, Place and Power in Modern Russia: Essays in the New Spatial History*, came out in 2010.

CATRIONA KELLY is Professor of Russian at the University of Oxford and author of many works on Russian cultural history. She is currently working on *St Petersburg: Shadows of the Past*.

RONALD GRIGOR SUNY is the Charles Tilly Collegiate Professor of Social and Political History at the University of Michigan. His many works include *The Soviet Experiment: Russia, the USSR, and the Successor States* (1998/2011).

NANCY CONDEE is Professor at the Department of Slavic Languages and Literatures, University of Pittsburgh. Her publications on Russian culture include *The Imperial Trace: Recent Russian Cinema* (2009).

BIRGIT BEUMERS is Reader in Russian at the University of Bristol. Her many works on Russian cinema include *A History of Russian Cinema* (2009).

DMITRY BARANOV is Curator at the Russian Ethnographical Museum, St Petersburg, and works on the history of Russian ethnography and the Ethnographical Museum.

ALBERT BAIBURIN is Malkhaz Abdushelishvili Professor of Anthropology at the European University, St Petersburg. He is currently completing a study of the Soviet passport.

VITALY BEZROGOV is Senior Research Fellow at the Institute of Pedagogical Theory and History, Russian Academy of Education, Moscow. He specializes in the history of education and history of childhood.

ANDREW JENKS is Associate Professor of History at California State University Long Beach. He is the author of *Russia in a Box: Art and*

Identity in an Age of Revolution (2005). His biography of the first cosmonaut, Yuri Gagarin, is to be published in 2012.

SERGEI ABASHIN is Senior Research Fellow at the Institute of Ethnology and Anthropology, Russian Academy of Sciences, Moscow. He is the author of *Nationalisms in Central Asia: In Search of Identity* (2007, in Russian).

DINA KHAPAEVA is a researcher at the Helsinki Collegium for Advanced Studies. She has published widely on historical memory and in the field of cultural studies. The English translation of her latest book, *Nightmare: From Literary Experiments to Cultural Project*, will appear in 2012.

ELZA-BAIR GUCHINOVA is Fellow of the Institute of Ethnology and Anthropology, Russian Academy of Sciences, Moscow, and the author of many works, including *The Kalmyks* (2006, in English).

VICTORIA ARNOLD is a cultural geographer who is completing her DPhil degree, 'The Experience of Sacred Space in Post-Soviet Russia: A Geography of Orthodoxy and Islam in Perm' Krai', at Hertford College, Oxford.

MICHAEL GORHAM is Associate Professor of Russian Studies at the University of Florida and the author of *Speaking in Soviet Tongues: Language Culture and the Politics of Voice in Revolutionary Russia* (2003).

OLIVIER FERRANDO is a political sociologist at Sciences Po, Paris/CERI. He works on ethnic minorities in Central Asia (e.g. 'Manipulating the Census: Ethnic Minorities in the Nationalizing States of Central Asia').

ANNA KUSHKOVA holds a candidate's degree in anthropology at the European University, St Petersburg, and is currently a doctoral student in anthropology at the University of North Carolina (Chapel Hill). Her study of *salat Oliv'e* (Russian salad) appeared in the leading Moscow journal *New Literary Observer* in 2005.

ALEXANDER PANCHENKO is Senior Research Fellow at the Institute of Russian Literature, Russian Academy of Sciences. His books include *Khristovshchina and Skopchestvo: The Folklore and Traditional Culture of Russian Mystical Sects* (2002).

GALINA MIAZHEVICH is the Gorbachev Media Research Fellow at Christ Church, Oxford. She is working on a project examining the relationship between grass-roots xenophobia and state media in the Belarusian nation-building project.

Acknowledgements

We would like to thank the Arts and Humanities Research Council, the University of Oxford and New College, Oxford, for sponsoring the research on which a number of the contributions here draw, 'National Identity in Russia from 1961: Traditions and Deterritorialisation', and our collaborators on the project, in particular Andy Byford, Hilary Pilkington, Elena Omelchenko, Josephine von Zitzewitz, Victoria Donovan, Rowenna Baldwin, and Edmund Griffiths, for their lively and stimulating contributions to the debates. Helpful discussions also took place at two international conferences, 'National Identity in Eurasia I: Identities & Traditions', and 'National Identity in Eurasia II: Migrancy & Diaspora', held at New College and at Wolfson College, Oxford, in 2009, and attended by scholars from all over the former Soviet Union and Eastern Europe, as well as the US, Australia, Germany, France, the Netherlands and the UK. We are also grateful to our anonymous readers for their guidance, and to the staff at Cambridge University Press, above all Linda Bree and Maartje Scheltens, for their invaluable support during the editorial and production process.

Library of Congress transliteration is used throughout the text, except in the cases of individual words and names where an alternative transliteration has become established (glasnost, Yeltsin, Ilyumzhinov etc.).

PART I

The status of national identity

Introduction: national subjects

Mark Bassin and Catriona Kelly

THE CHALLENGE OF IDENTITY

In the twentieth century the people on the territories between Libau and Vladivostok (the two ports to extreme west and east of the Russian Empire)[1] underwent two sociopolitical experiments on a massive scale. The first of these, the creation of a highly integrative Soviet culture which succeeded the formation of the new state in 1917–22, has been abundantly documented.[2] The second – the disintegration of the Soviet state in 1991, accompanied by express marketization (the aptly named 'shock therapy' programme of Yegor Gaidar) – is still in the process of being understood.

What happened to Soviet culture in 1991? To what extent was the upheaval predictable? What did being 'Soviet' actually mean, and how far have Soviet attitudes and behaviour patterns survived the demise of the state in which they were created? What was the relationship between 'Soviet' identity and *natsional'nost'* (national identity/ethnic identity)? These are some of the questions that we set out to examine here, twenty years after the collapse. Of the many ambivalences and contradictions woven into the fabric of Soviet civilization, nothing was more ambivalent and contradictory than the question of national identity. On one hand, the orthodox Marxist position – at least as articulated by Marx himself – was clear enough. Both as real/existing political 'nation states' and as the subjective sources of affective group identity, nations were stigmatized as reactionary 'remnants' of capitalist civilization which would have no place in the socialist order of the future. This was a position which most Bolsheviks prior to 1917 endorsed, and they believed with Marx that bonds of class solidarity would quickly and definitively replace those of ethno-nationality.[3] By the 1920s, however, the realities of managing the still nationally conscious population of the former empire had necessitated a more conciliatory approach, such that the concept of 'socialist nations' was accepted by the political leadership of the Soviet Union.[4]

Indeed, from this point on, the recognition and endorsement of nationality became one of the most fundamental political and social principles of the Soviet system. Ethno-nationality was the primary criterion for the political-administrative organization of the USSR as a federal state, and from the 1930s all Soviet citizens were required to maintain a sort of dual identity that was inscribed in their internal passports: on one level as Soviet citizens but more especially as members of a specific nationality who belonged to a particular national territory. The imperative for the precise territorialization of nationality was an indication of its critical importance to the Soviet system.[5] Across the country, boundaries were drawn to delimit ethnic homelands that had never really existed as such, and in those cases where there simply was no historical association with a particular region – most obviously the USSR's Jewish population – one was assigned arbitrarily.[6]

Despite the apparent importance of nationality and national identity in the USSR, however, their status remained highly ambiguous. Official disregard for the integrity of the cultures and identities of the Soviet nationalities was succinctly expressed in the Stalinist dictum 'national in form, socialist in content'. National identities would be tolerated, that is to say, only to the extent that they could be shaped and controlled by the central authorities. Moreover, the legacy of Marxist hostility to the principle of national identification and the determination that class solidarities should override and destroy the tribal bonds of attachment to national groups remained powerful. Beginning in the post-Stalinist 1960s, this emerged explicitly in the form of a powerful state-sponsored discourse about an emergent supranational and 'meta-ethnic' *sovetskii narod* or Soviet people, whose development would inexorably subsume existing nationality structures and render them irrelevant. Nikita Khrushchev went so far as to contemplate doing away with the ethno-territorial principle in Soviet federalism altogether, and although subsequent leaders carefully stepped back from this extravagant radicalism, the doctrine of *sliianie* or the merging of all Soviet nationalities into one continued to receive official endorsement.[7]

This ambivalence regarding the status of nationality was reflected in Western research on the USSR. A special category of study was devoted to so-called 'nationalities' issues, but for the most part this research tended to focus on the policies of the Kremlin leadership (or its regional representatives) for the day-to-day management of these issues. This management was effected through a complex array of legal structures, programmes of social mobilization and exclusion, party-political machination and ideological campaigns, the evolution of which was carefully tracked across the decades. In a country as highly centralized and authoritarian as the USSR, such an approach was entirely logical, and this research told us a great deal about many aspects of social and political development in the country.[8] But it did not tell us very much at all about just how important genuine national affections and identities really were among the Soviet population. If only implicitly, official narratives about an emergent 'Soviet people' were given a significant degree of credence in the Western literature, which seemed to suggest that affective attachments to local nationality identities were indeed being increasingly eroded and thus did not represent a significant autonomous force.[9]

The turbulence of the *perestroika* years and the ensuing collapse of the Soviet Union served to transform quite completely our understanding of the significance of identity as a political, social and cultural factor. Three separate elements of this transformation were of particular importance. On the one hand, the surge of ethno-national affirmation across the Soviet population, which spread with remarkable speed and intensity after 1985, ended all doubt about the ubiquity and enduring vitality of national identification in the country. Experts may argue as to whether or not this sustained wave of national mobilization was in fact the primary cause for the collapse of the Soviet Union, but there can be no question that it figured among the principal factors fatally destabilizing the *ancien régime*.[10] The second element was the final recognition by the country's largest and most dominant national group, the ethnic Russians, that they themselves were in fact a subject 'nationality' like all the others. Many Russians now decided that they had not benefited but suffered from their traditional identification with the Soviet state *in toto*. Indeed, they felt that over many decades they had been the primary object of a deliberate programme of state-sponsored discrimination, as a consequence of which they had suffered a sort of special national depredation qualitatively worse than that experienced by other national groups. Not merely had the Soviet state disrespected and destroyed their unique national traditions and values, it had never even recognized that they had possessed such distinctions in the first place.[11] From this standpoint it was entirely natural that the Russians opted to align with the other national groups in 1991, first in rejecting the supranational structures of the USSR in favour of national consolidation, and then in joining the post-Soviet project of redefining the precise contours and content of their national identity. As the papers in this collection indicate, this latter project continues unabated down to the present day, with issues such as language use, appropriate symbolism, national origins (what in the late Soviet period came to be known as 'ethnogenesis') and the relationships of one particular nationality with others (up to the level of overt declarations of superiority) all the subject of vigorous debate.[12]

The final element in this transformation related to the adoption of new analytical perspectives on the nature of nationalism and national identity. The disintegration of the cold war order engendered an entirely novel appreciation of the essentially volatile and protean nature of nationalism and national identity. Early in the 1980s a robust scholarly literature on these subjects began to develop powerful concepts such as the 'construction of nationhood' and 'imagined communities', arguing that identities were not fixed and static structures but rather dynamic, malleable and contested.[13] It was now suggested that, although nationalist narratives generally envisioned their respective nation as primordial and unitary, all nations in fact exist in multiple versions, which differ a great deal from each other in content and appeal to different constituencies within the group as a whole. Moreover, such national ideas or identities were open to ongoing manipulation and rearrangement, which did not necessarily weaken their appeal but indeed could enhance it decisively. Identities, that is to say, were essentially contingent: they were shaped by specific historical-political contexts, and had their primary meaning and effects within them. It is important to note, moreover, that the inherent variability of national identification did not in any way diminish its significance. Indeed, rather the contrary was the case. It was precisely the fact that identities were flexible and open to shaping that rendered them maximally appealing and effective.

The extent to which these insights contributed to altering our understanding of Russia became very clear after 1991. One of the areas most dramatically affected was the historiography of the Soviet period. The collapse of the Soviet Union called for a fundamental re-examination of the manner in which the country had been established and reasons that it had developed in the way that it did. Fresh research into these questions was of course aided immeasurably by the opening of previously closed archival sources, but it was also directly stimulated by the heightened appreciation of the inherent importance of identity as a driving dynamic of social and political organization. As a result, the early history of the Soviet Union has already been rewritten in significant ways, with notions of constructed nationhood and invented communities now placed at the very centre of inquiry. The pervasive importance of ethno-national identity in the establishment and organization of the Soviet state has been stressed in a series of analyses which show how the particular accommodations the Soviet Union eventually made with this factor served to determine the fundamental character of the state and its policies.[14] Over the decades and in all corners of the realm, the Soviet state devoted immense resources and efforts to manipulating (and occasionally effectively creating) the manifold identities of the Soviet population. The particular fate of ethnic Russia in this process has also been examined, and we can trace how the palpable ambivalences underlying Russia's position, apparent already in the 1930s, were repeatedly renegotiated right down to the end of the regime.[15] As part of this, the more general and abstract question about Soviet conceptions of the nature of ethno-national identity has become a subject of study in its own right.[16]

In regard to post-Soviet studies, the centrality of identity is yet more pronounced. As had been the case after 1917, so the rearrangement of political power and social allegiances after 1991 served to destabilize established categories of identification and to initiate new phases of renegotiation and redefinition. In contrast to post-revolutionary Russia, however, our heightened appreciation of the nuances of identity discourses today ensures that they are recognized and analysed as such. In a sense the former Soviet Union can be treated as a veritable laboratory of identity construction and manipulation, within which identity operates in different ways and at various levels. Most fundamentally, each of the fifteen newly independent nation states is engaged in its own process of so-called 'nation-building', whereby an aspiring leadership seeks to provide – along with novel constitutional arrangements and legal structures – freshly crafted narratives of national belonging.[17] The post-Soviet experience demonstrates, moreover, that the practice of identity construction is not restricted to these sorts of coordinated exercises in the macro-management of official state ideologies. Along with this, identity discourses today are highly fragmented, and can be driven not from the top but from below, by social sub-groupings within a given national context who are seeking to establish and defend their position in the novel social and political circumstances. Russia provides an indicative example of this. While the problem of defining a post-Soviet Russian national identity obviously stands as a principal challenge in its own right,[18] identity narratives now also play an explicit part in the mobilization of particular constituencies within Russia, defined by affinities such as gender, youth, sexual orientation, religion or geographical region.[19] The role of identity is also emphasized in analyses of migration, the Russian diaspora, globalization, national politics and even Russian foreign policy.[20]

PLACING NATIONAL IDENTITY

Early studies of post-Soviet culture generally emphasized rupture with the Soviet past: the overturning of political symbols, the creation of new national myths to replace the transnational myths of 'Soviet' belonging, the triumph of 'savage capitalism' and the cult of individual success, the explosion of consumerism that greeted the end of the shortage economy.[21] Since 2000, on the other hand, more hesitancy about the extent of deep change has emerged. It has become common to talk of 'nostalgia' – the longing for the return of the past, with the implication that the post-Soviet population regrets the disappearance of the communist system and is unprepared to confront the legacy of political repression.[22]

However, 'nostalgia', with its overtones of sentimental passivity, offers an unduly constrictive model for the understanding of the relationship between post-Soviet culture and its Soviet predecessor. 'Nostalgia' can be simply a lifestyle choice, an exercise in 'retro-chic', not much different from the commercialization of the past in other cultures – the phenomenon of the Irish pub, for example.[23] Contributors to the many online forums about the Soviet past are quite capable of waxing lyrical about the vanished taste of 1970s ryebread, yet also expressing cynicism about the political assumptions of state socialism.

In any case, if we are to understand the relationship between Soviet and post-Soviet culture, we need to look not only at topics such as the arguments over Soviet history – important as these are – but to raise the question of how social institutions, attitudes and practices have weathered change. We need to combine the study of memory (the conscious relationship with the past) and the analysis of tradition – the habits, institutions, practices and linguistic formulas that characterized Soviet society. A broad disciplinary range is also advantageous: work by anthropologists and sociologists, in particular, can help us understand the deeper levels of national affiliation, half-articulated and only partly conscious elements in collective belonging. The failure of political nationalists to make real headway in the post-Soviet world has been much emphasized.[24] Yet 'banal nationalism' (to use Michael Billig's term)[25] is endemic in post-Soviet society. The interethnic conflicts that specialists in politics and international relations profess not to find at the level of relations between successor states are rife in villages and cities, and lay assumptions about national characteristics make their way into important areas of political policy too, above all the handling of migrants.[26] The sense that Russian national identity, under Soviet power, was simply a 'blank space' (often adduced as an explicatory device for the nature of Soviet intranational politics)[27] is hard to sustain when one, say, studies closely the material that was used for teaching in the Soviet schoolroom.[28]

Soviet and Post-Soviet Identities is intended as an introduction to these issues, and to the ramifications of political changes in attitudes and social practices. We share the insights of recent work on the anthropology of post-socialist states, with its emphasis on the fact that categories such as 'ideology' and 'the economy' do not simply 'exist', but are constantly reinterpreted and debated, becoming discursive fields.[29] To polarize 'ideology' and 'daily life' or 'myth' and 'reality' would be misleading, because everyday practices are often shaped by highly self-conscious interpretations of the past, and by relationships with political institutions. In this sense, the collection acts not just as a companion to, but also an extension of, the collection edited by Simon Franklin and Emma Widdis, *National Identity in Russian Culture: An Introduction* (2004). Where that collection concentrated on 'Russian' identity (as manifested in art forms such as music, in ideas about language and everyday life etc.), and was primarily concerned with intellectual culture, this collection addresses the vexed issue of a 'Soviet' identity from a perspective shaped by the recent interest in the history of Soviet everyday life.[30] Innovative also is the detailed consideration given to the *late* Soviet period, which is just starting to be the subject of scholarly enquiry.[31]

The articles do not attempt to provide a potted history of what happened to different republics under Soviet power ('identity in Lithuania', 'nationalism in Uzbekistan' etc.) – which would be to risk repetition and an over-abundance of local detail. Instead, our case studies examine issues, ideologies and institutions that had an impact across the different Soviet republics. The opening articles by Ronald Suny and Nancy Condee address questions that are of central interest in the study of nationalism worldwide, as well as in the Soviet Union and its successor states, focusing on the role played by emotions in national identification, and on the contradictory heritage of nationalism, as both a path to freedom and a path to the subjugation of others. This is followed by articles assessing key institutions that disseminated national ideas to the Soviet population. Birgit Beumers addresses cinema, the art form nominated by Lenin as 'the most important of all the arts' for its propaganda values, the purveyor of ideas about the national and local past to the Soviet population, and more recently of concepts of 'the Soviet self' of a retrospective and nostalgic kind. Dmitry Baranov's article discusses the ethnographical museum, a repository for national memory and a didactic space where visitors were taught about the meaning of the constituent Soviet 'peoples' and about the overarching Soviet nationality. Albert Baiburin turns to the Soviet passport, the fundamental identity document that conferred a sense of collective belonging ('citizen of the USSR'), and the everyday practices and threshold rituals which reinforced the sense of its importance.

From institutions we move to myths, the invention of national histories and traditions that granted legitimacy to individual Soviet 'peoples' (particularly the so-called 'titular nationalities' of the republics, that is, those that enjoyed the status of the main national groups within a given republic, whose language was taught in schools – in the non-Russian republics, alongside Russian – and whose culture was promoted as the main focus of local identity). Vitaly Bezrogov looks in detail at the stories about origins and belonging that were purveyed in Soviet textbooks and in the post-Soviet didactic materials that succeeded them. While there was a good deal of change in these narratives over the Soviet period, the late Soviet representation of national identity has proved tenacious in post-1991 Russia, despite official commitment to multiculturalism. The section also assesses the legends of heroic self-sacrifice and death-defying endeavour that signified 'Soviet' in its highest possible meaning. Andrew Jenks's article about Yuri Gagarin analyses the cult of a hero whose persona was markedly different from the heroes of the early Soviet or war epochs: Gagarin was presented as more approachable and less severe than his predecessors, yet paradoxically this innovative figure came to stand, in the post-Soviet era, for a highly positive understanding of 'Soviet identity'. The section is rounded off by Sergei Abashin's discussion of nation formation in post-Soviet Central Asia, and of the role played in this by heroic visions of the pre-Soviet past, now represented as having been suppressed in the Soviet era itself. At the same time, he emphasizes that national self-assertion has taken different forms in the various republics; in by no means all of them is Russia seen as the 'historical enemy'.

The next section of the book shifts from myths about nation to the spaces of national identity – the sites of memory and sentiment where people constructed a sense of belonging. All Soviet citizens looked to Moscow as the ultimate capital, the focus of awe and the model of an 'exemplary socialist city', as examined in Dina Khapaeva's article. Khapaeva looks at how the celebratory rhetoric of the Stalin years has now been replaced by a Gothic vision of the post-Soviet Russian capital as a threatening and violent place, less the home of the 'bright future' than of the despoiled present. Local regions had their own centres, with their own hierarchy of construction and urban space, and our next chapter is a case study of one of these – Elista, the capital of Kalmykia. Elza-Bair Guchinova shows how, in the 1960s, 1970s and 1980s, the city symbolized the renaissance of the formerly disgraced Kalmyks, yet was at the same time thoroughly standardized. Thus, space could be at once profoundly meaningful in a local sense and the token of a wider sense of Soviet belonging. In the post-Soviet era Elista has become the centre of a reinvented Kalmykian past that owes much to a 'globalized' version of Chinese culture. The kitsch 'orientalization' described here is both specific to place (the entire point being to make Elista a town like nowhere else) and typical of other post-Soviet cultures, where zoomorphic sculptures and 'traditional' decorative elements are also used to destandardize a common architectural and sculptural legacy.[32] Victoria Arnold's discussion demonstrates the transformation of post-Soviet space from a different point of view. She shows how plans for the reconstruction and construction of mosques in different parts of the Russian Federation have initiated at times agonized debate on the rights to existence of the 'sacred spaces' belonging to different religious cultures. In all three papers the understanding that the construction of urban space represents a version of Soviet and post-Soviet culture to which all observers assent is challenged.[33] Here, city monuments and the city imaginary are shown to be the arena of conflict and uncertainty.

Identity could also be expressed in language. As Michael Gorham's contribution shows, there were 'all-Soviet' views of linguistic propriety that united the denizens of historically diverse areas, and this has resulted in a widespread sense that the violation of propriety (for example, through the use of obscene language on the Internet) signifies cultural breakdown and anomie on a large scale. Olivier Ferrando's essay shows the resonance of language in real-life choices. While Soviet language policy acknowledged the importance of linguistic diversity, the social function of communication was seen in homogeneous terms. The Russian language was not just a lingua franca, but a model of effective language use; parents were determined their children should be functional in Russian, sometimes to the exclusion of so-called 'native tongues'. Yet language was not simply about the espousal of a given tongue. It also had imaginative resonance. As Anna Kushkova's chapter shows, Soviet citizens responded to deprivation – a nationwide phenomenon – not just by complaining about deprivation and finding practical ways to combat this, but by talking about their experiences, converting their difficulties into stories that identified them as 'Soviet citizens', but also as individuals.

However, Soviet solidarity had its stresses, and not every aspect of identity formation proved viable in the post-Soviet era. Decades of religious propaganda left many of the population agnostic, if not actively atheist. But the multinational 'Soviet empire' was also an empire of different creeds. Particularly – but not exclusively – in rural areas, religious beliefs and practices proved tenacious. The least 'Soviet' members of the population before 1991, religious believers took a leading role in cultural change thereafter. At the same time, some aspects of religious belief – for example, the emphasis on rituals – had a strongly 'post-Soviet' character (in the sense of bearing the obvious traces of the Soviet past). The contributions in the final section of the book address these paradoxes. Catriona Kelly shows how the official conception of a 'Soviet identity' was one inimical to religious belief, but the everyday relations between representatives of the state and representatives of the Russian Orthodox Church were more complicated and flexible than was suggested in ideology. At the same time, the very success of the Church's survival strategies in the Soviet era was to sap the authority of the hierarchy in the post-Soviet period, including, implicitly, among believers themselves.

Alexander Panchenko is concerned with how believers' attachment to particular holy sites became politicized in the context of the planned society. Efforts to stigmatize the cult of sacred springs as representative of backwardness, ignorance and superstition were pervasive, but also unsuccessful (in part because there was, by 1917, already a long history of attempted control of such cults); yet the history of popular belief shows that it is subject to historical transformation too. Galina Miazhevich's article, on the other hand, is concerned not with efforts on the part of Soviet administrators or the Orthodox hierarchy to press for religious hegemony, but with the on-the-ground diversity of religious belief. The case of Belarus – a multi-faith population like many others in 'post/Soviet space' – is used to illustrate how believers' sense of affinity has not observed simplistic confessional lines, and how confession and ethnic identity do not easily overlap.

As several of the contributors to this volume emphasize, the roles of memory in post-Soviet culture are more diverse than the 'nostalgia' paradigm would allow. Painful memory may be censored and repressed (as Dina Khapaeva argues here); recollections of the Soviet past can combine with glorification of the pre-Soviet past (a phenomenon that Sergei Abashin discusses with reference to Central Asia) – a tradition that itself draws on the Soviet heritage of representing history in a straightforwardly moralistic way. And memories of the Soviet past can be reshaped to highlight motifs that are relevant to the present – thus, Anna Kushkova's informants, discussing their strategies for obtaining food in the days of deficit, disparage and downplay the role of support networks and emphasize their own resourcefulness, since portraying community participation has the distasteful resonance of official Soviet collectivism. Always, our contributors underline that the relationship with the past was not one of unquestioning replication, or helpless 'cultural inertia', but a dynamic process in which Soviet and post-Soviet human subjects constantly reassessed their heritage and its significance as a model for the present, and a guide to everyday behaviour.

The different 'snapshots' of Soviet and post-Soviet reality that are offered reflect some of the multiple processes of identity formation in this vast landmass. They move away from the traditional image of the (effectively or imperfectly) regimented and brainwashed subject of the communist utopia, *homo sovieticus*, to a subtler view of ordinary Soviet citizens as engaged in multiple beliefs, practices and institutions that they themselves helped to shape, to understand and to articulate.

NOTES

1. 'Mezhdu Libavoi i Vladivostokom' was also a proverbial phrase; cf. 'From Land's End to John o'Groats' in Britain.
2. See e.g. S. Kotkin, *Magnetic Mountain: Stalinism As Civilization* (Berkeley, CA, 1995); S. Fitzpatrick, *Everyday Stalinism* (New York, 1999); S. Fitzpatrick, *Tear Off the Masks: Identity and Imposture in Twentieth-Century Russia* (Princeton, NJ, 2005); J. Hellbeck, *Revolution on My Mind: Writing a Diary under Stalin* (Cambridge, MA, 2006); J. Sahadeo and R. D. Zanca, *Everyday Life in Central Asia: Past and Present* (Bloomington, IN, 2007); E. Dobrenko, *Political Economy of Socialist Realism* (New Haven, CT, 2007). Substantive discussion of Soviet identity is also available in journals (see e.g. *Kritika: Explorations in Russian and Eurasian History*, www.slavica.com/journals/kritika/kritika.html) and in works by Russian and post-Soviet authors, for example N. B. Lebina, Il'ya Utekhin, Konstantin Bogdanov, Gasan Guseinov, Natalia Kozlova, Irina Sandomirskaia and others.
3. W. Connor, *The National Question in Marxist-Leninist Theory and Strategy* (Princeton, NJ, 1984); E. Nimni, *Marxism and Nationalism: Theoretical Origins of a Political Crisis* (London, 1994).
4. J. Smith, *The Bolsheviks and the Nationality Question, 1917–1923* (Basingstoke, 1999).
5. R. Kaiser, *The Geography of Nationalism in Russia and the USSR* (Princeton, NJ, 1994).
6. In the Jewish Autonomous Region, founded in 1934, the population of the titular nationality never exceeded the 16.2% of the 1939 census, and had dropped to 8.8% in 1959.
7. Iu. Iu. Veingol'd, *Sovetskii narod: novaia istoricheskaia obshchnost' liudei. Sotsiologicheskii ocherk* (Frunze, 1973); M. P. Kim, *Sovetskii narod: novaia istoricheskaia obshchnost' liudei* (Moscow, 1975); S. T. Kaltakhchian, 'Sovetskii narod', in *Bol'shaia sovetskaia entsiklopediia* (Moscow, 1976), 25.
8. For an excellent example of this approach, see G. Simon, *Nationalism and Policy toward the Nationalities in the Soviet Union: From Totalitarian Dictatorship to Post-Stalinist Society*, trans. Karen Forster and Oswald Forster (Boulder, CO, 1991).
9. See e.g. A. Inkeles and R. Bauer, *The Soviet Citizen: Daily Life in Soviet Society* (Cambridge, MA, 1959); H. Alt and E. Alt, *The New Soviet Man: His*

Upbringing and Character Development (New York, 1964); M. Geller, *Cogs in the Soviet Wheel: The Formation of Soviet Man* (London, 1988); L. Attwood, *The New Soviet Man and Woman: Sex Role Socialization in the USSR* (Basingstoke, 1990). Where national content was recognized, it was usually limited to 'Russian' (see e.g. R. Hingley, *The Russian Mind* (London, 1977), which also deals with the Soviet period).

10. For opposing views, see e.g. R. Suny, *The Revenge of the Past: Nationalism, Revolution, and the Collapse of the Soviet Union* (Stanford, CA, 1993); S. Kotkin, *Armageddon Averted* (Oxford, 2001).

11. For a sympathetic discussion of this situation by a Western historian, see G. Hosking, *Rulers and Victims: The Russians in the Soviet Union* (Cambridge, MA, 2006).

12. We are not primarily concerned here with national extremism, whether practised by the institutions of state or as a grass-roots phenomenon. For recent discussions of this topic, see e.g. http://groups.yahoo.com/group/russian_nationalism/; www.sova-center.ru/.

13. Three of the most important and influential works on this subject were published in the same year, 1983. B. Anderson, *Imagined Communities: Reflections on the Origins and Spread of Nationalism* (London, 1983); E. Gellner, *Nations and Nationalism* (Oxford, 1983); E. Hobsbawm and T. Ranger, eds., *The Invention of Tradition* (Cambridge, 1983).

14. As well as Smith, *Bolsheviks and the Nationality Question*, see T. Martin, *The Affirmative Action Empire: Nations and Nationalism in the Soviet Union, 1923–1939* (Ithaca, NY, 2001); F. Hirsch, *Empire of Nations: Ethnographic Knowledge and the Making of the Soviet Union* (Ithaca, NY, 2004); R. G. Suny and T. Martin, eds., *A State of Nations: Empire and Nation-Making in the Age of Lenin and Stalin* (Oxford, 2001); H. Carrère d'Encausse, *The Great Challenge: Nationalities and the Bolshevik State, 1917–1930* (New York, 1992).

15. D. Brandenberger, *National Bolshevism: Stalinist Mass Culture and the Formation of Modern Russian Identity, 1931–1956* (Cambridge, MA, 2002); Y. M. Brudny, *Reinventing Russia: Russian Nationalism and the Soviet State, 1953–1991* (Cambridge, MA, 1998); V. Tolz, *Russia: Inventing the Nation* (London, 2001).

16. Hirsch, *Empire of Nations*; A. Weiner, 'Nature, Nurture, and Memory in a Socialist Utopia: Delineating the Soviet Socio-Ethnic Body in the Age of Socialism', *American Historical Review* 104:4 (1999), 1114–55. Also see the debate in *Slavic Review*: E. D. Weitz, 'Racial Politics without the Concept of Race: Reevaluating Soviet Ethnic and National Purges', *Slavic Review* 61:1 (2002), 1–29; A. Weiner, 'Nothing but Certainty', *Slavic Review* 61:1 (2002), 44–53; F. Hirsch, 'Race without the Practice of Racial Politics', *Slavic Review* 61:1 (2002), 30–43.

17. G. Smith et al., eds., *Nation-Building in the Post-Soviet Borderlands: The Politics of National Identities* (Cambridge, 1999); P. Kolstø, ed., *Nation-Building and Ethnic Integration in Post-Soviet Societies* (Boulder, CO, 1999); P. Kolstø, ed., *National Integration and Violent Conflict in Post-Soviet Societies* (Lanham, MD,

2002); P. Kolstø and H. Blakkisrud, eds., *Nation-Building and Common Values in Russia* (Lanham, MD, 2004). In addition, there are large numbers of studies devoted to specific states.

18. Tolz, *Russia*; V. Tolz, 'Forging the Nation: National Identity and Nation Building in Post-Communist Russia', *Europe-Asia Studies* 50:6 (1996), 993–1022; P. J. Piveronus, *Reinventing Russia: The Formation of a Post-Soviet Identity* (Lanham, MD, 2009); E. W. Clowes, *Russia on the Edge: Imagined Geographies and Post-Soviet Identity* (Ithaca, NY, 2011); R. Marsh, *Literature, History and Identity in Post-Soviet Russia* (Bern, 2007).

19. H. Pilkington, ed., *Gender, Generation and Identity in Contemporary Russia* (London, 1996); B. J. Baer, *Other Russias: Homosexuality and the Crisis of Post-Soviet Identity* (Basingstoke, 2008); J. Johnson, M. Stepaniants and B. Forest, eds., *Religion and Identity in Modern Russia: The Revival of Orthodoxy and Islam* (Aldershot, 2005); I. Gololobov, *Regional Ideologies in Russia: In Search of a Post-Soviet Identity* (Saarbrücken, 2008); A. White, *Small-Town Russia: Postcommunist Livelihoods and Identities* (London, 2004).

20. H. Pilkington, ed., *Migration, Displacement and Identity in Post-Soviet Russia* (London, 1997); G. Hønneland, *Borderland Russians: Identity, Narrative, and International Relations* (Basingstoke, 2010); R. Fawn, ed., *Ideology and National Identity in Post-Communist Foreign Policies* (London, 2003); D. Blum, ed., *Russia and Globalization: Identity, Security and Society in an Era of Change* (Baltimore, MD, 2008); P. Casula and J. Perovic, eds., *Identities and Politics during the Putin Presidency: The Foundations of Russia's Stability* (Stuttgart, 2009); A. P Tsygankov, *Pathways after Empire: National Identity and Foreign Economic Policy in the Post-Soviet World* (Lanham, MD, 2002).

21. See e.g. N. Condee, ed., *Soviet Hieroglyphics* (Bloomington, IN, 1995); H. Goscilo and B. Holmgren, eds., *Russia–Women–Culture* (Bloomington, IN, 1996); C. Kelly and D. Shepherd, eds., *An Introduction to Russian Cultural Studies* (Oxford, 1998); A. M. Barker, ed., *Consuming Russia: Popular Culture, Sex, and Society since Gorbachev* (Durham, NC, 1999); C. Humphrey, *The Unmaking of the Soviet Union* (Ithaca, NY, 2002).

22. See e.g. S. Boym, *The Future of Nostalgia* (New York, 2001); M. Nadkarni and O. Shevchenko, 'The Politics of Nostalgia: A Case for Comparative Analysis of Post-Socialist Practices', *Ab Imperio* issue 2 (2004), http://abimperio.net/cgi-bin/aishow.pl?idlang=1&state=shown&idnumb=37; S. Oushakine, *The Patriotism of Despair: Nation, War, and Loss in Russia* (Ithaca, NY, 2009). There is a substantial literature on political nostalgia in Russian as well, by Dina Khapaeva, Nikolai Koposov, Il'ia Kalinin and others.

23. 'Retro-chic' is the expression used by R. Samuels, *Theatres of Memory* (London, 1994), 51–137, to name the fashion for clothing, furnishings etc. in historic styles that became widespread in Britain during the 1970s. For a humorously ironic discussion of the Irish pub, see R. Foster, *Luck and the Irish: A Brief History of Change* (London, 2007). Boym describes this as 'commercial nostalgia', a disparaging term set against 'reflective nostalgia'; however, the latter, in her representation, is aimed at the pre-Soviet past, begging the question of

whether nostalgia aimed at the Soviet past can be reflective (cf. S. Oushakine, '"We're Nostalgic, But We're Not Crazy": Retrofitting the Past in Post-Soviet Russia', *Russian Review* 66:3, 2007, 451–82).

24. See e.g. Brudny, *Reinventing Russia*; R. Brubaker, *Nationalism Reframed: Nationhood and the National Question in the New Europe* (Cambridge, 1996); G. Sasse, *The Crimea Question: Identity, Transition, and Conflict* (Cambridge, MA, 2007).

25. M. Billig, *Banal Nationalism* (London, 1995).

26. See e.g. A. Regamey, 'Representations of Migrants and the Politics of Migration in Russia', *Forum for Anthropology and Culture* 6 (2011), http://anthropologie.kunstkamera.ru; 'Forum 8: Nationalism and Xenophobia As Research Topics', *Forum for Anthropology and Culture* 5 (2009), ibid.; M. Sokolov, 'The End of Russian Radical Nationalism?', ibid.

27. For the 'blank space' argument, see e.g. Y. Slezkine, 'The USSR as a Communal Apartment, or, How a Socialist State Promoted Ethnic Particularism' *Slavic Review* 53:2 (1994), 414–52.

28. See particularly Vitaly Bezrogov's discussion here.

29. Humphrey, *Unmaking*; D. Rogers, *The Old Faith and the Russian Land: A Historical Ethnography of Ethics in the Urals* (Ithaca, NY, 2009), 11–15.

30. Cf. Sahadeo and Zanca, *Everyday Life*, or C. Kiaer and E. Naiman, eds., *Everyday Life in Early Soviet Russia: Taking the Revolution Inside* (Bloomington, IN, 2006).

31. e.g. the collections edited by P. Jones, *The Dilemmas of Destalinization: Negotiating Cultural and Social Change* (Basingstoke, 2006); L. Attwood, M. Ilic and S. Reid, eds., *Women in the Khrushchev Era* (Basingstoke, 2004); J. Fürst, P. Jones and S. Morrissey, eds., *The Relaunch of the Soviet Project*, special issue of *Slavonic and East European Review* 86:2 (2008); M. Ilic and J. Smith, eds., *Soviet State and Society under Nikita Khrushchev* (London, 2009); D. Kozlov and E. Gilburd, eds., *The Thaw: Soviet Society and Culture during the 1950s and 1960s* (in press).

32. A similar process is in train, for example, in Almaty: see A. Sabitov, 'Kitsch in the Contemporary Urban Environment of Kazakhstan', in *National Identity in Russia from 1961: Newsletter* 4 (December 2009), 5–8, www.mod-langs.ox.ac.uk/russian/nationalism/newsletter.htm.

33. In the 1990s the reconstruction of urban space in socialist cities tended to be perceived as evidence for wide-ranging changes in political perception: see e.g. K. Verdery, *The Political Lives of Dead Bodies: Reburial and Postsocialist Change* (New York, 1999). For recent discussions of urban space, see M. Bassin, C. Ely and M. K. Stockdale, eds., *Space, Place, and Power in Modern Russia* (DeKalb, IL, 2010).

CHAPTER I

The contradictions of identity: being Soviet and national in the USSR and after

Ronald Grigor Suny

Prejudice and public opinion have often worked to shape popular attitudes, and even those of scholars, toward Russia and the Soviet Union,
easily distinguishing the diverse experience of that part of the world from
life in the West. One form of this supposed Russian exceptionalism is to
see the ethnic or national as natural and self-generated and the socialist or
Soviet to be an artificial imposition. But as with many commonsensical
constructions, the real situation was (and is) far more complicated.
However severe the ruptures of Russia's historical evolution, one of the
constants has been, at least in the last two hundred years, a tension
between empire and the national. Both the tsarist and the Soviet regimes
attempted to negotiate the difficult path between the imperatives of a great
and diverse state, on the one hand, and the more particular concerns of
ethnic and religious communities themselves adopting and adapting the
language and self-identification as nations. Rather than the usual Western
image of the ethnic or ethno-religious individual confronting the
Russifying Soviet regime – in one reading, *homo islamicus* versus *homo
sovieticus* – we can see a specifically Soviet subjectivity that managed both
to value one's ethnic culture and imbibe and even treasure the values and
norms of Soviet life. While the more familiar pattern of empire versus
nation is certainly evident, more surprising is the way in which the two
managed to live together, borrow from each other, and create hybrid and
shared political concepts. This intricate interweaving of loyalties and
identities, shifting over time, is the subject of this chapter.

AFFECTIVE COMMUNITIES

I begin with the proposition that nations are as much 'affective communities' as they are 'imagined communities', and that national identification

is not only with people with whom one has common interests but with whom one feels a special bond, a tie of some kind of 'kinship' and affection distinct from the feelings one has toward those of other nations. Beyond the actual or fictive kinship of ethnic groups, nations are grounded in imaginative relations of various kinds – common origins and ancestors, common history and destiny, blood or culture, belief in the spiritual unity of a people or commitment to shared political principles that constitute a powerful cultural synthesis. The signs of commonality are also varied, selective, shifting and often contested: language, religion, somatic features, foods, fashions, patterns of child raising, appropriate expression of emotion and so on.

Among the most suggestive insights of Benedict Anderson's seminal work *Imagined Communities* is the author's warning in the chapter 'Patriotism and Racism' that 'it is doubtful whether either social change or transformed consciousnesses, in themselves, do much to explain the *attachment* that peoples feel for the inventions of their imaginations – or, to revive a question raised at the beginning of this text – why people are ready to die for these inventions'.[1] He goes on to suggest that 'progressive, cosmopolitan intellectuals' (here he appears to mean primarily European Marxists) should move beyond insisting 'on the near-pathological character of nationalism, its roots in fear and hatred of the Other, and its affinities with racism' and remember 'that nations inspire love, and often profoundly self-sacrificing love'.[2] Positioned at the opposite end of political science from those who attempt to reduce the nation to rational calculation, Anderson insists on its affective connections. Political love, he notes, is expressed 'in the vocabulary of kinship (motherland, *Vaterland, patria*) or that of home (*heimat* or *tanah air* [earth and water, the phrase for the Indonesians' native archipelago])'.[3] And it gains its power from its relation to nature, inevitability, being unchosen and disinterested. '[T]he family has traditionally been conceived as the domain of disinterested love and solidarity,' and similarly 'for most ordinary people of whatever class the whole point of the nation is that it is interestless. Just for that reason, it can ask for sacrifices'.[4] As a leading Republican politician in the United States John McCain might have put it (in an exercise of partisan political manoeuvring): 'country above party, personal interests and politics'. Here the old warrior taps into the deep sense of what permits the ultimate sacrifice, dying for one's country, which Anderson contends 'comes only with an idea of purity, through fatality', rather than through self- or material interest.[5]

THINKING ABOUT THE NATION

Nations are quintessentially modern forms of political communities that are made up of people who imagine that by virtue of some shared character- istics – be it language, religion, common origins or historical experience – they have the right to self-determination, a right to rule themselves and to possess their purported 'national' homeland. Although groups such as nations have existed throughout history, the nation form in its full panoply became the hegemonic form of communal political identification only with the elaboration of a 'discourse of the nation' in the early modern period (roughly from the seventeenth to the early nineteenth centuries) in which the appropriate legitimization of political authority stemmed from its con- sent by a 'people' constituted as a 'nation'. Here culture, very often ethnic culture but at times civic-political culture, became the basis for political rights and legitimacy of the state authority.

It was precisely in what we might call 'the moment of the nation', the late eighteenth-century revolutions and the early nineteenth-century social upheavals, at the very time of the Romantic revolt against Enlightenment rationalism, that the discourse of the nation emerged, and primordialized national identities were fixed on to specific peoples. At roughly the same time a notion of nation as a community of people with common culture, aspirations and political endowments emerged as a central subject in historical writing. By the early nineteenth century statesmen and intellec- tuals across Europe were learning to 'speak national'. The concept of nation became common in political language, even as its meaning remained varied, unstable and highly contested.

I focus on this moment of origin in the late eighteenth and early nine- teenth centuries because it appears to me to be a conjuncture greatly overdetermined by both a revived interest in emotions and by the actual experience by individuals and groups of people of a cascade of related emotions. Scholars have long noted the intimate connection between emotion and nineteenth-century nationalism, born as it was in the age of romanticism. For Herder, in many ways the author of nationalism, feeling (*Gefühl*) was the means to thought and understanding. Through language, feeling apprehended reality with an immediacy that the senses could not achieve. Humans and the world were united in feeling, which then could be expressed through words, but every signification initially involved an emo- tional attitude toward the world. Poetry and music were not simply beau- tiful representations of the world but, for Herder, a means to understanding it through a 'logic of emotion'. 'A poet', he said, 'is the creator of the nation around him: he gives them a world to see and has their souls in his hand to lead them to that world.'[6]

Even as historians and theorists turned their attention to the sociological settings that made the nation and nationalism possible – the breakdown of older cultural systems and identities, greater social mobility and social communication, the development of print capitalism, the practices of absolutist bureaucracies, war and popular mobilization – we find the emotions of love, pride, fear and resentment consistently embedded in their narratives, often without acknowledgement.[7] Originating with a structural transformation that shook traditional identities, the move to the national may have been highly contingent, but once available the nation form became the vehicle to overcome the early modern and modern psychosocial crisis of identity.

Since the mid-nineteenth century, national identity construction has most powerfully been about a single, unitary identity, not a multiplicity of self-understandings, embedded in a long history and attached to a specific territory. The power of that identity lay within the broad transnational discourse of the nation, which justified both territorial possession and statehood to those with prior and exclusive claims, based on language, culture or race. As a new form of political legitimation, the nation brought culture together with a strong political claim to self-rule that ultimately found its sanction in a story about the past. The practice of finding deep ancestors and long genealogies certainly goes back to earlier forms of political legitimation, at least to the Bible if not even earlier, in the story of kings, who as sons had gained power by virtue of the connection to fathers.

National identity, then, begins with empathetic attachments to those included within the group, and distance and difference from those without. Shared narratives link the members of the nation together in a constructed community that – in the discourse of the nation – legitimizes the people's right to rule themselves through their chosen leaders who are like themselves. Threats to the group are threats to the individuals identified with that group; anxieties, resentments, fears and hatreds may be attached to that collective identity and make up the emotional disposition of the group out of which more specific emotional responses emerge when the requisite stimuli are experienced. From these dispositions and emotions predictable action tendencies occur. The result under certain circumstances can be conflict or violence. These affective communities with their attendant empowerment of the people and eventual commitment to democratic politics, their evident success in mobilizing popular armies for combat, proved by the early twentieth century to be the most serious threat to the then ubiquitous forms of polity, dynastic monarchies and empires.

Empire is a polity based on conquest, difference between the ruling institution and its subjects, and the subordination of periphery to the imperial centre. Justified by the power of the ruler and sanctioned by claims to divine favour and dynastic legacy, empire demands obedience and loyalty, and though it may desire love of the sovereign, it does not require it. Unlike the affective communities we call 'nations', empires have a quite different emotional valence. They are not primarily based on shared emotions of affection and kinship (*fraternité*) or horizontal equivalency (*égalité*). Rather, historically fear and awe of the ruling prince were integral to the arsenal of the political authorities. Muscovite rulers saw themselves in a paternal role, protecting their subjects, Russian and non-Russians alike, which presumed an affective tie between ruler and ruled. The tsar may have been *batiushka* (little father) to his people, but the relations of fathers to children, particularly stern fathers, differ greatly from idealized relations of brothers and sisters.[8] As Richard Wortman has demonstrated in his study of tsarist rituals, distance of power from people, rather than affinity and family connection, marked empire and differentiated it from the nation state of future centuries.[9] Even the models of rulership were foreign – Byzantium and the Mongol khans – and foreignness conveyed superiority. When that sense of paternalism and protection was lost in 1905, with no strong bond of nation in place, the empire became ever more vulnerable to the claims of radicals with rival notions of how Russia should be ruled.

The history of tsarism is of an empire that at times engaged in nation-making, but its nationalizing state practices were always in tension with the structures and discourses of empire. Tsarism never created a nation – that is, an *affective community* – within the whole empire or even a sense of nation among the core Russian population, even though it managed to engender great loyalty from important parts of the country's elite. The imperial tended to thwart if not subvert the all-inclusive national, just as the national worked to erode the stability and legitimacy of the hierarchical and differentiated imperial state, based as it was on embedded inequities, naturalized distinctions and the sense that the superior had the right to rule over the inferior without their consent. As Alexander Morrison has shown, Russians failed 'to develop a genuine form of Imperial citizenship'.[10] In contrast to overseas empires, however, the rigid hierarchies of *sosloviia* (social estates)[11] in Russia, the differential rights, obligations and privileges, and the far more repressive, even draconian, rule of the peripheries (consider the *karatel'nye ekspeditsii*, 'punitive expeditions', of 1905–7) – not to mention the vastness of the empire's territory, lack of density of means of communication and transportation, underdeveloped educational system and low level of literacy – all combined to make the coherence and solidarity that ideally mark nations acutely difficult for the Russians to achieve.[12] While Muscovy and imperial Russia were successful in integrating the core regions of the empire, often referred to as the *vnutrennie guberniia* (internal provinces), into a single nationality, diverse administrative practices, as well as the compactness of the local ethnicities and the effects of settlement policies, maintained and intensified differences between the Russian core and the non-Russian peripheries. In its last years the dynasty appeared increasingly to be incompetent and even treacherous. As Russians suffered defeats and colossal losses in the First World War, the fragile aura of legitimacy was stripped from the emperor and his wife, who were widely regarded as distant from, even foreign to, Russia. What the dynasty in the distant past had imagined was empowering – their difference from the people – now became a fatal liability. Elite patriotism, frustrated non-Russian nationalisms and peasant weariness at intolerable sacrifices for a cause with which they did not identify combined lethally to undermine the monarchy. The principles of empire, of legalized differentiation and inequality, were incompatible with modern ideas of democratic representation and egalitarian citizenship that gripped much of the intelligentsia and urban society. When the monarchy failed the test of war, its last sources of popular affection and legitimacy fell away.

THE SOVIET STORY

For much of the reading public and the Russian historical profession as well, the story of the collapse of the Soviet Union appears to be parallel to the tsarist story – the failure of empire before the inevitable onslaught of nationalism, the fragility of the transnational ties of Soviet identity overwhelmed by the powerful affective bonds of ethno-nationalism that the Soviets themselves had done so much over seventy years to promote, or, in a more common narrative, to undermine. My own contention is that we have tended to underestimate the connective elements, political, cultural and *affective*, that made the USSR a rather cohesive state until its very last years. While individual cases vary greatly, Soviet citizens often experienced identification both with the ethnicity or nation to which they were officially ascribed and, in different ways, with the Soviet Union as motherland or fatherland, and acceptance of the values and norms of Soviet life. The intensity of identification with – or in the case of some, such as Estonians and many Georgians, hostility to – the USSR and the political system varied greatly, but evidence for such a relatively positive affective relationship can be drawn from the lingering nostalgia of many for the old ways and regret at the Union's demise. The ethno-nation may have been family, and the Soviet slogan *druzhba narodov* (friendship of the peoples) may have been official sentimentality and wishful thinking, but millions of people felt attachment to the Soviet Union, ready to defend it, die and kill for it, and embrace it as *Rodina* (Motherland). The Soviet authorities and the creative intelligentsia successfully forged for several generations an emotional connection first to the Revolution and Civil War, the project of creating a new world, then to Lenin and Stalin as personifications of the Soviet project, later to the victory over fascism, a civic culture that connected persons with broad spaces and great power status. Later many would feel deceived that their faith was based on misrepresentation and ignorance of what was happening, what they didn't know or avoided finding out about. This ambiguity is expressed in Yevtushenko's post-Soviet poem:

> Farewell, our red flag.
> You were for us brother and foe.
> You were a pal in the trenches,
> the hope of all Europe,
> but the red veil
> that shielded the Gulag
> and so many unfortunates
> in ragged prison overalls.
>
> Farewell, our red flag.
> You rest, lie down,
> but let's remember all
> who do not rise from the grave.
> You led the deceived
> to the slaughterhouse,
> to the grinding mill,
> but they will remember you –
> you were yourself deceived.[13]

One of the many ironies of Soviet history is that a state that in many ways manifested the qualities of empire in fact over time created something like a multinational nation state with the aid of its internationalist ideology, its self-proclaimed historical project of building socialism and its promotion of nationality among the non-Russian peoples. As in any empire, sovereignty belonged only to the centre, the Communist elite, the metropole of the Soviet empire. The periphery, both Russian and non-Russian, was ruled in the name of its own *mission civilisatrice* (civilizing mission) that like the policies of the French and Portuguese overseas empires would elevate them into a higher civilization. Yet, more ambitiously, it sought to create a shared culture, in this case Soviet, in which the peoples of the USSR would draw closer together (consider the frequently used term *sblizhenie*) and perhaps ultimately assimilate (*sliiat'*) into an integrated Soviet People (*sovetskii narod*) free of nationalism and many national characteristics. Two projects that appear contradictory (one might say dialectical) coexisted. On the one hand was the promotion of ethno-national cultures of the non-Russian peoples (*korenizatsiia* or indigenization), complete with their own ethno-national territories and the trappings of statehood, and on the other was the acculturating, integrative programme of modernizing a 'backward' peasant country, in the confidence that the socialist solvent would homogenize the dozens of different social and ethnic groups. The Soviet Union was at one and the same time an empire state and a state of nations. The open questions that beg further research, however, remain. Did the USSR become a kind of Soviet nation? How deep were the affective bonds that tied the diverse peoples together in a single affective community?

The contradictions between empire and a multinational state of nations were never fully resolved, and they contributed to the deep structural problems and discursive confusions that marked the Soviet experience. While the ultimate collapse of the Soviet system and the dissolution of the Union (two different but related phenomena) were primarily the result of ill-considered decisions and practices of the very summit of the Communist Party, the underlying ethno-national structure provided capacities and possibilities that, at a moment of extreme vulnerability, thwarted Gorbachev's efforts to create a more democratic and decentralized state, and facilitated the transition to fifteen (or more) independent republics.

My own argument is that the making of the Soviet 'nation' was not a linear process but that national integration and affective connection rose and fell. The pre-war years were too early for such a grand project to have achieved great results. Indeed the first decade of Soviet power was far more about national restoration and reconstruction than about the effective achievement of a transnational Soviet national identity, beyond, perhaps, the enthusiasts of the Communist Party. In the 1930s Stalin embarked on such an integrative project, ending the extreme variant of non-Russian nationalization that had marked the Leninist and NEP years, attacking local and bourgeois nationalism, purging the first generation of national Communists, concentrating state power in Moscow and imposing a form of Great Russian Soviet patriotism on the country as a whole – Soviet in form, Russian in content. The upheavals of collectivization, the devastating famines and the Great Purges divided the population into multitudes of losers and a few victors, with contrasting and conflicting loyalties.[14] But nation steadily replaced class as a central signifier. Correcting Marx and Engels, Stalin asserted in 1931 that the proletariat now had a fatherland.

The Stalinist 1930s were the years of the formation of what David Brandenberger has called (following M. N. Riutin) 'National Bolshevism', the introduction of a 'new pragmatism' in Soviet ideology that 'eventually settled upon a russocentric form of etatism as the most effective way to promote state-building and popular loyalty to the regime'.[15] Nativist, even nationalist, this new direction was not aimed 'to promote Russian ethnic interest . . . so much as . . . to foster a maximally accessible, populist sense of *Soviet* social identity through the instrumental use of russocentric appeals'.[16] Brandenberger argues that the intention of Stalin and the Stalinists was 'to promote little more than a patriotic sense of loyalty to the party and state between 1931 and 1956', but they unwittingly generated 'a mass sense of Russian national identity within Soviet society' that 'proved durable enough to survive the fall of the USSR itself'.[17] In Brandenberger's view, Russian national identity was a more successful achievement than the pan-national Soviet identity. He seems to accept – and believe that Stalin accepted – that the emotional power of ethnicity was greater than the civic Soviet identity, and the former was deliberately used to enhance the latter.

The regime employed the language of emotions in its campaign. 'Soviet patriotism is a burning feeling of boundless love', *Pravda* editorialized in 1935, 'a selfless devotion to one's motherland and a profound responsibility for her fate and defence, which issues forth like mighty spring waters from the depths of our people.'[18] The new Soviet histories were, on Stalin's orders, to be replete with heroes and events and to eliminate the abstractions that had marked the Pokrovskian school of historiography.[19]

Along with scholars such as Geoffrey Hosking and Hubertus Jahn, I have emphasized the weakness of Russian national identity in the imperial period right through the first decades of the twentieth century. The Leninists actively discouraged Russian nationalism in the NEP period, and well into the thirties people could be punished for 'Great Russian Chauvinism'. In her study of popular opinion in the 1930s, Sarah Davies notes the fragility of a sense of Russian nationness among ordinary workers and peasants, and its articulation primarily at the margins of contact with others such as Jews and Armenians.[20] While Russians expressed ethnic pride and a sense of unique Russian characteristics in their proverbs and songs, or their visceral hostility toward the Jews and other Others, the broader identification with abstract nation remained amorphous. Yet the ascription of nationality, its fixedness in the internal passport after 1932, reified what earlier had been a more fluid identification.[21]

FRIENDSHIP OF THE PEOPLES

Druzhba narodov was introduced into the Soviet vocabulary in December 1935, partially supplementing the term *bratstvo* (brotherhood). Terry Martin argues that *druzhba* (friendship) replaced the Affirmative Action Empire of the 1920s and early 1930s (1923–33) to become the new national constitution of the USSR, the imagined community of the Soviet state. For Martin, the idea of 'brotherhood' retained Marxist notions of class conflict, whereas 'friendship of the peoples' emphasized the trust that had developed among nationalities and, particularly, with smaller nationalities overcoming their earlier distrust of the Russians.[22] My own sense is that the two terms were variously used for different purposes. While brotherhood implies greater intimacy, it also involves hierarchy between older and younger brothers, and everyone was aware of which nationality would soon become the *starshii brat* (older brother).[23] With friendship the diminution of the notion of a kinship tie had the advantage of an emphasis on equality among the Soviet peoples. Friends after all are equivalent to one another; their relationship is about trust, devotion, dependability, affection and reciprocity. Equality and hierarchy were brought together (dialectically!) in Stalin's toast of 8 November 1938: 'Old Russia has been transformed into today's USSR where all peoples are identical ... Among the equal nations, states, and countries of the USSR, the most Soviet and the most revolutionary is the Russian nation.'[24]

Of course, calling something dialectical does not eliminate the contradictions and tensions inherent to it. Stalin's conception of Soviet patriotism, as frankly Russocentric as it was, attempted not to descend into ethnonationalism, yet the lines between patriotism and nationalism were not merely blurred but impossible to draw. Discussions raged for the whole of the Soviet period over the meanings of these two terms – in Armenian it was *hairenasirutiun* (patriotism), which was acceptable, and *azgasirutiun* (nationalism), which was not – but without clear resolution. The point has often been made that in the war Sovietism was pushed aside in the name of Russian nationalism, but this formulation misses the peculiar amalgamation of the two that marked those years. In his first speech on the anniversary of the Bolshevik Revolution in 1941, Stalin told the 'nation' that 'you must draw inspiration from the valiant example of our great ancestors', and then went on to name them: Aleksandr Nevskii, Dmitrii Donskoi, Kuz'ma Minin, Dmitrii Pozharskii, Aleksandr Suvorov, Mikhail Kutuzov. Russians to be sure, but defenders of the fatherland. Here was a Georgian with his accented Russian calling these military leaders 'our ancestors'. They were not merely ancestors of ethnic Russians but of the Soviet people as a whole. In much wartime rhetoric, images from the Russian past blended with those of the Soviet past and present. In the famous Soviet poster by the Kukryniksy, the ghosts of Nevskii, Suvorov, and Chapaev call on the Red Army men forward.[25] Soldiers, men and women, went into battle and to their death shouting 'Za Rodinu, za Stalina!' ('For Stalin, for the Motherland!'). A supranational but Russified patriotism was grafted onto Leninist internationalism, replacing the class element with a new primacy placed on Russia's past. As party leader Aleksandr Shcherbakov suggested to journalist-novelist Ilya Ehrenburg, 'Borodino is closer than the Paris Commune'.[26]

The war was both interruption and acceleration, unbearable sacrifice and transcendent triumph. Soviet historians and party officials fought bitterly over the 'correct' formulation of Soviet patriotism and impermissible nationalism. Tsarist Russia as 'gendarme of Europe' and 'prisonhouse of peoples' was at least, in Zhdanov's rendition (1936), 'the lesser evil' for non-Russians.[27] Pride in the Russian past became sacrosanct even as some, like the historian A. M. Pankratova, tried to elevate the martial qualities of non-Russians. Film studios in the national republics put out their own versions paralleling *Aleksandr Nevskii*: Armenia's *David Bek*, Georgia's *Georgi Saakadze* and Ukraine's *Bohdan Khmelnytsky*. Ultimately no clear decision was taken, and the task of reconciling national histories with the Russian imperial story proved insurmountable. As Serhy Yekelchyk concludes in his study of Ukrainian historiography, 'The casualties of this cohabitation were many: historians accomplished little, ideologues could not completely control the writing and teaching of history, and teachers apparently struggled to instill in students both pride in their nation's past and an appreciation of Russian imperial credentials.'[28] But 'once the exigencies of 1941–1943 had faded, party ideology reverted to an extreme version of the post-1937 line on the Russian people's ethnic primacy within Soviet society', which, Brandenberger concludes, 'emerged from the wartime experience in a much more russocentric and etatist form than it had been before the outset of the conflict'.[29] As Stalin proclaimed in his famous toast in May 1945, the Russian people were 'the most outstanding nation of all the nations in the Soviet Union', 'the Soviet Union's leading force among all the peoples of our country', and possessed 'a clear mind, hardy character, and patience'.[30]

Diaries, letters, and official reports testified that the war heightened national feelings, both Russian and non-Russian, and ethnic pride was accompanied often by ethnic hostility toward others. There was a new expression of and a greater permissiveness toward anti-Semitism during and after the war that metastasized into the anti-cosmopolitan campaign and the Doctors' Plot.[31] In specific cases, such as western Ukraine or the Baltic region which were incorporated into the Soviet Union during or after the Second World War, nationalism was directed against the Soviets. But it would be wrong to conclude that all particularistic nationalisms were opposed to a broader Soviet patriotism. The lasting effect of the war on many was the construction of a highly effective political and affective integration of Soviet and national identifications. The Soviet Union became the Fatherland (*Otechestvo*) and even the Motherland (*Rodina*), and it became easier to imagine and experience loyalty simultaneously to both one's ethno-nation and the USSR, and more difficult to separate the two. Victory solidified and sanctified the Soviet regime and Stalin. History seemed to be truly on their side, and when the fruits of that victory were denied by the capitalist West, armed with nuclear weapons, insecurity and fear, pride and faith heightened the feelings of many toward the *patrie en danger*. As if to emphasize its distance from its earlier internationalism, the Stalinist leadership of the late 1940s turned xenophobia into a mark of loyalty to the socialist fatherland. Nativist pride in Russia's past was combined with deep hostility toward the West.

The post-war synthesis involved severely restricting non-Russian nationalisms (Stalin apparently told filmmaker Sergei Eisenstein: 'We must overcome the revival of nationalism that we are experiencing with all the [non-Russian] peoples'),[32] promotion of the Russian imperial historical narrative as the foundation of Soviet patriotism, and deploying the struggle and victory of the Great Patriotic War to solidify the pan-national identification with the Soviet Union. The diverse histories of non-Russians were brutally subordinated to the Russian narrative. In 1948 the Armenian Communist Party condemned scholars for 'idealizing the historical past of Armenia'. Three years later it castigated the nineteenth-century novel *Kaitser* ('Sparks') by the nationalist writer Raffi that it had approved for republication just four years earlier. Stalin's Russia/USSR – the two words were used interchangeably in the late 1940s and early 1950s – was an empire of nations with the Russians as the imperial nation, but unlike the tsarist empire the Soviet Union worked assiduously and consistently under Stalin to create a Soviet affective community, and it was largely successful in creating such a community. But the Soviet community coexisted with the national communities within the empire.

The Soviet national anthem adopted in 1944 to replace the Internationale neatly summarized the Stalinist national patriotic synthesis:

> Unbreakable union of free republics
> Forged through the centuries by Great Rus!
> Hail the united powerful Soviet Union,
> Created by the will of the peoples!

Nationality was sensed as a palpable reality that since Lenin's time had been made ever more real by Soviet nationality policy. One's ethnicity conferred advantages or disadvantages on individuals. Officially nationality was inferior to Soviet patriotism, but the close association of Sovietism with Russia presented hundreds of millions of Soviet citizens with the dilemma of reconciling their ethno-national connections with their supranational loyalties. Some, like most Estonians, simply rejected the Soviet Union and along with it Russia, and lived exclusively within their own ethnic community. Others, like the hundreds of thousands of Armenians who either lived in or emigrated to Russia and other republics, assimilated into Russo-Soviet culture. Although their nationality was indicated on their passports, they were effectively 'Russian' in language, culture and attitude; after a generation or two they intermarried, and even their passport identity might disappear. Between those two poles were others who tacked back and forth between identities or created hybrid identities, becoming situationally Soviet in some circumstances, ethnic in others. Nationality was so powerful a marker in late Soviet society that it was inevitably used instrumentally, e.g. for political or social advancement within a national republic or to emigrate from the Soviet Union (Jews, Germans, Koreans and others).

THE RISE OF RUSSIAN NATIONALISM

When reading the peculiarity of their own nation within the Soviet empire, many Russians saw the whole Soviet Union as their patrimony (since in the absence of Russian Republic institutions, all-Union institutions served in that capacity), while simultaneously complaining that Russians were in an inferior and exploited position vis-à-vis the non-Russian nationalities. As

Yitzhak Brudny puts it, '[T]he Russian population in general, and Russian nationalists, in particular, viewed the USSR as essentially a Russian nation-state rather than an empire. The problem with the USSR, they insisted, was that it was not Russian enough.'[33] The Soviet Union was a strange empire in which the peoples of the periphery, in the minds of many, lived better and had greater advantages than the people of the metropole.

Brudny usefully distinguishes between the official 'nationalism' of the Soviet state, which aimed to include all the peoples of the USSR in the imagined community of the *sovetskii narod* (Soviet people), and the Russian nation-making nationalism that arose in the last decades of the Soviet Union, which promoted an exclusively ethnic Russian nation (*russkaia natsiia*) and would eventually contest the civil nationalism of the Yeltsin years that proposed a nation of all citizens living in Russia (*rossiis-kaia natsiia*).[34] The story he tells about the emergence of post-Stalin Russian nationalism is quite compelling. Initially in the early and mid-1950s, led by the journal *Novyi mir* ('New World'), essayists (*ocherkisty*) and village prose writers (*derevenshchiki*) depicted the devastation of the Russian countryside with its implicit critique of the Stalinist legacy and its nostalgic appreciation of threatened peasant traditions and values. This tentative opening of a public sphere in the Soviet Union, I would note, was closely linked to Khrushchev's de-Stalinization campaigns and was only tangentially nationalist. But these mild critiques by poets and short-story writers were tolerated by the Khrushchev and Brezhnev regimes, even as more political writers were forced into the samizdat (illegal self-publishing) underground. As Marxist ideology lost its mobilizational force, and politics was reduced to administration, the Brezhnev regime sought support for its revitalization of agriculture by including the nation-alists within the permissible realm of expression. The party tolerated their control of the Russian writers' union and their publication in prominent thick journals such as *Molodaia gvardiia* ('Young guard') and *Nash sovre-mennik* ('Our contemporary'). Both liberal and conservative nationalists were soon joined by more radical nationalists opposed to the liberalization of Soviet politics and dedicated to a more statist vision. But the nation-alists proved difficult to tame, and they were shut down under Andropov. Even with a degree of state support, however, the nationalists' politics of culture failed to move beyond an intelligentsia discussion, and when civil society re-emerged in the Gorbachev years, nationalists were unable to succeed in the arena of mass politics. The alliance of conservative and radical nationalists was defeated in the 1990 elections to the RSFSR Congress of People's Deputies.

A P R È S L E D É L U G E

What is now only too self-evident is that in contrast to the expectations of both Marxism and modernization theory – that industrialization and urbanization in either its capitalist or socialist variant would lead to an end to nationality differences and conflicts – not only was nationality preserved in the Soviet Union, but the power and cohesion of nationalities and their elites were enhanced. National identities were reified and primordialized. Ostensibly equal as in a multinational nation state, in fact Soviet nationalities lived in a permanent state of advantages and disadvantages provided by who they were. Russians might be privileged in the centre, but not necessarily in Armenia or Georgia. Armenians thrived in Armenia, and if they were competent in Russian and culturally assimilated, they did well in Russia and other republics. They were, however, at a disadvantage in Georgia or Azerbaijan precisely because of their ethnicity. Distinctions and hierarchies of power and access to various social goods were revealing characteristics of the Soviet Union as empire. Rather than the 'withering away' of interethnic hostilities, social mobilization intensified interethnic competition for limited social resources, while urbanization and education led to 'heightened national self-consciousness and increasing national separatism among the more socially mobilized members of each national community'.[35] Russification occurred, both spontaneously and through government programmes, but in some of the Union republics (most notably, the Baltic and Caucasian republics and Ukraine) indigenous intellectuals defended and promoted their own culture and language. As Khrushchev and particularly Brezhnev permitted national Communists to remain in power for many years, entrenched ethnic elites emerged in the non-Russian republics. By the last decades of Soviet power, nationalities experienced an unprecedented degree of local autonomy.

In the post-Soviet world ethno-nationalism proved powerful at certain moments in several of the smaller republics, particularly in the Baltic region, Moldova and Caucasia, as well as western Ukraine, but it did not grip most of the Muslim republics or Belarus, and was not widespread in Russia, where it remained the expression of a dispossessed fringe.[36] The Yeltsin years were in many ways revolutionary, a kind of 'Bolshevik-style liberalism' that set out to change Russia radically into a capitalist democracy and set the country back on its 'natural' course of history from which it had been derailed by the Bolsheviks. The seventy years of Soviet power were imagined as a deviation, a distortion that must be reversed in order to restore Russia to its true and healthy path toward civilization. Russia's leaders and many

intellectuals abandoned the world in which they had grown up, a world that
had been experienced, even with all its repression, mundane imperfections
and corruptions, as one of order, progress and purpose, at least up through
the mid-1970s. In its place they took the country into a world of unpredict-
ability, embedded corruption and criminality, economic hardship, military
weakness and the precipitous decline of Russia from great power status to a
wounded, humiliated, truncated state.

Though many democratic and Western values gained greater acceptance
among Russians in the 1990s, the eradication of the Soviet value system
deeply divided the country between those who supported the general
direction of the economic and political changes initiated by Gorbachev
and Yeltsin and those for whom the rejection of the Soviet past as an
authentic part of Russia's history and tradition meant their ejection from
the rebuilding of the nation. People who had fought and suffered for that
system were overnight rendered disgruntled, disoriented red-flag-waving
marginals. The turn back to symbols and institutions of the pre-Soviet
past – the double-headed eagle, the imperial flag, the Orthodox Church, the
reburial of the last tsar's family (though not – yet – the revival of the
Romanov anthem, 'God Save the Tsar') – resonated negatively among
many former *sovki* (Soviets, literally 'dustpans'), not to mention the 20
per cent of Russia's population that is neither Orthodox nor ethnically
Russian.[37] Intellectuals and politicians skirmished over the question of what
constitutes the Russian nation and state, whether the former union should
be restored or be limited to Great, Little and White Russians, be constituted
as a republic of Russian-speakers or become a multinational state in which
'Russian' is both understood as ethnic Russian (*russkii*) and as citizen of the
republic (*rossiiskii*).[38] As Mark Bassin has argued, Eurasianism is a principal
reaction to the collapse of empire, and as Alexander Titov has demonstrated, its popularity in the 1990s can be explained by 'its psychological
compatibility with Soviet values'.[39] Writers, from liberals such as
Aleksandr Tsipko to Eurasianists such as Sergei Lavrov and Lev Gumilev,
regretted the fall of the Soviet Union, the loss of the country with which
they identified despite the personal wounds that so many suffered.

The USSR was never fully a nation state and could never be an ethno-
national state. It remained an empire even as Gorbachev attempted futilely
to transform it into a multinational state by stripping the Soviet structure of
its imperial elements. But within that empire, in contrast to the tsarist
empire, Soviet state-builders were able to lay the foundations of an affective
community, a supra-ethnic bond between various nationalities and the
Soviet enterprise as a whole. Pride in the achievements of socialism and

pain in the sacrifices of Stalinism and world war combined with love for dual motherlands and a willingness to sacrifice for a common future. Like many other identities, the identification with the Soviet project proved fragile during glasnost (openness) and perestroika (rebuilding) when the old verities were radically reconceptualized.

Soviet peoples had both an ethnic and a national identity, and the national extended for many to the Soviet Union as homeland as a civic identity. At times the two underpinned each other in a tense relationship; at other times they competed and even undermined one another. The broad Soviet civic identity eventually gave way, but only under extraordinary circumstances. The ethnic emerged and then had to deal with its own difficulties in making nations in the new post-Soviet states. The collapse of the Marxist-Leninist world-view, already frayed and tattered particularly among young people, left an ideological vacuum that was rapidly filled by a naive and romantic faith in the wonders of democracy, capitalism and nationalism. Available for exploitation, nationalism both in late Soviet and post-Soviet times was employed by politicians from Yeltsin to Putin. But rather than positive emotions of love and pride, the dominant affective disposition centred on envy, resentment and anxiety – the decline of Russia as a great power, the humiliation of defeat at the hands of the West, resentment at the treatment of Russia and Russians by the ungrateful formerly Soviet republics. The victory in the Second World War remained a rallying point for both the sense of Russia's deserved greatness and its lost prestige and power. Yet, in Russia, nationalism did not grip the wider public but remained a phenomenon limited to intellectuals, some politicians and relatively isolated groups of malcontents on the dispossessed fringe. And it competed with a bitter nostalgia for the Soviet Union.

The road to capitalism and democracy has been rough and rocky, and even former Communists quickly dressed in ethno-nationalist drag in order to stay in power. They carried out nationalizing programmes to reinforce the sense of nation within their new states. But teaching languages and patriotic histories is only the beginning of creating an affective community. If one considers the common good, the predatory governments in many post-Soviet states have not acted in the national interest. Elections have been manipulated or stolen; violence has been deployed to keep old elites in power; policies often are conceived to satisfy Western patrons and protectors rather than the population. In time Russian and post-Soviet market economies turned into a peculiarly piratical form of capitalism that produced poverty for most and obscene wealth for a few. Democratic hopes outside the Baltic republics died a slow death in the face of restored authoritarianism.

To a degree Putin righted the listing ship of state he inherited from
Yeltsin. With high oil prices in his favour, he managed to forge broad
coalitions across the political spectrum from the Communists to the
nationalists, excluding the discredited liberals. Where Yeltsin had tried to
bury the Communist past as if it had never happened, Putin merged pride
in Soviet achievements with the reforms that had ended the command
economy and monopoly of the Communist Party. As a neoliberal in
domestic policy and a hard realist in international affairs, he restored the
red flag for the military and the Soviet national anthem (albeit with
appropriate new lyrics), resurrecting symbols that still resonated for many.
What constituted the 'motherland' was less contested than in the Soviet
years, yet nostalgia for what had been lost was a persistent theme in the
media. In Russia a nostalgia television channel replayed old movies and
recycled memories of the USSR. The older generation in particular found it
hard to let go, but as one decade succeeded another, people accommodated
themselves to the way the world had become. The longing for what was no
longer possible and the clinging to what was left had already been captured
in a bitter late Soviet joke:

A young worm asks his father about life.
    'Dad,' says the young worm, 'what is it like to live in an apple?'
    'Oh, son,' answers the dad, 'living in an apple is wonderful; it's juicy, crispy,
delicious.'
    'Dad,' asks the son. 'What is it like living in an orange?'
    'Oh, son, living in an orange is incredible, it's liquid sunshine, it's California.'
    'But, Dad, why do we live in shit?'
    'Son! There is such a thing as the motherland!'

NOTES

1. B. Anderson, *Imagined Communities: Reflections on the Origin and Spread of Nationalism* (London, 1991), 141.
2. Ibid.
3. Ibid., 143.
4. Ibid., 144.
5. Ibid.
6. Cited in the article 'Johann Gottfried von Herder', *Encyclopaedia Britannica*, vol. XI (Chicago, IL, 1970), 418.
7. Borrowing from Friedrich Nietzsche, Liah Greenfeld employs the term *ressentiment* as the central theme in her mammoth study of five nationalisms. *Ressentiment* is the 'psychological state resulting from suppressed feelings of envy and hatred (existential envy) and the impossibility of satisfying these feelings'. It 'fostered particularistic pride and xenophobia, providing emotional nourishment for

the nascent national sentiment and sustaining it whenever it faltered': Liah Greenfeld, *Nationalism: Five Roads to Modernity* (Cambridge, MA, 1992), 15–16.

8. Valerie Kivelson, personal communication to the author.

9. 'In expressing the political and cultural preeminence of the ruler, foreign traits carried a positive valuation, native traits a neutral or negative one': R. Wortman, *Scenarios of Power: Myth and Ceremony in Russian Monarchy*, vol. I, *From Peter the Great to the Death of Nicholas I* (Princeton, NJ, 1995), 6.

10. A. Morrison, 'Aryanism, Asianism and Imperial Citizenship', paper presented at National Identity in Eurasia I: Identities & Traditions, 22–4 March 2009, New College, University of Oxford.

11. Prior to 1917, Russians were born into *sosloviia*, or 'estates': *dvorianstvo* (gentry/ nobility), *meshchanstvo* (plebeian townspeople), clergy and peasantry; these classifications were permanent and heritable.

12. Morrison, 'Aryanism'.

13. Translation by the author.

14. The Harvard Project on the Soviet Social System provides an excellent and easily accessible window into popular and intelligentsia attitudes about the effects of Stalinist nationality policies: www.hcl.harvard.edu/collections/hpsss/ index.html.

15. D. Brandenberger, *National Bolshevism: Stalinist Mass Culture and the Formation of Modern Russian National Identity, 1931–1956* (Cambridge, MA, 2002), 2.

16. Ibid., 4.

17. Ibid., 9.

18. 'Sovetskii patriotizm', *Pravda*, 19 March 1935 (cited in Brandenberger, *National Bolshevism*, 28).

19. i.e. the interpretative tradition led by Mikhail Pokrovskii, which dominated historical research and teaching up to the early 1920s.

20. S. Davies, *Popular Opinion in Stalin's Russia: Terror, Propaganda, and Dissent, 1933–1941* (Cambridge, 1997), 88–9.

21. There is a large literature on the Soviet passport as well as on the ascription of nationality. See, for example, D. Shearer, 'Elements Near and Alien: Passportization, Policing, and Identity in the Stalinist State, 1932–1953', *Journal of Modern History* 57:4 (December 2004), 835–81; Y. Slezkine, 'The USSR as a Communal Apartment, or, How a Socialist State Promoted Ethnic Particularism', *Slavic Review* 53:2 (Summer 1994), 414–52, reprinted in G. Eley and R. G. Suny, *Becoming National: A Reader* (New York, 1996), 203–38; R. G. Suny, *The Revenge of the Past: Nationalism, Revolution, and the Collapse of the Soviet Union* (Stanford, CA, 1993); T. Martin, *The Affirmative Action Empire: Nations and Nationalism in the Soviet Union, 1923–1939* (Ithaca, NY, 2001); K. Brown, *The Biography of No Place: From Ethnic Borderland to Soviet Heartland* (Cambridge, MA, 2003); and Albert Baiburin's contribution in this volume.

22. Martin, *Affirmative Action Empire*, 432, 436–42.

23. For these ideas I am indebted to discussions with my former undergraduate student Tom Hooker and his work on friendship in the 1930s.

24. Brandenberger, *National Bolshevism*, 284 n. 43.

25. 'We are fighting heartily and bayoneting daringly, grandchildren of Suvorov, children of Chapaev' (Kukryniksy, 1941; depicted in Brandenberger, *National Bolshevism*, 117).

26. I. Ehrenburg, *Liudi, gody, zhizn'*, 322; Brandenberger, *National Bolshevism*, 150.

27. Brandenberger, *National Bolshevism*, 50.

28. S. Yekelchyk, *Stalin's Empire of Memory: Russian-Ukrainian Relations in the Russian Historical Imagination* (Toronto, 2004).

29. Brandenberger, *National Bolshevism*, 130, 131.

30. Cited in ibid, 130–1.

31. A. Weiner, *Making Sense of War: The Second World War and the Fate of the Bolshevik Revolution* (Princeton, NJ, 2001), 114–22, *passim*.

32. Brandenberger, *National Bolshevism*, 187.

33. Y. M. Brudny, *Reinventing Russia: Russian Nationalism and the Soviet State, 1953–1991* (Cambridge, MA, 1998), 7.

34. Ibid, 7–8.

35. R. J. Kaiser, *The Geography of Nationalism in Russia and the USSR* (Princeton, NJ, 1994), 248.

36. For elaboration of this point, see R. G. Suny, 'Constructing Primordialism: Old Histories for New Nations', *Journal of Modern History* 73:4 (December 2001), 862–96.

37. *Sovok* (plural *sovki*) literally means 'dustpan', but in the late Soviet period it referred negatively to something or someone 'Soviet'. It has come to be an ambivalent reference to a Soviet person. For a discussion of the term, see G. Strashnyi, 'Chto takoe sovki' ['What are *sovki*?'], www.grisha.ru/zapiski/26.htm.

38. V. Tolz, 'Conflicting "Homeland Myths" and Nation-State Building in Postcommunist Russia', *Slavic Review* 57:2 (Summer 1998), 268, 289, 293–4.

39. M. Bassin, 'Eurasianism from Trubetskoi to Dugin', and A. Titov, 'Lev Gumilev and the Re-birth of Eurasianism', papers delivered at National Identity in Eurasia I: Identities & Traditions, 22–4 March 2009, New College, University of Oxford.

CHAPTER 2

Tales told by nationalists

Nancy Condee

THE ANTILOGY: PRELIMINARY REMARKS ON NATIONALISM

Tollendum esse Octavium. (Cicero, *Letters to His Friends* (II.479)).

As a concept, 'nationalism' is clear enough, if one takes it to mean the speaker's ardent advocacy of his or her own culture, loosely defined as a common linguistic community, territory or imagined collectivity. That beloved culture, the nationalist's claim goes, sustains certain dominant values, privileged attitudes or capacities less available to other cultures. In this regard, as Adrian Hastings suggests, 'nationalism is strong only in particularist terms, deriving from the belief that one's own ethnic or national tradition is especially valuable and needs to be defended at almost any cost'.[1] These qualities often entail the speaker's performative acts in ritual, rite and collective habit. To choose an oft-quoted example from Anthony Smith, nationalism is a sentiment 'emphasizing the symbols, ceremonies, and custom of national identity'.[2]

Such definitions as these – Hastings', Smith's and others, here and elsewhere – are functionally invaluable.[3] The fact that they tend to offer no specific information about nationalism's content is unimportant, since our understanding implicitly substitutes one culture's set of symbols, ceremonies and customs for another's. Nor need we mind that a cultural sentiment – so keenly felt that it may lead to voluntary physical self-sacrifice – may be replaced in another culture by a different sentiment, or the same one, no less keenly felt. All of this absent content is unproblematic to the definition's functionality.

What remains curious in standard definitions of nationalism has less to do with functionality than with affect. The grave disjuncture between the term's definitional emptiness and its gesture at passion so intense as to prompt us to die for our country is oddly compensatory, as if in response to the bland act of equating passions that prompt quite different citizens of another country to die for theirs. The alleged uniqueness and value of one's

37

life, abstracted to a definitional slot into which content may sequentially be inserted, is an unbearable juxtaposition that can be endured only within a relentless semantic insularity; the real conditions of the world outside – that which lies beyond semantics – must not intrude.

These concerns are more than intellectual. By Hastings' definition above, for example, how would we distinguish between Russian and Chechen nationalisms? It is one thing for polemical debate – for the sake of provocation, or simply counterfactually – to assert that these two nationalisms are identical. It is something quite different for a foundational definition to advance the task of their conflation. One needs be neither a Russian nationalist nor a Chechen nationalist but a mere philologist to see the conceptual shortcomings of this operation. What is absented in their conflation is the question of hegemony, with the result that Russian nationalism and Chechen nationalism – in social reality, antonyms to each other – appear to be conceptual synonyms. Perhaps this decontextualization is simply a feature of definitions more broadly, allowing them to function as placeholders emptied of any actual social meaning. Here, however, the absent real-world context most starkly renders the definition radically ineffectual.

The initial appeal of abstraction may spring precisely from its capacity to subdue the driving passions of nationalism. Highly functional because it 'properly' decontextualizes its subject, a definition of this kind suppresses the existing issues of sovereignty, thereby conflating the hegemon with the freedom fighter. History, too, is mysteriously elided: after all, in the Soviet decades of the 1960s and 1970s, certain elite cultural varieties of nativist Russian nationalism, most evident in the fiction of the village prose cluster, would disavow any existing hegemonic privilege, claiming instead that all Russians were indentured to the Soviet state, from which they dreamt of launching an emancipation project. As Ilya Prizel has persuasively argued, village prose writing could be seen as articulating the heartland's wounded nationalism, a nativist protest against the predations of the metropolitan centre.[4] In the retrospect of forty years, of course, cultural politics have selectively aggregated many of the village prose writers to the hegemonic nationalism of metropolitan state culture in ways that have blunted its oppositionalist critique, and nowadays the victimhood of this Russophile literary nationalism hardly resounds with the same pathos as that of a post-Soviet Chechen culture that has endured sustained military intervention. A definition of 'nationalism' that does not navigate these complexities is of little analytic use.

This instability within 'nationalism' is commented on in passing by Madina Tlostanova, who opines that Russian cultural politics have 'turned into an oxymoronic but (for Russia) typical *imperial nationalism*'.[5] Here several questions arise: how are these two terms – 'imperial', 'nationalism' – aligned as oxymoronic? Is this the only possible alignment – in other words, are they *unavoidably* oxymoronic? How is it that 'nationalism', conventionally signalling *liberation* from hegemonic rule, can come to signal *hegemonic* rule itself?

One is tempted to revert to the anodyne truth that Russia is a land of perpetual enigma, but something else, I would argue, is at work instead. At a purely semantic level, 'nationalism' comprises internally contradictory vantage points that do not lend themselves easily to dictionary practices, but rather to rhetorical ones, where discourse trumps semantics. The word's potential for internal contradiction – the nationalist as hegemon or freedom fighter? – suggests that it might be included in that class of words, such as 'cleave' ('to stick fast to' or 'to split apart') or 'sanction' ('to penalize' or 'to approve'), that are called antilogies by those who name things. It is not a mere matter of two meanings, but something inconceivable: a single word, incompatible to itself, that alternately excludes and insists upon each of its two internal meanings.[6] By 'quiddity', for example, do we mean the essential or the inessential? In each case – as in 'cleave' or 'sanction' – the isolated word hangs in a kind of temporary limbo: we are forced to wait for more information from the external context. Unlike other words weakly dependent on relational linkages, antilogies are heavily reliant on referentiality. Only the social context can break a Janus-faced word such as 'sanction' in one direction or the other.

Such is the case, I would contend, with 'nationalism'. This rhetorical volatility does not hamper, but – just the opposite – enhances the enormous productivity of the nationalist impulse for contemporary Russian culture. Felicitously (for the rhetorician), no commitment can be made in advance about two very different rhetorical projects: on the one hand, emancipation from a hegemonic culture; on the other, exaltation at a hegemonic victory over the minority culture. Both potential meanings have the power to haunt the word. To refer to director Nikita Mikhalkov, for example, as a nationalist is perpetually to allow for this slippage: his hegemonic pride in Russian culture may 'inexplicably' be inflected with intimations of victimhood, as if he were justly agitating for greater access to the heretofore restricted cultural treasures unevenly available in the discriminating empire, without any attending accountability associated with his position as a member of the dominant ethnicity in that social construct.

In Cicero's antilogy, quoted at the outset of this section, Octavian must be raised up (*tollendum*).[7] But the intended meaning may also have signalled its opposite: Octavian must be destroyed (*tollendum*). It is Hegel's *Wissenschaft der Logik* (1812–16) that draws upon exactly this rhetorical opportunity to describe the double action of sublation – elevating while cancelling out – and the citation has remained since then a prime example of the antilogy's irresolvable appeal (its antilogical dynamic, so to speak).[8] In keeping with this line of speculation, one might find in 'nationalism' a similar double action: if a core aim of nationalism is sovereignty, then a core aim of hegemonic nationalism is the sublation of sovereignty to that higher power we would call empire.

It is this distinction between empire-preserving nationalism and empire-dismantling nationalisms that has provoked some of the most interesting recent research since the 1990s, work that productively illuminates continuities across the dynastic, Soviet and post-Soviet polities. Here, for example, Alexei Miller attends to the strategies of the upper and lower bureaucracies of the late dynastic period:

We can see that part of the higher imperial bureaucracy began to consider the possibility of using nationalism in the empire's interest, while, at the same time, the rank-and-file bureaucrats ... invariably treated nationalism with suspicion because of its connection to democratic representation and demand for broader autonomy of public opinion.[9]

Miller is speaking here of the strategic investments of the late dynastic empire, yet one might read this sentence slightly differently as an inadvertent comment on contemporary Russian cultural politics, when two distinct notions of nationalism are also in play: those sources of nationalism that serve consolidating interests, as opposed to the sources of nationalism that threaten such multiple dangers as democratic representation, popular sovereignty and broader autonomy, as well as populist fascism, xenophobia and social disintegration.

Russia's empire-preserving nationalism is best captured in what Hugh Seton-Watson – with some terminological inaccuracy – called official nationalism,[10] the primary function of which has historically been the retardation and selective appropriation of those nationalisms that, occupying that space where civic or ethnic autonomy might seek linkages, would speak publicly back against the state unless appropriately restricted. Official nationalism provides the most historically familiar ideological system to ensure that the unmanageable business of nation formation is muted, but more importantly that such muting can itself be naturalized as the philosophical workings of *sobornost'* (communitarianism), the Russian idea, or other nineteenth-century constructions of knowledge. Nationalism is thus assigned a place remote from social institutions, from what many Western scholars, in their own conceptual shorthand, would call civil society.

To return, therefore, to Madina Tlostanova's 'imperial nationalism', the adjective provides crucial information that may steer the listener out of the antilogy's paralysing hesitation. The adjective–noun combination is indeed oxymoronic, if we understand 'nationalism' to imply a liberationist agenda, but it is something akin to tautology if 'nationalism' signals a hegemonic relation to contiguous cultures under the imperial umbrella.[11]

In a larger scope, it might be suggested that, at a time of accelerated globalization, the cultural texts of hegemonic nationalism – its state-endorsed films, novels, monuments, and above all television and radio broadcasts – are a project of extraordinarily strategic fluidity. Because their imperial afflatus must inevitably be rendered provincial in the global circulation of a larger cultural set, the nationalist hegemon's capacity for a sudden reversal of meaning permits a claim to potential victimhood in the context of a larger field that is global cultural power.

NATIONHOOD: A BAD FIT, BUT AN INTERESTING ONE

Let us turn back once more to Anthony Smith, quoted at the outset of this chapter. I return to his work not because of its weaknesses, but instead to stake out here a defined position in contrast to Smith's work on nationalism, where he is perhaps the leading figure. In *Warwick Debates*, Smith has defined the nation as 'a named human population sharing an historic territory, common myths and memories, a mass, public culture, a single economy and common rights and duties for all members'. As ever, there is little to which one could object in Smith's account, which has been put forth similarly in a number of monographs and articles.[12]

Smith's definitions, here and elsewhere, do not, however, easily help us distinguish the nation from, for example, my own university, or my colleagues' institutions at New College, Oxford, or Moscow State University, any one of which likewise claims a historic territory, common myths and memories, a public culture, a single economy, and common rights and duties for all members. As collectivities, our universities are not nations, except in a capriciously poetic sense or a deeply antiquated one.[13] The tautological quality to Smith's definition – named populations share

nameable commonalities – leaves something conceptually riskier unidentified in his definition of nationhood.

That risk is taken up by Smith's interlocutors, often referred to by the
loose umbrella term of constructivists. In the early 1980s an explosion of
constructivist monographs marked an invaluable turning point in the field
of nation theory, even becoming – in the critical assessment of Smith
himself – 'the dominant orthodoxy in the field'.[14] Whether we are speaking
of John Breuilly's political argument in *Nationalism and the State* (1982), of
Benedict Anderson's cultural contribution in *Imagined Communities* (1983),
of Ernest Gellner's sociological *Nations and Nationalism* (1983) or most
famously of Eric Hobsbawm and Terence Ranger's social history in the
collection *The Invention of Tradition* (1983), these constructivist volumes
played an enormous role in galvanizing debates on nation formation and
nation-sustaining practices.[15]

For all their differences and internal nuances, one might summarize the
constructivists' common assertions in four broad fields of agreement. In
various ways, most would argue that the concept of nationhood is, first, a
recent construction, dating from the mid- to late eighteenth century, a time
concomitant with accelerated industrialization, the rise of the bureaucratic
state, print capitalism, universal education and most importantly an intensified appeal to popular sovereignty. Second, nationhood in this modernist
understanding is conceived as a practice of continual renewal of civic
association through autonomous, horizontal linkages that sustain and differentiate the nation's activities from the practices of the state. Third,
nationhood involves the invocation of sustaining myths of equality, citizens'
answerability, collective agency as practices of a plural and allegedly unique
body. Fourth, the nation's legitimacy often involves claims that seemingly
disavow its modern, disruptive origins, substituting instead a soothing
naturalization that resituates those origins in a long tradition as if they
were always already there: eternal, essential, transparent, organic and (most
importantly) immune to further analysis. One might well speculate that
such reassurances are symptomatic of traumatic innovations that were in
practice associated with late eighteenth-century nation-construction: citizen
agency, the dismantling of the Christian universe, a rescission of the divine
right of kings and so forth.

However constructed these discursive categories, one cannot argue that
they are therefore artificial or do not really exist. Even such an opponent to
constructivism as Smith has acknowledged that 'Ernest has always insisted
that nations and nationalism are real and powerful sociological phenomena,
even if their reality is quite different from the tale told about them by

nationalists themselves.'[16] 'Ernest' (Gellner) was Anthony Smith's teacher and his great interlocutor, by then at Prague's Centre for the Study of Nationalism. Their exchange in 'The Warwick Debates' of 24 October 1995, less than two weeks before Gellner's death on 5 November 1995, has been invaluable in making sense of the tales told by nationalists.[17] Thus, the core difference between the constructivists – broadly speaking – and Smith's ethno-symbolist position (as he himself has called it) is not the constructed quality per se, but its modern invention.[18]

For those of us in the humanities, these tales about the nation with their double meanings – the logical lapses of nationalism – form the most interesting aspect of the field, because they strain to breaking point evidentiary information and usher us instead into the realm of conjecture, where data and imagination utterly fail to account for each other. Out of this failure comes the productivity of cultural analysis, however profoundly interpretive it is doomed to be. The artist-nationalist, who stares keenly backwards in time until he is finally able to 'discern' an ancient, national origin, is the creative provisioner of the plural self. For scholars of culture, it is less important to set him straight than to make interpretive sense of his labour. The constructivist appreciation of the illogic – the necessary lapses of empirics – in the narration of nationhood happily focuses on the disjuncture between the nation's recent history and its imagined story: if the former is relatively short, the latter is as long as its minstrel can insist on its being.

BAL MASQUÉ

But what good are these debates for local scholars of Russian culture? What is their purchase? At the heart of my position is the view that the usefulness of nationhood as an interpretive frame for Russian culture is radically distorting; the category is an unsalvageable misfit. The process of nation formation, as an institutional phenomenon emergent in late eighteenth-century Europe and elsewhere, is a process to which Russia eventually became, in an unmediated sense, largely peripheral. As Hosking and others have suggested, the Russian imperial tradition – unlike other imperial traditions – has not been strongly marked with a drive toward nation formation, at least in the constructivist sense of the term. 'The Russian nation', Hosking argues, 'has never been able to develop to the full its own political, economic or cultural institutions, since these have been distorted or emasculated for the needs of the empire.' And, as Ronald Suny has unambiguously argued, after 1917 'no Soviet *natsiia* [nation] was "created," only a Soviet *narod* [folk]'.[19]

At the same time, the ways in which the discursive category of 'nation' does *not fit* Russia have produced some of the more useful and interesting moments in contemporary representations of Russian collectivities. While the arguments of such constructivists as Gellner, Breuilly and Anderson are compelling in *unmediated* ways in other contexts, the core value for Russianists of these volumes is not what the texts tell us about Russia, but what they provide as *contrastive* background.

Yet, in both elite and demotic cultures since the early nineteenth century, Russia's eventual disinclination toward sustained nation-formation – for reasons that might at first seem paradoxical – has not precluded the emergence in recent years of robust nationalist movements, organizations and parties, both state-sponsored and independent. Here one might appreciate in a new spirit Gellner's remark that nationalism 'invents nations where they do not exist'.[20] It is by no means the case, he argues, that the already-existing nation gives voice to nationalism, or that nationalism is somehow empirical confirmation of a nation's existence. Indeed, it might be more compellingly argued that the blusterings of a robust nationalism are the measure of a weak, absent or imperilled nation formation; moreover, in the case of *official* Russian nationalism – whereby the state stands in for those practices of civic association and popular sovereignty that would, in the nation state, function autonomously – its constructions of citizen loyalty might be taken as symptomatic of an etiolated nationhood. In this regard, nationalism must be thought of as a wish state.

My larger point is this. If we could tolerate this disjuncture – in broad-brush strokes: that weak nation formation may easily persist alongside powerful nationalisms – rather than rushing to assume that where there is strong nationalism there must also be strong nationhood, we could perhaps savour the contradictions of contemporary culture in ways otherwise unavailable to us.

For students of culture, the value of these vexing contradictions is their explanatory power for precisely the cultural text, with all its circumlocu-tions, misrepresentations of historical and contemporary reality, and stra-tegic lacunae. I have written earlier of Ivan Aivazovskii's seascapes as a kind of imperial display, an imaginary thalassocratic mummery of life as overseas empire.[21] The artist's painterly engagement with the maritime dominion produces an imaginative status at once British and not-British. While Aivazovskii's interest in British seascapes certainly has its historical roots in the painter's admiration for and acquaintance with English Romantic seascape painter J. M. W. Turner (1775–1851), whom he met in 1842, this biographical fact alone does not require our attention if what we are looking at instead is the set of ideological (and therefore artistic) compatibilities from one of his painterly empires to the next: *The Mary Caught in a Storm* (1892), for example, or his *View of Constantinople by Moonlight* (1846), and the later *View of Odessa by Moonlight* (1860). It is in this analytic resistance to the biographical imperative that Aivazovskii's work becomes newly interesting.

A similar line of inquiry could be opened up, for example, concerning Karl Briullov's *Last Day of Pompeii* (1830–3), which invites us to overlay the Roman imperial catastrophe onto a potentially incipient Russian one, or Acmeist Nikolai Gumilev's poems about the Abyssinian empire, which invites implicit comparison with his own non-Abyssinian counterpart. In these cases or others, the content might be thought of as a kind of creative impersonation: not therefore fraudulent or ill-intended, but the foundational act of culture, which characteristically misconstrues itself as this or that. The artist's speculation (more accurately, an 'imagined inevitability': a 'what if') requires us to ask how we could ever take at face value the self-presentation of any cultural text.

And this line of argument leads to a final set of questions: if the artistic representation of one empire may masquerade as another empire – the continental expanse of Russia as a maritime power, or a gloomy, augural Russia as Rome in time of catastrophe, or the northern Russian empire as a southern African empire, and so forth – then it is a small step to consider that the imperial culture's imagination might also freely play at nationhood, without Russia's ever being a nation in the material, infrastructural or civic sense. Why would it not? And, if so, what would it mean?

The last of these questions is an enormous one and I have no illusions that it could be answered in a single chapter. Let me at least map out conjecturally how such imperial 'nation-play' might be addressed in the cultural sphere with which I am most familiar, namely contemporary Russian cinema.

THE IMPLICATIONS FOR CONTEMPORARY CULTURE: COMMENTS ON CINEMA

But in this case [in Chechnya] the war was between people who speak the same language. Their cultural background and education were the same. So in a way they were relatives. (Aleksandr Sokurov)[22]

My argument to this point concludes, among other things, that 'imperial nationalism' is not another orientalizing oxymoron, in the long tradition of casting Russia as eternally paradoxical, but rather an attempt to stabilize the innate ambiguity of 'nationalism' by employing it in an adjective–noun compound that offers a kind of sublated sovereignty over the multi-ethnic panorama, lending coherence to what might otherwise be nationalism's disruptive potential.

Were we to be able to overcome our own liberal resistances to its habit of mind, we might find that, in various modes, imperial nationalism informs contemporary Russian culture to a far greater extent than we perhaps had reckoned. I will restrict my comments to three contemporary filmmakers who are as different from one another as might be imagined, but who nevertheless share an orientation inflected by this habit of thought. My interest in no way lies in a substantive or comprehensive analysis of the directors' work; such scholarship is amply available elsewhere.[23] Instead, this inquiry asks how we can understand their work in the larger cultural environment.

I will begin with the recent work of Aleksandr Sokurov, whose remarks in the epigraph above refer to his 2007 film *Aleksandra*, a text that (like his comments in the epigraph above) carries a message of political kinship in its choices of narrative strategy, casting, camerawork and plot structure to offer us war as an allegory of temporary family disharmony.[24] Sokurov, of course, may write and shoot as he wishes: his understanding of Chechen–Russian relations as a kinship does not require scholarly refutation, any more than his assertion that the cultural backgrounds of Chechens and Russians are 'the same'. Whether or not we take these assertions as true, a different thing here is worthy of our attention: Sokurov is remarkably incurious about the historical context of the shared language, as if it were an inevitable consequence of family resemblance, rather than of military conquest. His representations here, both in his recent film and in interviews that extrapolate from that work, exist as a specific kind of discursive Russia, one in which Chechnya is inscribed as internal to Russia's dominion, and therefore – apparently, without further reflection – a family member. Within the diegesis of Sokurov's film, the brief visit of a Russian grandmother to her grandson at the edge of the empire is elaborated through a subplot that suggests the visit of one elderly grandmother to another elderly female relative within a larger family expanse, as Aleksandra goes to the bombed-out home of a female market trader whom she meets on the outskirts of Groznyi. Aleksandra's closing invitation to the three generations of Chechen women that they pay a return visit to her northern home acts as visible plausibility of their common story of an extended family, contributing the warmth of kinship as a substitute for the armoured necessities of occupation.

Sokurov's comment above, therefore, is not an isolated interview remark in conversation with film scholar Ian Christie. On his website, *Island of Sokurov* [*Ostrov Sokurova*], the director's comments on the Chechen wars reveal a similar orientation. Speaking here, too, of Russian–Chechen relations, Sokurov writes:

When an intonation of trust emerges, all else remains insignificant, all the more so if everyone speaks in a single language – in Russian … Therefore a great deal of attention is devoted to the unifying significance of the Russian language … [A]bove all else, it is the language of unification.[25]

With their homogenizing claims to the empire's periphery, Sokurov's assurances here (as in the script of *Aleksandra* itself) effortlessly stitch together the language of empire with the language of nationhood, the horizontal dialogue of the brothers and sisters, as Anderson characterizes it.[26] Nationhood in this respect is a valuable imaginative resource, satisfyingly fraudulent; its real institutional incompatibility with the political realities of contemporary Russia is of no concern whatsoever. We may individually object to Sokurov's project – his overwriting the imperial relationship as one of benign, inter-generational national subjects in voluntary cohesion and reciprocal respect – but this is a separate matter. 'We need a strong state,' Sokurov has argued elsewhere. 'For me, there is enormous significance when a citizen serves the state … This is, by the way, our Russian tradition, very important and deeply rooted.' And further: 'I, of course, cannot mute in myself an attraction to the military. I am after all a Russian.'[27]

Let us next turn to a second, very different Russian filmmaker. Aleksei Balabanov is a confounding figure for Russian and Western scholars and journalists alike. His nationalist episodes, explicitly affirmed as such in press conferences and interviews, have become part of his cinematic signature. They are Balabanov's equivalent to Muratova's twins – as most recently in *Minor People* (*Vtorostepennye liudi*, 2001; also known in English as *Second-Class Citizens*), *Tuner* (*Nastroishchik*, 2004) and *Melody for a Barrel Organ* (*Melodiia dlia sharmanki*, 2009) – or Vadim Abdrashitov's train, as most recently in *Play for a Passenger* (*P'esa dlia passazhira*, 1995), *Time of the Dancer* (*Vremia tantsora*, 1998) and *Magnetic Storms* (*Magnitnye buri*, 2003), and engender equivalent critical speculation.[28] Even those who deeply admire his work have trouble finding a descriptive category for Balabanov himself: racist? anti-Western? nationalist? As Jonathan Romney suggests, 'Balabanov has a reputation for elusiveness, baffling journalists with the assertions that he's a patriot and an Orthodox Christian and that "the future is Russian".'[29] In several recent films, most notably the action film *Brother 2* (*Brat 2*, 2000), *War* (*Voina*, 2002) and the comedy *Dead Man's Bluff* (*Zhmurki*, 2005), both Westerners and non-Russian minorities are treated with a kind of xenophobic provocation that flickers between mockery and rage. In interviews Balabanov is even less ambiguous ('I am against things foreign,' he explains in an interview with Roger Clarke).[30] If Balabanov's work might be described as nationalist, it manages to be so in both senses described above – pridefully (if often self-parodically) disrespectful toward both the hegemonic West and domestic ethnic minorities. While one cannot account for all the reasons why Balabanov may baffle journalists, it is reasonable to venture that they lie precisely in this apparent contradiction between hegemonic and liberationist nationalisms.

In several of Balabanov's films – in particular *Brother 2* and *War* – Balabanov's Russian protagonist struggles against the larger world order of New York and London in an allegory of liberationist self-assertion, interlarded with ready insults to non-Russian ethnicities, such as 'Eggplant', the black character in *Dead Man's Bluff*. The Russian protagonist's fragile honour has at stake real consequences, not only within the diegetic reality of a specific film, but also in the larger social drama of Russian cinema's drive for distribution networks, box-office draws and global ranking, for which Balabanov's hero is a symbolic placeholder. In Balabanov's cinema (and implicitly not only there), the Russian protagonist will never beat Hollywood, but his ceaseless counter-assault seeks the larger stakes of self-definition, social agency and independence – symbolically performing in miniature the nation's struggle for autonomy – in ways that drape the collective identity of the local cinematic event in the robes of little nationhood. It would be foolish to make accusations about the deceitfulness of this practice, as if deceit were not a feature of culture itself. Instead, we might ask ourselves about the ways that the enduring antilogy of nationalism helps to structure and naturalize this apparent incompatibility: in global cinema, Balabanov's impassioned drive for an emancipation from Hollywood's dominion; in the domestic arena, the mocking disregard of the entitled lumpen for the swarthy subordinates in the shrunken multi-ethnic empire.

And a final example: Nikita Mikhalkov's affinities to what might be described as an explicit imperial nationalism are perhaps the most consistently on view among these three directors. Beyond his directorial work, his other cinematic contributions might be seen as similarly programmatic. As an actor in his own films, for example, he offers the spectator a range of Russian military, state and security figures, from Colonel Kotov in the melodrama *Burnt by the Sun* (*Utomlennye solntsem*, 1994) to Alexander III in *Barber of Siberia* (*Sibirskii tsiriul'nik*, 1998) to the unnamed FSB security officer in the courtroom drama *12* (2007), all positioning Mikhalkov as cinema's key agent of hegemonic nationalism. At the same time, the alternative – a Russian nationalism resistant to hegemonic Western values – informs such films as *Barber of Siberia*, with its disruptive US predators, and the 1987 romance *Dark Eyes* (*Ochi chernye*), with its jaded European intruder.

Mikhalkov's nationalism intertwines this display of local hegemonic power – as the parade of state figures suggests – with the freedom fighter's bravado at the periphery, making a self-conscious counter-declaration against 'Hollywood values'. If Sidney Lumet's original 1957 courtroom film *Twelve Angry Men* vaunts the jury system as an American virtue that – in Hollywood's casuistry – bears evident vulnerabilities, yet triumphs in the end, Mikhalkov, in *12*, rewrites Lumet's script as if in collaboration with Konstantin Pobedonostsev, whose 1896 *Moscow Collection* (*Moskovskii sbornik*) exposed the Western jury system as an unsalvageable travesty of higher justice. Jousting with Hollywood and US society more broadly, Mikhalkov maps out a distinctly different path for the Russian legal system from the one enacted in Hollywood's courtroom, one sceptical towards Western-imported institutions and favouring a spiritually inflected dispensation of justice.

The uncertain global stature of Russia's lead directors underscores the vexing issue of Russian culture's place in the larger world order, in its historical relationship first to Europe, then to the US and – at least as far as cinema is concerned – to Hollywood, where Russia's status is always potentially located at the colonial periphery of global hegemony and where the very internal contradictions of 'nationalism' cannot help but trigger the other, emancipatory meaning of the word itself.

The figure of antilogy is the key discursive trope of this overland empire, where empire-preserving and empire-dismantling drives are mobilized across the same contiguous space. Unlike the decolonization of the Third World from the First – a decolonization played out between discrete units, set apart by the third space of ocean – Second World decolonization is a dynamic internal to itself, and its contradictions likewise remain internal to the contiguous space. Likewise, its nationalisms contain complex inter-determinations of empire-preserving and empire-dismantling impulses, entanglement and disentanglement, like ravelled fabric, simultaneously ravelling up into a knot and ravelling out into individual threads.

NOTES

1. A. Hastings, *The Construction of Nationhood: Ethnicity, Religion and Nationalism* (Cambridge, 1997), 4.
2. A. Smith, *National Identity* (Reno, NV, 1993), ix.
3. See, for example, Smith's working definitions in A. Smith, 'Dating the Nation', in *Ethnonationalism and the Contemporary World: Walker Connor and the Study of Nationalism*, ed. D. Conversi (London, 2002), 53–71; A. Smith, 'Ethnosymbolism', in *Encyclopaedia of Nationalism*, ed. A. Leoussi (New Brunswick, 2001), 84–7; A. Smith, 'Gastronomy or Geology? The Role of Nationalism in the Reconstruction of Nations', *Nations and Nationalism* 1:1 (1994), 3–23; A. Smith, 'The Warwick Debates', www.lse.ac.uk/collections/gellner/Warwick.html. A more elaborated argument than can be permitted here would discuss Smith's distinctions between perennialist, modernist and postmodernist nationalisms (see in particular Smith, 'Gastronomy', 18–23), as it would likewise discuss conceptual distinctions in the work of other scholars, such as Alter's *risorgimento*, reform and integral nationalisms in P. Alter, *Nationalismus* (Suhrkamp, 1985); Billig's extremist and banal nationalisms in M. Billig, *Banal Nationalism* (London, 1995); Greenfeld's individualistic, collectivistic and ethnic nationalisms in L. Greenfeld, *Nationalism: Five Roads to Modernity* (Cambridge, MA, 1993), and 'Nationalism in Western and Eastern Europe Compared', in *Can Europe Work? Germany and the Reconstruction of Postcommunist Societies*, ed. S. E. Hanson and W. Spohn (Seattle, WA, and London, 1995); Hall's 'nationalism from above', as opposed to one based on desire and fear, in J. A. Hall, 'Nationalisms: Classified and Explained', *Daedalus* 122 (1993), 1–28; Hechter's state-building, peripheral, irredentist and unification nationalisms in M. Hechter, *Containing Nationalism* (Oxford, 2000), especially 15–17; Mommsen's liberal, imperialist, fascist and contemporary nationalisms in W. J. Mommsen, 'The Varieties of the Nation State in Modern History: Liberal, Imperialist, Fascist and Contemporary Notions of Nation and Nationality', in *The Rise and Decline of the Nation State*, ed. M. Mann (Oxford, 1990), especially 210–26; and Gellner's whimsical Sleeping Beauty and Frankenstein's monster nationalisms in E. Gellner, *Nations and Nationalism: New Perspectives on the Past* (Ithaca, NY, 2009), especially 48.
4. I. Prizel, *National Identity and Foreign Policy: Nationalism and Leadership in Poland, Russia, and Ukraine* (Cambridge, 1998), 194.
5. M. Tlostanova, 'The Imagined Freedom: Post-Soviet Intellectuals between the Hegemony of the State and the Hegemony of the Market', *South Atlantic Quarterly* 105:3 (Summer 2006), 637–59; quotation on 654. Emphasis in the original.
6. Cf. Hamlet (5.1): 'Where be his quiddities now, his quillets, his cases, his tenures?'
7. Cicero, *Letters to His Friends*, trans. W. Glynn Williams, 3 vols. (Cambridge, MA, 1929), 479.
8. G. W. F. Hegel, *Werke in 20 Bänden*, vol. v, ed. E. Moldenhauer and K. M. Michel (Frankfurt am Main, 1969–71), 114.

9. A. Miller, *The Romanov Empire and Nationalism: Essays in the Methodology of Historical Research*, trans. S. Dobrynin (Budapest, 2008), 212.

10. H. Seton-Watson, *Nations and States: An Inquiry into the Origins of Nations and the Politics of Nationalism* (Boulder, CO, 1977), 83–7, 148. Sergei Uvarov's original term, from which Seton-Watson's analysis is derived, had been *narodnost'* (not *natsional'nost'*), a difference that now takes on greater significance in the context of an argument about the political expectations attending to *narod* (folk) and *natsiia* (nation).

11. Perhaps because of this internal instability, 'nationalism' seems to attract other potentially contradictory formulations: see, for example, S. Levinson, 'Is Liberal Nationalism an Oxymoron? An Essay for Judith Shklar', *Ethics* 105:3 (April 1995), 626–45.

12. For a similar definition, see, for example, Smith's 'Dating the Nation', 54, 65.

13. I have in mind here the fourteenth-century universities of Paris and Prague, divided into a French, Saxon or Polish *natio* (nation).

14. Smith, 'Dating the Nation', 54.

15. J. Breuilly, *Nationalism and the State* (Chicago, IL, 1994); see also his interview for H-Nationalism with D. H. Doyle and S.-M. Grant (London, 29 March 2006), online at www.h-net.org/~national/Breuilly.html; B. Anderson, *Imagined Communities: Reflections on the Origin and Spread of Nationalism*, 2nd edn, rev. (London, 1991); E. Hobsbawm and T. Ranger, eds., *The Invention of Tradition* (1983; Cambridge, 1992).

16. A. D. Smith, opening statement, 'The Warwick Debates', www2.lse.ac.uk/researchAndExpertise/units/gellner/Warwick.html.

17. Gellner and Smith, of course, are not unique in this regard: many scholars have written about what Balibar has described as nationalism's 'retrospective illusion': 'it consists in believing that the process of development from which we select aspects retrospectively, so as to see ourselves as the culmination of that process, was the only one possible, that is, it represented a destiny'. Of value here is the dialogue between Gellner and Smith as otherwise quite opposed figures, rather than the uniqueness of their views. See E. Balibar in E. Balibar and I. Wallerstein, *Race, Nation, Class: Ambiguous Identities* (London, 1991), 86.

18. 'For nationalists themselves', writes Smith, 'the role of the past is clear and unproblematic ... The task of the nationalist is simply to remind his or her compatriots of their glorious past, so that they can recreate and relive those glories.' Smith, 'Gastronomy' 18.

19. G. Hosking, *Empire and Nation in Russian History*, The Fourteenth Charles Edmondson Historical Lectures, 3–4 February 1992, Baylor University (Waco, TX, 1993), 9; R. Suny, 'Studying Empires', *Ab Imperio* 1 (2008), 205–13; quotation on 211.

20. E. Gellner, *Thought and Change* (London, 1964), 169.

21. N. Condee, 'Mediation, Imagination, and Time: Speculative Remarks on Russian Culture', *Ab Imperio* 1 (2008), 177–92.

22. I. Christie, 'Grandmother's Russia', *Sight & Sound* 18:10 (October 2008), 40–1, 54.

23. Among recent English-language discussions of Sokurov's work, see J. Alinez, 'Mythopoeia, "Metahistory", and Aleksandr Sokurov's *Sun* (*Solntse*), 2004', *KinoKultura* 10 (2005), www.kinokultura.com/reviews/R10-05solntse.html; I. Christie, '*Russkii kovcheg* / *Russian Ark*', in *The Cinema of Russia and the Former Soviet Union (24 Frames)*, ed. B. Beumers (London, 2007), 242–51; D. Kujundzic, 'After "After": The "Arkive" Fever of Alexander Sokurov', *ARTMargins*, 5 May 2003, www.artmargins.com/index.php/6-film-a-video/272-after-qafterq-the-qarkiveq-fever-of-alexander-sokurov. On Balabanov, see N. Condee, *The Imperial Trace: Recent Russian Cinema* (New York, 2009); J. Graffy, 'Brother', *Sight & Sound* 10:5 (May 2000), 44, www.bfi.org.uk/sight-andsound/review/322 [accessed 12 January 2011]; A. Horton, 'Lynch Pin? The Imagery of Aleksei Balabanov', *Kinoeye* [*Central Europe Review*] 2:18 (9 May 2000), www.ce-review.org/00/18/kinoeye18_horton.html [accessed 12 January 2011]; S. Larsen, 'National Identity, Cultural Authority, and the Post-Soviet Blockbuster: Nikita Mikhalkov and Aleksei Balabanov', *Slavic Review* 62:3 (Autumn 2003), 491–511. On Mikhalkov, see B. Beumers, *Nikita Mikhalkov* (London, 2005); S. Graham, 'Mikhalkov, *12* (2007)', *KinoKultura* 19 (January 2008), www.kinokultura.com/2008/19r-twelve.shtml; E. Prokhorova, 'Svoi sredi chuzhikh, chuzhoi sredi svoikh', in *Cinema of Russia*, ed. Beumers, 168–78.
24. I have elaborated this argument in 'Endstate and Allegory (Late Sokurov)', in *The Cinema of Alexander Sokurov*, ed. B. Beumers and N. Condee (2011).
25. A. Sokurov, *Island of Sokurov*, www.sokurov.spb.ru/isle_ru/isle_ftr.html.
26. Anderson, *Imagined Communities*, 177.
27. A. Sokurov, 'Teni zvuka', television interview for TV-6 Moscow with Petr Shepotinnik, Asia Kolodizhner and Liubov' Arkus, *Iskusstvo kino* 12 (1994), 13–17, quotation on 15–16.
28. A. Horton, 'Lynch Pin?'; A. Horton, 'Oh, Brother! Balabanov's *Brat 2*', *Central European Review* 3:5 (5 February 2001), www.ce-review.org/01/5/kinoeye5_horton.html; A. Horton, 'War, What Is It Good For?', review of Aleksei Balabanov's *War*, *Kinoeye* [*Central Europe Review*] 2:2 (21 January 2002), www.kinoeye.org/02/18/horton18_no3.php; V. Rizov, '*Cargo 200*: An Unflinching, Quasi-Comedic Portrait of 1984 Russia', *Village Voice*, 31 December 2008, www.villagevoice.com/2008-12-31/film/cargo-200-an-unflinching-quasi-comedic-portrait-of-1984-russia/; D. Seckler, 'Aleksei Balabanov, *Dead Man's Bluff* [Zhmurki] (2005)', *KinoKultura* 10 (2005), www.kinokultura.com/reviews/R10-05zhmurki.html; S. Toymentsev, 'Grigorii Konstantinopol'skii: *Pussycat* (*Koshechka*, 2009)', *KinoKultura* 31 (2011), www.kinokultura.com/2011/31r-koshechka.shtml.
29. J. Romney, 'Brat-Pack', *New Statesman*, 10 April 2000, www.newstatesman.com/200004100043.
30. R. Clarke, 'Film: Freaks and Film-makers', *Independent* (London), 20 August 1999.

PART II

Institutions of national identity

National identity through visions
of the past: contemporary Russian cinema

Birgit Beumers

BOY: And you lied. There is no Koktebel' in the Crimea. I checked the atlas.
FATHER: Koktebel' was renamed Planerskoe in 1944. Got it? . . .
BOY: Why did they rename Koktebel' Planernoe?
FATHER: Planerskoe. Koktebel' is a Tatar word. The Tatars were deported at the
end of the war. And there was a big airfield for planes and gliders [*planery*].
Hence the name.

(Dialogue from *Koktebel'*, dir. Aleksei Popogrebskii and
Boris Khlebnikov, 2003)

On the one hand, the dialogue above echoes the common confusion over place names after the renaming of streets, cities and countries following the collapse of the Soviet Union; on the other, it predicates the impossibility of an understanding between Soviet fathers and Russian children. The child does not know the history, which has randomly changed the poetic name of the land of sky-blue hills (*köktöbe*) to a functional label, and back again, leaving the post-Soviet generation doubtful of the facts of the present and reticently curious about the country's history. Without knowing the past, the boy cannot even find Koktebel'; having learnt about the history, he finds every single word of the father's story to be a lie: there is no Koktebel' in the Crimea, at least not the one that the father evokes in his memory. (And moreover, there is no monument to a glider as his father says, but just its ruins.) Destabilizing the commonly accepted view of the past is one of the main objects of a cinema that defines itself by reference to the past: as *post*-Soviet.[1]

This chapter looks at some films produced during the Putin era and set in the Soviet, post-war past – a period remembered nostalgically in a number of ways in contemporary Russia. There are virtual museums (Muzei '2oi vek', www.2oth.su), television and radio stations (Nostal'giia TV and Radio Nostalgie), themed restaurants (Gastronom No. 1; Stolovaia No. 57)[2] and artefacts such as the objects sold in the gift shop Ministerstvo podarkov (which uses Soviet-style objects for designer gifts) or by the jeweller Gourji.[3] There continue to be even Soviet-style sweets, produced for example by the confectionary labels of Babaevskii (Red Moscow, *Krasnaia Moskva*, and Cosmic, *Kosmicheskie*), Krasnyi Oktiabr' (Alenka; Stratosphere, *Stratosfera*; and Metropolitan, *Stolichnye*) and RotFront (Moscow Woman, *Moskvichka*), all of which invoke the traditions of the Soviet past in their chocolate wrappings. This nostalgia for the post-war Soviet past also helps to explain the phenomenal appeal of the television show *Lately* (*Namedni*), where the presenter Leonid Parfenov collated footage and chronicled Soviet life to build a catalogue of the past:

The TV programme *Lately* was designed to be a farewell [to the Soviet past]. Time passes and approximately since the second term of Putin's presidency, since 2004, it has become clear that Russian [*rossiiskoe*] doesn't mean Russian at all. It doesn't work like in montage – return to the cut of 25 October 1917 and paste the next onto it. The Russian is a continuation and development, and even repetition of the Soviet. It's become clear that the Soviet was the template ... We live in an era of a renaissance of Soviet antiquity.[4]

In the preface to his book accompanying the series, Parfenov defines the Putin era as a time when 'the country celebrates holidays and serves the army, elects the rulers and watches television, sells hydrocarbons and receives an education, supports football teams and gets cured in hospitals, sings the anthem and threatens foreign countries – in Soviet style'.[5] It is a time when Soviet childhood is remembered with warm feelings and a sense of nostalgia that does not, however, aim to restore that past, but rather to celebrate its collective spirit.[6] A desire to rebuild links with the past can further be observed in documentary cinema's bio-chronicles,[7] but also in social networks such as Classmates (odnoklassniki.ru), which help to find those lost friends of the (largely Soviet) past and simulate a sense of collective that is no longer extant in the current capitalist climate governed only by self-interest. Significantly, all those areas of nostalgia detect positive aspects in Soviet everyday life (*byt*) rather than the official discourse. Such a 'harmless' return to the past – through chocolate wrappers, gifts, jewellery and other collectibles – also lies at the heart of the popularity of memoirs, both in literary and cinematic form. These include Pavel Sanaev's autobiographical story *Bury Me Behind the Baseboard* (*Pokhoronite menia za plintusom*), published in 1996 and turned into a film by Sergei Snezhkin in 2008,[8] and Lilianna Lungina's memoir *Word-for-Word Translation* (*Podstrochnik*), published in 2010 and turned into a film by Oleg Dorman released in 2009. It also goes some way to explain the growing number of literary adaptations that have brought Russian (and Soviet) classics onto the television screen, largely in a serialized form – making available for home-viewing those classics that were once reserved for the intellectual elite: Fedor Dostoevskii's *Idiot* (2003), Vasilii Aksenov's *The Moscow Saga* (2004), Anatolii Rybakov's *Children of the Arbat* (2004), Mikhail Bulgakov's *Master and Margarita* (2005), Liudmila Ulitskaia's *Kukotsky's Case* (2005), Boris Pasternak's *Doctor Zhivago* (2005), Nikolai Gogol''s *Dead Souls* (2005), Il'ia Il'f and Evgenii Petrov's 1920s satire *The Golden Calf* (2005) or Aleksandr Solzhenitsyn's *In the First Circle* (2006), to name but the first few that come to mind.[9]

The Soviet past thus fulfils a social function, reasserting the value of friends and a collective that is lacking in the present, and turning into 'mass culture' what used to be the privilege of the Soviet elite. In both cases a moral and ideological value system – plainly absent in contemporary Russia – is also offered. However, when this value system is threatened or shattered, the public rebels, as we shall see from the responses to cinematic returns to the Soviet past.

The return to the past in post-Soviet culture has yet another function. Issues of the formation of a national identity through various media, and cinema in particular – both with regard to the Soviet identity formulated during the 1930s (building the Soviet empire) as well as to a Russian identity in the post-Soviet era (resurrecting an imperial past, Soviet or pre-revolutionary) – have been the object of much scholarly debate.[10] Both periods of identity formation have frequently been compared with each other, and the return to the 1930s in 1990s culture – be it in reworkings of the past or parodies in sots-art style – has been widespread. The void left by the demise of the Soviet Union (and its ideology) has shifted the historical focus onto the imperial, pre-revolutionary past, which served as a reference point for the new Russian identity in the 1990s. Oleg Sulkin has argued that the Soviet past was filled with an ideological content that disappeared after the collapse of the Soviet Union in 1991.[11] He suggests that this ideological vacuum is replenished in two ways in post-Soviet Russia: first, through an imperialist and orthodox view, including state capitalism; and second, through liberal and democratic approaches supportive of bourgeois values and individual liberties.

If the late 1980s and early 1990s saw a surge of films about the Stalin era and the Purges,[12] which strove to disclose the crimes of the regime and fitted onto the agenda of glasnost and perestroika (and thus within an ideological framework), then post-Soviet cinema has chosen different periods in its attempt to fill the 'ideological vacuum', while at the same time offering models for a national identity. The 'imperialist view' can be traced through films that focus either on legendary heroes – from the rebel Ermak to the Soviet inventor Sergei Korolev and the heroes of the *bylina* in recent Russian cartoons – or on periods that inspire a sense of national pride, especially the Second World War. Moreover, it can be detected in films about the pre-revolutionary era, from Nikita Mikhalkov's *Barber of Siberia* (*Sibirskii tsiriul'nik*, 1999) and films about the resistance to Bolshevism, including Andrei Kravchuk's *Admiral* (2008) about Aleksandr Kolchak, or Oleg Fomin's *Gentlemen Officers: Save the Emperor* (*Gospoda ofitsery*, 2008), which both rewrote the role of the Whites in 1917.

The second discourse, suggesting a more nuanced view of the recent Soviet past, manifested itself fairly late in the 1990s and thrived during the 2000s. This perspective glorified neither Soviet heroes – from the Second World War to fighters against Bolshevism – nor the 'everyday' golden Soviet past in the style of *Old Songs about the Main Thing* and the popularity of Soviet films during the Yeltsin era; instead, it critically reviews recent Soviet history. While films promoting the imperialist discourse tended to seek a larger audience, the liberal view has usually been adopted in films for festival audiences, although it is difficult to speak about blockbusters and auteur cinema at a time when the film industry and infrastructure still lay in ruins.

We have thus identified two paradigms for the revisioning of the Soviet past: the confirmation or challenge of the old Soviet value system, and the tendency for the imperial discourse to speak to the masses and the liberal discourse to speak to more critical audiences. Furthermore, the colouring of reality plays a decisive role in the reception of films about the past. The perestroika era had been dominated and doomed by the *chernukha* genre,[13] revealing the bleakness and squalor of contemporary, everyday existence. This was cinema's response to the Soviet film production system's request for a varnished reality, glossing over screen versions of past and present alike. Now the time had come to peel off the varnish, from past and present. If we scrutinize the visual representation of the 1950s in Vladimir Men'shov's *Moscow Does Not Believe in Tears* (*Moskva slezam ne verit*, 1979) or Nikita Mikhalkov's *Five Evenings* (*Piat' vecherov*, 1978), we find a meticulous reconstruction of the past, varnishing details to romanticize the 'old days'. By contrast, the 'authentic' everyday life of the 1990s was shown in bleak colours in the *chernukha* films, which provoked a nostalgia for the Soviet past in mass culture. This was apparent especially in the television scheduling and viewing practices of the late 1990s, which relied almost exclusively on old Soviet films,[14] but also in the advertising practices that appealed to Brezhnev era goods ('Indian Tea', 'Lianozovo Milk') in an attempt to boost sales of domestic products in a market that was flooded by imports.[15] This return to things Soviet was partly motivated by the desire to instil a sense of safety: in advertising, the translation of foreign ads had led to confusing messages, while the proliferation of domestic *chernukha* and crime films had estranged audiences.

At the end of the twentieth century, cinema seemed to offer no new visions for the future or recipes for a new identity. Contemporary reality was bleak, while the past was often harrowing. The Soviet legacy was so alienating that it could replace the image of the enemy of the West (now a friend) and address the Soviet past as the alien 'other', in an attempt to distance oneself while also modelling the new identity on the rejected Soviet project (what Lev Gudkov has termed 'negative identity').[16] The past was the antithesis to the present, but what did this 'negative' image, the Soviet 'other', look like?

Let us first survey the historical periods represented in recent Russian cinema in the order of their appearance on the screens: Pavel Chukhrai's *The Thief* (*Vor*, 1997), set in 1952; Aleksei Iu. German's *Khrustalev, My Car!* (*Khrustalev, mashinu!*, 1998), set in 1953; Viacheslav Sorokin's *Totalitarian Romance* (*Totalitarnyi roman*, 1998), set in 1968 and among dissident circles involved in the protest against the USSR's invasion of Czechoslovakia; Valerii Ogorodnikov's *The Barracks* (*Barak*, 1999), set in the Urals in 1953; Leonid Mariagin's *101st km* (2001), set in the Moscow suburbs in the 1950s, dealing with criminal teenage life; Vadim Abdrashitov's *Magnetic Storms* (*Magnitnye buri*, 2003), set in the Urals during the privatization of factories in the late perestroika period; Pavel Chukhrai's *A Driver for Vera* (*Voditel' dlia Very*, 2004), set in 1962–3; Aleksei Uchitel''s *Dreaming of Space* (*Kosmos kak predchuvstvie*, 2005), with a background of the events unfolding in Murmansk between 1957 and 1961; Aleksei Balabanov's *Cargo 200* (*Gruz 200*, 2007), set in Leninsk in 1984; Karen Shakhnazarov's *Vanished Empire* (*Ischeznuvshaia imperiia*, 2008), set in 1973, with an epilogue in the present; Aleksei A. German's *Paper Soldier* (*Bumazhnyi soldat*, 2008), set in 1961 between Moscow and the cosmodrome Baikonur; Valerii Todorovskii's musical *Hipsters* (*Stiliagi*, 2009), set in Moscow in 1955; Aleksandr Proshkin's *Miracle* (*Chudo*, 2009), set in 1956, and based on the so-called 'Standing of Zoia';[17] and Garik Sukachev's hippie film *House of the Sun* (*Dom Solntsa*, 2010), set in the late 1960s and shifting between Moscow and the Black Sea.

As is obvious from this brief catalogue, the interest in the Soviet past sees a notable rise in the period between 2007 and 2010. The list (which includes the best-known films in domestic and international distribution) comprises a diverse group of filmmakers who tackle the Soviet past for different reasons. However, the relative stability of the Putin era has allowed the revisioning of the Soviet past in a critical light: there is no longer a desire to return to the golden Soviet times (as can be found in advertising of the late 1990s), but a distanced, critical view of the Soviet era – even those years that might have been the most hopeful, such as the Thaw and glasnost, or which offered reasonable living conditions, such as the early Brezhnev years. Filmmakers who largely lack first-hand experience of these times look back with nostalgia – not wanting a return, but attempting to find a reason for their present identity (or lack of it) in a past that they share with the nation.

I discuss here some of the more popular films that revisit the Soviet past. My aim is to assess the shift in the manner of representation of the past (authentic, staged, artificial) in order to establish a connection between representation and reception. Broadly speaking, I explore how films debunk the myth of a happy Soviet past promoted in mass culture. They review the Thaw as a time when the hope for change is obstructed by the system that crushes man along with his aspirations – for the conquest of space, the cosmonauts in *Paper Soldier* and *Dreaming of Space* respectively, or for a just power, the general in *Driver for Vera* and the priest in *Miracle*. The period of stagnation (or *zastoi*) in the 1970s features rarely as a setting, and is characterized by counter-culture (*House of the Sun*) and a rise of subculture (*Vanished Empire*) – a time when the dominance of the political system over its victim, the individual, was reaffirmed. The perestroika era is discredited as a time of latent or rampant violence (*Magnetic Storms*, *Cargo 200*). Generally, all these films tend to be concerned not with major historical events or political figures, but with the personal and everyday aspect of Soviet life. Where historical leaders appear, they do so from a deeply personal angle, such as the figure of Lenin in Sokurov's *Taurus* (*Telets*, 2000), depicted as a sick man who despairs over his inability to control his body. In *Miracle*, Khrushchev may be decisive, but he also suffers from sleeplessness and the weather conditions like any ordinary man. Such de-heroicization is typical of the Thaw, but it also provides a contrast to the official Soviet narrative – historical or social – by emphasizing the personal life of heroes and leaders.

REVISITING THE THAW THAT NEVER WAS?

The revisioning of the past beyond the terror of the Stalin era began with a turn to the immediate post-war period and attempted to reappropriate the past as a personal (hi)story. Filmmakers meticulously reconstructed the past, less through props and decor than through an emotional personal memory. The plot of Chukhrai's *Thief* functions in this manner, touching the viewer through an emotional portrayal of the downward spiral of crime that governs post-war Soviet society and – the finale suggests – leaves the future of the country in the hands of orphaned children. German's *Khrustalev, My Car!* also exemplifies this approach, showing life under Stalin through the eyes of a child, the son of General Klenskii, who himself heads the medical team caring for the sick leader. These films carefully restore the emotional hardship of those years, a feature also strikingly translated in *The Barracks*, which shows everyday life in one of Stalin's construction projects of the 1950s. Films about the early 1950s, then, reconstruct the atmosphere of the time through emotional experience (*perezhivanie*, also enacting this on the viewer), with an emphasis on the everyday rather than the heroic narratives that were typical for that time. Here cinema places the spotlight not on the war heroes who are unable to adapt to post-war reality (as in Thaw cinema), but non-heroic characters, criminals and victims of the system.

Pavel Chukhrai's *A Driver for Vera* marks a significant break away from the Stalin era into the Thaw. The film is set in 1962, but extraordinarily uses an approach typical of 1990s cinema about the 1930s – i.e. the exposure of the cruelty of the system – while setting this in the most hopeful period of Soviet history, the Thaw. Indeed, the opening frames show the hopefulness for a new life during Khrushchev's reign. Standing on the viewing platform on Sparrow Hills, Cadet Viktor poses for a camera, leaning on the new black Volga car he drives for an army general. The scene, which captures Moscow State University's new building, is filmed in reverse perspective: the clicking camera takes pictures not of Viktor, but of the newly-weds standing near the balustrade and outside the camera's frame. The film cuts from these sun-drenched images of happy life (a marriage, Viktor's job, the country's future education) to a sterile, cold morgue, where a post mortem has been carried out on the body of Major Kraikov after his alleged suicide. The colourful joy of everyday life is cancelled by a gruesome and bleak political reality. Life's appearances are treacherous. People may wear bright dresses, carry radios and take snapshots, and they may have acquired material wealth, but this surface reality hides political intrigues that will ultimately destroy lives. A sense of reversal informs the film's narrative, where joy turns into sorrow, and happiness into a nightmare.

The action moves from the capital to the Black Sea, where General Serov, commander of the Black Sea Fleet, resides. The new spirit of hope can be sensed far from the centre, too: Elvis Presley, the twist and the Spanish love-song 'Bésame Mucho' play in the background, and Vera's behaviour reveals an open attitude towards Western lifestyle. The availability of radios and tape recorders and the leisure activities of people walking on the promenade or partying on yachts, as well as theatre and variety performances or visits to restaurants – all these activities paint a vivid and detailed picture of the 1960s, showing a relaxed country and echoing the emphasis on leisure facilities promoted by Khrushchev. Moreover, the locals mingle with Cuban soldiers stationed at the Black Sea. Yet again, these are only superficial and misleading indicators of a happy life.

Against the background of the events that unfold in the film stands the Cuban missile crisis in October 1962. Serov's crippled daughter Vera had an affair with a Cuban soldier and is expecting his child: what might have been acceptable in the summer of 1962 is no longer tolerated in the autumn, and Vera has to hide the identity of the father of her unborn child and agree to a 'white' marriage to Viktor to save the general's face. The film also takes up current political issues when making a reference to a sunken vessel, whose crew perished because no fire brigade was allowed on board, for the ship carried uranium. This incident hints at the tragedy of the *Kursk* submarine on 12 August 2000, but in Chukhrai's scenario it is the reason for the downfall of the general, whose responsibility it had been to carry out the orders from the centre, resulting in the death of dozens of sailors. The incident reflects how Khrushchev's liberalism abruptly turned into rigid internal control, while the hardliners – the KGB officers in the film – remain in control at all times. The surveillance through the secret service is an example of this: Viktor is to denounce Serov to Savel'ev, who serves as adjunct to the general and master-minds his downfall. So the film remarks both on the power of the secret service then as well as now, pointedly alluding to the political background of the president at the time of the film's making, Putin having begun his career in the ranks of the KGB.

The shifts in international politics (the Cuban missile crisis), as well as the internal control through hardliners that eventually brought about Khrushchev's fall, all impact directly on the life of the characters because of their social standing. Vera may be spoilt but remains simple at heart: a motherless child raised by her father, who showers her with love. She needs none of the luxury goods her father can procure, for it is his home-made potatoes with butter that really bring her happiness. Yet her life is cut short, for she and her father die at the hands of the KGB, while her baby girl is saved by the orphaned Viktor, who lost his own little sister. At the end of the film, the former maid Lida is pictured holding the general's grandchild like a Madonna with infant, evoking compassion for the continued endurance of suffering.

There is no future where all personal and family relations are cut off. Vera is separated from her Cuban lover and then killed, her father also is murdered, and Viktor has to run from the arms of the KGB, with his army career ruined.

The survival of the system rather than the individual re-enforces the social nightmare where the family, together with its values of humanism and love, perishes. No future is offered in the film. The army and the secret service turn reality into a nightmare. Chukhrai's film inverses the historical perception of the Thaw as a period of possible optimism, and it relegates the 1960s to that part of Soviet history which witnessed the oppression and destruction of moral and social values of family and love. Chukhrai rejects any nostalgia for the Soviet past, not for ideological reasons, but in the context of the loss of universal values. He trashes any nostalgic feeling by exposing the impossibility of happiness in a society whose families were 'crippled' and deprived of mothers and fathers. Chukhrai dismantles the myth of the Thaw, turning the hope for the future into the nightmare of Soviet life in the 1960s. Although the film grossed US$2 million at the box office (a significant amount, considering the time of its release), audience responses to the film were negative, with bloggers accusing it of darkening reality and inaccurately representing history.[18] As Liliia Nemchenko comments on the responses: 'Probably a lot of those who rejected the film would have happily accepted the concept of the filmmaker, but in a Stalinist decor.'[19] She accurately points at two aspects that appear to have tainted the film's reception: on the one hand the bleak outlook on the Thaw as a period of repression, and on the other the accuracy of the setting (and the acting), which facilitated an emotional identification with the fate of the main characters. In that context, the past as shown on screen is no longer a past with which the viewer wishes to identify.

By contrast, the approach adopted by Valerii Todorovskii in his film *Hipsters* had almost the opposite effect. By creating a deliberately playful and stylized representation of the Thaw era, he generated a box office of US$16 million – and positive responses on blogs. Set in 1955, after the death of Stalin but before the Twentieth Party Congress of February 1956, the film uses the musical genre, which facilitates a more distanced (and distancing) approach to the past. The 1950s are shown as a period dominated by uniformity, where any otherness was suppressed. However, this crushing of rebellious youth remains on the level of a game, without inviting the viewer to identify with the characters – to use theatrical terms: demonstration (*predstavlenie*) rather than experience. The film's style, with its close-ups and crane shots, musical interludes and colourful dresses (which could never have been captured on Soviet colour film stock so brightly), deliberately sets itself apart from the style of the 1950s in order to underline the artificial quality of the (pseudo)-historical setting and thereby emphasize the performative nature of the

Figure 3.1 A scene from *Hipsters* (*Stiliagi*, Valerii Todorovskii, 2009).

film. Todorovskii himself called the film 'some fantasy about our fifties'.[20] The playful opposition to uniformity is conveniently set in a most suitable arena: the world of the *stiliagi*, the style-hunters and dandies, who dressed in Western fashion and were famously parodied in a caricature in *Krokodil* in 1949.[21]

History is faked, but this does not matter, and 'small inaccuracies do not spoil the film's impression but rather strengthen it' (blogger Roman, Ufa, 23 December 2008).[22] On the contrary: the film's appeal lies precisely in recognizable, rather than authentic, voices and tunes. The songs of the *stiliagi* imitate rock and jazz melodies of the 1950s, but were actually composed by a multiplicity of contemporary, post-Soviet, popular bands and their leaders, such as Nol' and Fedor Chistiakov, Bravo, Maik Naumenko, Garik Sukachev, Andrei Makarevich, Vladimir Shakhrin and Chaif, Slava Butusov, Natal'ia Pivovarova of Kolibri, and Viktor Tsoi – all lend their voice to the dissonant voices of underground culture. By contrast, the youth organization of the Communist Party, the Komsomol, is a dull and monotonous chorus (Figure 3.1). The film treats the past as an aesthetic phenomenon rather than searching it for social or historical issues. It dwells on the parallels between then and now musically, but also in social terms, comparing the hipsters to present-day punks; indeed, as a blogger remarked: 'they resemble more contemporary punks' (blogger Erna, 2 January 2009).[23] And most importantly, the ending of the film is triumphant: dreams might not have come true then, but they do now.

Hipsters observes the transformation of the former *komsomolets* Mels, who turns into a *stiliaga* not for ideological but for personal reasons (he falls in love with Polza). Mels – a common Soviet name at the time – was formed as an acronym from the initials of Marx, Engels, Lenin and Stalin, but our hero drops the 's' to become the *stiliaga* Mel. This simple act turns into an ideological scandal, since it signals disloyalty to Stalin, and Mel at the instigation of the *komsomolka* Katia has to surrender his Komsomol membership card. Again, this is an act of personal revenge rather than ideological punishment, because Katia is in love with Mel(s) but loses him to the *chuvikha*[24] Polza (Polina), whose nickname, too, is an acronym – of 'Remember Lenin's Testaments' (*Pomnim Lenina zavety*) rather than a variant of the Americanized name Polly.

When Polza conceives a child after a one-night stand with a black African visiting Moscow – the encounter with the Other being the driving force – Mel stands by her in an almost conventional marriage. The reference to Grigorii Aleksandrov's popular musical *The Circus* (*Tsirk*, 1936) is too obvious: Marion Dixon and her black child are integrated into the Soviet collective represented by the circus audience and supported by the blond, blue-eyed Soviet hero Martynov. Polza, on the other hand, becomes an average Soviet mother, concerned with the child and household chores rather than trendy outfits. Normality replaces rebelliousness. Moreover, Mel's dreams are shattered when his friend Fred tells him that a *stiliaga* would stand out even on New York's Broadway. Otherness turns out to be an invention, and a myth. The film's finale sings a song of praise to the present rather than the past, for allowing genuine multi-cultured-ness, otherness and difference – precisely those ideals, that is to say, that were advanced in Soviet propaganda. Only now, in present-day Moscow, on Tverskaia Street, can the *stiliaga* Mel – the ancestor of a multi-cultured society – stand amid a crowd of skinheads and punks (representing the otherness of today). In this sense, *Hipsters* debunks the *stiliaga* myth as an illusion and shows the time and place for genuine variety as the Moscow of today, playing into the hands of liberal and democratic ideologies.

If we compare the responses to these two films, which were made at the beginning and towards the end of Putin's presidency and which deal with the early and late Thaw, we can see a shift away from the marginal location of the Black Sea (where much of the Soviet ambience is still preserved for today's filmmakers, allowing them to use an authentic setting) to the central location of Moscow. Moreover, the filmmakers abandon the method of psychological realism in favour of an artificial approach and a staged performance of the past. Neither Chukhrai nor Todorovskii reconstruct the past: their films are not an exercise in myth-making, nor do they create a fact-based spectacle of the past (à la *The Storming of the Winter Palace*). Moreover, both films contain a number of contemporary references, be it to political events or the visual merger of past and present, thus preventing a complete immersion into the past. Finally, we see a move away from a bleak portrayal to a cheerful one. The *stiliagi* did not overturn society, and the regime did not tolerate otherness, but this was also true for other countries at the time, and things have changed now. This optimistic message is not unrelated to the film's reception, but more importantly it points to a particular use of the Soviet past.

However, *Hipsters* adopts a fundamentally different approach to the Soviet legacy. It neither duplicates the past nor glorifies it, but rather involves the viewer in a playful journey to the past as a subculture that is constructed and artificial, exaggerated and overdone, in order to allow for a mix of past and present. The past is not reconstructed, but stylized. The songs may sound like they are from the 1950s, but they are not. The colour of the clothes is almost too blunt and shrill: commonly images of the period are in black and white, with a few colour drawings of cartoons in news-papers, so the film appears to overdo the style as we are used to seeing it. *Hipsters* turns into a performance, a demonstration of a life that never existed in that form: bright and amazing.

Ol'ga Shaburova effectively demonstrates this playful approach to the Soviet past in consumer culture, where for example the Central Department Store (GUM) turns the Soviet experience into a spectacle to allow the New Russians (*novye russkie*) to 'play at' living in the USSR – for promotional events. Of course, none of the props, decorations or goods would have been as perfect in Soviet times. Shaburova compares this staged return to a sanitized, cleansed and purified Soviet past to another experi-ence, that of a lunch at the children's department store Detskii mir, which closed only in 2008. Until then, an old-style real *stolovaia* (called Café Nostalgie) could be found on the top floor, which received no attention whatsoever, but still offered the original Soviet experience.[25] The staged version of the past suggests that one can visit the Soviet times for a brief spell and safely return to the present, and there is no possible harm in such a brief revisitation. Films such as *Driver for Vera*, however, unsettle the viewer, in that they deny him or her the belief in a happy past, and by implying that the structures and errors of the past have an impact on the present, they destabilize the viewers' fragile construction of a (positive) identity that encompasses the Soviet past as one's own (rather than the other, the enemy). Chukhrai reads history as a closed system: there is no future for any of the characters, except perhaps the maid and the baby, the (not) mother and (not her) infant at the film's end.

PERESTROIKA: THE END OF THE SOVIET UNION

The period of stagnation has not formed the setting for many films, the most significant exception being Shakhnazarov's *Vanished Empire* (grossing $1.5m at the box office and securing a US release). The film unfolds as a flashback to 1973, when three students get involved in the subculture and the rising shadow economy, tasting the forbidden fruit of Western consumerism available through illegal trade while longing for a 'normal life'. The film's structure, with a narrative frame from the present, excludes the possibility of turning time back, because the past is firmly labelled as 'the past'. The format of the flashback, along with the filmmaker's suggestion to return to the ancient, eastern roots in search of the self, sets this film apart from those already discussed in this chapter. If the stagnation period is almost absent from the screen, the latent violence inherent in the perestroika period has recently caught Russian filmmakers' attention. Bearing in mind that the majority of cinema-goers are aged between eighteen and thirty-five, they will largely not remember the perestroika period first-hand as adults, but this is nevertheless the time of their childhood. Therefore, when this time is soiled on screen, audiences often become quite touchy in their response.

Abdrashitov's *Magnetic Storms* opens with a long sequence that confronts the spectator with monochrome scenes of nightly gang fights in a factory, shot in a blue-grey tint that veils the two opposed sides in a cloth of uniformity. Indeed, they are all workers of the same factory engaged in fist-fights, which are paced and look almost choreographed, never showing any physical injury sustained in the fight, but rather the movement of the racing feet and the beating fists. This scene shows a balletic performance rather than a historical document. The absence of an overview and the breathtakingly fast movement of the camera create a sense of dizziness for the spectator, almost like the Danish Dogme films shot with hand-held cameras. Similarly, the context for the events is hard to understand: Abdrashitov's lens is so close to the action that it is impossible to grasp the background for the events, despite some clues. Man is in the grip of historic events that gush like a thunderstorm and shake up human lives – which is one explanation for the film's title.

The events are set in the late 1980s, during the period of factory strikes following attempts to privatize state-owned enterprises. The workers stand divided between Markin and Savchuk, two bureaucrats who seemingly haggle over the ownership of the factory. Yet the bosses have long since struck a deal and use the workers for their own political goals: they pay the strike leaders to kindle the strike and the confrontations, until the army is brought in to pacify the situation. Such protests were part of an organized campaign to discredit Gorbachev's reforms in the late 1980s: they served to undermine the privatization of state property and to cover up the local deals between party bosses over ownership.

Yet Abdrashitov dwells on the romantic plot through the relationship between the couple Marina and Valera. The strikes literally intrude into their lives: the strikers force their way into their home and continue fighting in their bedroom. Corruption extends not only to the secret deals of the factory management, but also to the private sphere. Marina, who narrowly escapes rape after returning from the fields where they have been stealing potatoes, understands that she faces a choice: sooner or later, being raped by the local workers, or going with her sister to Moscow to be 'raped' and paid, i.e. to prostitute herself. She chooses the latter, leaving Valera behind. At the end of the film the workers march towards the factory, in unison, this time to work. Their marching is choreographed in the same way as the opening scene, but this time it is one-directional and takes place in daylight: the magnetic storm of uncoordinated, chaotic movement, socially and literally, is over. Stability has returned, but happiness has vanished, and the individual has no future outside the collective. Like Chukhrai in *Driver for Vera*, Abdrashitov debunks the myth that the perestroika period was full of hope. Unlike Chukhrai, he stages the events, blurs the historical context and leaves the viewer with a melodrama that ultimately could have happened any time. As a result, the film elicited neither an outcry nor audience support.

Aleksei Balabanov's *Cargo 200*, by contrast, caused much controversy owing to its portrayal of violence, crime and corruption in late Soviet society. Balabanov detects the first cracks in the surface of the happy Soviet times in the year 1984, and he focuses his gaze on the rampant violence of the state (Afghan war, prison camps, corrupt police force) that is replicated on a personal level (rape, murder).[26] Violence replaces human and verbal relations.

Cargo 200 offers a bleak view of the 1980s, exposing the abundant corruption – moral, sexual, physical, ideological. Balabanov suggests that neither liberalism nor orthodoxy can replace the absence of the Soviet value system, because the whole of society is infected by corruption. Lev Gudkov has formulated this process thus: '[Balabanov] concisely shows the necrosis of human features, the decay, the crisis, where violence is the code of conduct.'[27] Moreover, Balabanov not only destroys the illusion that the contemporary viewer might have had a happy childhood during perestroika, but he also implies that the young generation was raped, killed and murdered in the name of the state (the Afghan war; the policeman; the convict forced to commit the rape), denying the spectator any possibility of a return. It is this outright denial of nostalgia through an exaggerated, unreal, nightmarish portrayal of the past which makes *Cargo 200* such a destabilizing experience. Gudkov perceives a direct link between the latent aggression of the present and nostalgia:

Our sociological research shows that the higher the level of inner aggression, the stronger the nation's nostalgia for the Soviet past and the fact that it has gone. The Brezhnev era is seen as a golden time, quiet, well-to-do, stable, when the state guaranteed some welfare and so on. Its idealization is particularly obvious against the background of the crisis during the 90s. The same can be said about the persistent love for old Soviet films, the envy for those rosy times and stories with simple (simplistic to cartoon level) romantic heroes. This is nostalgia for cynical, exultant social masks. Many people will be averse to *Cargo 200* precisely because it is the strongest attack on their nostalgic feelings and memories, on their current view of their former lives.[28]

CONCLUSION: TURNING TIME BACK?

Although not set during perestroika, Timur Bekmambetov's blockbuster *Night Watch* (*Nochnoi dozor*, 2004) should not be ignored in a discussion of films about the Soviet past, because the narrative frame of *Night Watch* and its sequel *Day Watch* (*Dnevnoi dozor*, 2006) involves an exercise of rewriting the past – with the 'chalk of fate' (the subtitle of the sequel).[29] Anton Gorodetskii, worried that his wife has betrayed him with another man and carries the latter's child, consults a sorceress (Schulz) to bring about a miscarriage. Unbeknown to him the magic spell fails. When his son Egor sides with the dark forces of Zawulon, Anton has to find the chalk of fate in order to reverse his spell and bring Egor back onto his – the right (and light) – side. If we read the film as an allegory for the rampant and destructive capitalism that characterized the decade, then we could say that Egor – a child born in the chaotic 1990s – temporarily finds a father figure in the evil Zawulon rather than in his birth father Anton, who turns time back so he can give Egor the family that had become dysfunctional after the intervention of the sorceress Schulz (a foreign, Western influence). Fathers – real, not surrogate ones – need to take action to change society. Asserting Russia's inclination to patriarchal rule, *Night Watch* also offers a reassuring view of our relationship to the past: time can be turned back, spells undone and mistakes corrected.

But does the spectator want to turn time back to any of the Soviet epochs as presented in recent Russian cinema? The 1950s are shown as a period where hope for the future turns into a nightmare of perpetuated corruption and where otherness is only an illusion or an adolescent prelude to conformity. The most radical denial of a happy past concerns the decade when the Soviet Union collapsed along with its ideology and value system: through choreographed movement Abdrashitov reveals the coordinated deceit of the people, depriving them of control over their lives and stripping the state of its property: a legacy that dooms Russia's economy to the present day. Balabanov shows the Soviet era as a harrowing past which holds nothing worthy of preservation, even if it stands for the precious and happy childhood of the contemporary viewer. This view destabilizes the assumed (dis)continuity from Soviet to post-Soviet values by representing the past not in bleak but in grotesquely violent and exaggerated forms. As time passes, films no longer show the Soviet past in terms of psychological realism (as appropriate for the romantic or melodramatic genre), but through a playful and performative exploration or repelling exaggeration. The myth of nostalgia for the Soviet past – so prominent in mass culture – has been dispelled in these recent films; the present is dissociated from the Soviet past.

In her study on nostalgia Svetlana Boym has defined two types of a longing for the past that correspond broadly, and in more general terms, to the distinction Oleg Sulkin makes with regards to cinema: one kind of nostalgia restores the imperial past (corresponding to the imperialist and orthodox view Sulkin describes); the other offers a critical and ironic view, challenging the truth about the past (reflecting what Sulkin calls a liberal and democratic approach):

Restorative nostalgia stresses *nostos* and attempts a transhistorical reconstruction of the lost home. Reflective nostalgia thrives in *algia*, the longing itself, and delays the homecoming – wistfully, ironically, desperately. Restorative nostalgia does not think of itself as nostalgia, but rather as truth or tradition. Reflective nostalgia dwells on the ambivalences of human longing and belonging.[30]

While restorative nostalgia takes us back to the construction and building of a new society, a new country, and a new empire, the reflective kind invites the observer to dismantle, destabilize and question. In this chapter I have explored largely films that engage in a reflective nostalgia for the post-war Soviet period. It is a nostalgia deprived of the longing, dwelling instead on the shared home, a common space. But this common space is one of suppression, victimization and destruction, increasing the pain of longing and making a return undesirable, if not impossible. Filmmakers debunk the myth that the Soviet system has ever instilled hope, faith or confidence in its citizens – even in the most hopeful times of Thaw and perestroika. According to the films discussed here, the Soviet past is nothing but a series of attempts to victimize the people, and their common home may not have been as happy as the nostalgia mode of the 1990s suggested. It is rather the source of violence and collapse, on a domestic and state level. Its legacy is only destruction, emigration or a void – one that very recent films fill with neither a restorative nor a reflective nostalgia, but a pseudo-nostalgia for an artificially recreated and staged past that never was, but that can inspire pride, as the success of Todorovskii's *Hipsters* amply shows.

NOTES

1. See also L. Nemchenko, 'Traditsii sovetskogo poeticheskogo kinematografa v postsovetskom kino', in *Sovetskoe proshloe i kul'tura nastoiashchego*, ed. N. Kupina and O. Mikhailova, 2 vols. (Ekaterinburg, 2009), vol. 1, 87–100; here 87.
2. D. Tsivina, 'Back in the USSR', *Kommersant*, 11 April 2008, www.kommersant.ru/doc.aspx?DocsID=877499 [in Russian].
3. O. Shaburova, 'Nostal'giia: strategii kommertsializatsii, ili Sovetskoe v glamure', in *Sovetskoe proshloe*, ed. Kupina and Mikhailova, vol. 1, 33–44.
4. A. Garros, 'Bog melochei', interview with Leonid Parfenov, *Ekspert*, 17 November 2008, www.expert.ru/expert/2008/45/bog_melochei/.
5. L. Parfenov, *Namedni: nasha era 1961–1970* (Moscow, 2009), 6.
6. G. Tarasevich, O. Andreeva and S. Sheikhetov, 'Khochu v SSSR!', *Russkii reporter*, 6 December 2007, www.expert.ru/russian_reporter/2007/27/hochu_obratno_v_sssr/.
7. S. Oushakine, 'Totality Decomposed: Objectalizing Late Socialism in Post-Soviet Biochronicles', *Russian Review* 69:4 (2010), 638–69.
8. Pavel Sanaev, b. 1969, writer, filmmaker and actor, is the stepson of the actor Rolan Bykov. Lilianna Lungina (1920–1998), wife of scriptwriter Semen Lungin and mother of filmmaker Pavel Lungin, was a translator.
9. See B. Beumers, 'The Serialization of Culture or the Culture of Serialization', in *The Post-Soviet Russian Media: Conflicting Signals*, ed. S. Hutchings, N. Rulyova and B. Beumers (London, 2009), 159–77, esp. 166–7.
10. See, for example, E. Dobrenko, *Stalinist Cinema and the Production of History* (Edinburgh, 2008); B. Beumers, ed., *Russia on Reels: The Russian Idea in Post-Soviet Cinema* (London, 1999); Nancy Condee, *The Imperial Trace* (Oxford, 2009).
11. O. Sulkin, 'Identifying the Enemy in Contemporary Russian Film', in *Insiders and Outsiders in Russian Cinema*, ed. S. Norris and Z. Torlone (Bloomington and Indianapolis, IN, 2008), 113–26, esp. 113.
12. See, for example, Tengiz Abuladze's *Repentance* (*Pokaianie / Monanieba*, 1984, released 1986); Aleksei Iu. German's *My Friend Ivan Lapshin* (*Moi drug Ivan*

Lapshin, 1983, released 1985); Ivan Dykhovichnyi's *Moscow Parade* (*Prorva*, 1992);
Sergei Livnev's *Hammer and Sickle* (*Serp i molot*, 1993); and Nikita Mikhalkov's
Burnt by the Sun (*Utomlennye solntsem*, 1994).

13. See S. Graham, 'Chernukha and Russian Film', *Studies in Slavic Culture*
    1 (2000), 9–27.
14. B. Beumers, 'Cinemarket, or The Russian Film Industry in "Mission
    Possible"', *Europe-Asia Studies* 51:5 (1999), 871–96.
15. B. Beumers, *Pop Culture Russia!* (Santa Barbara, Denver and London, 2005), 316–30.
16. L. Gudkov, 'Ideologema "vraga"', *Negativnaia identichnost'* (Moscow, 2004),
    552–649. For a discussion of the 'Other' in recent Russian cinema, see
    T. Kruglova, 'An Artistic Diagnosis of Modern Russian Cinema: The Little
    Man vs. the Big Other', *KinoKultura* 30 (2010), www.kinokultura.com/2010/
    30-kruglova.shtml; and Beumers, 'The Self and the Other in Recent Russian
    Cinema', *KinoKultura* 30 (2010), www.kinokultura.com/2010/30-beumers.
    shtml.
17. On the 'Standing of Zoia', see Alexander Panchenko's chapter in this volume.
18. One of the film's blogs can be found at http://kino.otzyv.ru/opinion.php?
    id=766; all box-office data from www.kinopoisk.ru.
19. Nemchenko, 'Traditsii sovetskogo poeticheskogo kinematografa', 94.
20. L. Smolina and V. Zakharov, 'Seks, komsomol, rok-n-roll', interview with
    Valerii Todorovskii, *Empire* [blog], 18 November 2008, www.vokrug.tv/
    article/show/Valerii_Todorovskii_o_Stilyagah_dengah_sekse_i_kinokritike/.
21. D. Beliaev, 'Stiliaga', *Krokodil*, 10 March 1949, 10.
22. Blog on Russian cinema: http://ruskino.ru/mov/forum/7915.
23. Ibid.
24. *Chuvikha* is a slang word meaning 'bird' or prostitute; for the *stiliagi* the term
    was used for girls who appreciated American culture and dressed in American
    fashion.
25. Shaburova, 'Nostal'giia', 43–4.
26. For an analysis of violence in Russian culture, see B. Beumers and M. Lipovetsky,
    Performing Violence: Literary and Theatrical Experiments of New Russian Drama
    (Bristol, 2009).
27. Lev Gudkov, 'Raspolzaiushcheesia obshchestvo', *Iskusstvo kino* 7 (2007) http://
    kinoart.ru/2007/n7-article4.html.
28. Ibid.
29. On the literary foundation of these films, see Dina Khapaeva's chapter in this
    collection.
30. S. Boym, *The Future of Nostalgia* (New York, 2001), xviii.

CHAPTER 4

Archaizing culture: the Museum of Ethnography

Dmitry Baranov

Ethnographical museums, with their representations of the culture of different peoples, were among the most important vehicles for the official understanding of national identity in the nineteenth and twentieth centuries, and among those operating in Russia, none was more prominent than the State Museum of Ethnography of the Peoples of the USSR in Leningrad (now the Russian Ethnographical Museum), a centre for the dissemination of Soviet views of ethnic affiliation (*etnos, natsional'nost'*).[1] The middle of the twentieth century saw dramatic changes in the strategies of exposition and exhibition adopted, which were provoked as much by the crisis in museum ethnography of the 1930s as by the shifting ideological conditions and altering public mood characteristic of the immediate post-war period. This article will address in particular the questions of how and why the principles guiding the representation of the Russian people changed, and what the results of these changes were.

If scientific research, collection and conservation work establish relatively impenetrable institutional boundaries for the outsider (i.e. the non-museum worker), then the exhibition, as a specialized form of communication developed by the museum to relay specific images and meanings to the outside world, is the aspect of this work that is most sensitive to both the demands of the 'mass public' and the exigencies of ideology.[2] The representational strategies employed by a museum are largely determined by factors that are beyond its control, i.e. by the ideological apparatus of the state, whether the particular task in hand is to demonstrate the after-effects of colonialism, to raise awareness about 'ancient, disappearing, primitive ways of life' or to exhibit 'positive national experience'. At the same time the influence of ideology in this domain should not be overestimated, given that the special nature of museum 'language' (which is first and foremost a language of things) imposes certain boundaries on the information communicated. To put it another way, exhibits bring with them a trail of meanings determined by their previous contexts, and thus the manipulation of these meanings has certain limits.[3]

The special status of the State Museum of Ethnography was largely a result of its close association with the state establishment[4] and of the public perception of it as an authoritative institution created for the conservation, study and exhibition of concrete objects of cultural heritage. This in turn made it vulnerable to attempts to integrate its exhibitions into whatever ideological discourse happened to be considered appropriate at a particular time. The important point here was not simply the issue of how the state interfered with museum affairs, but also the fact that it felt such interference to be necessary in the first place. This indirectly reveals the important role assigned to the museum in justifying the implementation of policies concerning the peoples living within the territory of Russia/the USSR.

The most serious infringement of the museum's institutional boundaries, that is, of external interference in the conceptual basis of museum practices, which led the museum into a protracted crisis, came at the end of the 1920s, and lasted well into the first half of the 1930s. Up until this time the academic and ideological conceptions for the representation of the peoples of Russia in the museum had been in a state of relative equilibrium. These conceptions were founded on the idea of an ethnic hierarchy with the Russian people at the top, which received official endorsement during the reign of Alexander III and was the basis for the museum's strategies of collection and exposition–exhibition. In exhibitions which opened in 1923, the so-called 'principal nationalities' – for which read, the Eastern Slav peoples – were separated out, and the Russians placed at the pinnacle of these. As a result, the Russians, unlike the other peoples, were assigned three halls rather than one. The exhibition itself was arranged as a series of themes, whose selection fully corresponded with the priorities of museum ethnography at that time. The themes of 'occupations' and 'art' were exhibited in the most detail, the latter incorporating almost all ornamented objects of any kind. Women's clothing was also exhibited in large quantities, since it constituted, according to the exhibition's organizers, the most vivid expression of ethnographic characteristics. The subjective nature and appraisal of what was exhibited was obvious both in the choice of exhibits and in the way in which these were ordered, in other words in the very structure of the exhibition.

The emphasis on a holistic, that is, a general, all-inclusive and widely accessible, depiction of 'the lives of the people' was the central factor behind the structuring of the Russian exhibition.[5] This emphasis was central to the didactic aims of the exhibition and, by extension, to its role in shaping identity. The apparently 'definitive' title of the exhibition, 'The Russians', masked the conditional, fragmented and subjective character of the displays. It made explicit the attempt to demonstrate an overall cultural unity with clearly defined boundaries, when in fact neither the cultural boundaries nor the structure of what they determined were at all concrete. In a certain sense, then, the exhibition served the purpose of 'imagining ethnic culture'.

Exhibitions at this time tended to function according to a common principle in their treatment of ethnicity, underlining the unique character of a given people and its distinctness from others. Dissimilarities were thus more topical than commonalities. Festival dress, embroidery samples, objects of folk art, scenes from rituals and so on became obligatory components of the 1920s exhibitions, and it was with the help of these exhibits that the display organizers traced the boundaries of ethnicity.

The illusion of authenticity was founded on a conception of objects as providing 'material evidence of an era' and signifying the 'materialized reality of culture', and hence being a means to 'objectively' depict ethnographic reality. It was supported by the specific methods employed in the exhibition to represent ethnographic activity. Thus, for the first time, prearranged 'sets' began to be used in museums: certain ethnographic practices – rituals, trading activities, interiors and so on – would be replicated in the minutest detail. In most cases, these sets were taken to be valid reflections of reality by visitors.[6]

The contextual presentation and thematic structure of the exhibition thus exposed a strong tendency for exhibition methods to depend on master narratives. This type of presentation would function from this point forward as an instrument for implementing the ideological goals of the time – albeit not always a very effective instrument, as became clear in the 1930s.[7]

Having burgeoned in the second half of the 1920s, signs of ideological pressure became even more tangible between the end of the 1920s and the beginning of the 1930s, emerging in the form of a series of government decrees. From this point onwards, through its exposition of cultures, the museum was expected to provide a 'progressive analysis of the destructive influence of capitalist civilization on pre-capitalistic structures, juxtaposing the policy of tsarist Russia and the colonial activity of the imperial dynasty with the national policy of the Communist Party and the economic-cultural growth of the peoples of the Soviet Union'.[8] In 1928 a decree was passed by the Central Executive Committee of the Communist Party and by the Council of People's Commissars, 'On the Construction of Museums in the RSFSR', in which the transformation of the museum into a centre of propaganda was openly discussed.[9] Exhibitions had to contain 'evidence of the nation-forming process and of national politics and national culture in

the Soviet period and in the period immediately preceding the revolution'.[10]
At the First All-Russian Museum Congress established in 1931, the slogan
'Replace the "Exhibition of Things" with the "Exhibition of Ideas"' began
to be tossed around.

It was at this point in particular that the notion of 'traditional culture'
obtained unambiguously negative connotations, becoming synonymous
with anachronism, backwardness and ignorance. All exhibitions at the
museum were immediately reconfigured in accordance with the official
objective of demonstrating that the contemporary period (1920s–1930s)
had brought huge advances in the lives of the Russian people as compared
with the pre-revolutionary era. New contexts were created in which the
pre-revolutionary past was juxtaposed with Soviet contemporaneity in the
case of each individual theme.[11]

The new exhibitions, unlike those arranged at earlier periods, combined
two principles for the selection of exhibits. Decorative and characteristically
'ethnic' objects were predominantly used to exhibit old ways of life. In the
case of traditional Russian culture,[12] this created an 'archaic-festive' impression. But modernity, on the other hand, was represented by urban and
decidedly *un*ethnic ('socialist') objects,[13] making the Soviet part of any
exhibition appear detached from reality, emasculated, repetitive and boring,
no matter which particular people happened to be the subject of
the exhibition. The extraordinarily rich collection of objects from the
1890s and 1900s, and the colourful set designs depicting this period,
completely overshadowed the photographs and diagrams depicting village
life in the 1920s.

In this case the aesthetics of the individual artefacts triumphed over the
ideological thrust of the exposition as a whole, making the exhibitions, to
use the lexicon of the period, 'politically harmful'.[14] In addition, it turned
out that the manipulation of exhibits was not wholly effective to begin with;
the trails of former meaning, a 'metonymic residue' of sorts, did not allow
things to be organically subsumed into new narratives.

For perhaps the first time, the Museum of Ethnography had shown its
inability to fully control the primary meaning generated by the objects in its
exhibitions.[15] The balance between scientific and ideological concepts had
been disrupted. It is perhaps no coincidence that in the 1930s a kind of
phobia with regard to authentic objects developed among museum workers,
and that, in connection with this, a peculiar process that one can only term
'suppression' of objects on display began. Items began to be removed from
the exhibitions, while at the same time the walls and display units filled up
with slogans and citations, schedules, photographs and tables of figures.[16]

In the words of the director of the museum at that time, E. A. Mil'shtein, 'the object constitutes an illustration of a particular historico-ethnographic theme'.[17] To quote V. G. Bogoraz-Tan, then employed at the Kunstkamera (Leningrad's other ethnographical museum, under the direction of the Academy of Sciences), 'Once you are free from things, these objects will no longer attack you, they won't commit the acts of violence against the exhibition organizers that they used to, whether in old museums or in new ones.'[18]

At the time the exhibition's lack of success was attributed to purely 'objective' factors: 'The novelty which has already entered the lives of the peoples of this country has yet to express itself in new sorts of material culture or folk art.'[19] In other words, a new life had dawned but was yet to 'materialize' as such; for the moment it remained disembodied. The museum's disregard for contemporary cultural reality, and its denying the latter ethnographical status, was revealing: the realia of Soviet rural life were simply not compatible with the ideological requirements of the day.

Several exhibitions in fact closed in quick succession, since, in the words of a study published in the late Soviet era, 'the comparison was not advantageous for modernity, and imbued the exhibition with an improper political flavour'.[20] Thus, the attempt to establish a new cultural reality by means of a new kind of ethnographical exhibition inevitably ended up coming to grief. The distance between reality as the viewers understood it and its representation in the exhibition was just too great. The representations were based on ideological constructs which visitors could simply not 'read'.

The attempt to transform the Museum of Ethnography (or the State Museum of Ethnography, as it was known after 1934) into an 'institution for political instruction'[21] thus ended unsuccessfully. Many of the exhibitions that were supposed to enlighten the public were considered so disastrous that they were simply closed down.

The second half of the 1930s was characterized by a slight easing of ideological pressure (see Figures 4.1 and 4.2). The appearance of several pre-war exhibitions with a decidedly art-historical orientation marked a new trend in representational practices. These included 'The Arts and Crafts of Russian Artisans in the Northern Regions of the RSFSR', 'Popular Art of the Chuvash and Mari Peoples' and 'Arts of the People of Georgia'.[22] There was also a cautious rehabilitation of ethnographic objects or, more precisely, of those objects which could be classified as works of folk art.

The interpretation of exhibits as works of art was only possible in the absence of a rigorous presentation of these objects in terms of their ethnographic context. At the same time, the recognition of the aesthetic

Figure 4.1 'Red Tea-House', from the exhibition 'Uzbeks in the Past and the Present', 1935.

Figure 4.2 'Collective Farm Worker's House', from the exhibition 'Russians of the Central Black-Earth Region', 1936.

value of ethnically marked objects was a first step towards a re-evaluation of objects, and also of folk traditions. But this was at best a tentative step back towards 'ethnography' in the pre-revolutionary sense, given that 'the art of the people' was generally exhibited as the product of Soviet creative enterprises, that is, the sort of creative output that was produced under conditions of tight political and aesthetic control.

In the immediate post-war period, three more art-historical exhibitions were opened: 'Popular Art of the Slavs' (1945) in the Recreation Park on Nevsky prospekt, 'Dress and Popular Art of the Slavs' (1946) in the Kirov Central Park of Culture and Recreation, and (the first exhibition to be held in the State Museum of Ethnography after this reopened following repairs to war damage) 'Popular Art and National Dress of the Slavic Peoples' (1948).[23]

The revitalization of the long-dead theme of Slavdom was no accident. With the wave of patriotic feeling that swept over the country after victory in 1945, interest in questions of ethnic identity began to grow. Workers at the museum saw the significance of the exhibitions in the fact that the 'leading role of the Slavic peoples and, above all, the Russian people in the universal defeat of fascism arouses increased interest in the history and culture of these peoples'.[24] Responses to the exhibitions regularly made the equation 'the USSR/Soviet people = Slavdom'. For example, 'With the Soviet people as its allies, Slavdom is indestructible!'[25] 'The USSR is the authentic stronghold of Slavdom!'[26] Statements such as these smack of the Pan-Slavic rhetoric of the second half of the nineteenth century, offering a reinterpretation of this rhetoric in the light of the USSR's ambitions towards Eastern Europe.

The Slavic theme also started to dominate the collection work of the museum. In the museum targets for the 1947–50 period, it was stated that

the majority of expeditions and study visits to collect concrete ethnographic artefacts and fieldwork records for academic purposes are to be conducted in those regions and among those peoples that are intended for exhibition, that is, among the Russian populations of the central, southern, and northern regions of the RSFSR. The study and collection of materials on Ukrainians, Byelorussians [are also required].

Moreover, the goal of 'commencing the systematic study and collection of materials on the western and southern Slavs' was identified.[27]

In the preamble to the thematic-exposition plan for the 1948 exhibition, mention was made of the 'exceptionally important political significance of academic propaganda in connection with the Slavic question'.[28] Thus the exhibition 'should assist ... the propaganda of Soviet scientific state ideas concerning the question of Slavdom'.[29]

This period was dominated by the idea of the 'Slavic brotherhood' at the level of high politics, and in the cultural world too, which naturally shaped the conceptualization and disciplinary approaches of Russian academics, particularly historians and ethnographers.[30] Indeed, the main purpose of the exhibitions at this time was to illuminate the shared roots of Slavic folklore and Slavic culture generally, which underlay the 'aesthetic coordinates' of the era.

It was at this period when an incipient conflict between the ethnographic and the aesthetic approaches to exhibition work began to brew in the State Museum of Ethnography. Contextualized/ethnographic presentations of the classic kind put the emphasis not on the individual artefacts, but rather on the meaning generated by local cultural situations. This sort of approach in some sense excluded local cultures from a global context. After all, the products of folk art were not exhibited in 'galleries of international masterpieces', such as the Hermitage. By contrast, the exhibition within the ethnographic museum of objects as masterpieces, whose presentation did not require contextualization, permitted the museum to break free of the limits of its parochialism in order to portray the ethnic aspect as a part of world cultural heritage, which one could and should take pride in and which, as a consequence, constituted an important part of one's identity. In the exhibition response book, visitors with monotonous regularity expressed the sense of exultation and feelings of pride in 'their' people that the exhibition had given them: 'I am leaving with the sense that the Slavic peoples are peoples of great culture and knowledge. Culture and art will develop in close friendship, the hand of which was offered by the Russian people'; 'The museum helps us to understand our people and come to love them'; 'You feel a sense of pride for your great nation'; 'The museum presents a vivid picture of the diversity, elegance, and taste of the Slavic people ... proving to the world their limitless creative potential'; 'The present exhibition gives a good reflection of the national art of our great ancestors. It stirs a feeling of pride in the heart of every Russian for the accomplishments of the nation.'[31]

Yet the exhibition provoked concern among both members of staff at the State Museum of Ethnography and visitors that the ethnographic profile of the museum might be diluted as a result of the 'aestheticization' of the exhibitions. At a meeting of the lower Academic Council in 1947 which was dedicated to the discussion of the thematic-exposition plans for the exhibition 'Folk Art and National Dress of the Slavic Peoples',[32] the danger of 'departing from the ethnographic profile of the museum in the direction of straightforward art studies' was voiced.[33] As a result, this exhibition later acquired a somewhat 'ethnographic hue'. The first three rooms were reserved for the presentation of the culture of the Russian people, and thus exhibited their living arrangements; occupations; popular art, including games and festivals (in particular Christmastide, since it incorporated notable pre-Christian motifs); and theatre. The fourth and fifth rooms were dedicated to the Byelorussians and Ukrainians, and the last room portrayed the 'national dress and ornaments of the eastern, western, and southern Slavs', and concluded with the theme, 'Friendship of the Slavic Peoples'.[34]

The exhibition's art-historical emphasis nevertheless continued to influence its reception by visitors: 'Thank you [to the museum workers] for collecting such a great wealth of the art of our people'; 'The exhibition is great! (at least, the old section, the nineteenth century) Our era is worse, or decadent, or is yet to be defined . . . The new era will provide us with new art forms. The heritage of the past, [. . .] the art of our ancestors, it's your job to make sure it gets exhibited!'; '[I want] to say something about its [the museum's] role in bringing our people closer to the peoples of other Slavic countries and its role in educating us about the art of the Russian people.'[35] In addition, workers at the museum understood that the shift towards an aesthetic vision of culture was a way of allowing them to avoid the 'slippery' themes and undesirable interpretations produced by the ethnographic approach. Consider, for example, the following excerpt from the minutes of a meeting devoted to the discussion of the exhibition's conceptual design: 'This tendency [to emphasize the role of clothing and its various elements as lucky charms] . . . cannot be considered healthy. It is a reflection of the idealistic trends in ethnography.'[36] Naturally, this kind of rebuke made museum workers cautious.

The opening of several exhibitions devoted to popular art forms at the same period of the late 1940s unexpectedly raised questions concerning the museum's self-definition by means of its representational practices and the maintenance of its disciplinary (ethnographic) boundaries. In visitors' responses, the State Museum of Ethnography of the Peoples of the USSR frequently got mixed up with the Russian Museum, the famous museum dedicated to Russian art that was right next door: 'The exhibition is nice, but where the heck are all the paintings by famous Russian artists?'; 'We would really like to give our opinion of our visit to the Russian Museum. Now we can actually talk about the beauty of the Slavic people'; 'We liked the exhibits at the museum of Russian art very much'; 'Let's hope that this is only the start of a future museum of peoples' art!!!'[37]

Faced with the danger of totally undermining its ethnographic profile, the museum was forced to return to ethnographic practices in its presentation of the cultures of peoples in the pre- and post-revolutionary periods.[38]

But the newly opened exhibitions inherited the shortcomings of the 1930s, in particular the preponderance of documentary photographs, tables, maps, quotations and the 'inevitable repetitiveness of the uniform, pan-Soviet materials in the sections about modernity'.[39]

Finding a solution to the 'crisis of representation' was only possible if a new conceptual framework for museum exhibitions that would conform with changing ideological goals could be established. By the start of the 1950s, energetic efforts were being made to develop the idea of an inherently new, pan-ethnic community, which was given the title of 'the Soviet people'. The artificial character of this move, its role as an abstract construct, was never a secret: 'This community of contemporary peoples is the consequence of one nation's embrace of the best national traditions of another; it is the result of the gradual realization of the Soviet government's policy on nationalities.'[40] Yet, in a certain sense, this new ideologeme was also consistent with reality, in as much as the modernization of society really had led to the emergence of certain all-Soviet cultural features.

While the notion of 'the Soviet people' was articulated clearly only much later, in 1971, the term had in fact first appeared as a linguistic signifier considerably earlier, in the second half of the 1930s. This chronological background may well indicate that the notion of *sovetskost'* (Sovietness) was a modification of sorts of the pre-revolutionary idea of *rossiiskost'* (Russianness in the supra-ethnic sense, the characteristics of a citizen of the Russian Empire).

Though not created in the museum, the notion of a Soviet people unexpectedly turned out to be a way of resolving the prolonged crisis of what and how to exhibit. As a result, it was developed extensively within the museum space. According to the 'General Plan for Museum Exhibitions' adopted in 1956:

The Soviet period . . . should not be exhibited separately for each individual people, it should incorporate all peoples and be presented in a room specially marked off for that purpose. This will allow us to present both the national particularities in the ways of life and cultures of different peoples and the emergence of common characteristics; it will reveal the existence of a political, economic, and cultural community of peoples and the drawing together of nations and peoples.[41]

Rather than each exhibition containing a section that depicted the Sovietization of that particular people, there was now to be a separate generic Soviet room to offer a triumphant culmination to *all* the national stories.

'The Russians from the End of the Nineteenth to the Beginning of the Twentieth Centuries' was the first permanent exhibition to appear with the 'Soviet section' removed. It comprised five rooms (the first four of which were opened in 1956–8, and the fifth in 1959) which were dedicated to the following themes: 'Principal Occupations', 'Trade and the Formation of the Working Class', 'Housing and Implements of Workers and Peasants', 'Dress of Workers and Peasants' and 'Spiritual Culture of Workers and Peasants'.[42]

In the event the removal of the Soviet material did not mean that all problems were now resolved. Perhaps the greatest difficulties were encountered when setting up the room containing the exhibition of spiritual culture, which, according to standard ethnographic classification, should have included the popular ceremonial practices that were so frowned on in Soviet political culture. The authors were faced with the rather quixotic ideological objective of demonstrating that 'the Russian people's spiritual culture was founded on a materialistic understanding of the surrounding world', and that 'the entire life of the Russian people and their spiritual culture was in a state of organic progress towards revolution'.[43] As a result, the emphasis was put on the 'positivist-rational', aesthetic and recreational components of culture, in particular art, folklore, people's theatre, games, rituals (presented in an artistic context), knowledge and entertainment.

A certain easing of ideological pressure was nevertheless detectable in the Russian exhibition. This pressure now shifted to exhibitions about modernity, in particular 'The Art of the Peoples of the USSR' (1957), 'The Art of the Soviet Republics' (1960), 'The USSR: A Fraternal Union of Equal Peoples' (1964), 'The Art of the Contemporary Nations of the USSR' (1966), 'The New and Traditional in the Housing and Dress of Contemporary Nations' (1972) and 'Contemporary Ceremonies and Festivals of the Peoples of the USSR' (1988).

At the same time, the new, integrative take on Soviet culture did not result, as might have been expected, in the modernization of all or most of the exhibitions. The result was the opposite. With the Soviet present hived off, there was nothing to offset the ideal vision of the 'ethnographic past' of Russian culture (the end of the nineteenth and beginning of the twentieth centuries) as presented, which pretended to the status of a definitive and unified depiction, and included such elements (then considered essential) as the principal occupations, trades, lodgings, implements, elements of costume, festivals and art forms. The exhibitions became less, not more, modern in this period.

The conspicuous temporal divide between visitors and the culture exhibited brought about an 'exoticization' of the latter, achieving, in a somewhat paradoxical manner, a colonial vision of 'our' people.[44] This colonial perspective, which would soon provide the context for representations of the cultures of all the other peoples of Russia as well, created a favourable backdrop for demonstrating, in the exhibitions dedicated to modernity, the success of the Soviet government's civilizing activities.

The culture of the Soviet peoples was represented as the passive object of external forces (the Communist Party, the state), thanks to which their lives were modernized and included in the historical process (and specifically in the process of Sovietization). Highlanders descended to the plains, and nomads started to lead a settled life: 'The peoples of Siberia have executed a sharp jump forward from their former existence, patriarchal and half-savage, and have passed by the capitalist phase to arrive at socialism; they have transformed their economy, culture, and daily life';[45] 'The shepherds and goatherds of Kazakhstan, the hunters of Altai, the highlanders of Dagestan, [have been sent] into higher education, so they can be turned into engineers and technicians.'[46] The most remarkable feats were those that had been executed by the supposedly most primitive peoples: 'The more backward a people was in tsarist Russia, the greater the transformations that have been wrought in its daily life [under Soviet rule].'[47]

As at earlier stages of the museum's history, these exhibitions became a crucial arena for a play of meanings that was primarily associated with ideological, rather than academic, discourse. One of the principal objectives for the presentation of modernity was declared to be the 'propaganda of the Soviet way of life through the language of the exhibition, the representation of contemporary national processes within the country as a whole and in its separate regions'.[48] A stark dichotomy of values was established. On the one hand lay old, nefarious traditions which had to be uprooted; on the other, new ones ('Soviet traditions') with a positive ideological content, which needed to be espoused. The status of the traditional and the ethnic aspects in exhibitions about modernity was ambiguous: the museum was concerned about the danger of 'exaggerating the role of national traditions in the contemporary life of the people', but was confronted with the task of conveying an 'accurate impression of the tenacity of traditional-everyday culture and of the extent of its interaction with contemporary culture'.[49]

Exhibition practices began to be employed as weapons in the battle against the 'relics of the past', 'against such remnants of the past as the subordinated position of women, the ritual abduction of young girls, the exchange of bride-money, the survival of blood feuds, national violence, religious anachronisms, etc.'[50] The museum had turned out to be more than a mere institution for the preservation and exhibition of cultural heritage; above all else it had become an instrument for constructing new cultural realities, in this case a new pan-ethnic community. The common traits of Soviet culture could be discerned not only in the ethnically untainted generic housing, dress and mass-produced implements that were displayed in the new exhibitions, but also in those 'new', artificially generated forms of popular art, for example the 'Bashkurti Khokhloma' (Bashkurti lacquer in the Russian style) or Kazakh ceramics 'in the Ukrainian style', which were intended to give explicit evidence of the formation of a well-defined and unified cultural entity, 'drawing attention to the cultural synthesis between individual peoples'.[51]

In this 'colonial perspective' the Russian people was accorded two separate roles. On the one hand, it was the dominant force, the conduit of progress, initiating a project of Russification which met with varying success from place to place. References to 'the great Russian people' were ubiquitous, becoming a positive cliché in the post-war era. The relationship between Russians and other Soviet peoples was consistently presented according to an 'enlightenment/backwardness' contrast: 'The party dispatched engineers, scientists, scholars, and skilled workers to the periphery so they could give aid to the backward regions.'[52] 'As a result of contact with the great Russian people, a gradual rise in class and national consciousness [comes about]'; 'the art of Soviet Turkmenistan ... develops under the direct influence of the best traditions of the great Russian people'.[53] The phrase 'great Russian people' worked like a kind of tactful rephrasing of the pre-revolutionary usage 'Great Russians', which in the 1930s had become taboo (cf. the phrase 'Great Russian chauvinism').[54] But Russian peasant culture was itself stigmatized as an assemblage of 'religious survivals from the past and superstitions' that was ripe for extermination. This interpretation was fostered by the atheist campaign launched at the end of the 1950s, which led to the appearance of many ethnographical studies devoted to the 'survivals of the past' ripe for imminent disappearance. The ambivalent place of the Russian people in the Soviet modernizing project – as both object and subject of the process of social transformation – has led some recent observers to speak of 'Russian schizophrenic Orientalism'.[55]

The ideologically motivated exhibitions dealing with the Soviet period remained in place until the late 1980s and early 1990s, when they quietly shut down for good and all, at the same time as the disappearance of the object they were depicting. Fate had something else in store, however, for the exhibitions dedicated to the Russian people. With only the slightest of modifications, these are still on show today, directing the gaze of the visitor to the exotic 'archaic-festive' image constructed by the unstinting efforts of generations of museum workers.

With the collapse of the Soviet Union in 1991, the State Museum of Ethnography of the Peoples of the USSR suddenly found itself with two conflicting missions. Its holdings and academic departments embraced the entire area of the former USSR, but the museum had traditionally been supposed to deal with the ethnographical study of the nation state in which it was located, which had now shrunk to the Russian Federation. The renaming of the institution as the Russian Ethnographical Museum in 1992 helped to conceal the tension, but still left the museum with half its exhibition space devoted to the non-Russian republics of the former Soviet Union. This was to become a ticklish diplomatic issue in the years immediately following, as various countries in the CIS and the Baltic attempted to press their claims on items in the collection that they held to be associated with 'their' cultures. The very fact that the REM was housing items from the cultures of 'foreign' peoples was invoked in the new post-colonial rhetoric of the time as a sign of Russia's still unburied imperial ambitions. However, since the REM did not evolve any new overall conception of its role, the assumption remained, by default, that its coverage was to go on including not just the peoples of Russia, but those of the regions surrounding the country. From the point of view of academic study as such, this conservatism could be seen as neutral enough (continuing to collect material from areas adjacent to Russia, where historically contact has been close, has an obvious rationale, and helps to facilitate comparative work). But once again, ideology continues to rear its head – as in the late nineteenth century, so in the early twenty-first century, museum workers do not always avoid the temptation, when focusing on the cultures of regions adjacent to Russia, of showing exclusively how, as D. A. Klements once put it in 1901, 'Russian political, economic, or moral influence' impacts upon these.[56]

Translated by Victoria Donovan

NOTES

1. For a discussion of the State Museum of Ethnography (or GME) in the 1920s and 1930s, see F. Hirsch, *Empire of the Nations: Ethnographic Knowledge and the Making of the Soviet Union* (Ithaca, NY, 2005), 187–227. For a general discussion of the role of the ethnographical museum in the national and imperial project, see 'Forum', *Forum for Anthropology and Culture* 4 (2007), 149–248.
2. Evidently the ideological constituent is extremely important even within this strictly academic sphere, but, in general, it exists in a latent form and is not always recognized by museum workers themselves as existing.
3. Sue Pearce provides a slightly different interpretation, emphasizing the entire contingency of meaning inherent in the postmodern approach. See her

'Thinking about Things', in *Interpreting Objects and Collections*, ed. S. M. Pearce (London, 1994), 125–32.

4. The museum, founded on the order of Emperor Alexander III and established in 1902 as the Ethnographic Department within the Russian Museum, was conceived as a grandiose imperial project, the main task of which was to present a picture of the 'ethnographic sweep of our native land, a picture of the peoples dwelling in Russia and its immediate vicinity'. Throughout the Soviet period (in 1934 it was separated into an independent museum and began to be called the State Ethnographic Museum; in 1948 it became the State Museum of Ethnography of the Peoples of the USSR and from 1992, the Russian Museum of Ethnography) and right up to this day it has remained an 'Institution of Federal Significance', i.e. the central national museum in its area.

5. In accordance with the ethnographic division of the Russian people which existed at that time, the three rooms of the exhibition were dedicated to the North Russian, Central Russian and South Russian ethno-cultural zones respectively.

6. This impression was created by the binary decoding which objects were subjected to upon arriving first in the museum, and then in the exhibition: (1) from metonymic to metaphorical form, whereby the object breaks free of its natural environment and is included in the classificatory system determined by the museum discourse (in semiotic terms – the paradigmatic chain), and (2) from metaphorical to metonymical, whereby the object enters a new, artificial context, becoming part of the exhibition (syntagmatic chain). In general, these semantic shifts are concealed from the visitor's gaze; he or she interprets the exhibits not as metaphors or symbols of the ethnographical activity represented, but rather as its exact reflection.

7. It should be noted that the quest for simplicity and semantic transparency was articulated as early as the very beginning of the twentieth century: 'The general appearance of the room must serve as a prospectus for the observer when he first enters it, and as a résumé when, on leaving, he takes one final browse around' (I. Smirnov, 'Neskol'ko slov po voprosu ob organizatsii Etnograficheskogo otdela Russkogo muzeia', *Izvestiia Imperatorskoi Akademii Nauk* 15, 1901, 232).

8. Quoted from T. V. Staniukovich, *Etnograficheskaia nauka i muzei* (Leningrad, 1978), 203.

9. I. I. Shangina, *Russkii fond etnograficheskikh muzeev Moskvy i Sankt-Peterburga: istoriia i problemy komplektovaniia, 1867–1930 gg.* (St Petersburg, 1994), 130.

10. Ibid., 75.

11. T. A. Kriukova and E. N. Studenetskaia, 'GME narodov SSSR za piatdesiat' let sovetskoi vlasti', *Ocherki istorii muzeinogo dela v SSSR* (Moscow, 1971), 37.

12. The exhibition 'The Russian Population of the Black Earth Regions of the RSFSR' was created in 1936.

13. I. I. Shangina, 'Kontseptsiia komplektovaniia sobranii etnograficheskikh muzeev (30–50-e gody XX v.)', *Iz istorii formirovaniia etnograficheskikh kollektsii v muzeiakh Rossii (XIX–XX vv.)* (St Petersburg, 1992), 143.

14. The exhibition 'The Ukrainian Village before and after the October Revolution' (1931) and 'Byelorussians of the BSSR' (1932) were closed for 'distorting Soviet

reality', 'The Contemporary Kolkhoz Village' never opened and 'The Leningrad Region and Karelia' (1937) was closed for being 'anti-Soviet' (AREM [Archive of the Russian Ethnographical Museum], f. 2, op. 1, d. 365; I.I. Shangina, 'Etnograficheskii muzei Moskvy i Leningrada na rubezhe 20kh–30kh godov XX v.', *Sovetskaia etnografiia* 2, 1991, 77).

15. See in this regard J. Clifford, *Routes: Travel and Translation in the Late Twentieth Century* (Cambridge, MA, 1997), 138.
16. Kriukova and Studenetskaia, 'GME', 68; Staniukovich, *Etnograficheskaia nauka*, 200.
17. E. A. Mil'shtein, 'Gosudarstvennyi muzei etnografii', *Sovetskaia etnografiia* 1 (1948), 218–22.
18. Staniukovich, *Etnograficheskaia nauka*, 200.
19. Kriukova and Studenetskaia, 'GME', 37.
20. Ibid.
21. Mil'shtein, 'Gosudarstvennyi muzei etnografii', 221.
22. In addition to those stated above, the following exhibitions were opened at this time: 'The Uzbek SSR (Uzbeks Past and Present)', 'The Turkmen SSR', 'Peoples of the Finno-Ugric SSR', 'Peoples of the Murmansk Region (Sami)', 'Peoples of the Northern Caucasus', 'Jews in Tsarist Russia and the USSR' and 'Peoples of Siberia' (Chukchis, Koryaks, Evenks, Oirots, Khakass).
23. AREM, f. 2, op. 1, d. 919, ll. 4 and 7; ibid., d. 961, *passim*.
24. Ibid., d. 919, l. 4.
25. *Pravda*, 12 May 1945.
26. AREM, f. 2, op. 1, d. 919, l. 7.
27. Ibid., d. 596, l. 2.
28. Ibid., d. 961, l. 27.
29. Ibid., l. 29.
30. On the general political background, see I. I. Shangina, 'Pervye gody posle voiny', *Rossiiskii etnograficheskii muzei, 1902–2002* (St Petersburg, 2001), 50–3.
31. Response Book [Kniga otzyvov], AREM, f. 2, op. 1, d. 920, ll. 10, 11, 12 ob., 11 ob.; d. 1032, l. 13. The ethnocentrism of visitors' conceptions of the exhibition needs investigation in its own right. I will note here only that the 'Russian component' was particularly prominent in responses to this exhibition (apart from those making a comment who identified themselves with other nations). The phrase: 'We liked the art of the Russian people best of all' emerges as the refrain of the response book as a whole. But ethnocentrism can also be detected in the particular sensitivity of some visitors to the shortcomings of the exhibition, for example: 'tedious, horrid models and crumpled costumes. If only it had been done realistically, and not in this vulgar popular-print naturalistic way ... As a Russian, I took offence that our nation has been portrayed so shoddily, and a non-Russian would just think we were useless' (ibid., d. 920, l. 25).
32. This temporary exhibition (*vystavka*) occupied several halls that had recently been reopened to the public and was open for a relatively long time, and so was sometimes referred to as a 'permanent exhibition' (*ekspozitsiia*) in the documents produced by the museum.

33. AREM, f. 2, op. 1, d. 964, l. 10.
34. L. Potapov, 'Ekspozitsiia po slavianskim narodam v GME', *Sovetskaia etnografiia* 2 (1948), 216; AREM, f. 2, op. 1, d. 961, ll. 17–72.
35. Response Book, AREM, f. 2, op. 1, d. 920, ll. 9 ob., 13, 28 ob.
36. AREM, f. 2, op. 1, d. 964, l. 42.
37. Response Book, AREM, f. 2, op. 1, d. 920, l. 29 ob.; d. 1032, ll. 13 ob., 7, 18 ob.
38. 'Ossetians' (1949); 'Kabardins' (1950); 'Peoples of the Volga Region: The Chuvash and Mari People' (1950); 'Peoples of the North: Nenets and Evenks' (1951); 'The Turkmen' (1952).
39. I. I. Baranova, 'Pokaz sovremennosti v GME narodov SSSR (poiski i problemy)', *Sovetskaia etnografiia* 2 (1981), 29.
40. P. I. Kushner, 'Programma po izucheniiu kul'tury i byta kolkhoznogo krest'ianstva', *Kratkie soobshcheniia IE za 1950 g.* 12 (1950), 103.
41. 'General'nyi plan na 1956 g.', AREM, f. 2, op. 1, d. 1209, l. 1. See also Kriukova and Studenetskaia, 'GME', 70.
42. AREM, f. 2, op. 1, d. 1330, l. 1.
43. *Kratkii putevoditel': GME narodov SSSR* (Leningrad, 1959), p. 4; AREM, f. 2, op. 1, d. 1330, l. 3.
44. The colonial vision was more marked in the case of those exhibitions dedicated to non-Russian peoples. In this case, it was absolutely mandatory to develop the themes of the 'progressive influence of the Russian people, and the inter-penetration of peoples and their cultures'. M. E. Sazonova, 'GME narodov SSSR', *Sovetskaia etnografiia* 2 (1963), 22.
45. *Sovremennoe narodnoe iskusstvo RSFSR: kratkii putevoditel'* (Leningrad, 1958), p. 2.
46. AREM, f. 2, op. 1, d. 1230, l. 16.
47. AREM, f. 2, op. 1, d. 1157, ll. 3–4.
48. Baranova, 'Pokaz', 27.
49. Ibid., 30.
50. Ibid., 4.
51. N. M. Romanova, *Metodika pokaza v ekspozitsiiakh i na vystavkakh sblizheniia natsii i narodnostei SSSR i formirovanie novoi istoricheskoi obshchnosti – sovetskii narod* (Leningrad, 1986), p. 27; V. Z. Gamburg, A. S. Morozova and E. N. Studenetskaia, *Problema sootnosheniia traditsionnoi kul'tury i sovremennosti v ekspozitsii GME narodov SSSR* (Moscow, 1964), p. 6. Curiously, at this period attempts were made to 'neutralize' the national question, reconfiguring it in 'spatial-geographic' terms: ethnicity was reconceptualized as the emergence of local variants of an all-Soviet culture.
52. AREM, f. 2, op. 1, d. 1230, l. 14.
53. Ibid., d. 1447, ll. 1, 31.
54. The term 'Great Russian' was removed from the captions and annotative material in the exhibitions at the start of the 1930s, and from then onwards was used only in citations from historical texts etc. This practice has continued to the present day.

55. See e.g. K. Kobrin, 'Ot paternalistskogo proekta vlasti k shizofrenii: orientalizm kak rossiiskaia problema (na poliakh Edwarda Saida)', 2008, http://magazines. russ.ru/nz/2008/3/kk5.html.

56. AREM, f. 1, Protokoly predvaritel'nykh soveshchanii po voprosam ob ustroistve i organizatsii Etnograficheskogo Otdela Russkogo Muzeia (1901 g.) [PSO], d. 11, l. 4.

CHAPTER 5

Rituals of identity: the Soviet passport

Albert Baiburin

The Soviet internal passport was the most important identity document available to the Soviet population generally. It had a crucial role in the official existence ('file self') of the citizen,[1] determining both personal and collective identity. It denominated the individual characteristics of each separate holder ('1. *Surname* IVANOV; 2. *Name and patronymic* Sergei Borisovich; 3. *Date of Birth* 13 December 1924; 4. *Place of Birth* Leningrad; 5. *Nationality* Russian'), and also his or her Soviet citizenship. In practice the binary status of the passport as an identity document was usually dissolved, and the passport was assigned a single concrete function, acting either as 'the passport belonging to Ivanov S. B.' or as 'a Soviet passport' generally. For the most part it served as an identity document in the first sense (when one's right to reside in a certain place (*propiska*) was checked, when one signed up in a library or visited a clinic, when one moved to a new job etc.).

The passport could be a preventive device – to stop people from migrating at will.[2] It could also be an instrument of discrimination (the so-called 'point five', nationality, i.e. ethnic identity, was regularly used to reject Jewish applicants for study and work, while at some periods members of certain ethnic groups, for example Kalmyks, could not obtain passports at all). It made information which in some societies would be considered private (e.g. whether the holder was married, single or divorced) available to any official who chose to open it.[3] However, it is possible to look at the document the other way round as well. It facilitated movement and access to certain places, conveying full rights of citizenship.[4] By extension, when signing up for passports and using them, Soviet citizens made decisions (not always under coercion) about what to call themselves, when they were born and what 'nationality' they belonged to.[5]

If the passport's role as an identity document was dynamic, the subject of constant negotiation, its status as a primary signifier of Soviet identity was unvarying, and so to some extent invisible. At the same time there were occasions when this status was given central attention. One such was when the holder received the passport for the first time. Sometimes this happened in a very low-key way, as we shall see. But in the late Soviet era, Soviet propaganda started to represent as the ideal a formal ceremony at which young people were solemnly presented with their first passport, and their 'entry into citizenship' was stressed. As well as relating to the passport as such, this ceremony belonged to the important category of 'Soviet rituals' (or if one prefers, 'invented traditions'), which played a crucial part in the social construction of identity.[6] These rituals began to proliferate on a large scale in the late Soviet period, and their development at this stage was testament to new understandings of social belonging, as is obvious if one compares them with the rituals of the first post-revolutionary years, which were key instruments of Sovietization in their time.

SOVIET RITUALS IN THE 1920S AND 1930S

The creation of new Soviet rituals began soon after Soviet power itself, and their primary purpose at this stage was to foster a new, secular, society. By 18 December 1917 the Decree on Civil Marriage, Children, and the Introduction of a Registry of Civil Ceremonies[7] had announced that all legal acts relating to the social status of the citizenry that had previously been under the jurisdiction of the Church were now transferred to the jurisdiction of state institutions. From now on, only civil marriages and records of births or deaths set down in a state registry office were recognized as proof that a person had married, been born or died.[8] This effected a radical change in the nature of family relationships, and also a change to the rituals marking new phases in a person's identity.

In April 1918 a special decree was passed bringing to an end the traditional Easter bonus in places of employment.[9] Unsanctioned absences on Church holidays were severely punished, while people received extra leave if they volunteered to work on these days. The introduction of the 'uninterrupted working week' (*nepreryvka*) on 26 August 1929 not only ended the recognition of religious holidays, but also abolished the special status of Sundays, since the day of rest could now fall on any fixed day.[10]

Yet privately Church holidays retained much of their appeal. The new, Soviet, calendar felt empty and unfamiliar.[11] Naturally, embellishing the calendar with new holidays, this time sponsored by the state, became a major priority for the fledgling regime. Some of these echoed religious festivals, but in politicized form. The holy days of the Church calendar were contested by parody events ('Red Easter' and 'Red Christmas'), or existing festivals were replaced with new ones, such as the Day of the Paris Commune (18 March).

The situation with family celebrations, as opposed to calendar ones, was different. Existing rituals were reworked to expel their religious colouration and 'family' significance, and infuse them with new socialist content. At 'red christenings' the traditional 'godparents' were renamed 'civil sponsors', and those officially taking part in the ritual included members of the mother's and father's work collective, not to speak of workers from Soviet and party organizations (who took over the functions of the priest). These people would read aloud a 'decree' announcing that the newborn had been accepted into the ranks of the citizens of the Land of the Soviet. For their part the baby's parents would be presented with an 'Exhortation from Soviet Society'. An example dating from 1932 and preserved in the local museum of Serov, in the Urals, runs like this:

We bless you not with the sign of the cross, not with holy water and prayers, but with the legacy of slavery and darkness, with our red flag of struggle and labour, shot through with bullet holes, ripped by bayonets ... We order the parents of this newborn girl to raise their daughter as a faithful warrior for the liberation of toiling people all over the world, an ally of science and labour, an enemy of darkness and ignorance, a burning defender of Soviet power.[12]

A straw poll was taken and the newborn named 'Oktiabrina' (October Girl) by majority vote. Other names of the time included Vilor (Vladimir Il'ich Lenin – organizer of the Revolution), Lentrosh (Lenin, Trotsky, Shaumian), Dazrasmygda ('Long live the Fusion of the City and the Country') and so on.

New festivals at this period generally resembled Soviet political meetings. A presidium and president would be elected; speeches, a vote and a resolution would follow. Sometimes there would even be a show trial (of something or someone associated with 'obsolete daily life'). But 'red funerals' with official speeches instead of a church requiem and 'red weddings' with orations by fiery warriors for the bright future and a reception with tea and no vodka had little chance of becoming acceptable alternatives to 'obsolete rites', especially in the country. Here, people were notoriously conservative, though occasionally Komsomol workers did organize new rituals of some kinds, for example celebrations of 'harvest festivals'.[13]

By the middle of the 1920s the creation of new rites of this kind had fallen out of favour. A sign of the times was a speech by V. V. Veresaev:

In the past, the funeral rite had a completely clear rationale. People gathered round the coffin of the deceased to pray for his soul; the corpse itself had something mysterious and sacred about it, sacred as a temple, since it was the place where the immortal soul of a person lived ... But we put the decaying body in a box of a particular shape covered with red fabric and mount a guard of honour that changes every 10 minutes (and what are they guarding, when you think about it?). Music plays away in the background. What is it all for? What on earth is the point?[14]

When Veresaev's comments were made, it was only a year since the funeral of Lenin, and it was clear that he had in mind not just new rites 'in general', but one quite concrete example of the genre.

Yet the so-called 'Five-Year Plan of Militant Atheism', announced in 1932, injected new life into the campaign to create alternative holidays. Over the ensuing years, such occasions as elections to the Supreme Soviet, Constitution Day and the 'jubilees' (landmark birthdays) of Stalin himself now started to be celebrated as national festivals.[15] In 1931 the First Parade of Physical Culture Enthusiasts took place, initiating a new tradition of grandiose sports displays. More than 100,000 young people took part in the physical culture parade organized in 1933; through the efforts of the 'Ready for Labour and Defence' movement, the numbers of enthusiasts continued increasing from year to year. The propaganda of sport and health appears to have had considerable success among the youth of the time. For the generation born in the late 1920s, Physical Culture Day was, by the late 1930s, almost as important a festival as 7 November and 1 May.[16] However, during the Second World War and in the years afterwards, the drive to create new rituals died down.

LATE SOVIET RITUALS

In the late 1950s another phase in the creation of 'new Soviet man' by means of rituals and festivals began. As late as 1956, officials in the Culture Section of the Central Committee of the Communist Party had responded to a proposal to create new rituals by describing them as 'serving no purpose'.[17] However, just three years later, in 1959, a campaign to implant such festivals was launched in *Izvestiia*.

At this point the wider social context of rituals, and the attitude to them, altered significantly. The point was now social integration, rather than the conversion of the population to communist values. By the 1960s, traditional rituals – previously seen as obsolete – began to be viewed in a positive light, provided they were not obviously religious. Elements of new Soviet rituals themselves began to be directly adopted from folk precedents (e.g. the presentation of bread and salt, and the shouting of 'bitter, bitter!' to get the bride and groom to kiss, during wedding ceremonies).

In terms of the way that new rituals were described in official documents of the time, this phase of Soviet history differed from earlier phases of ritual creation. Where previously the new rites had been imposed on people 'from above', it was now claimed that dozens of letters to the newspapers had pointed to the need for new festivals and rites that would be 'in tune with the times': festivals of labour and friendship, hammer and sickle festivals, age of majority festivals, Komsomol weddings etc. The recognized purposes of 'rite creation' had also altered. If, in the 1920s and 1930s, the struggle with religion had been the leading motive behind the invention of new rites (a purpose that remained relevant, especially since official anti-clericalism reached a peak in 1959–64), there were now other aims in view as well. The new rites were supposed to make Soviet people more 'cultured' (by encouraging them not to drink, for instance), and also to inculcate the ideals of collectivism and internationalism.

According to some of the brochures about new rituals, the movement to create these originated in the Baltic States (though there were also other acknowledged centres, for example Leningrad, where a palace of marriages, 'the first in the country', opened in 1959). For instance, the so-called 'age of majority festival' was allegedly first celebrated in Latvia (1956, and in Estonia a year later). Latvia was also the first Soviet location where the 'Day of the Child' began being celebrated (in 1957).[18] The leading role of the Baltic States may be explained by the fact that people here realized, more quickly than anywhere else, that they could preserve religious rites such as confirmation and baptism if they made them look sufficiently 'Soviet'.

By the start of the 1960s the 'grass-roots' campaign to revive old rituals and create new Soviet ones was starting to acquire the level of top-down control that the authorities considered essential. A landmark was the organization in 1964 of the First Conference on the Implantation of New Soviet Rituals.[19] At this, 'rite creation' was declared to be a central task of activists in regional party organizations, and it was claimed that one of the basic problems with work to date in the area had been the weak level of theorization of the subject, and the lack of any academic discussion of experience so far and of the issues this had raised.[20] Those called upon to work on the development of new rituals included ethnographers, folklorists, musicologists and other academic specialists.[21] The importance of the new rituals was also regularly mentioned at congresses of the Komsomol.[22]

It was customary to divide festivals and rituals into three categories: (1) Soviet and international state festivals (7 November, 1 May, 8 March etc.); (2) workplace and professional festivals (Initiation into Professional Life, First Wage Packet Day, Harvest Festival, Reindeer-Herders' Day etc.

etc.); (3) civic and family festivals and rites attached to particular dates (New Year, 'Farewell to Winter', a Sovietization of the old Shrovetide) and to important events in the life cycle (age of majority, entry into the army, marriage etc.). It was to this last category, 'life cycle rituals', that the Solemn Presentation of the Soviet Passport belonged.

THE PASSPORT RITUAL

The Solemn Presentation of the Soviet Passport began being organized on a small scale in the early 1960s.[23] But the ritual started to spread only once the 'general passportization' of the Soviet nation had been announced in 1974 (this process was initiated on 1 January 1976, as passports began being issued, for the first time in Soviet history, to the entire adult population).[24]

The selection precisely of the passport as a crucial point in the life cycle was thus related not just to the rise of ritual, but to the increasingly prominent role of this document in the Soviet person's existence. Normal life was quite impossible without the passport. It was needed to travel around the country (to use an aeroplane or a hotel), indeed, to move around at all, since at any moment holders might be stopped and asked to show their passport to prove their identity and the fact that they were registered with the police as legally required. It was needed not just to move to a new job, but also to register children at school; one even needed it to collect a package at the post office. It is no accident that it was at this point that an ironic saying came into use: 'Every respectable Russian consists of three parts: soul, body and passport.' With more and more Soviet citizens being granted a passport, and the ritual of showing it becoming ever more common, it became important to raise the passport above the level of routine, to make it seem more than a tedious piece of paper that was required for merely mechanical purposes. Significantly, these years also saw the introduction of a new model of the Soviet passport. Dark red rather than green, it also had a more imposing appearance, with a much more prominent state emblem on the cover.

The age at which people received passports was also important. Sixteen was a notable age threshold in Soviet tradition, the stage at which some-one was considered to be fit for full adult employment (fourteen- and fifteen-year-olds might not work a full day) – though the age of majority was in fact officially eighteen.[25] Hence, references to work and to adult life appeared prominently in the passport ritual. The fact that the age for receiving passports and the age of majority did not coincide had no effect on the passport ritual – even though those receiving the passport were, legally speaking, not yet adults, they were still congratulated on receiving citizenship and beginning a new, 'adult' phase of life. The symbolic status of the passport itself – as a sort of testimony to attaining adulthood – took precedence over the biological age of those who acquired the document.

The title of the ritual ('the Solemn *Presentation*') is also important. Those involved in the ceremonial were not just *receiving* the passport (having simply reached the right age). The passport was being *presented* to them as a gift from the state, and they were therefore rendered indebted to the state – as they were for their happy childhood, education and so on.[26] The debt could only be repaid (and then only in part) by heroic feats of labour or in defence of the Motherland (an incessant motif in Soviet propaganda). In this sense the 'Solemn Presentation of the Soviet Passport' was one among many episodes in a specific exchange system between state and citizen, but a particularly important one.

Sometimes a different name was used for the ritual – 'Festival of the Age of Majority', 'The Sixteen-Year-Olds' Festival' etc. The most widespread alternative was 'Initiation into Citizenship'.[27] This particular title appears to have caused those who invented it some embarrassment, since it drew attention to certain anomalies requiring explanation (the person being presented the passport was considered a 'citizen' already, though one with limited rights, but on the other hand, it was only two years after receiving the passport that he or she would become a citizen in the full sense). Yet in fact this was to prove the most lasting of the alternatives, its popularity surviving into the post-Soviet period. The reasons for the persistence of this slightly inappropriate title will be suggested below.

The ritual of the Solemn Presentation, like other new rites, was the living illustration of a construct. In early Soviet propaganda, 'red marriages' were celebrated; in practice, couples queued up, signed the book and exited through the door. Similarly, in the late Soviet period, most sixteen-year-olds got their passports in a totally routine fashion at the so-called 'passport desks' of the local police station. It was a select few who were given their passports ceremonially.[28] One was supposed to earn one's right to the ceremony by good school work (passports would be handed out to a group of sixteen-year-olds at one time). The fact that the ritual was not 'just for everyone' of course increased the importance of the event in the eyes of those who were organizing it.

It was common for official brochures to emphasize the superiority of the Solemn Presentation over the usual practice of simply handing out passports to those who had reached the age of sixteen: 'Someone gets his passport . . . Here he is, coming into the local police station, standing in line in the corridor, then they let him into a little stuffy room. He signs the receipt, pays his thirty kopecks and hasn't time for a proper look at his first adult identity document before the shout of "Next!" rings out.'[29] A memoir of 2002, however, is more ambivalent:

I was dying to get my first passport, I was hoping I'd get it before I was supposed to. By the time my turn came round, the district committee of the Communist Party had thought up some idiotic procedure called 'Initiation into Citizeniship of the USSR'.[30] But to start with, I'd had a basinful of the Twenty-Sixth Congress [in 1981] by then, all those synopses and political indoctrination sessions and 'lessons in courage', and I was also dying to start my adult life. And so, three days before the Solemn Presentation I went to the head of the passport desk and showed him my press card from *Moskovskii komsomolets*, and told him I had to go on a business trip and that I'd miss the ceremony. The police major stubbed out his cigarette in his skull-shaped ashtray, wrinkled his eyes as the smoke rose up, reached into a safe the size of a bookcase, fished out my booklet and . . . I set off into adult life. I seem to remember that Andriukha, another boy from my class, and I split a bottle of port[31] between two for the first time in our lives that evening.[32]

At the same time, not everyone remembered receiving their passport in such a cynical way. In villages, particularly, mass passportization was the source of joy: 'The whole village was there, we drank and we danced. It was . . . we were all human beings now. All equal. We could visit the town and be equal there. We could go somewhere. We had our "document" in our hands.'[33] Participants as well as creators thus sometimes fostered the process by which, like every ritual, the Solemn Presentation of the Soviet Passport sought to create a special alternative type of reality, unlike that in everyday life, with the chaos and rudeness that obtained in actual Soviet offices acting as anti-ideal.

The second (semiotic) type of reality constructed by the Solemn Presentation conformed to the principles obtaining in Soviet festivals and rites generally. The scenarios for these were usually written in special commissions for the implantation of new rituals or in local sections of the *Znanie* (Knowledge) Society; they were rubber-stamped by party and city, or local, administrations.[34] The concrete forms according to which any rite was realized were up to local administrations, but the spirit of the rite was supposed to remain inviolate. What this meant was that individual commissions worked to convergent patterns. The model scenarios published in brochures were strikingly homogeneous, and so were the unpublished texts that were actually used for performance in different places.[35]

In the eyes of those who created it, the ritual was supposed to inspire those being presented with the passport with a feeling of pride in their motherland

and a sense of responsibility because one was now becoming a citizen of the Soviet Union. The presentation was often arranged on a festival day of some kind. The most suitable was usually held to be the Day of the Soviet Constitution (5 December), since the ritual was supposed to confer on participants the rights and duties listed in the Soviet constitution. However, it did not necessarily take place on a festival day at all, since the presentation itself was supposed to make any day a festive occasion. The venue was usually a club or a house or palace of culture; in summer, it might be a park. Whichever way, it would be somewhere suitably imposing that could hold large numbers of people, since this was very much a public occasion.

In order to lend weight to the ceremony and by extension to the Soviet passport itself, the organizers would try to create a 'solemn atmosphere'. There were various well-tried means for doing this. The hall and most particularly the platform, stage or dais would be decorated with banners, with the state emblem of the Soviet Union and the particular Soviet republic in which the ceremony was being held, and with portraits of Soviet leaders and posters. From loudspeakers poured recordings of patriotic songs; sometimes there would even be a live brass band. Alongside the heroes of the hour, those being presented with the passports, would appear Communists of many decades' standing, war veterans and veterans of labour, and 'leaders of production' (all described as 'representatives of public life'),[36] representatives of the local administration (party and government officials), teachers, parents and some members of the younger generation (usually a Pioneer troop). The selection of these people was explained by the fact that the idea of the 'relay race of generations' underlay the ritual – as was also the case with other rituals of maturation at this period.[37] In a kind of Soviet variant of magic initiation ceremonies, participants received their passports from bigwigs such as heroes of labour and party chiefs, and were supposed not only to perpetuate their remarkable feats but to excel these. Pioneers would solemnly greet those being presented with passports, and would symbolically take the place of the latter as 'passport holders in waiting', striving to earn the great honour of being granted a Solemn Presentation in their turn. The parents and teachers who had raised this 'new shift'[38] would pass on their congratulations and accept congratulations from others.

As in any classic ritual, there was no division between spectators and actors – everyone was considered a participant. In this way a kind of ritual model of Soviet society was created, as different generations executed an exchange of symbolic values. As was expected in Soviet systems of exchange, this was markedly asymmetrical, since those receiving their passports and waiting to receive them in the future were indebted to everyone else present, not to mention such virtual participants as the Motherland, party, Komsomol and so on.

The ritual would open with music. Usually this included 'Song of the Motherland' ('Broad is my motherland / In her are many fields, forests and rivers'), the famous lead number in Aleksandrov's 1936 film *The Circus*. Then there was usually a reading of Maiakovskii's 'Verses on the Soviet Passport', with the stress falling on the final lines: 'Read and eat your hearts out: I'm a citizen of the USSR!' The poem was actually about a Soviet foreign passport (the internal passport was reintroduced only in 1932, three years after it was written), and Maiakovskii's original addressees were foreign border guards (moving 'along the front line of couchettes and wagons-lits', at whom he aimed the 'red bomb' of his passport). But this historical irony never interfered with the sense of emotional elevation. For Soviet citizens, *pasport* meant 'identity card'; it was a 'foreign' passport (*zagranpasport*) that required qualification.

In their speeches the veterans and bureaucrats would talk about the role of the passport in the life changes that sixteen-year-olds were experiencing. A standard speech by a veteran went like this: 'When you receive your passport today, you will become a full citizen of the Union of Soviet Socialist Republics, you will have great rights and important duties conferred on you, as set out in the Constitution of our country' and so on.[39]

The passport was presented by a representative of the state. Most often this was the head of the local passport office. Then a party or government worker congratulated the young person on receiving his or her passport. Then a people's deputy from the district or village soviet would read out a Soviet vade mecum along the following lines:

Dear comrade!
Today you, young citizen (citizeness) of the Union of Soviet Socialist Republics, have, in receiving your passport, acquired the high and honourable title of Citizen of the USSR. Bear it proudly and carefully all your life! Remember that you can only do so by means of honest labour, a clear conscience, by a great sense of truth and justice, by fidelity to your Motherland. Let the bright sun of reason shine down always on your path . . . Be worthy of the high title of Citizen of the Union of Soviet Socialist Republics![40]

In response one of the recipients would read out a solemn oath.[41] The details might vary,[42] but the general drift was always the same: those receiving their passports swore to be faithful and not spare themselves for the good of the Motherland (or the Fatherland, or both). After this oath had been recited, the recipients would sign their names – not in their passports (in case nerves made them make a mistake), but in a presentation book, *I'm a Citizen of the USSR*. The occasion would be rounded off by the Soviet national anthem.

Such was in outline the scenario for the Solemn Presentation of the Soviet Passport. If we compare it with the memories of receiving one's passport the ordinary way cited earlier, it becomes clear that pretty well the only thing the two experiences had in common was that one ended up with a copy of the identity document in question. Everything else about the Solemn Presentation was a realization of official ideas about what a festival celebrating this document should be like.

If we turn to the substance of the ritual, it becomes obvious that not all the official organs involved in the ceremony considered actually being presented with one's passport as a sufficiently remarkable event in itself to justify such a high occasion. Hence the constant attempts to load more symbolic signification on the ritual and to assign a more elevated meaning to it. The commonest strategy was to represent the passport as the central symbol of Soviet citizenship.[43] In this case the entire ritual acquired a slightly different significance. It was not just presentation of the passport, but acquisition of citizenship that was at stake (in some countries an event of this kind would be reserved for foreigners taking the citizenship of the receiving country). The result was to transform the individual identity which it was a passport's essential function to record into a generic Soviet identity, which then became the defining identity for the passport holder. It is intriguing to record that there was no variant of the passport ritual that included even a hint of the personal identity intrinsic to the idea of an identity document. However, collective Soviet identity (entry into the circle of those who are 'really one's own', into the Soviet family) was emphasized at every point. The rite hinged on a double peripeteia: along with receiving one's passport, one received citizenship, and instead of one's individual identity one received a collective identity. This was accompanied by another type of transformation (one that was natural in a ritual context). Participants received their passports as members of a collective, rather than one by one (as when people went to collect their passports in the ordinary way: cf. the official's cry of 'Next!' in the story about receiving one's passport at the 'passport desk'). While this might seem simply to amount to a multiplication of the original situation, in fact it totally transformed this. A procedure of private, even personal significance became a collective public event.

That was not the end to the shifts in significance. From the point of view of a sixteen-year-old, the passport was above all a symbol of adulthood: in the first place it signified independence, the capacity to do what adults do but was formerly forbidden (for instance, drink alcohol, smoke, watch 'grown-up films' and so on).[44] In official Soviet rhetoric, however, adulthood meant something quite different – the chance to labour on behalf of the Motherland or to defend her from the assaults of enemies. Further, in official discourse adulthood was linked with the acquisition of rights and duties, not to speak of responsibilities (cf. the reminder of one's debt to the Motherland).

It was precisely these appreciations of the significance of receiving one's passport (the equation of 'passport' in the concrete and abstract citizenship, the emphasis on the transformation from individual to collective and legal minor to adult) that determined the character of the ritual. They also made themselves felt in its rhetoric. The audio-visual components of the ritual were grouped round two basic nexuses of signs. One of these was associated with the idea of *citizenship* (the flag, the state emblem and other state symbols, the constitution, the leader portraits), and the other round the *official under-standing of adulthood* (representations of heroic feats of labour and war, banners with slogans and proverbs about labour, and so on). The same ideas, essentially, were expressed also in the verbal components of the ritual. In the speeches, poems, the vade mecum, the oath – everywhere the central point was the high calling of Soviet citizens, and the victories on the field of labour and, if necessary, war that awaited them.

Such shifts and substitutions in meaning did not derive from a desire to hoodwink the public. Rather, they were intended to transform into ritual a social practice that was considered vitally important. One might say that the ritual by its essential nature demanded an ontological shift, an elevation in status of all the components involved. Yet, given that none of the ritual components were in fact related to the essence of the ceremony, practically speaking (the young person would get his or her passport whatever rite was used) most people did not care too much about how they received their passport. If some people who did not receive their passport ceremonially were disappointed to have missed out on the ceremony, others were pleased that they had not had to waste their time on such nonsense.

Soviet rituals (like so-called 'traditional' ones) did not require to be understood in the usual sense of the word, or reflected on in any way. They did not appeal to reason, but to emotional perceptions. It was not words but collective practices, including discursive practices, which were at stake.[45] As in any ritual, pre-existing texts were collectively re-enacted. Essentially, the entire performance of the ritual comprised a selection of quotations. Even the participants were 'quoting', since their role was to 'enact' the primary composition of Soviet society. In an increasingly individualized society, these features of the ritual elevated it above ordinary life, but at the same time ran the risk of making it seem insincere and artificial.

This chapter has examined the ways in which the internal passport shaped citizens' sense of national identity and their view of themselves as subjects of Soviet rule. It has shown that a crucial role in emphasizing the collective and patriotic significance of the passport was played by the Solemn Presentation of the Soviet Passport, a ritual that began to be promoted on a mass scale in the mid-1970s, to accompany the wholesale 'passportization' of the Soviet population. While only a small minority of sixteen-year-olds actually went through the ritual, it was widely publicized, and increasingly became accepted as the appropriate (if not necessarily the typical) way of entering 'Soviet citizenship'. The ritual also crystallized many of the key features of Soviet rituals in this period, not to speak of official perceptions of these as expressions of collective belonging and 'Communist education'.

With the collapse of the Soviet Union, Soviet passports disappeared. However, the 'Russian' (Lithuanian, Kazakh, Armenian etc. etc.) identity cards that were created by the new governments were usually strikingly similar, in terms of their appearance and the information they contained, to their Soviet counterparts.[46] In Russia the Solemn Presentation of the Passport was one of the few Soviet rituals to survive 1991 (another example would be the wedding ceremony as organized in the palace of marriages).[47] By the early twenty-first century, Solemn Presentations had vanished from Moscow and St Petersburg, but the ritual was still regularly performed in provincial towns.[48] However, this circumstance was probably not an indication that a miracle had happened, and a newly invented ritual had been transformed into a dynamic, naturally developing one. It was more a case of psychological inertia (people's idea of how to celebrate important occasions was entirely dependent on Soviet stereotypes) and *faute de mieux*. The other maturation rituals that once clustered around the age of sixteen or so (entry into the Komsomol or into the 'working classes') disappeared in 1991, along with the Komsomol itself. For those who wanted an official way of marking transition to adulthood – something that parents and teachers, if not young people themselves, saw as important – only the Solemn Presentation was left.

As for the passport itself, it remained indispensable after 1991. Indeed, anxiety about 'terrorism' and draft-dodging meant that passports were examined more often. In 1990s Russia it became impossible to buy rail tickets without showing one's passport, and there began to be regular spot-checks (particularly on young men of a 'non-Slavic' appearance) at metro stations. By the early twenty-first century, traders regularly cruised public transport offering plastic cases to protect this precious document. A standard sales pitch was that the cases were necessary to stop the pages wearing out, because 'we have our passports checked all the time'.[49] Thus, the passport represented an important and rare case of the persistence of a central Soviet social institution, and the rituals associated with it, into the post-Soviet period. This situation derived not just from state paranoia, but from rank-and-file citizens' own sense of what was fitting (after the removal in 1997 from the passport template of the 'fifth point' detailing nationality, there were protests not just from Russians, but from representatives of some ethnic groups, such as Bashkirs, who felt that the public affirmation of their national identity was being impeded). Just as in the Soviet period, the passport remained much more than an identity document pure and simple. It was a central constituent both of individual and of collective identity. Like Soviet citizens before them, citizens of the Russian Federation continued to be composed of 'three things: body, soul and passport'.

Translated by Catriona Kelly

NOTES

1. For the use of the term 'file self' in a Soviet context, see S. Fitzpatrick, *Tear off the Masks! Identity and Imposture in Twentieth-Century Russia* (Princeton, NJ, 2006).
2. There is a large literature on migrancy control by means of the passport and *propiska*. Works in English include M. Matthews, *The Passport Society: Controlling Movement in Russia and the USSR* (Boulder, CO, 1993); M. Garcelon, 'Colonizing the Subject: The Genealogy and Legacy of the Soviet Internal Passport', in *Documenting Individual Identity*, ed. J. Caplan and J. Torvey (Princeton, NJ, 2001), 83–100; C. Buckley, 'The Myth of Managed Migration: Migration Control and Market in the Soviet Period', *Slavic Review* 54:4 (1995), 896–916 etc.
3. It was customary for hotel staff to refuse to assign a double room to people not registered as married – unless they were of the same sex.
4. In this context, a passage in Colin Thubron's travel book *In Siberia* (London, 2000), 132, comes across as rather crass. Thubron describes how an elderly man from the Evenk people he encountered had suffered a terrible fire in his home, and was able to rescue only one thing: 'What had he carried out, I wondered, in those few seconds? Had he salvaged a few hoarded roubles, a precious garment, a sentimental photograph? "What did you save?" I strained to catch his voice. It came tiny, self-satisfied. "My *pasport*."' Thubron comments, 'I sensed his degradation'. But this ignores the obvious: the man, from a population group only recently entitled to possess a passport, was *proud* of his possession of the document, which he associated with full membership of the Soviet collective. Cf. Ol'ga Berggol'ts's recollections, in her 1949 diary of a visit to the village of

Staroe Rakhino, of young people's indignation when the local collective farm chairman tore up their passports to stop them leaving: 'Why bother with finishing school, they'll never let us out, yet they give us all this stuff about "every road is open to the young"' (*Ol'ga: zapretnyi dnevnik*, St Petersburg, 2010, 151). The chairman herself asked why people had 'armed our youth with passports' (ibid., 150).

5. For example, members of some non-Slavic nationalities (e.g. Latvians, Lithuanians and Estonians) did not traditionally have patronymics, but the Soviet registration system forced them to acquire these. Dates of birth were by custom vague in peasant society ('at the start of Shrovetide'), but had to be determined when people acquired passports (and 'adjusting' dates so that one could defer military service, or hasten the receipt of a pension, was a widespread practice). See A. Baiburin, 'K antropologii dokumenta: pasportnaia "lichnost'" v Rossii', in *Status dokumenta v sovremennoi kul'ture*, ed. I. Kaspe (in press). The category of 'nationality' was also flexible: passport-holders chose their identity at sixteen, a choice that was officially supposed to be based on the 'nationality' of their parents, but which might require negotiation with officials who insisted on assigning a given 'nationality': see A. Baiburin, 'Nepravil'naia natsional'nost'', in *Lotmanovskie chteniia 2010 g.* (in press).

6. There is an extensive literature on Soviet rituals. Several hundred publications appeared around the time of the First Conference on the Implantation of New Soviet Rituals (1964) alone. See L. M. Saburova, 'Literatura o novykh obriadakh i prazdnikakh za 1963–1966 gg. (osnovnye voprosy i tendentsii izucheniia)', *Sovetskaia etnografiia*, no. 10 (1966), 173–81. (For an outline list, see www.mod-langs.ox.ac.uk/russian/nationalism/bibliography.htm.) For the most part, such publications are useful exclusively as primary sources – guides to the ideals and mentality of the time (e.g. I. V. Sukhanov, *Obychai, traditsii i preemstvennost' pokolenii*, Moscow, 1976; V. A. Rudnev, *Sovetskie prazdniki, obriady, ritualy*, Leningrad, 1979; L. A. Tul'tseva, *Sovremennye prazdniki i obriady narodov SSSR*, Moscow, 1985). But some publications were a little more substantive. For example, the well-known folklorist and writer Dmitry Balashov, 'Traditsionnoe i sovremennoe', *Nauka i religiia* 4 (1966), 29, argued that you actually cannot create new rituals – an idea that was, by the standards of the time, subversive. But thoughtful work of this kind was in very short supply. Work by Western scholars on Soviet festivals generally addressed the social functions of the new traditions, their roles in propagandizing Soviet ideology, their effects on different social strata etc. See e.g.: J. McDowell, 'Soviet Civil Ceremonies', *Journal for the Scientific Study of Religion* 13:3 (September 1974), 265–79; C. A. P. Binns, 'The Changing Face of Power: Revolution and Accommodation in the Development of the Soviet Ceremonial System', *Man*, n.s., 15:1 (1979), 170–87; C. Lane, *The Rites of Rulers: Ritual in Industrial Society – The Soviet Case* (Cambridge, 1981). In the 1990s the new accessibility of archive materials and the rise of interest in Soviet mass culture generated more thoroughly researched and argued discussions: see e.g. K. Petrone, *'Life Has Become More Joyous, Comrades': Celebrations in the Time of Stalin* (Bloomington, IN, 2000). M. Rolf, *Sovetskii massovyi prazdnik v Voronezhe i*

Tsentral'no-Chernozemnoi oblasti Rossii (1927–1932) (Moscow, 2009) and S. Malysheva, *Sovetskaia prazdnichnaia kul'tura v provintsii: prostranstvo, simvoly, mify (1917–1927)* (Kazan, 2005) look in detail at the Soviet provinces, drawing evidence from extensive consultation of local newspapers and archives.

7. *Dekrety sovetskoi vlasti*, vol. I (Moscow, 1957), 247–9.

8. The situation with the Anglican Church in England today is partly analogous: a record of marriage made by a member of the clergy is still legally valid, though a record of christening or burial does not equate to a record of birth or death.

9. *Dekrety sovetskoi vlasti*, vol. II (Moscow, 1959), 99.

10. M. Gumerova, '"Nepreryvka" i antireligioznaia agitatsiia', *Konstruiruia 'sovetskoe'? Politicheskoe soznanie, povsednevnye praktiki, novye identichnosti* (St Petersburg, 2011), 58–63.

11. Even now the Julian calendar has not completely lost its hold. It is quite common in villages to hear people say 'I last saw him on St Peter's Day', and so on. In Russian cities this is less common, but everyone still knows when 'Old New Year's Eve' falls (13 January).

12. V. M. Ivanov, *Zhizn' rozhdaet novye obriady* (Minsk, 1964), 69.

13. Such 'harvest festivals' were introduced in different parts of Russia and were organized to coincide with the traditional 'Apple Saviour' festival (19 August). See L. A. Tul'tseva, *Sovremennye prazdniki i obriady narodov SSSR* (Moscow, 1985), 42.

14. Veresaev's speech dates from 1925, and the following year it was published as *Ob obriadakh novykh i starykh* (Moscow, 1926). Quotation here from p. 6. The little 32-page brochure came out in a print run of 5,000, which, by contemporary standards, was quite sizable.

15. These festivals are analysed in detail in Petrone, *Life Has Become More Joyous*.

16. See Happiness-PF9–10: interview with man b. 1929, Leningrad, conducted by A. Piir, St Petersburg 2007; transcript held in interviewer's own archive. For a more detailed discussion of Soviet physical culture celebrations and the role of physical culture in the formation of 'new Soviet man', see M. O'Mahony, *Sport in the USSR: Physical Culture – Visual Culture* (London, 2006), esp. 57–96.

17. Russian State Archive of Recent History, Moscow, f. 5, op. 34, d. 14, l. 3.

18. The festival was introduced by the UN in 1949.

19. The Second Conference on New Soviet Rituals took place in Kiev in October 1978.

20. P. P. Kampars and N. M. Zakovich, *Sovetskaia grazhdanskaia obriadnost'* (Moscow, 1967), 34.

21. A decade or so later, in 1977, conferences dealing with changes in the lives of the peoples of the USSR began being organized, with much attention being paid to the development of new rituals. N. S. Polishchuk, 'Vsesoiuznaia konferentsiia po voprosam etnograficheskogo izucheniia sovremennosti', *Sovetskaia etnografiia* 6 (1977), 104–12.

22. See e.g. *Semnadtsatyi s''ezd Vsesoiuznogo leninskogo kommunisticheskogo soiuza molodezhi, 23–27 aprelia 1974 goda. Stenograficheskii otchet* (Moscow, 1975), vol. II, 215, 244.

23. One of the first methodological guides to organizing the Solemn Presentation of the Soviet Passport was published by the Board of Culture of the Regional Committee of the Communist Party, Perm province: E. Klimov, *Torzhestvennyi akt vrucheniia pervogo sovetskogo pasporta (metodicheskoe posobie v pomoshch' kul'turno-prosvetitel'nym rabotnikam* (Perm, 1961). The scenario proposed consists of five parts: (1) arrival of the guests and organization of informal relaxation before the ceremony begins; (2) the Solemn Presentation of the Soviet Passport; (3) mass entertainments, games, dances, instruction in singing mass songs; (4) cordial chat over a cup of tea; (5) departure of the guests.

24. Until 1974, villagers were not entitled to receive passports – or to be more accurate, workers at state farms were entitled to receive them, while workers at collective farms were not (with the exception of some skilled workers, such as tractor drivers). According to the census of 1970, collective farm workers accounted for around 50 million people, or 20.5% of the entire Soviet population.

25. From the age of sixteen, some restrictions relating to age were lifted: for example, children could now watch 'adult' films (with the endorsement 'banned for viewing by children under 16') and visit public places in the evenings without adults; in Leningrad the latest time at which children under fourteen were allowed to appear on the streets unaccompanied was stipulated in 1940 at 9 p.m., and in 1944 it was 10 p.m. (but now the restriction was extended to children under sixteen). 'O meropriiatiiakh po bor'be s detskoi besnadzornost'iu (obiazatel'noe postanovlenie)', *Biulleten' Ispolkoma Lengorsoveta* 11 (1940), 2; 'O pravilakh povedeniia detei v obshchestvennykh mestakh (v teatrakh, kino, tramvaiakh, na stadionakh i t. d.) i na ulitsakh goroda Leningrada', ibid., 12 (1944), 8. It is interesting to note that the age when people received their first passport was stable for many decades (only in 1997 was it changed – at this point, children started to receive their first passport at fourteen).

26. On the general motif of gratitude, see J. Brooks, *Thank You, Comrade Stalin! Soviet Public Culture from Revolution to Cold War* (Princeton, NJ, 2000).

27. The idea of 'citizenship' is evoked also in the titles of such publications on the passport as V. S. Gurkov and N. K. Dubovik, 'Posviashchenie v grazhdanstvo: stsenarii', *Novye grazhdanskie obriady i ritualy* (Minsk, 1978) etc.

28. An idea of the scale of participation is given by a timetable for such ceremonies in the different districts of Leningrad (a city whose population was then over 4 million) during March 1975. Forty-five ceremonies were held in 'palaces of culture' etc. across the city and its outskirts, as one-off occasions, not on a regular basis (Tsentral'nyi gosudarstvennyi arkhiv literatury i iskusstva, St Petersburg [TsGALI-SPb.], f. 105, op. 2, d. 1160, ll. 1–2). The ceremony was being promoted especially energetically at this point, because of the new passport issue of 1974–6 (see above). Figures in ordinary years were presumably lower.

29. E. Klimov, *Novye obriady i prazdniki* (Moscow, 1964), 100.

30. In the original the plural of citizens, *grazhdane*, is misspelled *grazhdaniny*.

31. A low-rent fortified wine, *portvein*, the equivalent of US Thunderbird or 'British sherry' as the preferred drink of impecunious topers.

32. A. Fedorov, 'Gerbastyi orlastyi', *Avtopilot* 4 (2002), 2.

33. Oxf/AHRC-Evp-08 PF-3 IN, p. 4: interview with woman b. 1934, village of T., southern Russia, conducted by I. Nazarova, Evpatoriia, 2008; transcript held in the Oxford Russian Life History Archive, www.ehrc.ox.ac.uk/lifehistory. Rural residents lucky enough to receive passports at earlier periods also treated this in a celebratory way: e.g. E. Filippovich, *Ot sovetskoi pionerii do chelnoka-pensionerki (moi dnevnik). Kniga 1 (1944–1972)* (Moscow, 2000), entry for 15 May 1952 (the writer and the rest of her class dressed up in their best to receive their passports).

34. After the Conference on the Implantation of New Civic Rituals (1964), the Council of Ministers of the USSR set up a 'Council on the Creation and Implantation of New Civic Rituals', including among its members writers, artists, composers, theatre directors and other theatre workers, and later academics, above all ethnographers and folklorists.

35. See, for example, the unpublished scenario from Leningrad (1975), TsGALI-SPb., f. 105, op. 2, d. 1160, ll. 3–4.

36. It was such people who were first to receive the new-style passport first given out in 1976.

37. 'The relay race of generations' was a standard metaphor for a stable process of cultural transmission in which older generations were supposed to pass the 'baton' of Soviet values to the next.

38. As in 'factory shift', another standard metaphor for those waiting their turn in the alternation of generations.

39. *Prazdniki, obriady, ritualy: tsikl semeino-bytovykh ritualov i obriadov* (Novgorod, 1984), 22.

40. *Novye grazhdanskie obriady i ritualy* (Minsk, 1978), 18.

41. *Prazdniki, obriady, ritualy*, 24.

42. See e.g. the extended version in *Novye grazhdanskie obriady*, 21.

43. This idea was constantly revisited in the endless brochures on Soviet rites, but in V. S. Gurkov, 'Obriad posviashcheniia v grazhdanstvo', *Prazdniki i obriady v Belorusskoi SSR* (Minsk, 1988), 266, it is set out directly: 'The passport is a symbol of Soviet nationality.'

44. Certainly, there were (as with other age thresholds, e.g. the age of criminal responsibility) different ages at which drinking was permitted at different phases of Soviet history. Until 1958 there was no prohibition on the sale of alcohol to children (see A. Sakharov, 'Alkogol' i prestupnost' nesovershenno-letnikh', *Sovetskaia iustitsiia* 16 (1965), 22–4). Once an age boundary had been fixed, it kept changing (from sixteen to eighteen, and later to twenty-one – which it remains at present). But attitudes to drinking are of course not just a matter of official prescription. There was also the issue of unofficial control by 'adults'; whatever the formal prohibitions, this control weakened or was abandoned altogether after young people received their passport.

45. Cf. Konstantin Bogdanov, 'The Rhetoric of Ritual: The Soviet Sociolect in Ethnolinguistic Perspective', *Forum for Anthropology and Culture* 5 (2009), 179–216.
46. In addition, Soviet passports issued just before the collapse continued to be in use for many years after the regime had disappeared.
47. The general principle of the corporative 'show' has survived as well: for an interesting case in point, see L. L. Adams, *The Spectacular State: Culture and National Identity in Uzbekistan* (Durham, NC, 2010).
48. As will be indicated by an online search for *torzhestvennoe vruchenie pasporta* in Cyrillic.
49. e.g. in the St Petersburg metro, September 2010.

PART III

Myths of national identity

CHAPTER 6

'If the war comes tomorrow': patriotic education in the Soviet and post-Soviet primary school

Vitaly Bezrogov

Patriotism is the love of one's Fatherland's riches and glory, and the desire to further these in every respect.

Nikolai Karamzin

The cherished pages of books
Help people live –
And work, and learn,
And treasure the Fatherland.

Sergei Mikhalkov

'EVERY RUSSIAN CITIZEN HAS ONLY ONE HOMELAND – RUSSIA'

Among the central methods of instilling a sense of identity and 'imagined community' in citizens is the content of the school curriculum.[1] Both during the Soviet period and afterwards, this included much attention to 'patriotic education', meant to shape a positive relationship towards the 'homeland' on the part of those being educated, to generate, in the words of a pedagogical textbook of 1941, 'love of the fatherland'.[2] The purpose of such education was seen as being to inculcate a love of 'the great state that protects us',[3] and to delimit a clear boundary between 'us' and 'them' (in extremis 'the enemy'). In a utopian society such as the Soviet Union, patriotic education also entails the cultivation of hope that utopia will be achieved.[4] Hence, in the Soviet Union patriotic education was not concerned with the realities of the 'homeland' but always constructed an image of what this 'homeland' *ought* to be – or, to be more exact, of what it would become.

In Soviet times the idea of a 'homeland' (in Russian *rodina* – derived from the verb *rodit'sia*, 'to be born', and therefore meaning 'native land') was inseparably linked to the image of 'the USSR' itself. A 'Soviet person' was meant to love his or her 'homeland – the Soviet Union'. The imaginary 'homeland' was constructed by a wide variety of different means:

113

manipulated statistics, spurious historiography, an artificial literary canon that did not reflect readers' tastes, the production of all manner of 'fakelore', the evolution of a language policy that presented Russian as the state's lingua franca, the confection of canonical visual imagery (for instance, the many allegorical representations of the Motherland in posters, statues etc.) and so on. The official construction of 'our Soviet Homeland' or 'our Socialist Homeland' entailed a poorly differentiated, yet hypnotic, image of *the USSR as a whole* – a homeland where, 'from one end to the other', 'the sun never sets'. The mass renaming of towns, streets and territories, which redrew this space historically as well as geographically, did not work to undermine patriotic education, since such renaming was considered tantamount to an ongoing perfecting of the homeland, bringing it nearer and nearer to the bright communist future. In the Soviet era the homeland was understood as a unified space, both historically and geographically. It was vital to love *the whole* of this 'homeland' *all at once*, since, in the conditions of a totalitarian culture, the ideal simply could not be divided or fragmented.[5]

The collapse of the Soviet 'Motherland' and the emergence of separate republics made patriotic education into potentially a much more complex problem. Not only did the overarching concept of a 'Soviet nationality' disappear (requiring the search for some other focus of collective identification), but all the constituent republics of the USSR were in fact multiethnic, though they each had an official 'titular nationality', making the crystallization of national identity round just one ethnic group a matter of considerable sensitivity. Yet the established, highly integrative conceptions of patriotic education (and its subcategories 'political education', 'civic education' and 'military education') that predominated in the USSR before 1991 continued to be reproduced in the 1990s and 2000s. What happened in Russia exemplifies this process in a striking way.

In the words of a definition from the 2000s, 'Patriotic education ... represents a systematic and purposeful endeavour of both state authorities and civic organizations to create among the country's citizens a high level of patriotic consciousness and a sense of loyalty to the fatherland, and to ensure the citizens' readiness to fulfil their civic duty and constitutional obligation to defend the interests of their homeland'.[6] Noteworthy here is the absolutely typical reference to state and public organizations as the only bodies that have a right to engage in patriotic education, and the equation of 'patriotic education' and military training (the term 'civic duty' here can be taken to refer explicitly to service in the armed forces). In this interpretation, 'love for the Motherland' means loyalty to the state and to its political leadership.

There are some elements in this paradigm that became more explicit in the post-Soviet period than they were in the Soviet period – for example, it was now emphasized that the aims of patriotic education were best fostered by 'active attempts to combat' the 'distortion and falsification of history'.[7] Comparable formulations could be found in academic publications as well, for example the claim that 'the feeling of patriotism ... embraces concern for the interests of our great country, pride in the heroic past of our country and in the scientific, technological and cultural contribution made by our people to world civilization ... a respectful attitude to the historic past and to the traditions of Russia'.[8]

The primordial attitudes that prevailed in the 1940s (as in claims that village children were 'closer to nature' than city ones, and that feeling for nature was a starting point for patriotic feeling) were alive and well in the early twenty-first century:

For human beings, an especial spiritual affinity with the native spaces where they spent their childhood, where their parents and ancestors worked, for that confined stretch of the globe with which the events in human fate are linked, is entirely natural. It is above all on this territory where humans feel most unconstrained, where everything is most understandable and dear.[9]

The broad, indeed global, ambitions and vague phrasing are typical. The highest professional-pedagogical echelons in charge of developing patriotic education in Russia in the 2000s viewed it as a way of optimizing social life itself. They interpreted it as '*the* basis ... for the preservation of the country's sociocultural space'.[10] The tenacity of the Soviet legacy makes it important to begin by analysing the characteristics of patriotic education before 1991.

AN APPROACH TO THE STUDY OF PATRIOTIC EDUCATION

In order to show how patriotic education constructed an 'official homeland' in Soviet times, and what patriotic education offered pupils after 1991, I propose to examine a series of ABCs, readers, Russian-language primers and elementary textbooks on 'the world at large', produced by both central and regional publishers in the USSR (particularly the RSFSR).[11] I shall focus on material for primary schools, since full secondary education (eleven to seventeen) was introduced only in 1970, and since the basic efforts to mould children's perceptions were especially assiduous at the primary stage of school education.

The elementary school textbook – to list only the characteristics of the genre that are most significant for its role in patriotic education – is the result of a compromise between accepted representations of the world, the perceived abilities of the child at a particular stage of development, and the national and political agenda of patriotic education itself. It is a way of modelling and creating a system of values for assessing the world's phenomena, and depends both on explicit and implicit images of the desired world.

The original source of patriotic education in Russian primary education was the text 'Our Fatherland', which appeared in the textbook *Children's World*, published in 1861 by the renowned Russian pedagogue K. D. Ushinskii. This text was used actively in Russian schools up to 1917, but fell into oblivion in the Soviet era. However, it was returned to primary-school textbooks in 1992.[12]

Between the 1920s and the present, patriotic education went through several transformations. First it evolved from a genuinely internationalist orientation in the 1920s to the idea of the USSR as a fatherland of the world's labouring masses created specifically by the Great Russian people. From the mid-1930s to the 1950s the patriotic education agenda shifted quite explicitly to the imperial conservatism characteristic of National Bolshevism.[13] In the 1960s–70s this was followed by an emphasis on the pseudo-internationalist 'struggle to save the world beyond the Iron Curtain'. During the 1980s–90s there was an increasing acceptance of more locally oriented patriotic education, which was allowed to thrive alongside the overarching state-wide project, which led to struggles between the patriotic education agendas of 'the centre' and 'the locality', which in turn resulted in the development of new and sometimes ambiguous regional patriotic identities. Finally, in the 2000s, after a period of vigorous regionalization at the political level (1991–2000), patriotic education once more revived the dream of an overarching Russocentric state; this went hand in hand with a considerably reduced role of internationalist and globalist orientations.

Soviet textbooks were instruments that did not educate the pupil for his or her own benefit, but for the benefit of the country itself. Even in purely formal terms, these textbooks were owned not by children, but by the educational system itself. The books thus acted as representatives of the state in the pupil's own home. They presented children with an official version of the world and of the child's place in it. This explains the emergence of an alternative movement in the 1970s and 1980s that was driven by a passion for history and local studies, whose representatives sought to rediscover 'the homeland' as if it were a kind of Atlantis – built over and renamed so many times that it had become unrecognizable.

The beginnings of the 1990s were characterized by a popular-romantic search for 'roots', a search that was understood as an embodiment of post-Soviet liberalization. Local systems of patriotic education were formed at the level of either a distinct region or of a distinct ethno-cultural subject. However, the term 'Homeland' itself moved to the forefront of the discourse of patriotic education. In what follows I shall examine more closely the different phases that the use of the concept of 'Homeland' went through in Soviet/Russian primary schooling from the 1920s on.

PHASES IN THE USE OF THE TERM 'HOMELAND'

The 1920s to the first half of the 1930s

In this early period the term 'homeland', used in primary-school textbooks, had a purely functional meaning – one's 'place of birth/origin':

> *Velika moia sem'ia*
> *Gde rebiata – tam i ia.*
> *Gde rebiata – tam i khata,*
> *Tam i rodina moia.*
> My family is really huge,
> Where other kids are – I am too,
> Home is for us one and all,
> My motherland is with them all.[14]

The 1930s to the beginning of the 1940s

Concepts such as 'our Soviet, native, remarkable, happy country' or 'our kolkhoz, forest, river' etc. outnumbered explicit references to the 'homeland' itself. The USSR was presented as the 'fatherland of the world's working class' (with reference to Stalin's speech of 1931).[15]

The 1940s to the 1960s

This was the crucial period when the canonical traits of a 'Soviet Homeland' as an ideological myth were constructed and then applied as the key instruments of Soviet patriotic education. These traits included: the Homeland's 'vast expanses', its natural riches, its unprecedented progressiveness (understood simultaneously as economic self-sufficiency and avant-garde political stance), and the role of Moscow as the idealized 'heart' of 'our beloved Homeland-Mother'. The 'Soviet Homeland' was presented as the joint achievement of the whole of the Soviet working class, requiring unremitting protection so that its wonders should not fade. The theme of the transformation of nature was also popular (social relations were treated as already fully transformed).

The end of the 1950s also saw the establishment of a canonical textbook layout of texts and images of the Homeland. These were placed mostly on the opening and closing pages of the textbook. But there were also cases where the discourse on 'the Homeland' was dotted throughout the whole textbook (it is worth noting that in imperial Russia, as in contemporary Germany, Austria and other European countries round the turn of the nineteenth and twentieth centuries, the first and last pages of primary-school textbooks usually featured prayers and texts of a religious kind):

> *Rabotai, uchis' i zhivi dlia naroda,*
> *Sovetskoi strany pioner!*
> Work, study, and live for the people,
> O Soviet Young Pioneer![16]

> *Za novye shkoly, za svetlye shkoly,*
> *Spasibo, liubimaia Rodina-mat'!*
> For new schools, for bright classrooms,
> Thank you, dear Motherland![17]

And so on and so on.

The 1970s to the 1980s

In the late Soviet era the educational establishment sought to tie the following elements together into a patriotic education system: (a) love of Lenin, (b) devotion to the Russian language (as the language in which Lenin spoke and constructed Communism), (c) loyalty to the party, (d) service to the state, (e) love of labour (as *the* embodiment of 'true patriotism'), (f) civic discipline (where a citizen is conceived of as a 'cog' in the state machine), (g) the unflinching conviction and heroic will to victory of the Soviet state, and finally (h) summing up all of the above – 'the enormous love of the Homeland'. Lenin, the party, 'the People' (instead of 'the working class'), the country, the army, the Homeland, the language. These were the key concepts on which late Soviet patriotic education was constructed in elementary school. The Homeland was invariably identified with the state.[18] A rationalized pride in the progressiveness of 'our system', of 'our' technological achievements and social relations, and so on, and the formation of an emotional attachment towards the Homeland were strengthened by nurturing in pupils a sense that the Homeland itself (as the state) looked after its citizens in a whole variety of complex ways. 'Care' (*zabota*) was one of the buzzwords of this era. Attachment to one's 'little homeland' (*malaia rodina*), i.e. the development of regional identifications, was underplayed: much more important was the interiorization of the entire 'Soviet Homeland' as a sign and a myth. The official aim of patriotic education in primary education of this period was the formation of 'literate and hard-working citizens of our great Homeland – the Union of the Soviet Socialist Republics', capable of 'living as upright citizens', giving their all in the workplace, and 'deeply loving and protecting' their Homeland.[19]

As the preface of an ABC advised its readers: 'You are learning to read and write, and for the first time, you are writing the dearest and most precious words for all of us: mama, Motherland, Lenin.' The order is significant – in previous decades, Lenin would definitely have been far more important than the other entities mentioned; now he trailed along in third place. 'From it [the alphabet book] you will learn how great and wonderful is our Motherland,' the book continued. The central point was then spelled out in capitals: 'OUR MOTHERLAND IS THE USSR.' Finally, towards the end of the book, came an extended eulogy:

Your Motherland and mine is the USSR. Wonderful native land! Fields, woods, seas and rivers! New factories are being built. Tractors plough the fields. Trains and aeroplanes rush everywhere. Boats sail the seas and rivers. High-high in the sky fly swift-winged Ils, Tus, Iaks, Ans [abbreviations of different Soviet aircraft types]. The USSR is a land of peace and labour.[20]

The 1990s to the 2000s

In the post-Soviet era, ideological emphasis shifted wholly onto the term 'Homeland' (*rodina*) itself, together with its synonyms, such as 'Fatherland' (*otechestvo* or, more poetically, *otchizna*). Previously, in the Soviet era, the Homeland had been directly associated with Lenin, the party, the International etc. The myth of Lenin, in particular, had performed certain functions of the myth of the Homeland (his hand always on the latter's pulse). According to post-Soviet patriotic education, however, what had to be loved above all else was the Homeland/Fatherland, both in the sense of the country as a whole and in the sense of one's own native part or corner of this country. Migrating beyond one's 'native land' was frowned upon and was considered tantamount to a betrayal of both the little and the greater Homeland.

At one level, the thesis 'one man – one homeland' stemmed from the ideology of the Iron Curtain and from the negative attitudes towards both emigration and immigration that obtained in the Soviet era.[21] Yet post-Soviet patriotic education went even further in this direction. If late Soviet primary-school textbooks permitted the use of the figurative expression 'my second homeland' (to refer to a land that one had fallen in love with), in post-Soviet patriotic education such an expression effectively became inadmissible and was nowhere to be found in primary textbooks. Even extracts from Soviet authors were 'airbrushed' to exclude the expression.[22]

The importance of the Homeland in post-Soviet primary education was underlined and confirmed by the placing of patriotic texts at the beginning or the end of the textbook or at the beginning and end of the entire Russian-language syllabus. At the same time there were also situations where the topic of the Homeland was the core theme in the study of Russian language and literature more generally. Hence, as well as appearing at the beginning and end of textbooks, references to the Homeland were also dotted throughout these. There was an obvious unity between the layout of post-Soviet books and the canonical layout of textbooks that had been established in the 1950s. Though pre-revolutionary textbooks exercised influence as well, there were greater affinities between post-Soviet books and textbooks published during the Stalin era, and especially under Stalin, at the structural and visual levels.

Post-Soviet textbooks, like their Soviet predecessors, emphasized the defence theme, drawing a direct line between emotional and practical commitment to *Rodina*: 'loving the Homeland' = 'living in the Homeland' = 'defending the Homeland'. A new environmental theme could also be found: 'protecting the environment' = 'protecting the Homeland'. Images of 'the Homeland' and of 'the Mother' were fused. The Homeland's 'immense size', communicated both textually and visually, was presented as unquestioningly positive – a quality that enabled the Homeland to overcome any difficulty, to endure anything, defeat anyone, solve any problem.[23] Thus, these Russian-language primers were practically unusable as textbooks for Russian-speakers living outside Russia itself, whether in the so-called 'near abroad' (former Soviet republics) or beyond. And the textbooks produced for Russian teaching among the ethnic minorities of the Russian Federation whose native language was not Russian included much more overtly ideologized blocks of text dealing with the 'little' and 'greater' Homelands (mostly in terms of their unity with the main Soviet state) than did those aimed at the mainstream Russian population.

In post-Soviet textbooks the love of the Fatherland was linked to a sacralized love for nature and the historical past. Love of the Homeland equalled love of olden times, the appreciation of the Homeland's ancient heritage. All forms of antiquity were emphasized: (a) linguistic 'archaisms', (b) the old ways of life, such as traditions, customs, folk epics, (c) architectural monuments, (d) the coats of arms of ancient towns, and so on and so forth. Pupils were taught how close the life of their ancestors was to them, how wise were the policies of their country's past rulers.[24] They were told that only in one's Homeland could everything be truly 'one's own', that creative life was possible only on one's native soil and in one's native tongue. The significance of 'Mother Moscow' for Russia as a whole – the country and its people – was ground into readers.[25] Children were taught that it was the duty of every Russian to defend the honour of the Russian Federation against anyone who offended it.[26]

The concept of the 'Homeland' in post-Soviet textbooks reflected the drive of the contemporary political elite to eulogize the Soviet past, but it was also rooted in the real need of Russian society to acquire a new type of identity, a new object to love and believe in. At the same time, quite what to love inspired a degree of confusion – as in the bewilderingly tautologous formula, 'My country is my native land.'[27]

Textbooks designed for non-Russian ethnic minorities tended to have more developed sections on the distinction between the 'little' and the 'greater homeland'. In ABCs and language books for ethnic minorities (both those in the minority language and those in Russian) definitions of the 'Homeland' were characterized by several contradictory features. There was great emphasis on the importance of the 'little homeland', which each person was meant to have, regardless of where he or she had ended up later on – this was one's place of birth, childhood, upbringing. Yet at the same time this 'little homeland' was inevitably linked not just to one's 'native republic', but also to Russia as the 'greater homeland', in the sense that every individual's patriotic duty was to defend the borders of the Russian Federation as a whole. There was emphasis on the history of unity – the fact that the brotherhood and friendship of a given people or region with Russia was eternal.[28] Past uprisings against the autocratic Russian Empire, for instance, were considered as frankly irrelevant to the present close relationship between the 'little homeland' (essentially the ethnic republic) and the Russian Federation.[29]

Texts about the Homeland in post-Soviet primers for Russian children produced by centrally based publishing houses rarely mentioned the fact that in 'their' Homeland lived other peoples who had the same right to this homeland as they did; more precisely, there was no mention of the fact that every citizen of this country, regardless of ethnicity, had the same rights. In textbooks for minorities, on the other hand, statements to this effect were much more common; however, here too the Russian people was allocated the number one spot in the hierarchy of peoples, while the minority in question was routinely allocated second rank, with all the other peoples in the Federation following behind (so in Tatar textbooks the hierarchy would be Russian–Tatar–the rest; in Chuvash textbooks, Russian–Chuvash–the rest, and so on). Such textbooks stressed that 'our homeland' was that 'great country' – Russia. The homeland identity of one's 'native republic' was left rather vague.[30]

'I'VE LOVED YOU SINCE CHILDHOOD, MY BELOVED COUNTRY'

The inability of such a closed state as the Soviet Union to rely exclusively on the idea of 'class' as a way of differentiating its population prompted the development in the Soviet education system not just of 'international socialist' but also of 'patriotic' education.[31] Throughout the history of the Soviet Union the interaction between these two approaches determined the peculiar blending of slogans championing the struggle for communism in the world at large and yet also the protection of the socialist fatherland.

Soviet patriotic education grew not out of the past, but out of an awaited future. The notion of 'homeland' in the structure of patriotic education fulfilled the task of fusing the individual and 'the country', of subjugating individuals to the state and of rooting them to their place of residence and work.[32] Creating the image of a future Homeland was meant to make the child love the present one. Detail was avoided; the child was airily assured that 'the Russian people always loved its homeland'.[33] The love of the Homeland that was demanded of pupils was supposed to be 'active' – the child was to be drawn into labour or military activities that were to be of help to 'our entire great homeland', which might mean schoolwork, but might equally well mean work on a kolkhoz field, or military service.[34] Love, thus embodied in action, allowed the notion of the 'Homeland' to become the means of dissolving individual consciousness in the collective, enabling the regime to absorb the individual through the identification of personal interests and aims with the interests of 'the country'. The homeland in the mental constructions that resulted became synonymous with the state (i.e. the government and the party), the country, the people, the authorities.[35]

In pre-revolutionary Russia the model hierarchy inculcated in children had looked something like this: God, father, mother, the Russian ethnos, tsar, one's homeland (the country in the geopolitical sense, in which the Russian ethnicity was 'the sovereign and the ruler'). The most important primary-school subject was Holy Scripture, followed by Russian geography (understood as 'fatherland/homeland studies').[36] In Soviet patriotic education 'the homeland' featured in an equivalent hierarchy, but it was placed below Lenin, the party leaders, Communism, the party itself, five-year plans and so on, although it was higher than either the school or the family. For many decades 'the school' ranked higher than 'the family', but still below 'the country' (*strana*) and 'the people' (*narod*).

In textbooks written after the collapse of the Soviet Union, texts about the Homeland suddenly acquired much greater significance than in Soviet times. Since everything that had once been ranked above the 'Homeland' in Soviet patriotic education had been unceremoniously dumped, the 'Homeland' itself could move up the ranks and take up the position previously occupied by Lenin and the party. Texts about the Homeland in school primers now became analogues of the Lord's Prayer and the national anthem, used for indoctrination in the Orthodox theocracy of the Russian Empire and the totalitarian USSR respectively.

The results of post-Soviet patriotic education of this kind made themselves felt, for instance, in an essay by a fourteen-year-old schoolboy from Orlov, written in 2004–5 as an entry in a regional competition: 'A Russian must understand that there is no better place for him than his Homeland.'[37] These words could stand as a summary epitaph to this chapter. A Russian of the 2010s who had been through the correct patriotic education would now be anxiously scrutinizing his or her future, understanding it as inseparable from the future of his or her Homeland, shaken by the post-2008 world crisis. The long-term success of post-Soviet patriotic education seemed likely to depend on the extent to which the state as a 'politically organized Homeland'[38] was able to continue representing itself as an object of compulsory love and pride, requiring protection from each and every one of its citizens, in circumstances where national boosterism seemed more vulnerable than it had before 2008.

Translated by Andy Byford

NOTES

1. Classic studies of such material include B. Anderson, *Imagined Communities* (London, 1991), and E. Weber, *Peasants into Frenchmen: The Modernization of Rural France* (Stanford, CA, 1976).

2. B. P. Esipov, 'Vospitanie sovetskogo patriotizma i proletarskogo internationalizma', in *Spravochnaia kniga uchitelia nachal'noi shkoly*, ed. M. A. Mel'nikov (Moscow, 1941), 195.

3. N. A. Churakova, *Literaturnoe chtenie: uchebnik. 4 klass*, 2 vols., 2nd edn (Moscow, 2008), vol. II, 169.

4. Cf. Stalin's speech at the First All-Soviet Congress of Workers in Socialist Industries: 'In the past we had no fatherland and could not have had a fatherland. But now that we have overthrown capitalism and the workers are in power, we do have a fatherland and we can defend its independence … We must step forward in such a way that the working class of the entire world can look at us and say, yes, there is our advance battalion, there is our brigade of shock-workers, there it is, my fatherland' (Esipov, 'Vospitanie sovetskogo patriotizma', 195–6).

5. Cf. A. Confino: 'The Heimat idea functioned … as a *unifying national memory, a never-never land* that was impervious to political and social conflicts … a *simultaneous representation* of the locality, the region, and the nation' (*The Nation as a Local Metaphor: Württemberg, Imperial Germany, and National Memory, 1871–1918*, Chapel Hill, NC, 1997, 100–1; emphasis added). Mass renaming was a persistent feature of Soviet rule, extending to cities (Perm to Molotov etc.) as well as streets and institutions.

6. *Moskvichi o patrioticheskom vospitanii i effektivnosti provodimykh meropriiatii: po materialam issledovaniia N. P. Pishchulina i S. N. Pishchulina* (Moscow, 2004), 4.

7. Ibid., 5. For comment on the official campaign against the 'falsification of history', see e.g. N. Koposov, 'Istoricheskaia politika pytaetsia prikryt'sia Niurnbergom', www.cogita.ru/syuzhety/kultura-pamyati/nikolai-koposov-o-tom-kak-istoricheskaya-politika-pytaetsya-prikrytsya-nyurnbergom.

8. A. Degtyareva, 'Narodnaia pedagogika i patriotizm', *Mir obrazovaniia – obrazovanie v mire: nauchno-metodicheskii zhurnal* I (2003), 176–7.

9. V. F. Shapovalov, 'Rossiiskii patriotism i rossiiskii antipatriotizm', *Obshchestvennye nauki i sovremennost'* I (2008), 125. Notable is the neo-Ushinskian note in all this (see below). For the 1940s material, see e.g. V. A. Gruzinskaia, 'O vospitanii sovetskogo patriotizma na urokakh geografii', in *Nachal'naia shkola: sbornik statei. Posobie dlia uchitelei*, vol. II, ed. M. P. Malyshev, comp. B. P. Esipov (Moscow, 1949), 134.

10. Quoted from a statement by the pro-rector of the Volgograd Institute for Further Pedagogical Education (Volgogradskii institut povysheniia kvalifikatsii rabotnikov obrazovaniia): see N. A. Grigor'eva, 'Gosudarstvennaia politika i praktika razvitiia sistemy patrioticheskogo vospitaniia v sovremennoi Rossii', in *Idei otechestvennoi pedagogiki: istoriia i sovremennost': materialy nauchno-prakticheskoi konferentsii (24–25 April 2008)*, ed. L. I. Gritsenko (Volgograd, 2008), 124.

11. Some 318 textbooks published between 1922 and 2008 make up the corpus of material on which my remarks are based.

12. In the Soviet period, this text was usually quoted in abridged versions, with selected phrases used as the focus of the citation. I will cite the full original version here to show the starting point:

Our fatherland, our motherland is Mother Russia. We call Russia our father-land, because our fathers and grandfathers lived there from the dawn of time. We call her the Motherland because we were born there, we speak our native tongue (*rodnoi iazyk*) and everything there is dear (*rodnoe*) to us, and she is our mother because she has fed us with her bread, given us her water to drink, taught us her language, like a mother, she defends us and protects us from all our enemies, and when we fall asleep for ever, she will also cover our bones.

Our motherland is great – our mother the sacred land of Russia! She stretches west to east 11,000 versts wide, from the north to the south 6,000 versts long. Not just over one part of the earth does Russia spread herself, but over two, Europe and Asia.

The largest part of Russia in terms of area is in Asia: this part is called Siberia. In Siberia, the population is also not large: savage non-Russians wander there, but there are some fairly good Russian cities and rich villages there now. Siberia is a rich region. In her mountains and rivers are many metals, including precious metals, and in her dark forests are many animals with valuable fur.

The most populous and educated part of Russia lies in Europe. There are two capitals in European Russia: St Petersburg and Moscow, and in the Kingdom of Poland is [another capital], Warsaw; there are many provincial capitals and district capitals, and the villages are beyond number.

Russia has more than 80 provinces, many different tribes and peoples, and the land feeds more than 75 million people. All these provinces, all these millions of people are the subjects of a single sovereign – the Orthodox Russian Tsar. Alongside Russia, there are also many other admirable states and lands in the world, but man has only one mother, and in the same way, he has only one motherland.

K. D. Ushinskii, *Detskii mir i khrestomatiia: uchebnik i sbornik klassicheskoi literatury dlia shkol'nogo i domashnego chteniia*, vol. 1 (Moscow, 2003), 225–6

13. For a discussion of this period, see D. Brandenberger, *National Bolshevism: Stalinist Mass Culture and the Formation of Modern Russian National Identity, 1931–1956* (Cambridge, MA, 2002).

14. A. M. Peshkovskii, M. N. Andreevskaia and A. P. Gubskaia, *Pervye uroki russkogo iazyka: grammatika, pravopisanie, razvitie rechi, stil'. Vtoroi god obuche-niia: kniga dlia uchenika*, 4th edn (Moscow, 1931), 32.

15. See e.g. N. M. Golovin, *Bukvar'* (Moscow, 1937); A. A. Kutovoi, *Bukvar': uchebnik russkogo iazyka dlia 2 klassa khakasskikh natsional'nykh shkol* (Abakan, 1942). In 1936–40 the concept 'Motherland' in the sense 'our entire country' was pervasive in other genres of Soviet culture, for example posters ('Our happy Soviet children have a lovely motherland', Galina Shubina, 1936). In summer 1938, one of the two most important bomber planes in the country, the ANT-37, which had been adapted to facilitate flights right across the USSR as a form of magical legitimation of the borders, had the symbolic name of 'Motherland' (see the memoirs of I. I. Shelest, *Lechu za mechtoi* (Moscow, 1973), http://militera.lib.ru/memo/russian/shelest_ii3/04.html).

16. Sergei Mikhalkov, in M. L. Zakozhurnikova and N. S. Rozhdestvenskii, *Russkii iazyk: uchebnik dlia 4 klassa nachal'noi shkoly*, ed. M. A. Mel'nikov, 4th edn (Moscow, 1958), 3.
17. Zakozhurnikova and Rozhdestvenskii, *Russkii iazyk*, 7.
18. 'State' and 'Motherland' were dissociated only with reference to the pre-Soviet past: cf. the following passage from T. A. Ladyzhenskaia, M. T. Baranov, L. T. Grigorian, I. I. Kulibaba and L. A. Trostentsova, *Russkii iazyk: uchebnik dlia 4 klassa srednei shkoly* (Moscow, 1987), 200: 'When the Ul'ianov children [Lenin and his siblings] grew up, they would all walk the path of revolutionaries. Love for the Motherland, honesty, hard work, high ideals, deep knowledge and an extraordinary capacity for friendship would be the distinguishing characteristics of all the members of the Ul'ianov family' (quoting Z. I. Voskresenskaia).
19. M. D. Pushkarev et al., eds., *Rodnaia literatura: uchebnik-khrestomatiia dlia 4 klassa*, 15th edn (Moscow, 1986).
20. V. G. Goretskii, V. A. Kiriushin and A. F. Shan'ko, *Bukvar'*, 4th edn (Moscow, 1984), unnumbered preface, 3, 77.
21. V. Zhdanova, 'Russkaia kul'turno-iazykovaia model' prostranstva i osobennosti individual'noi orientatsii v nei', in *Russkie i russkost': lingvo-kul'turologicheskie etiudy*, ed. V. V. Krasykh (Moscow, 2006), 56, argues that negative mobility of the population was generally regarded as a positive feature back in the Soviet period. But one has to be careful about this, given the state's reliance on forced mobility of the labour force, accompanied by the promotion of voluntary migration programmes for its own purposes, such as increasing the Russian population of different Soviet republics.
22. For instance, the phrase 'second homeland' started to be systematically removed from the literary excerpts set for study in class. In 1986 the writer Konstantin Paustovskii was still allowed to refer to Meshcherskii district as his 'second homeland', but in 1993 these words disappeared from textbooks.
23. The idea of the enormous size (literally, 'unembraceable character', *neob"iatnost'*) of 'our Motherland' as a positive characteristic and subject of pride appears to go back to the 1930s and 1940s, and the idea that socialist 'rule by the people' originated and exists in the world's largest country. This idea acted as a socio-psychological substitute for the 'theory of world revolution' and for the representation of the workers' international as the ideal form of social organization in the future. It allowed the USSR to continue being presented as the fatherland of all labouring peoples the world over and all the progressive forces on the planet.
24. Among other bits of boosterism, note, for example, 'The Soviet Constitution is just and wise' (Ladyzhenskaia et al., *Russkii iazyk*, 36).
25. L. I. Tikunova and T. V. Ignat'eva, *Propilei-stupen'ki: chistopisanie. 4 klass: rabochaia tetrad'*, vol. 1 (Moscow, 2007), 23).
26. See e.g. E. Iu. Davydova and I. A. Kuz'min, *Azbuka istokov: zolotoe serdechko. Uchebnoe posobie dlia 1 klassa obshcheobrazovatel'nykh uchebnykh zavedenii*, 4th edn (Moscow, 2007), 36–7. The concept of defence of the Motherland against 'enemies', set against a background of state symbolism and military themes, was

also elaborated in the well-known Soviet view of the USSR as a country plagued by enemies because 'our country' was bringing peace and socialism to the working people of the entire planet. But in the post-Soviet period, the hostility of Russia's enemies is not so easy for patriots to explain as it was back in Soviet days. The tendency therefore is to trace it to biological ('genetic') rather than ideological or political factors. See e.g. O. N. Fedotova, G. V. Trofimova and S. A. Trofimov, *Nash mir: uchebnik. 2 klass*, vol. ii (Moscow, 2003), 117.

27. V. G. Goretskii, V. A. Kiriushkin and A. F. Shan'ko, *Bukvar': uchebnik dlia 1 klassa trekhletnei nachal'noi shkoly*, 15th edn (Moscow, 1996), 78.

28. Compare Elza-Bair Guchinova's remarks on Kalmykia in her chapter of this book.

29. The formula 'My Motherland (or 'motherland') is Tuva, Bashkortostan, Tatarstan etc.' is found in post-Soviet locally published textbooks, but strangely enough (given the widespread emergence of regionalism in other respects), far less often than the formula 'My Motherland is Russia'.

30. It is interesting – though in some respects predictable – that the school Russian-language textbooks being produced in other former republics of the Soviet Union during the 1990s after independence set out a completely different concept of Russia, which acknowledged the ambiguity of the country and saw it as possible (essential) to defend both Russia and one's 'native land' (see e.g. D. Pashkauskaite, *Russkii iazyk: tretii god obucheniia*, Kaunas, 1995, 132–53).

31. Introductory quotation from L. V. Fedorova, ed., *Iamal'skii kaleidoskop: uchebnoe posobie po literature i literaturnomu kraevedeniiu. 2 klass* (Tiumen', 2003), 145.

32. The idea of tying people to one particular 'place of residence' has proved remarkably tenacious in the current conceptual baggage of post-Soviet officials and politicians. See e.g. a speech made by the minister of education and science of the Russian Federation, A. A. Fursenko, on 24 March 2006 at a sitting of the State Council, 'On the Development of Education in the Russian Federation': 'At all levels of professional education, the most important issue is the fit between the orientation and quality of training and the requirements of regional development, the provision to enable the citizens of all Russia's regions to receive a high quality of education in their place of residence and appropriate employment in the place where they have received their education.'

33. Gruzinskaia, 'O vospitanii sovetskogo patriotizma', 141.

34. The contention that patriotic education is 'the science of hatred' for 'enemies of the Motherland', 'those who grind us down', 'enslave us' etc., runs through all the textbooks of the Soviet period and can still be found in textbooks today (especially in regional ones, but not only in them). See, for example, S. Redozubov, *Bukvar' dlia negramotnykh* (Moscow, 1945), 74ff., and N. Kostin, *Bukvar'*, 2nd edn (Leningrad, 1947), 127ff., and cf. V. Voronkova et al., *Chtenie: 4 klass* (Moscow, 2005), 88 ('Our Motherland has many friends in different countries. But she also has bad and nasty enemies. They hate our peaceful, hard-working country. But the Russian Army keeps our Motherland safe from harm'), or G. Grekhneva and

K. Korepova, *Literaturnoe chtenie: 2 klass*, part 1, 7th edn (Moscow, 2007), 130 ('The Motherland is [our, your] mother, learn how to stand up for her), etc.

35. Such a concept of 'motherland/homeland' is – at least to a limited extent – internationalist, since it assumes the shared interests of all the ethnic groups in the country with their 'great and inseparable', and 'their own' (for each) but shared motherland. On the assimilation of the words 'state' and 'country', 'people', 'powers that be/government', see E. I. Kuz'min, *Bibliotechnaia Rossiia na rubezhe tysiacheletii: gosudarstvennaia politika i upravlenie bibliotechnym delom. Smena paradigmy* (Moscow, 1999), 52–3.

36. P. I. Kovalevskii, *Natsional'noe vospitanie i obrazovanie v Rossii* (St Petersburg, 1910), 62 etc.; I. Z. Skovorodkina, *Etnopedagogicheskii podkhod k obrazovaniiu narodov Rossii: istoriia, teoriia, praktika* (Moscow, 2008), 58–68.

37. V. G. Eremin, ed., *Mir, v kotorom ia zhivu: sbornik detskikh tvorcheskikh rabot* (Orel, 2008), 245. It is remarkable that the author of these words, and indeed his teachers and the jury of the regional competition into which the essay from which they are taken was submitted, totally failed to grasp just how grotesque this account of Soviet history was, with its effort to exculpate 'in one fell swoop' the treatment of Soviet villagers, trapped by the denial to them of identity cards in starving villages, the post-war concentration camps, the suffering of those forced to live on contaminated land and so on. This ameliorative formula lays bare what would appear to be the main underlying drive of current state-sponsored patriotic education. The theme of the unity and uniqueness of the Motherland is shared by both Soviet and post-Soviet textbooks – indeed, it is often heard more strongly in the latter. It is notable that in other countries with a strongly nationalist past, such as Germany, the topic of 'native land' is treated with a great deal more neutrality. For instance, a textbook intended for the fifth and sixth classes of non-specialist, non-selective schools can begin with the sentence, 'No-one wants to leave his Motherland', and a page or so later deal with four émigré children who have arrived in Germany from Bosnia, Kazakhstan, Nigeria and Turkey (P. Gaffga et al., *Weltkunde: Klasse 5/6 für Schleswig-Holstein*, Brunswick, 2008, 104–17; cf. C. Forster et al., *Trio 1: Gesellschaftslehre*, Brunswick, 2008, 144). It is interesting to note that, by contrast, the topic of emigration was treated in a much more balanced and unemotional way in Russian textbooks of the 1910s, as was migration into Russia. See e.g. K. M. Kurdov, *Otechestvovedenie: Rossiia sravnitel'no s glavneishimi gosudarstvami mira. Kurs srednikh uchebnykh zavedenii* (Moscow, 1912), 57–8.

38. I. Demidov, 'Edinaia Rossiia' – 'Molodaia Gvardiia' – 'Russkii proekt', www.kreml.org/topics/144887069; I. Demidov, quoted in 'Tezisy o politicheskom patriotizme', 10 November 2007, www.kreml.org/opinions/165202735.

CHAPTER 7

Conquering space: the cult of Yuri Gagarin

Andrew Jenks

Forty years after the tragic death of the first man in space, an American filmmaker released *Fallen Idol: The Yuri Gagarin Conspiracy*. This 2008 documentary rehashed the old canard that Gagarin's flight into space on 12 April 1961 was a sham, an elaborate cover-up of a failed launch just four days prior to the 'alleged' flight. It pursued the logic of all conspiracy theories: the evidence is the absence of evidence, which was supposedly destroyed by the conspirators. Gagarin, according to the documentary, was tortured by the secret of his falsely earned fame and descended into a downward spiral of alcoholism and depression before dying (mysteriously, of course) on a routine flight on 27 March 1968, just three weeks after his thirty-fourth birthday.

Fatuous though the film may be, its very existence points to the dynamism of the Gagarin cult, its ability to generate interest (and money) nearly twenty years after the collapse of the Soviet Union. Indeed, as the fiftieth anniversary of Gagarin's flight approached, the celebrations of Gagarin's life and myth intensified. In October 2009 a company called Kremlin Films registered with the Russian patent office to receive rights for the trademark 'Yuri Gagarin'.[1] In the meantime, cosmonauts and friends and relatives of Gagarin coordinated ever-bigger commemorations of Gagarin's birthday (9 March) and of the day of his flight (12 April). On 12 April 2009 nearly 200,000 people gathered on the field near Saratov (now known as 'the Gagarin Fields') where Cosmonaut Number One landed in the *Vostok*. Fighter jets flew overhead, teenagers drank beer and raced dirt bikes, and a VIP list of cosmonauts and politicians gave speeches on heroism and martyrdom. Aleksei Leonov, a cosmonaut and Gagarin's friend, noted in March 2009: 'While we are still alive we need to stimulate interest [in Gagarin].'[2] Gagarin is dead. Long live Gagarin!

A number of factors transformed the world's first space traveller into that rarest of cultural artefacts: a Soviet icon that survived the collapse of the Soviet Union. State support was certainly one factor. Soviet leaders wanted

children to be like Gagarin – selfless to the point of martyrdom in defence of
the Soviet state, willing to obey any order, cheerfully patriotic. He was
merely the latest in a long line of state-generated heroes who propagated the
official values of the regime. But state support alone was not enough to
create the Gagarin phenomenon. His celebrity endured precisely because it
was one of those rare instances when enthusiastic support from society
complemented the sanction and backing of the Soviet state.

ANTICIPATION AND ECSTASY

In the nearly four years from *Sputnik* in 1957 to Gagarin's flight in 1961,
Soviet citizens experienced a powerful 'premonition of space', to borrow an
apt phrase from the title of a 2005 movie. With an intensity bordering on
religious fervour, they anticipated the day when someone would travel to
the stars. So great was the atmosphere of anticipation that Soviet society was
swept with rumours of a manned space flight in the weeks leading up to the
historic launch. Little wonder, then, that fulfilment of the foreseen, though
supposedly secret, event provided a kind of euphoric climax (Figure 7.1). To
enhance the public mood, on the day of Gagarin's flight Soviet radio
broadcast 'The Poem of Ecstasy', a symphonic poem by the pre-
revolutionary Russian composer Alexander Scriabin, whose work, in an
earlier Soviet era, had been condemned as bourgeois, decadent, mystical and
escapist. 'The Poem of Ecstasy' also wafted out across Red Square for
Gagarin's triumphal Moscow return on 14 April.[3]

The combination of Gagarin and Scriabin projected Khrushchev-era
fantasies of escape from an imperfect and corrupted world. Many Soviets
believed that the launching of a man into space presaged the dawning of a
new age – as if rockets could somehow liberate people from the cramped
apartments, tedium, petty arguments, boring jobs, gritty poverty and
injustices of daily life. A schoolteacher from a village in Tatarstan, echoing
the sentiments of many of her compatriots, said the flight meant a better life
was on the way: 'A 6–7 hour working day, 2 days off a week, a happy life,
and a pension when you get old'. Others anticipated a more abstract pay-
off. The actor and singer Vladimir Vysotskii, a tragic figure/celebrity just
like Gagarin, remarked on the common belief that 'physics was going to
unveil the ultimate secrets to humanity – and then right away cosmonauts
would fly to the planets and stars, and the entire universe with its treasures
and other civilizations would reveal its mysterious depths'.[4]

These dreams were so intense precisely because they drew on earlier
currents in Russian and Soviet culture. Technological utopianism was a

Пламенный привет первому
советскому герою-космонавту
Юрию Алексеевичу ГАГАРИНУ

Figure 7.1 One of the many thousands of leaflets dropped from aeroplanes over Soviet
cities after Gagarin's flight.

central feature of Bolshevik ideology. In a 1924 animated film, *Interplanetary Revolution*, the Bolsheviks vanquished the bourgeoisie of Mars and brought justice and peace to oppressed humanoids in the solar system's hinterland. The film hit Soviet theatres five years before the Soviets were creating the foundations of communist agriculture, herding millions of peasants into collective farms (and starving millions in the process).[5] Such early works drew on an established Russian tradition of fascination with space (as expressed in the science fiction of Konstantin Tsiolkovskii and Aleksandr Bogdanov) and laid the foundations for a vibrant Soviet culture of science fiction.[6]

The mentality of the technological fix was especially appealing to those concerned about the viability of a socialist revolution in a backward, agrarian society – which is to say, just about everyone. As Lenin put it in 1920, 'Communism is Soviet power plus electrification of the entire country.' Stalin also viewed technology (along with terror) as a universal remedy: the Moscow metro, hulking steel factories and massive hydroelectric dams were preludes to a promised time of communist plenty.

Space conquest, however, was more than just the latest in a long list of technological fixes. Gagarin was a sign that communism was imminent. 'I believe in our bright future which is now just around the corner,' wrote one young woman in response to Gagarin's feat. A village schoolteacher was confident that 'the bright future of communism will arrive precisely tomorrow'. Those were typical sentiments – especially among letter writers from the peasantry and working class.[7]

Russocentric propaganda in the late Stalinist era had also piqued the atmosphere of anticipation. A reader of textbooks from that era would be convinced that ethnic Russians had made practically every meaningful discovery in human history. Their dams, factories and planes were the biggest; their leaps of development the fastest; their scientists the wisest (Mendeleev, Pavlov et al.). And who else but the Great Russians – whom Stalin toasted in victory rather than the Soviets – could have defeated the Nazis? In the words of one cosmonaut in training, nearly everyone 'wanted, anticipated and demanded that we be first in space'.[8] How wonderful it was, then, when Russians discovered that Gagarin was not just a Soviet citizen – but an undeniably Russian fellow, a real *muzhik* who knew what it was like to have dirt under his nails.

Eliding the boundaries between fact and fiction, science and fancy, Soviets filled Gagarin's flight with terrestrial as well as cosmic meanings. Many connected Gagarin's conquest of outer space with the placement of new virgin lands under the plough in Kazakhstan. Responding to a call on 13 April 1961 from *Komsomol'skaia pravda*, thousands of Soviets headed off to create collective farms named 'Gagarin'. 'The Virgin lands of Mars are ours!' proclaimed one student. 'Now we have no borders!' said another.[9] Gagarin's feat was so extraordinary that mere prose could not suffice: instead of letters to the editor, more than 300 Soviets composed poems to the editor. Said one letter writer, prefacing his poem with mundane prose: 'If you did a calculation, 12 April 1961 would be a record day for the production of poetry in the history of humankind.'[10] The thoughts expressed in these and many other unpublished and published writings from ordinary Soviet citizens contained the building blocks of Soviet Russian space culture: subjugation of space (on Earth as in the cosmos), dreams of imperial occupation, messianic tendencies.

It is striking how Gagarin – who was, after all, just a passenger – came to be the personal embodiment of the triumph of the Soviet space programme and of the hopes and dreams of Russian culture. The peculiar demands imposed by the Soviet military-industrial complex provide one explanation. Owing to the strict regime of secrecy and national security – the Soviet space programme, unlike NASA, was managed by the military – journalists were allowed to publish virtually nothing about the engineers whose technology had launched Gagarin into space. Sergei Korolev, the father of Soviet rocketry, was referred to publicly as 'the chief builder'.[11] Soviet journalists solved the problem by focusing on the biographies of the cosmonauts. The upshot was an intense personality cult focused on Gagarin.

By 13 April, Gagarin's visage was everywhere, from the ubiquitous posters featuring his dreamy gaze to the thousands of portraits dropped from planes onto the streets of Moscow and other major Soviet cities. Citizens struck a reverential pose – with their heads cocked back and eyes fixed on a cosmos filled with Soviet power. 'Verticality and great height have ever been the spatial expression of potentially violent power,' remarked the sociologist Henri Lefebvre.[12] For some, Gagarin replaced the banned image of Stalin; for others he filled in for the holy icons of the Russian Orthodox tradition – a Soviet miracle worker.[13]

Whatever their preference, many Soviets removed themselves from the rut of everyday life as they contemplated Gagarin's feat, going from a state of merely existing (in Russian, *byt*) to experiencing life on a higher plane (*bytie*). The two concepts, linked linguistically by the same root for being or existence, framed the mass reception of Gagarin's flight.[14] One Soviet sociological survey in the spring of 1963 discovered a similar distinction. Respondents defined 'socialist existence (*bytie*)' as 'an extremely heroic existence, the capacity to achieve heroic deeds day after day'. They connected communist utopia with a world in which heroism became commonplace and the boring attributes of everyday life had disappeared.[15]

Gagarin's biography followed precisely this trajectory from mundane to exalted existence. Born on an impoverished collective farm in Smolensk province, Gagarin spent the tender years of youth under Nazi occupation and then in ramshackle, unheated schools where he prepared for a career as a steelworker. Only a series of seemingly random encounters diverted him to a vastly more interesting occupation. Gagarin's story connected the most ordinary life imaginable in Soviet society – born and raised on a collective farm – to the ultimate achievement of his time.[16] Gagarin, in the words of Korolev, 'gave people confidence in their own capabilities, in their own potential, he gave them a reason to be braver and bolder'.[17]

Gagarin was *nash*, 'one of us' – not only a 'simple Soviet citizen', according to letters sent to the Academy of Sciences, but also 'our Russian man', 'our Soviet Russian man'.[18] Said a blue-collar pensioner in an unpublished letter to the newspaper *Izvestiia*, using the informal *ty* in Russian when referring to Gagarin: 'I am proud of you, a simple Soviet guy.' A man from Taganrog, in an unpublished letter, declared, 'Let all Russian Yuris, Ivans, Mikhails, Nikolais, Andreis and the rest of the good names live eternally and grow in strength, glorifying the banner of our proletarian background.'[19] Gagarin's story, in this instance, created a chain of connections that led from Gagarin to the individual and then back again to the state. Those connections allowed people to acquire, in the words of one scholar, 'a sense of self as a subject and responsible agent in the world, and a recognition of the interconnection of one's own narrative with that of others'.[20]

A feeling of familiarity and closeness was a typical response to modern celebrities, who 'combine knowability with distance'.[21] By appearing to be a normal Russian guy, and yet a cosmic superhero, Gagarin promoted the self-esteem of his society – something especially critical given the profound sense of insecurity Russians had long experienced relative to the outside world (and their own government).

GAGARIN AND THE MEDIA

Any attempt to explain the intensity of responses to Gagarin's flight, as well as its cultural and political effects, must consider the technologies that produced his story for public consumption. Radio had transformed the flight into a mass media event, allowing nearly everyone to experience Gagarin's birth as a public figure on the morning of 12 April 1961. Gagarin's triumphal return to Moscow on 14 April was broadcast by television and radio to millions of Soviet citizens.

These dramatic broadcasts heightened the sense of participating in a historic event and of belonging to the community that had witnessed it.[22] Audio and visual imagery, however, would not have been so effective had it not been for Gagarin's charisma, which was ideally suited for radio and television. Of course, there were plenty of writers in Gagarin's case, but they played an increasingly secondary role to the moving images of Gagarin that were simultaneously entering Soviet homes on millions of televisions just as Gagarin completed his flight. Those millions of televisions, alongside the millions of radio receivers, projected Gagarin's charm directly into Soviet Russian life in a way that printed words on a page could never have done.[23]

Radio waves literally filled Soviet air space, indoors and out, public and private. Whether it was news about enemies of the people or the feats of Soviet aviators circumnavigating the North Pole, the Soviet authorities used the radio network to grab people's attention – radio sets physically could not be turned off. The unifying potential of radio was greatly enhanced during the Second World War, when Soviets huddled around the radio receiver. They hung on every word in anticipation of triumphal or tragic news – usually getting both simultaneously.[24]

Adding to the drama for the listening public, Soviet radio conveyed news of Gagarin's flight in near real-time – announcing his flight before the craft had actually landed. As the flight neared completion, and as Gagarin's commanders were sure he had not perished on re-entry, they launched news of the nearly completed flight into the broader Soviet radio broadcast system.

The near real-time radio broadcast (viewers believed it was live) made the event emotionally riveting – and forever memorable.[25] And so, too, did the voice that broadcast the news. The famous radio announcer Yuri Levitan had chronicled the Great Patriotic War for Soviet audiences. When he solemnly conveyed news of the flight in his signature cadence and voice, listeners immediately connected Gagarin's triumph with the whole gamut of complex emotions evoked by his broadcasts during the war.[26] The connection between Levitan's voice and war was so strong that many listeners on 12 April 1961 assumed Levitan was preparing to announce the invasion of the Soviet Union by NATO forces. When he heralded Gagarin's flight instead, listeners went from agony to the anticipated feeling of ecstasy in a heartbeat. The voice of Levitan had transported them, as during the war, from tragedy to triumph.[27] Levitan himself remembered that tears welled up in his eyes as he announced Gagarin's flight: 'It was just like 9 May [1945], when I read the act of surrender by Hitler's Germany.'[28]

If radio presided over the birth of the Gagarin cult, television was its midwife. There were 5 million television sets in the Soviet Union at the time of Gagarin's flight, compared with just 15,000 ten years earlier. The force of Gagarin's personality on the small screen provided a sense of immediacy, intimacy and community, 'at just the moment when mass modernity made everything in city life seem so anonymous and fragmentary'.[29]

The triumphal reception on 14 April was the Soviet public's first opportunity to get a televised peek at their idol in all his seeming sincerity, heroic

splendour and humility. The cameraman to the cosmonauts had a grand-
stand view of the celebrations. He set up his cameras along the route from
the airport to Red Square, beginning with Gagarin's landing on a Soviet
Ilyushin 18 jetliner, accompanied by fighter jets – an honour previously
reserved only for heads of major foreign states. The cameraman described
the scene through the lens of his camera:

Gagarin appears at the doorway of the plane, rapidly comes down the stairs and
starts to march along the carpet strip towards the stand to the accompaniment of a
military band. Through the eyepiece of the camera I see that one of his boot-laces
has got loose. He casts a quick glance on it and keeps on marching. He stops in
front of Khrushchev, salutes him and reports briskly that the government assign-
ment has been successfully fulfilled.

The journalists assembled to watch him remembered a feeling of terror:
would he trip over his shoelace in front of the whole world?[30] Gagarin,
tellingly, came to the film-editing room to review the footage from the
festivities after the day's celebrations. There was a brief debate about cutting
out the scene with Gagarin's untied shoelace. Gagarin insisted the footage
should remain: it created the image of sincerity and truthfulness that he
preferred to project to his adoring public.[31]

    Vladimir Sappak, an early pioneer in Soviet television, saw Gagarin,
along with other newly minted idols in Soviet society, as products of the
television age in its infancy. What distinguished these new Soviet heroes
from previous generations of heroes was a particular talent for appearing
sincere and honest, thereby putting people at ease. And that was also in the
spirit of the Khrushchev thaw, which set the tone for public displays of
sincerity with his 'secret' speech condemning Stalin. Television, of course,
was heavily mediated and censored, just like the Soviet press. Still, for many
Soviets in the early 1960s, television created the illusion of immediacy and
authenticity that newspaper articles, or newsreel clips, could never replicate.
It had not yet dawned on most Soviet viewers that Gagarin's posture of
sincerity could be just that – a practised and studied pose.[32]

    For surviving Soviet eyewitnesses the day of the flight and the celebra-
tions in the days that followed remain the most vivid moments of their
lives – etched into their memories like letters in a granite monument.
A sociological survey conducted by *Komsomol'skaia pravda* in March and
April 1962 found an amazing similarity in descriptions of respondents to
Gagarin's feat – people huddled around radio receivers, mesmerized by
Levitan's voice, tears of joy streaming down their faces, strangers hugging
and kissing. Those memories were so hard-wired among those who lived in

that era that even four decades later they were virtually unchanged.[33] So dramatic was the impact of that moment that it even transformed the perception of time: Soviets began to divide the passage of historical time into before and after the flight, just as the Second World War had earlier marked an instant of radical discontinuity with the pre-war Soviet period.

Soviet and Russian culture took a new form on the day of Gagarin's flight, reconfiguring itself around an obscure and completely unknown provincial lad with a big smile.[34] A new official holiday ('Cosmonautics Day', first celebrated on 12 April 1962 and still an official Russian holiday) emerged after Gagarin's flight. Cosmonautics Day, while celebrating the beginning of the era of manned space exploration, placed the long-standing Russian dream of escape from Earth's seemingly intractable problems at the centre of the ceremonial calendar.

THE CULT OF THE SON

If the cult of Gagarin had emerged in a climate of intense anticipation, amplified by radio and television, and carried aloft on fantasies of escape from poverty, it also was born in the midst of Khrushchev's policies of de-Stalinization, which gained new momentum in 1961 and 1962.

Foreign journalists and Soviet citizens were struck by the contrast between the condemnation of Stalin and the emergence of a new cult around Gagarin.[35] One unpublished letter to the editor of *Komsomol'skaia pravda* was alarmed by the trend: 'Praise of him has reached the point where his mother, wife and even his children are practically heroes ... they have started naming kolkhozes, sovkhozes, streets, squares and other things after him. They even had a reception for him in the Kremlin ... In a word, the cult of personality, which has been condemned, is now blossoming anew with relation to Gagarin.'[36]

Most Soviets, however, were proud to live on a street or square freshly dubbed 'Gagarin'. Indeed, workers in factories and peasants on collective farms often originated the demand that their region or workplace be named in honour of the first cosmonaut – just as the first museum devoted to Gagarin in 1965, in the city of Saratov, was a product of local initiative and operated outside the official museum bureaucracy. For many Soviets, Gagarin provided a kind of glue that joined Soviet society (especially the Russian part of it) to the Soviet state at a time when condemnation of Stalin threatened one of the main things that had linked the two together for nearly thirty years.[37] Yet Gagarin was more than a replacement for Stalin. The idea of a 'son' as a banner of the nation, as opposed to a 'father', dramatically shifted the position

Figure 7.2 Gagarin as the son and brother so many had lost during the war.

of the subject toward the state. Stalin had been the creator: he created 'us'. Gagarin was the creation: 'we' created him. If there was not much one could do about a father – especially one like Stalin – the whole nation could participate in the creation of a son (Figure 7.2).[38]

In the spirit of Khrushchev's thaw, which had emphasized collective endeavours, many Soviets had a sense that their labours, in some small way, were responsible for Gagarin. When Gagarin visited his technical college in Saratov in 1965, his matronly cafeteria cook elbowed her way to the front of the receiving area, still wearing her apron and chef's hat. 'What's wrong?' she snapped to irritated school officials who were on the receiving end of her sharp elbows. 'Didn't I feed Gagarin!'[39]

People felt for Gagarin an intimacy and closeness that few had ever felt for Stalin. Everyone seemed to be on the familiar '*ty*' with him, referring to him by his diminutive Yura or Yurochka. For so many mothers and grand-mothers, who frequently surrounded him at public gatherings, he was the son they had lost during the war. When Gagarin went back to the technical college in Saratov where he studied in the mid-1950s, his female teachers assembled around him at the banquet, head in hands, and stared longingly and lovingly at their beloved Yurka. 'The teachers stroked the soft hair on Yuri Alekseevich's head, like mothers.'[40] Among those who remembered him, it was commonplace to repeat the claims of Gagarin's mother that he was a thoughtful, considerate and doting son – both for his biological mother and for the motherland that he served.[41]

If Yuri was a motherland's favourite son, he was also a Soviet father's pride and joy. The older designers and engineers, as well as political leadership, developed a fatherly relationship with the cosmonauts, adopting them as sons and worthy successors, or so they hoped, to the generation that had defeated the Nazis. When Gagarin came to Moscow for the triumphal celebration of his feat on 14 April 1961, the Soviet news agency TASS reported that, 'Nikita Sergeevich Khrushchev took off his hat, and like a father hugged the hero-cosmonaut, kissing him and for a long, long time not releasing him from his embrace.'[42] Following German Titov's successful flight on 6 August 1961, Titov and Gagarin joined Khrushchev atop the mausoleum to review a celebratory parade. The photo was splashed across the pages of the Soviet press and on Soviet television. The beaming Khrushchev looked like 'a proud father with his sons. All three were smiling and happy'.[43] The Soviet martyr-hero of the 1930s, the boy Pavlik Morozov, was a filial rebel; according to legend, he had denounced his father and was killed by his family. By the 1960s the sons had become models of filial piety; patriarchy was to be praised, not denounced.[44]

That public image of harmony, of course, sometimes masked generational tensions – especially between the fathers and the sons. Some (though not many) front-line veterans (*frontoviki*) resented Gagarin's rapid promotion to major, arguing that his heroism could not compare with the sacrifices they had made during the Great Patriotic War. But those too young to fight in the war resented their elders, especially the front-line servicemen, who seemed always to answer the ambitions of the younger generation with the question: 'What did you do during the war?'[45] For the first time, they seemed to have their own hero.

The tendency to think in terms of kinship was typical for the late Soviet period, when Russian nationalists gained increasing sympathy in party ruling circles.[46] It was also characteristic of modern nation-building. As one scholar has noted, 'National ideologies are saturated with kinship metaphors: fatherland and motherland, sons of the nation and their brothers, mothers of these worthy sons, and occasionally daughters.' Having a lineage, being able to place oneself in time, was especially important in the communist case because the Soviet Union had begun as a radical break with the ancestors worshipped before the Revolution. The more that past markers of identity were effaced, the more Russians hungered for new manifestations of their 'homeland' identity – their *rodina*, or motherland. The Gagarin clan functioned as a metonym for Soviet Russia's ancestral beginnings – revolutionary and Soviet yet also Russian and traditional. It was 'a kind of ancestor worship, a system of patrilineal kinship, in which national heroes occupy the place of clan elders in defining a nation as noble lineage'.[47]

Gagarin's mother, who died in 1984, became the most prominent of the Gagarin sub-cults, immortalized today by a life-size bronze figure of her sitting on a bronze park bench. Always surrounded by wreaths of fresh flowers, it greets pilgrims in the garden of her home in Gagarin, which became part of the 'Unified Gagarin Memorial Museum Complex'. Like her son, she relished the role of a public icon, transforming her biological connection to Gagarin into a full-time job as manager of the family (and thus national) cults.[48] She became the de facto director and tour guide at the museum devoted to her son in the town of Gagarin. Thousands of museum-goers and children sat down to tea with her as she recounted the story of her son's early years. She consciously designed these tea-and-biscuit rituals to reproduce the feelings of intimacy and closeness associated with the Gagarin image – and with the Russian nation, which prided itself on its hospitality (*gostepriimstvo*) to visitors.[49] Her hospitality was so legendary that the Soviet government in the early 1980s built her a hotel and apartment, called the 'House of Cosmonauts', where she enveloped visitors with her matronly warmth and regaled them with stories of Yuri's childhood games. With the aid of ghostwriters from the newspaper *Pravda* she penned a book on her son titled simply *About My Son*. First published in 1983, it went through three editions by 1986. Becoming a kind of Soviet 'agony aunt', Gagarina dispensed advice to children and parents alike.[50] Her personal secretary helped her manage correspondence from her fans, which she conducted on her own letterhead: 'From Anna Timofeevna Gagarina, the Mother of the First Cosmonaut of the USSR Iu. A. Gagarin.'[51]

If Gagarin's mother was an ideal matron, his wife, Valentina, played the role of the good wife. As a prototype of the ideal Russian woman, Valentina Gagarina conveyed the message that a woman should sacrifice everything for her man – especially if he was fulfilling his duty to the state. Khrushchev reinforced the image of the dutiful wife after Gagarin's flight, when he suggested that behind every Soviet male hero was a quiet, humble and self-effacing woman. That seems to have resonated positively with many Soviet women – or at least with those who bothered to send letters to newspapers. Without the sacrificing wife, who 'calmed his nerves and preserved his health, creating a benign and calm atmosphere at home', there would have been no

Gagarin. All 'Soviet women', said one letter writer, owed this 'humble woman' a debt of gratitude, which they could pay by reproducing her selfless devotion to their own husbands.[52] Following her husband's untimely and tragic death in 1968, Valentina has preserved the image of a grieving widow, scrupulously maintaining a public pose of grief and emotional distress.[53]

Since the Gagarin family was a sacred object, its representation could not tolerate those whose lives could not be shoe-horned into the idealized image. Some family members were therefore conspicuous by their absence. Soviet (and post-Soviet) discussions of the Gagarin family scarcely mentioned Gagarin's younger brother, Boris – beyond the fact that he was tortured by the Gestapo under Nazi occupation and nearly died. That part of his life suited the national narrative of victimization and suffering, but his life after the war, when he became a drunk and eventually committed suicide in the mid-1970s, went unremarked. His fate remained the family's (and the nation's) dirty little secret.

A perhaps more inexplicable missing family member was Gagarin's father. While journalists and party propagandists heaped praise on Gagarin's mother, they said almost nothing about his father, Aleksei. Taciturn and gruff, he seems to have had little enthusiasm for playing his assigned role, unlike his famous son and increasingly famous wife. There is some indication that his political views – especially disappointment over Khrushchev's downfall – may have disqualified him from cult status. According to one story, he refused to take down a portrait of Khrushchev after the latter was ousted, despite repeated requests from party officials in Gzhatsk and Smolensk. He later objected to his home town of Gzhatsk carrying his surname of 'Gagarin' after his famous son's death. When he was shown a ceremonial badge celebrating the town's 250th anniversary in the mid-1970s, in which the iconic image of his son was featured, he said: 'Why is it always Gagarin this and Gagarin that. He didn't found the city, he didn't build it. For 250 years people have lived and worked in the city. You have to respect history.'[54] The Soviet system's response to his frankness was to write him out of the Soviet Russian family.

By and by, however, a more appropriate father figure for Gagarin was found. He was Sergei Korolev, the 'chief builder' whose identity was finally revealed after his untimely demise in 1966 from a botched haemorrhoid operation (the reason for his death was never mentioned). While Korolev seems to have had genuine affection for Gagarin, treating him like the son he never had, he also emerged as the chief father-figure in the public presentation of the Gagarin cult – even in Gagarin's home-town museum, which devotes far more attention to Korolev than to Gagarin's father.[55]

Bonds of kinship had to be validated by loyalty and service to the state. Korolev and Gagarin thus formed a filial bond through service to the state that trumped Gagarin's biological father–son relationship. Through the 1980s, and especially after the collapse of the Soviet Union, Korolev's status as a father cult, and specifically as a father to Gagarin, intensified.[56] A life-size bronze statue in Taganrog, where the cosmonauts sometimes relaxed, features the father, Korolev, on a park bench, his arm draped around Gagarin, the son, 'as if they are dreaming about future conquests of space'.[57]

THE NATIVE SIDE OF THINGS

These images of the harmonious Russian Gagarin family provided a frame-work that simplified and humanized Soviet space, collapsing it into some-thing Russian, familiar and provincial, in contrast to the 'scale and complexity of modern, human-made environments' which were often incomprehensible.[58] The link to the state completed the family circle. To say that Gagarin was the 'first' was therefore not merely to refer to his entry into space, but also to highlight his status as progenitor of a new (yet paradoxically ancient) tribe/state. The heartland of this Russian nation, as seen through the prism of the Gagarin clan, was not in Moscow but in Gagarin's home town of Gzhatsk, in the provincial backwater of the Smolensk region. In the words of one ode to Gagarin, entitled 'The Native Side of Things', he grew up among vast 'expanses of flax and thick meadows of clover', surrounded by honeybees and butterflies, yet at the centre of the country. Rivers and rivulets flowed northward to Leningrad and southward 'to the Mother Volga, and then meandered their way to the little father (*batiushka*) Dnieper'.[59]

If people celebrated the native side of things through Gagarin, they also honoured the Russian traditions that had nurtured him in that land of clover and flax. Beginning in the 1970s, the museum devoted to Gagarin in his home town began researching and promoting his childhood amuse-ments – games such as *gorelki* (a kind of hide-and-seek), *lapta* (a traditional Russian ball-and-stick game) and *volchok* (like pin the tail on the donkey). By studying Gagarin's youthful diversions, children would learn a new culture of play linked to Russian folk traditions. The effort drew inspiration from a revival of Russian folk culture in the late Soviet era, when folklorists and propagandists promoted traditional Russian culture as a way to solidify Russian identity and to staunch the supposedly corrosive impact of more modern and cosmopolitan cultural practices. In the 1970s, children began playing 'Gagarin games'. The practice intensified as the Soviet Union collapsed.[60] In 1990 ethnographers, with children from Gagarin's home town in tow, embarked on eleven expeditions to the Russian provinces to interview old-timers about the games they played in their youth. The culminating point of their travels was Gagarin's birth village of Klushino, where the first cosmonaut lived as a boy until the end of the Second World War. When they entered the village, with microphones and notebooks in hand, they played the *baian*, a traditional Russian instrument, and sang Russian folk songs. Those exchanges have continued to this day, inspiring a mini-industry in ethnographic research and papers such as 'Yuri Alekseevich Gagarin: The Games of a Son of the Russian Land'.[61]

These ethnographic expeditions also re-enacted Gagarin's own peregrinations after his flight. From 1961 to 1968 Gagarin criss-crossed provincial Russia on a perpetual speaking tour, joining centre to province and province to centre, stitching those spaces together into a national community. The Arcadian values supposedly associated with his rural upbringing rooted Gagarin's journey firmly in Russian tradition, validating it as a national path. Moscow in turn celebrated the feat of its provincial son, weighing down his chest with every conceivable medal of honour – a prelude to pilgrimage rituals that brought the centre back to the supposed source of its national soul. Beginning in the 1970s, nearly 100,000 people a year boarded buses in Moscow and headed for a visit to Gagarin's ancestral homeland – a place that had, in addition, heroically endured the onslaught of both Napoleon's armies and Hitler's *Wehrmacht*.[62] A staple of the visit to Gagarin's birthplace of Klushino was a trip to the water well from which he drank as a boy, right next to the dug-out in the ground, faithfully preserved, where he lived under Nazi occupation. Drinking deeply from that well, pilgrims connected themselves to the spirit of the family that also contained the nation's essence.

CONCLUSION

That sense that the Gagarin clan was a prototypical 'Russian' family, validated by both its provincial roots and service to the state at the centre, is perhaps one of the most enduring facets of the Gagarin cult. Gagarin's provincial status connected him with earlier Soviet heroes such as the provincial Pavlik Morozov, who was 'imported from the periphery, repackaged, and then exported for the edification of Soviet provincials ... The legend came at once from the ideological heart of the country, and from the muscle and bone of its provincial everyday'.[63] As a symbol of filial piety rather than rebellion, however, Gagarin and Morozov could not have been more different. The cult of Gagarin abounded with positive metaphors of

family, kinship, motherhood, faithful filial relations, sisterhood, brotherhood, fatherhood. Gagarin's mother once wrote that her son 'was a son of
his native Earth and not some suspicious stepson. And that was why he was
able to perform a miracle'. She added that it was his status as a Russian,
rather than global citizen, that constituted the true source of his greatness,
for Gagarin 'and My Russia will live for eternity. Our character is in our
blood, the special way of the people'.[64]

By the late 1980s the native side of things seemed a far more inviting place
than foreign realms outside the fields of flax and clover – even as the Berlin
Wall fell and travel restrictions for Russians were lifted.[65] Into the twenty-
first century, Gagarin had largely been transformed from a symbol of a
common socialist future that would encompass the whole universe –
Gagarin as a space traveller and thus quintessential border-crosser – into
something very different: a figure at the centre of a Russian provincial idyll
situated firmly in the imagined folkways of the past.

At the same time Gagarin provided an important element of cultural
continuity with the Soviet period. At least one day a year, on Cosmonautics
Day, Gagarin has kept the dream of making a heroic escape from everyday
life (and the provinces) alive. Imagining themselves in space, looking down
upon their problems and enemies, many Russians have experienced a
sensation of empowerment – a typical human and not simply Russian
response. 'Spaciousness is closely associated with the sense of being free.
Fundamental is the ability to transcend the present condition, and this
transcendence is most simply manifest as the elementary power to move.'[66]
Those old dreams of transcending one's homeland and crossing borders
have not disappeared entirely.

Gagarin's legend has also helped many post-Soviet Russians, especially in
the provinces, negotiate and transcend the humiliation and confusing
welter of events in the 1990s. The Gagarin cult thrived against the backdrop
of economic catastrophe and a sharp decline in standards of living. 'There
was a breaking point in our lives,' said Gagarin's niece in 2007. 'People were
completely confused, they lost their bearings. Throwing out the old life was
not so simple.' As in the Soviet era, Gagarin gave provincial Russians
confidence that they could make the transition to the post-Soviet era with
their national community intact, 'a connecting point between the past and
the future', as his niece put it.[67] One poet at the annual 2006 Gagarin
conference in Gagarin declaimed a composition to a packed audience
entitled, 'The City of Gagarin: The World's Most Famous Province'.
This paean to all things provincial and Russian declared that, 'We are all
born in a province, all of us come from these rivers, peasant huts, and

forests, from these countryside towns.' Russians had reverted to the land during the economic collapse of the 1990s – just as they had during the Second World War – nurtured by their own labours on the soil. 'Russianness (*Russkost'*) can be found in every detail of provincial life,' the poet declared. But provincial Russia would rise again from the 'plough to the heavens' – as indeed it seemed to be doing, if ever so slowly, in the Putin era. The poet concluded: 'The world is awaiting new Gagarins from the provinces. And they will arise! Indeed, they already have. They are being reared like a simple, blue-eyed miracle, preserving the province, like a talisman in one's soul!'[68]

As in Soviet days, the promotion of Gagarin has remained both a popular and a state-driven phenomenon (Figure 7.3). The cult's survival was partly rooted in the well-noted feeling of nostalgia for the supposedly good old Soviet days, but not only in this. For the Russian space industry the cult of Gagarin was a way to popularize space conquest – and thus build public support for funding. Local boosters in Gagarin's home town and in Saratov also hatched grand plans to create massive tourist complexes centred on

Figure 7.3 Model of a proposed palace to be built on the site where Gagarin landed just outside Saratov.

Gagarin's feat – just as they had recreated 'Gagarin' clubs for post-Soviet generations of Russian children. Nostalgia for their Soviet youth was part of this, but so too was their desire for tourist roubles. Various politicians (with visible support for space programmes from both Vladimir Putin and Dmitrii Medvedev) joined those efforts, as did Gagarin's relatives, one of whom emulated Gagarin's own conquest of the centre. Gagarin's daughter Elena was appointed general director of the Kremlin complex of museums in 2001 – becoming, like her grandmother, a keeper of the nation's holy relics – and had connections leading to the heart of Russian power. Both state support, which increased dramatically in the run-up to the fiftieth anniversary of Gagarin's flight in 2011, and the support of volunteers have thus perpetuated Gagarin's life and legend as fundamental aspects of Russian national identity in the post-Soviet era.

NOTES

1. A. Klenin, 'Patent na Gagarina', *Ezhednevnaia delovaia gazeta*, 29 October 2009, www.rbcdaily.ru/2009/10/29/media/439070. Gagarin's daughter Galina owns exclusive worldwide rights to the trademark 'Iurii Alekseevich Gagarin' and to 'Pervyi kosmonavt Iurii Gagarin'. The copyright covers use of those terms for beer, watches, weapons, clothing and so forth.
2. A. Emel'ianenkov, 'A tret'im byl Kheminguei', *Rossiiskaia gazeta*, 5 March 2009, www.rg.ru/printable/2009/03/05/leonov.html.
3. 'Le Poème de l'extase (The Poem of Ecstasy), Op. 54', *New York Philharmonic* (January 2008), 35.
4. Russian State Archive of the Economy (RGAE), f. 9453, op. 1, d. 36, l. 53; op. 1, d. 37, l. 85; as cited in V. Zubok, *Zhivago's Children: The Last Russian Intelligentsia* (Cambridge, MA, 2009), 132.
5. J. T. Andrews, *Red Cosmos: K. E. Tsiolkovskii, Grandfather of Soviet Rocketry* (College Station, TX, 2009), 60–1; J. T. Andrews, 'Storming the Stratosphere: Space Exploration, Soviet Culture, and the Arts from Lenin to Khrushchev's Times', *Russian History* 36 (2009), 77–87.
6. A. Siddiqi, *The Rocket's Red Glare: Spaceflight and the Soviet Imagination, 1857–1957* (Cambridge, 2010), 76, 80. On the parallel cult of aviators, see S. Palmer, *Dictatorship of the Air: Aviation Culture and the Fate of Modern Russia* (Cambridge, 2006), 4.
7. RGAE, f. 9453, op. 1, d. 35, ll. 17, 67, 69.
8. V. Ponomareva, *Zhenskoe litso kosmosa* (Moscow, 2002), 243.
9. RGAE, f. 9453, op. 1, d. 36, ll. 17, 48, 55, 60, 66; d. 37, l. 64; d. 35, l. 91; Archive of the Russian Academy of Sciences (ARAN), f. 1647, op. 1, d. 260, l. 38.
10. RGAE, f. 9453, op. 1, d. 38, l. 1.
11. *Gagarinskii sbornik: materialy XXXIII obshchestvenno-nauchnykh chtenii posviashchennykh pamiati Iu. A. Gagarina* (Gagarin, 2007), 492.

12. H. Lefebvre, *The Production of Space* [1974], trans. D. Nicholson-Smith (London, 1991), 98.

13. V. Pop, 'Viewpoint: Space and Religion in Russia. Cosmonaut Worship to Orthodox Revival', *Astropolitics* (May 2009), 150–63; RGAE, f. 9453, op. 2, d. 21, l. 31; d. 34, ll. 6–7.

14. S. Boym, 'Kosmos: Remembrances of the Future', in A. Bartos, *Kosmos: A Portrait of the Russian Space Age* (Princeton, NJ, 2001), 85.

15. B. A. Grushin, *Chetyre zhizni Rossii v zerkale oprosov obshchestvennogo mneniia: zhizn' 1-aia epokha Khrushcheva* (Moscow, 2001), 427–8.

16. For example: RGAE, f. 9453, op. 1, d. 35, ll. 133–4; d. 36, ll. 17, 73; d. 35, l. 71; op. 2, d. 32, ll. 4, 34; d. 34, ll. 60, 116, 121, 128, 206, 216, 246.

17. *Gagarinskii sbornik: materialy obshchestvenno-nauchnykh chtenii posviashchen- nykh pamiati Iu. A. Gagarina (1996–1997gg.)* (Gagarin, 1998), 78.

18. ARAN, f. 1647, op. 1, d. 256, ll. 9–10.

19. *Gagarinskii sbornik: materialy XXVIII obshchestvenno-nauchnykh chtenii pos- viashchennykh pamiati Iu. A. Gagarina 2001 g.*, ch. 2 (Gagarin, 2002), 324; RGAE, f. 9453, op. 2, d. 34, ll. 5, 138.

20. J. N. Entrikin, *The Betweenness of Place: Towards a Geography of Modernity* (Baltimore, MD, 1991), 65.

21. F. Inglis, *A Short History of Celebrity* (Princeton, NJ, 2010), 11–12, 16.

22. V. Sappak, *Televidenie i my: chetyre besedy* (Moscow, 1963), 117.

23. RGAE, f. 9453, op. 2, d. 32, l. 82.

24. Party Archive of Saratov Province (PASO), f. 594, op. 2, d. 4711, l. 11.

25. RGAE, f. 9453, op. 2, d. 32, l. 80; op. 1, d. 36, l. 14; d. 38, l. 64.

26. *Gagarinskii sbornik . . . XXVIII*, ch. 1, 35.

27. RGAE, f. 9453, op. 2, d. 34, ll. 155, 180, 218; op. 1, d. 36, l. 12.

28. 'Gagarin, Iurii Alekseevich', *Imia Rossiia*, http://top50.nameofRussia.ru/person. html?id=64.

29. PASO, f. 594, op. 2, d. 4711, l. 54; Inglis, *Short History*, 10; Sappak, *Televidenie i my*, 117.

30. V. Suvorov and A. Sabelnikov, *The First Manned Space Flight: Russia's Quest for Space* (Hauppauge, NY, 1997), 70; Ponomareva, *Zhenskoe litso*, 57.

31. A. Adzhubei, *Te desiat' let* (Moscow, 1989), 162; Suvorov and Sabelnikov, *First Manned Space Flight*, 73.

32. I treat Gagarin's lies in 'The Sincere Deceiver: Yuri Gagarin and the Search for a Higher Truth', in *Into the Cosmos*, ed. J. T. Andrews and A. Siddiqi (in press).

33. Grushin, *Chetyre zhizni*, 426. On mass media and national identity formation: B. Anderson, *Imagined Communities: Reflections on the Origins and Spread of Nationalism*, rev. edn (New York, 2006).

34. Gagarin's smile was a major part of his appeal and of course constituted a crucial revision to the image of the non-smiling, implacable hero current in the early decades of Soviet power and during the Second World War.

35. Gosudarstvennyi arkhiv Rossiiskoi Federatsii, f. 4459, op. 43, d. 1011, l. 289.

36. RGAE, f. 9453, op. 2, d. 34, l. 149.

37. On the confusion caused by Khrushchev's attack on Stalin's legacy and cult, see M. Dobson, *Khrushchev's Cold Summer: Gulag Returnees, Crime, and the Fate of Reform after Stalin* (Ithaca, NY, 2009).

38. Iu. Ustinov, ed., *Bessmertie Gagarina* (Moscow, 2004), 116.

39. V. I. Rossoshanskii, *Parni iz nashego goroda* (Saratov, 2004), 152–3.

40. Ibid., 161; RGAE, f. 9453, op. 2, d. 34, l. 262; op. 1, d. 37, l. 133; G. N. Mozgunova, *Syn zemli smolenskoi: k 70-letiiu so dnia rozhdeniia Iu. A. Gagarina* (Smolensk, 2004), 48.

41. RGAE, f. 9453, op. 2, d. 34, l. 102, 145, 223; *Gagarinskii sbornik: materialy XXVII obshchestvenno-nauchnykh chtenii posviashchennykh pamiati Iu. A. Gagarina 2000 g.*, ch. 2 (Gagarin, 2001), 99.

42. *Syn zemli*, 46.

43. B. Chertok, *Rockets and People*, vol. III, *Hot Days of the Cold War* (Washington, DC, 2009), 196.

44. C. Kelly, *Comrade Pavlik: The Rise and Fall of a Soviet Boy Hero* (London, 2005).

45. RGAE, f. 9453, op. 1, d. 37, l. 51; op. 2, d. 30, l. 1; d. 34, l. 264.

46. On this tendency, see N. Mitrokhin, *Russkaia partiia: dvizhenie russkikh natsionalistov v SSSR, 1953–1985* (Moscow, 2003).

47. K. Verdery, *The Political Lives of Dead Bodies: Reburial and Postsocialist Change* (New York, 1999), 41.

48. *Syn zemli*, 58.

49. Tatiana Vladimirovna Egorova, interviewed by A. Jenks, Gagarin, 25 July 2007.

50. A. T. Gagarina, *Slovo o syne*, 3rd edn (Moscow, 1986), 156.

51. V. Tsybin and S. Khoruzhaia, *Neizvestnyi Gagarin* (Engels, 2002), 6–7.

52. RGAE, f. 9453, op. 1, d. 36, l. 7; op. 1, d. 37, l. 81.

53. See, for example, the photographs of Valentina in *Iurii Gagarin: stat'i, rechi, pis'ma, interv'iu. K 10-letiiu poleta v kosmos Iuriia Alekseevicha Gagarina* (Moscow, 1971).

54. *Syn zemli*, 75.

55. Adzhubei, *Te desiat' let*, 161; N. Koroleva, *Otets*, kn. III (Moscow, 2007), 55.

56. M. I. Gerasimov and A. G. Ivanov, eds., *Zvezdnyi put'* (Moscow, 1986).

57. Koroleva, *Otets*, 156.

58. Entrikin, *Betweenness of Place*, 44.

59. *Gzhatsk-Gagarin: 300 let. Stikhi, poemy, pesni* (Moscow, 2007), 54–6.

60. M. Sidlin, 'Ot gurchalki do stantsii "Mir"', *Nezavisimaia gazeta*, 9 June 2001, www.ng.ru/printed/18481.

61. *Gagarinskii sbornik: materialy XXIX obshchestvenno-nauchnykh chtenii posviashchennykh pamiati Iu. A. Gagarina 2002 g.*, ch. 1 (Gagarin, 2003), 244; Tamara Dmitrevna Filatova (Gagarin's niece), interviewed by A. Jenks, Gagarin, 8 August 2007; *Gagarinskii sbornik . . . XXVII*, ch. 2, 96–7.

62. Tamara Dmitrevna Filatova, interview, 8 August 2007.

63. Kelly, *Comrade Pavlik*, xxv.

64. *Gzhatsk-Gagarin*, 53.

65. On these anxieties and their relationship to a patriotism based on victimization by outsiders, see S. A. Oushakine, *The Patriotism of Despair: Nation, War, and Loss in Russia* (Ithaca, NY, 2009).
66. Y.-F. Tuan, *Space and Place: The Perspective of Experience* (Minneapolis, MI, 1977), 52.
67. Tamara Dmitrevna Filatova, interview, 8 August 2007.
68. *Gagarinskii sbornik . . . XXXIII*, 520–7.

CHAPTER 8

Nation-construction in post-Soviet Central Asia

Sergei Abashin

In his book *Imagined Communities* Benedict Anderson refers to the nation as a community whose members do not necessarily maintain direct contact with each other. For this reason, the emergence and existence of the nation relies heavily on a process of what he calls 'imagination'. Beliefs about common origins, a shared culture or common language are all points of agreement or disagreement, and they are used to draw the boundaries of the imagined nation and to create its symbols. Anderson also describes how the West European empires – among them the USSR – artificially introduced concepts of 'nation' and 'nationality' into their colonies in Asia. Referring to empires and anti-imperial nationalisms, he notes that 'one might go so far as to say that the state imagined its local adversaries, as in an ominous prophetic dream, well before they came into historical existence'.[1]

Within the system of social coordinates created by the Soviet Union, 'nationality' came to play a leading role. The use of nationality as the basis for the administrative and political division of Central Asia in the 1920s, together with the subsequent policy of *korenizatsiia* or 'nativization', resulted in a situation which transformed the classification of nationality from a speculative design into one of the most fundamental principles of state life and one of the chief instruments of administrative control.[2] The very same nations which were fostered and encouraged by the Soviet state, however, were subsequently to become an instrument that could legitimately challenge the very existence of the USSR. Thus, the collapse of the Soviet Union was carried through and justified as the break-up of an 'empire' into 'national states', which thereby acquired their right to 'self-determination'.

Today the former Central Asian republics are attempting to rebuild themselves as national states, and they appeal to the concept of the nation in order to explain the choice they have made. As they do so, they draw on a pool of discursive and explanatory models that, as Graham Smith has argued, may be described in terms of three characteristics: (1) they 'essentialize' and 'primordialize' the nation by describing ethnic identities as linear, eternal and uniform; (2) they 'historicize' the nation by locating its origins in ancient times, redolent of a 'golden age' and 'national heroes'; and (3) they 'totalize' the nation by levelling out all individual differences and characteristics among its individual members, who become 'collective individuals' with a collective memory, a collective homeland and so on.[3] All of these models were formed and actively articulated in a process of controlled (as it seemed at the time to the powers that be) nation-building in the Soviet Union. The nationalisms of the post-Soviet period have fully adopted and assimilated these models into their own ideological systems.

Along with this emphasis on the common features of the nationalisms in the post-Soviet states of Central Asia, however, it is important to keep in mind that each of these countries remains distinctive in terms of its respective historical, spatial-demographic, political and economic characteristics. All of these factors are configured differently in the different states, and they correspondingly give rise to different variations of nationalism. Indeed, in regard to certain parameters these variations might even be asymmetrical.

CENTRAL ASIAN NATIONS AND THE RUSSO-SOVIET LEGACY

The collapse of the USSR in 1991 turned the former national republics instantaneously into independent national states recognized by the international community. Not one republic in Central Asia had a mass secession movement or its own dissidents prior to the actual Soviet break-up; indeed local leaders remained loyal to the central Soviet leadership to the very last moment, never raising any demands for autonomy or independence. Despite this, the collapse of the USSR at the beginning of the 1990s and movement of the new states beyond the sphere of direct Russian influence has been represented by the Central Asian political elites as the long-awaited liberation from imperial shackles, resulting from national aspirations and ongoing struggle. The fact that these nations were themselves created in the period of Russo-Soviet rule has been completely forgotten, or more accurately ignored.[4]

All of the new states proclaimed their days of 'national independence', which symbolized the historic break with the recent past and a return to authentic national statehood. A prominent element in the movement of 'national liberation' became the renaming of cities and streets, with the names of 'non-titular' public figures (i.e. those not from the nationality that under Soviet rule was deemed to be the governing nation in a given republic) and Communist public figures gradually disappearing from the map of the region. The capital of Kyrgyzstan (in Soviet times called

Frunze after the Bolshevik leader who was born there) regained the name
Bishkek, as it was known when it was a small nineteenth-century settlement. The largest city in northern Tajikistan (in Soviet times Leninabad)
again became Khujand, while Tselinograd was transformed into Astana
and became the new capital of Kazakhstan. At the local level the numerous
kolkhoz farms originally called 'Communism', 'Socialism', 'CPSU
Congress' etc. were renamed after all kinds of heroes from the pre-
Soviet past. However, the exact place of the Russo-Soviet legacy in the
ideology of 'national independence' in Central Asia remains a complex
question. Despite a general drive in this region to describe the Soviet era as
an imperialist one, different Central Asian states have also preserved their
own idiosyncratic national memories of the Soviet past.

The presence of a large Russian-speaking community and elite
in Kazakhstan and Kyrgyzstan has forced local powers in these countries to
be much more cautious and flexible in their pronouncements about the era
of Russo-Soviet dominance. For example, there was a major debate in
Kazakhstan about whether the Kazakhs had been originally conquered by
Russia or whether they had joined the Russian empire voluntarily: neither of
these two opposing points of view emerged unambiguously victorious.[5] The
most important focus of criticism of Russo-Soviet imperialism in Kazakhstan
was the 1916 uprising and the early 1930s collectivization, both of which had
led to numerous casualties as well as the dispersal of much of the local
population to the surrounding regions. Some Kazakh nationalists are also
negative about the policy of Russian colonization that had started at the turn
of the twentieth century and continued during the cultivation of the virgin
steppe lands in the second half of the century. In Kyrgyzstan one sometimes
hears bitter reminders about past victims, but overall the Kyrgyz incorporation into the Russian Empire and the Soviet Union is viewed as mostly
positive – as something that had protected the Kyrgyz from their more
powerful neighbours and that had, in fact, helped them preserve much of
Kyrgyz culture and sovereignty.

In Tajikistan, where a Russian community is not a factor, the attitude
towards the Soviet past is also fairly positive. Here people are also grateful to
Russia for establishing a Tajik state and for ensuring the protection of its
culture and language, which, it is assumed, were threatened with extermination by the Uzbeks and the Afghans. It is not the Russians who are perceived
as the historical enemies in this state. The Tajik president, Emomali
Rakhmon, persistently refers to the 'cult of the other', arguing that today
'the worship of what is foreign is manifest again, but now in a new guise', and
that the achievements of Tajik history are ascribed to 'neighbouring peoples

and countries' or are 'considered to be the joint achievements of the Tajik and other neighbouring peoples'.[6] It is not difficult to guess that 'the other' here is the Turks, or more precisely the Uzbeks, from whom Russia had previously saved the Tajiks.

Academician Rakhim Masov has formulated the pivotal ideas of Tajik nationalism, revealing its logic. The Revolution of 1917 was a 'great event' in the history of the Tajik people, and the separation of distinct ethnic nationalities at this time undertaken by Soviet authorities was historically necessary and justified. However, this was then ineptly put into practice, with the pan-Turkic ideologists ('the Great-Uzbek chauvinists') instigating 'the beginnings of genocide of the Tajik people'.[7] Yet one of the paradoxes in this scenario is that many if not most of the 'pan-Turkic ideologists' who were creating Uzbekistan could easily have become 'Tajiks', had the situation in the 1920s turned out differently (and many of them did in the end). As a result, the theme of Uzbek aggression is invariably combined with the theme of betrayal, as for example in the formulation of Emomali Rakhmon: 'Some of the Tajik political figures became accomplices and instruments in the hands of pan-Turkic chauvinists'.[8] This theme of betrayal is also invariably accompanied by a search for individual people's 'authentic' ethnic roots. Yet what is symptomatic here is that the search for Tajik roots among the leaders and public figures of Uzbekistan (from Faizullah Khodzhaev to Islam Karimov) is matched by a similar search for compromising Turkic roots among the leaders and public figures of Tajikistan. Not a single Tajik leader has been able to escape such suspicions and accusations.

Turkmenistan, however, displays a negative attitude towards past Russo-Soviet domination. The heavy defeat suffered by the Turkmen Teke military battalions against the Russians at the Geok Teppe fortress in 1881, commemorated with a memorial day on 12 January, has become, in the ideology of independence, the symbolic beginning not of national rebirth but of national subjugation by foreigners. The Turkmen president Saparmurat Niyazov labelled the Soviet era the years of 'anguish, depression and hopelessness'. However, in Turkmenistan, criticism directed at Russia has come second to the eulogizing of the new authorities. Niyazov sought simply to tear out the Russo-Soviet page from his country's history as quickly as possible and then forget about it.

In Uzbekistan, at first, almost the entirety of the Russo-Soviet heritage was labelled foreign. The Uzbek leadership instigated the official policy of complete dissociation from the past, characterizing the last 150 years as a century and a half of subjugation, repression and exploitation by Russia.

Many opponents of Russia and the USSR became national heroes, along-side their victims. The Jadids were canonized as the ideological precursors of independent Uzbekistan, the Basmachi revolt was recognized as a 'movement for national liberation', and Faizullah Khodzhaev and Sharaf Rashidov were turned into veritable anti-Soviet dissidents, who had defended the independence of the Uzbek state and were then repressed by Moscow because of this. It is true that within the Uzbek intelligentsia, whose roots go back to the Soviet era, discussions continue about the pluses and minuses of Uzbekistan's colonial past. In the early 2000s the anti-imperial rhetoric of the Uzbek leadership softened to a degree. However, the overall conception, according to which the Uzbek people had been a victim of Russian imperialism, remains as prominent as before.[9]

The political and economic structure of Central Asian states continues to bear traces of the prolonged Russo-Soviet presence, during which these structures first emerged and grew. Many of the customs and traditions on which the contemporary life of these states is being built have their roots in the era of Russo-Soviet domination. This situation forces the local elites and societies in general constantly to return to the theme of the Russo-Soviet legacy and to look in it for a basis of their own identity.

THE NATION AND ITS HISTORY

No less complex for post-Soviet Central Asian nationalisms has been the question of the authenticity of pre-Soviet and pre-Russian imperial national history. Each Central Asian state strives to reconstruct the canonical image of its 'titular' nation – its traditional dress, cuisine, architecture, folklore, songs, dances, codes of conduct, moral values, rituals and so on. Many traditional elements have been incorporated into contemporary political structures: the *mahalla* (a local Islamic administration system) in Uzbekistan, the *aqsaqal* courts in Kyrgyzstan, the popular council in Turkmenistan and so forth. Many traditional elements have become a compulsory component in architecture, in monuments and in various political and social rituals. On the one hand, tradition has started to be viewed as the main source of legitimacy of national states, their way of representing themselves to the rest of the world and of endowing their existence with a deeper and longer-standing meaning. On the other, tradition has become a means of manipulating public opinion and a weapon that competing nationalisms can use against each other – and hence a source of new problems.[10] The greatest wealth of material for the construction of 'one's own' distinct national history is in the hands of Uzbekistan, on whose territory are located the most important cultural monuments in this region. This is something that the Uzbek elite has not hesitated to use, organizing, with the help of international bodies, a whole series of sumptuous celebrations of city anniversaries: in 1997, 2,000 years of Khiva and 2,500 years of Bukhara; in 2002, 2,500 years of Termez; in 2006, 2,700 years of Karshi; in 2007, 2,750 years of Samarkand and 2,000 years of Margilan. These and other similar celebrations, devoted to a host of various historical personages or events, have become a visible demonstration of the unquestionable antiquity and cultural wealth of today's Uzbekistan, and of its ability to consider itself equal to other great peoples of Europe and Asia.

In addition to representing the country as ancient and cultured, the Uzbek leadership has found it important to identify one particular historical figure and epoch that would serve as the brand label of Uzbek greatness. Such symbols were found in the ruler Tamerlane (Timur) and in the era of the Timurid dynasty, which lasted only for a relatively brief period – from the fifteenth to the sixteenth century – but which had left numerous historical traces of successful military conquests, grandiose construction work and the flourishing of literature. An entire Tamerlane 'industry' has now emerged in Uzbekistan.[11] His 660th anniversary, 1996, was proclaimed to be the year of Tamerlane: a Tamerlane museum was founded, all sorts of events were staged in his honour, countless books and articles were published about him, and a statue of Tamerlane on horseback replaced that of Karl Marx. In 2006 the 670th anniversary of the medieval ruler was celebrated in similar style. The image of this formidable military leader, who in his day terrified the West as well as Russia with his ruthlessness, has become for the Uzbek elite the symbolic embodiment of their greatest political ideals and national aspirations. The historians and politicians of Uzbekistan do not seem to be disconcerted by the fact that the Timurids did not see themselves as 'Uzbeks' – a term that was, in fact, used for their enemies, who came from the territory of today's Kazakhstan.

Kyrgyzstan and especially Tajikistan have followed a similar path, hopelessly seeking to copy the Uzbek example. In doing so, they try to compensate for the lack of material symbols of their national histories with more ambitious historical claims. For the Kyrgyz authorities the key historical reference point in the development of their nation has become the first mention of the so-called Yenisei Kyrgyz – the ancient Turkic-speaking tribes that formed a tribal union on the territory of Siberia. In 2003 this was turned into an opportunity to celebrate the 2,200th anniversary of Kyrgyz statehood. In 2000 the Kyrgyz state celebrated the so far record-breaking 3,000th anniversary of its second-largest town of Osh. The figure around which the Kyrgyz have built their own industry of symbolic production is the mythical hero of an ancient epic, Manas. Local scholars claimed that the Manas saga was exactly 1,000 years old in 1995.[12]

The ideologists of Tajik nationalism have traced their historical genealogy back to the Aryan era and Zoroastrianism through pan-Iranian roots and mythology. President Emomali Rakhmon has personally devoted his work *The Tajiks in the Mirror of History* to this idea. The year 2006 was officially proclaimed the year of Aryan culture.[13] In 2002 the 2,500th anniversary of the city of Ura Tube (Istaravshan) was celebrated, and in 2006 the 2,700th anniversary of the city of Kulob (Kulyab). In order to strengthen Tajikistan's connection with ancient states, the Leninabad province has been renamed Sughd and the Kulob province, Khatlon. However, the main symbol of Tajik statehood is the ruler Ismail Samani and the Samanid Empire, which existed in the ninth–tenth centuries. In 1999 Tajikistan triumphantly celebrated the 1,100th anniversary of the Samanid state. In 2000, in the centre of Dushanbe, in the place where the statue of Lenin stood in Soviet times (and which had earlier been temporarily replaced by the statue of the Persian poet Ferdowsi, the creator of the Iranian epic *Shahname*), the Tajik establishment erected a grandiose complex with the figure of Ismail Samani at its centre.[14] The highest mountain peak, previously known as the Peak of Communism, and which had once also borne the name of Stalin, has now become the Peak of Samani. Yet the Tajik elite seem hardly disconcerted by the fact that Ismail Samani actually ruled from Bukhara and that the Samanid Empire predominantly occupied today's territory of Uzbekistan.

The Kazakh authorities, by contrast, have a rather different stance, insofar as, for them, it is more important to demonstrate the achievements of modernization than of traditionalism, and to show that they are turned towards the future rather than the past. To be sure, in Kazakhstan too, heroes of the past are remembered – especially Abul Khair Khan and Ablai Khan, who were able to unite a considerable number of Kazakh tribes in the eighteenth century in the struggle against the Dzungars. A particularly important figure in Kazakh historical mythology is also Genghis Khan, the ancestor of Abul Khair Khan and Ablai Khan. Many nationalists seek to link the famous Mongol conqueror of the thirteenth century with the history of the formation of the Kazakh people. Furthermore, in 2000, Kazakhstan celebrated the 1,500th anniversary of the city of Turkestan, which sports an ancient mausoleum constructed by Tamerlane. Finally, in 2002, Kazakhstan celebrated 2,000 years of the city of Taraz. However, all these historical associations and symbols come second to the extolling of Kazakhstan's recent, post-Soviet achievements.[15]

Turkmenistan has created its own, in many ways unique, variant of national history which combines the traits of other nationalisms. Saparmurat Niyazov, leader of Turkmenistan, took charge of this personally, publishing in 2001 the work *Ruhnama* (the second volume of which appeared in 2004).[16] All of the presidents of Central Asian states have made their mark in the literary sphere, but Niyazov's work, devoted to the history and culture of the Turkmen people, has gone furthest by acquiring the official status of the principal 'spiritual' book of the nation, second only to the Quran – it is compulsory reading in all Turkmenistan's schools and universities, and regularly cited in the press and in inscriptions on monuments (including mosques). Niyazov's book takes the form of a personal monologue about the antiquity and history of the Turkmen, their moral code, their cultural values and customs. His own reflections were thereby transformed into an official, never questioned, account of the essence of the Turkmen nation.

In his work Niyazov did not focus on any one particular historical figure or period. Instead, the entire history of the Turkmen and their ancestors has been divided into a series of stages, each with its own prophet: Oghuz Khan, Gorkut Ata, Gorogly and others. All states that ever existed on the territory of today's Turkmenistan have been proclaimed Turkmen. Numerous Eastern rulers and dynasties have been transformed into Turkmen. All significant figures have their monuments and anniversaries. Thus, an entire cosmogony of Turkmen nationalism has been created, with the wholesale renaming of territories and cities, and even with changes being made to the names of months and days of the week. The final outcome of Turkmen history is the current epoch, headed by a new prophet – Niyazov himself, who, in 1993, received the official title of Turkmenbashi, leader of all Turkmen. Considerable attention by both state and society was devoted to his honour and to the honour of his late mother, who died in the earthquake of 1948. The personality cult of the Turkmenbashi combined the past and the present, creating a unique national mythology.

Thus, the history of Central Asia, just like its territory, appears to have been divided between the new national states.

THE NATION AND ITS LANGUAGES

Central Asian nationalisms are linguistic in their internal organization. Language plays the role of one of the main symbols of the nation, its 'soul' and core value. Care of the language is considered to be one of the primary duties of Central Asian politicians who have the task of building their national states. Common to all countries in Central Asia is the aim to make the language of the titular nation into their respective state's principal means of communication, thereby avoiding dependence on Russia in the symbolic realm, while also facilitating the social mobility of the rural population, for whom the lack of knowledge of Russian has been a persistent obstacle to development. Laws about state languages, which promoted the status of the languages of titular nations, were among the first laws to be passed in the new Central Asian states.

Another common tendency is the search for and the construction of an authentic national language. Here there is a contradiction between the desire, on the one hand, to make this language understandable and truly 'one's own' and, on the other, to make it both diverse and functional. In each of the five Central Asian states the problem of language has its own idiosyncrasies.

In Kazakhstan and Kyrgyzstan the most troubling question has been the country's relationship to Russian, which used to be the principal language of most people who were ethnically not Kazakhs or Kyrgyz, as well as of many Kazakhs and Kyrgyz themselves, especially the elite. In 1994 Russian regained official status in Kyrgyzstan and in 2000 it was proclaimed the second official language alongside Kyrgyz, the latter retaining the status of the state language. In internal state communication Kazakh and Kyrgyz leaders use Russian alongside their respective 'titular' languages in equal measure, sometimes even mixing the two together. Nevertheless, certain legal clauses that limit the rights of Russian-speaking citizens have remained in place – such as the stipulation that the knowledge of the titular language is a prerequisite for any candidate for the president of Kyrgyzstan. This is linked to the conception of Russian as, symbolically, the language of 'the other', incompatible with Kazakh and Kyrgyz identity. This in turn creates sociocultural distinctions within the population, questioning whether a Kazakh or a Kyrgyz whose principal language is Russian is 'authentic' or 'inauthentic'.

In Kazakhstan and Kyrgyzstan, laws instigating a shift from the Cyrillic alphabet to a Latin-based script have been prepared, but remain at the blueprint stage. By contrast the Turkmen and Uzbek authorities have been very radical in their linguistic reforms.[17] They not only unequivocally proclaimed their respective titular languages as the only official ones, completely excluding Russian from this sphere, but they also swapped the Cyrillic alphabet for the Latin one. Turkmenistan passed such a law in 1993 and Uzbekistan followed suit in 1995 (Karakalpakstan, an autonomous republic within Uzbekistan, had introduced its own version of the Latin script in 1994, but corrections needed to be made to it later on). In the mid-1990s the Latin script had started to be taught in Uzbek and Turkmen schools. This gesture, common to many Turkic-speaking elites in the former Soviet space, symbolized a total break with the Russian past. At the same time, the choice of a Latin-based rather than an Arabic-based alphabet pointed not towards the past of the region, but to a completely different, secular-modernist tradition of Kemalist Turkey, in which the Uzbek and, to some degree, the Turkmen elite had always sought an alternative to the Soviet path of modernization. It is true, though, that in everyday life, in the press and in book-publishing, the Cyrillic alphabet has not retreated completely even in these countries. Russian is still used since it remains the native tongue of the 'non-titular' section of the population as well as of many members of the titular intelligentsia. Indeed, the official functions of titular languages as national symbols are to a large extent out of step with real-life linguistic practice. In Tajikistan, which the Russian-speaking population by and large deserted during the civil war in the 1990s, there were no special laws defining the status of the Russian language, although the latter continues to play an important role in the life of the Russian-speaking Tajik intelligentsia. In the 2000s there were some discussions about gradually abandoning Russian in the official sphere. In 2007 President Rakhmon publicly announced the need for an official dictionary of personal and place names that would conform with the norms of the Tajik language. At the same time the question of the alphabet has stayed outside the authorities' purview. A totally separate sore topic for Tajikistan is the question of the language (and hence the ethnic identity) of the Pamir peoples occupying the autonomous province of Gorno-Badakhshan.

THE NATION AND ITS RELIGION

The most vexed question of contemporary Central Asian nationalisms is their relationship to Islam as the principal religion of all the titular nations in the region. In Central Asia, nations were formed in the 1920s as a result of a tacit agreement between the Bolsheviks and the local elites. One of the compulsory conditions of this agreement was the secular nature of nationalism – i.e. a rejection of religion as a source of legitimacy and identity. Religious heritage was accepted only if it was understood as part of national cultural traditions, devoid of any kind of religiosity.[18] At the beginning of the 1990s this agreement ceased to function and the authorities in the region were compelled to develop their own relationship with Islam. Islam offers tempting opportunities, but also creates new risks. On the one hand, its legalization allows the new states to make a clearer break with the Soviet past and offers the national ideologues many new instruments for resurrecting an 'authentic' national history. On the other hand, the strengthening of religious sentiments as well as of radical Islamist activism presents a serious threat to the internal stability of these countries and to the survival of the existing Central Asian regimes. Islam's universalist rhetoric challenges the very principle of national statehood in Central Asia. However, the balance of opportunities and risks is different in different parts of the region.

In Kazakhstan and Kyrgyzstan a considerable proportion of the titular population has reacted rather passively and indifferently to the idea of reviving religious values and institutions. For them religiousness has retained significance only as an element of ritual practice, which was something already characteristic of the Kazakhs and the Kyrgyz in the past, when their nomadic communities only weakly adhered to Islamic dogma, combining it readily with other customs. A certain, by no means large, section of the population of these two states, especially those in the southern regions, on the border with Uzbekistan, has welcomed the Islamic revival much more enthusiastically. Here one even finds adepts of radical Islamism. Finally, some Kazakhs and Kyrgyz have also converted to various neo-Protestant sects. Thus, the Kazakh and Kyrgyz authorities are forced to manoeuvre between these three numerically quite unequal groups, while also taking into account the interests of the non-Muslim Russian-speaking population and the more intensely Islamized Uzbek minority.

In Turkmenistan, the display of religiosity has been introduced into official Turkmen nationalism and placed under close state supervision. The Uzbek authorities follow a similar strategy, doing everything to retain Islamic tradition within a national framework, eradicating any illicit deviations. However, the complex composition of Uzbek society, an influential religious heritage, social problems and a stronger influence of external forces all work to limit the ability of the Uzbek elite to retain total control over the country's religious practices. The most direct conflict between nationalism and Islam is evident in Tajikistan, where, during the civil war in the mid-1990s, the opposing factions offered contrasting models of the interaction of state and religion. In trying to mobilize supporters, the opposition, headed by the leaders of the Islamic Renaissance Party of Tajikistan, at first insisted that Islamic values and laws must be at the centre of Tajik state-building. However, Tajik society reacted rather warily to such a proposition. After the conclusion of peace in 1997, the Islamic Renaissance Party acquired legal status, but gradually lost mass support and in the end had to relinquish several of its most radical slogans, shifting the emphasis of its rhetoric from religion to nationalism. Secular nationalism became victorious at this stage, proving that nationalist slogans were stronger than religious ones for uniting society and resolving its internal conflicts. The Pamir ethnic groups deserve separate mention, since for them the 'revival' of Ismailism and of the idea that they belong to the 'empire' of Aga Khan has had the effect of strengthening their independent identity.[19] Nevertheless, the Tajik authorities have so far managed to keep this separate ethno-religious identity within the boundaries of the Tajik nation.

THE NATION AND ITS TERRITORY

In Central Asian nationalisms, territory is not only the space that a nation occupies but also a key source of the national imagination. The landscape, the climate, the flora and fauna – all of this is seen as belonging to the nation, is intimately connected with it, and is lauded and represented together with other national symbols. The cult of the horse in Turkmenistan, the cult of Lake Issyk Kul in Kyrgyzstan, cotton as one of the symbols of Uzbekistan, the cult of the mountains in Tajikistan, the Aral Sea in Karakalpakstan, the endless steppes of Kazakhstan – all these are visual icons of particular types of Central Asian nationalisms. Territory roots the nation in nature and gives its people a sense that they live in their own home, on the land of their ancestors, on the land where they were born and that belongs to them. Accordingly, each titular Central Asian nation portrays itself differently on the mental map of the world. All Central Asian states, with the exception of Tajikistan, fuse their real territory with an imagined one. However, national territory does not necessarily fully coincide with state borders. Indeed, as a rule it extends beyond them and spreads onto the territory of the neighbouring states. Nevertheless, specific territorial claims and border disputes are not of themselves dangerous, nor do they inevitably destabilize the region as a whole.

More controversial is the question of what represents the 'centre' or 'core' of Central Asia. Uzbek nationalism aspires to the role of such a regional centre insofar as it has the largest human resources as well as the main historical symbols. In the early 1990s President I. Karimov came up with the idea of a union dubbed 'Turkestan – our common home', which presupposed the lead role of Uzbekistan in Central Asia. However, this idea, with its emphasis on Uzbek 'centrality', did not inspire much enthusiasm in the surrounding states. President Nursultan Nazarbaev proposed instead the alternative of Kazakh leadership, via the project of a Eurasian Union. At its base lay the economic achievements of Kazakhstan and its energy resources, connecting Central Asia to Russia and Europe. Nazarbaev's plan has been partially realized in the structures of the Eurasian Economic Community. Other variants of 'centrality' can be found in Turkmenistan's idea of 'international neutrality' and the idea of Kyrgyzstan as 'the most democratic country in Central Asia'.

By contrast the spatial image of the Tajik 'nation' has formed into something rather different and rather more problematic. The Tajik elite is not happy with the boundaries within which Tajikistan was confined in the 1920s. In the 1990s there emerged the concept of 'Historical Tajikistan', which, according to the interpretation of academician Numon Negmatov, 'occupied the entire western foot of the high ranges of "Upper Asia", the mountain knot of the Himalayas and Tibet, the entirety of the Tian Shan, Pamir-Altai and Hindu Kush mountain ranges, the Iranian plateau, the basins of the rivers Amu Darya, Syr Darya, Morghab and Geri Rud'.[20] In AD 1000 'Historical Tajikistan' was therefore supposed to occupy the entire territory of today's Uzbekistan and Tajikistan and a considerable part of Kyrgyzstan and Turkmenistan, as well as sections of the territory of today's Kazakhstan, China, Afghanistan and Iran! This definition has, nevertheless, practically assumed official status and is represented in particular Tajik state symbols. On the central square of the Tajik capital Dushanbe, next to the complex devoted to the memory of Ismail Samani, there also appeared a stone map showing the boundaries of this 'Greater Tajikistan'.

However, the notion of 'Historical Tajikistan' puts before Tajik nationalism the difficult question of the relationship between the Tajiks and the Iranians (Persians). Some ideologists propose that the Tajiks should be considered part of a 'Greater Iranian Nation'.[21] On the one hand, this allows the Tajiks to make legitimate claims to everything that belongs to Iranian cultural and historical heritage; on the other, however, it places the Tajiks in a subordinate and peripheral position in relation to the more powerful and larger Iran, undermining the independence of Tajik statehood. The task of protecting 'Tajik-ness' and of preventing it from dissolving into 'Iranian-ness' creates huge problems, since the difference between the Tajiks and the Iranians is mostly religious in nature (the former being Sunni and the latter Shia Muslims) rather than cultural or linguistic.

The idea of 'Historical Tajikistan' with the capital in Bukhara (now in Uzbekistan) also generates in Tajik nationalism a sense of trauma over the loss of its 'primordial' or 'core' territory. For expansion, Tajik nationalism looks not southwards, towards Afghanistan and Iran, where there are millions of Iranian-speaking Sunnis, but northwards, towards Uzbekistan, where lie the supposed principal 'Tajik' cities of Bukhara and Samarkand. The 'sacred' land of Bukhara is present even symbolically in the Ismail Samani complex in Dushanbe, substituting for the evident lack of 'centrality' of Tajikistan's actual capital. In this respect Tajik nationalism is the mirror image of Uzbek nationalism. The leaders of Tajikistan are not prepared officially to assert their territorial claims over Uzbekistan, but nor are they ready to forget their territorial 'losses' since this idea of traumatic loss plays such a pivotal role in Tajik nationalist ideology.

There is one other nationalism in Central Asia – that of the Uyghur – whose ideology is similarly based on the memory of a forsaken homeland. The Uyghur (in the past the Taranchi and the Kashgar), who have been living in Central Asia in compact groups for many generations, continue to view themselves as 'newcomers' to this area, whose homeland is still in China. Other, smaller, nationalisms in the region – the Dungan, the Korean, the Arab etc. – have a similar character.

THE NATION AND ITS DIASPORA

One of the problems of Central Asian nationalisms is the issue of diasporas. 'Compatriots' living outside their 'proper' state can provoke all manner of positive national feelings towards themselves, such as pride, curiosity, expectations and concerns for their wellbeing. At the same time, however, they can also be vaguely experienced as a potential threat or competition, and as a source of some unacceptable interpretations of the national idea. Each of the five Central Asian states has a distinct way of dealing with this problem.

In Kazakhstan and Kyrgyzstan interest in the Kazakh and Kyrgyz diaspora has not dominated public consciousness. 'Compatriots' living abroad were remembered only when the nationalists became aware of the need to increase the proportion of the titular nationality in the overall ethnic composition of the country. In the 1990s Kazakh and Kyrgyz nationalist ideologues worried over the fact that their respective titular nationalities barely formed an absolute majority in 'their' countries (only 50 per cent of the population of Kazakhstan being Kazakh and 60 per cent of Kyrgyzstan, Kyrgyz). This has led to the setting up of programmes for 'repatriating' the Kazakhs and the Kyrgyz from abroad. Some migrants were attracted by this programme, but such 'repatriation' never became a mass movement. Moreover, these migrants often discovered that they were culturally very different from their supposed compatriots.

The Tajik elite experiences the question of its diaspora as something particularly painful. When ethnic groups and territories were being divided in the 1920s, a considerable proportion of the Iranian-speaking population of Central Asia (including those who were bilingual) ended up living in republics surrounding Tajikistan, especially Uzbekistan, where they were registered as 'Uzbek'. The leaders and ideologues of Tajik nationalism cannot hope to create their 'Greater/Historical Tajikistan' in reality, but they are not abandoning the idea of rebuilding it into a conglomerate of Tajik diasporas clustering around contemporary Tajikistan. For this purpose they organized a Global Summit of Tajik and Persian-Speaking Peoples of the World, which was first staged in 1992 and then met regularly in subsequent years. The Tajik strategy towards its diasporas amounts to 'reminding' the 'Tajiks' who live outside Tajikistan that they really are Tajik. The ethnicity to which Tajik nationalists are appealing is emphatically objectivist: it does not matter how these 'Tajiks' actually feel or what they call themselves (since they often call themselves 'Uzbeks'); what is important is whether they speak Tajik, whether they have European facial features, and whether their lifestyle and culture happen to be settled – if this is the case, they are 'Tajik' regardless of what they themselves might claim. Tajik nationalists focus primarily on the Iranian-speaking population of Bukhara and Samarkand, where there are people ready to call themselves 'Tajik' and portray themselves as a diaspora. 'Potential' Tajiks of the Fergana Valley, Kyrgyzstan and Kazakhstan are of less interest to them. There is also little active discussion of the 'Tajik diaspora' in Afghanistan.[22]

In Turkmenistan the understanding of the Turkmen diaspora is extremely contradictory. In 1991 the state formed a Humanitarian Association of the Turkmen of the World, which was presided over by Saparmurat Niyazov and which staged international summits. However, the country's pride in the fact that there are so many Turkmen (and those who can be represented as Turkmen) living outside Turkmenistan (mostly in the Middle East and other parts of Central Asia) is combined with a complete absence of any government policy with regard to the integration of these Turkmen into a single community.

The position of Uzbekistan towards its diaspora is very different. Since Uzbek nationalism frames itself more in terms of its nation state and less in terms of its ethnic culture, it displays minimal interest in Uzbeks who are citizens of other states. In one of his books Islam Karimov states: 'there is only one Uzbek nation in this world and there are no national differences between the Khorezmians, the Ferganians or the Surkhandaryans – they are all Uzbek'.[23] In this list any Uzbeks who live outside Uzbekistan are effectively 'forgotten' and arbitrarily excluded from the 'Uzbek nation'.

THE NATION AND ITS MINORITIES

The logic whereby the state shows interest only in its titular nation naturally raises the question of the status and the rights of peoples and groups who do not belong to the titular nation. Central Asian nationalisms unequivocally treat the Russian-speaking population as 'aliens' and 'newcomers', even when these people have lived in these areas for over a century and a half (and in some parts of Kazakhstan even longer than that). Even more complicated is the status of 'minorities' who have been living there longer still. In Kazakhstan and Kyrgyzstan, for example, there is a substantial Uzbek community; in Tajikistan, a large Kyrgyz and Uzbek one; in Turkmenistan there are many Kazakhs and Uzbeks; in Uzbekistan there are Kazakh, Kyrgyz and Tajik groups. All these non-titular populations experience problems with preserving their native languages, with pursuing their education, with social mobility, with getting work in state institutions and with obtaining positions in political structures. They are often frustrated and perceive themselves to be suffering discrimination. This is not to say that Central Asian leaders and elites do not understand the difficulties of dealing with minorities. The prevailing ethnic dimension of Central Asian nationalisms creates insurmountable fissures in these societies, splitting them between 'us' and 'them', between the 'loyal' and 'disloyal' parts of the population, which in turn threatens political stability and creates obstacles to economic development.

In all Central Asian states there are strategies for integrating 'ethnic minorities' into societies where priority is still reserved for the titular nation. The most popular forms of integration are the creation of ethno-cultural societies for minorities and the organization of 'ethnic assemblies', as well as the setting up of informal quotas for representatives of minorities in organs of power at different levels. In fighting the real or illusory threat that ethnic minorities appear to pose, the authorities of all Central Asian states are generally dedicated to weakening them as much as possible, which is why they encourage their fragmentation into smaller ethnic or pseudo-ethnic communities. In Tajikistan an experiment was carried out during the census in 2000 where the 'Uzbeks' were divided into further ethnic subcategories of independent tribes, such as the Lokaians, the Kungurats etc.[24] However, such strategies fail to eliminate the fundamental problem of the division of these countries' citizens into 'us' and 'them'; on the contrary, they only further underscore ethnic differences, strengthening them through political and social practice.

Another strategy for solving the problem of minorities is their assimilation into the titular nation. This strategy is used in one form or another by all Central Asian countries, but the most consistent and firm policies in this direction have been implemented by Uzbekistan. The principal targets of assimilation are Uzbekistan's Iranian-speaking inhabitants. President Karimov, who, it is asserted, himself comes from this section of Uzbek society, proclaimed in one of his speeches that: 'we are essentially one people who speaks in two different languages, Tajik and Uzbek'.[25] This idea did not lead to any further theoretical development by Uzbek ideologists, but in practice it has become something of a semi-official ideology. In Karimov's work *Uzbekistan on the Threshold of the Twenty-First Century*, alongside the usual discussions about the antiquity of the Uzbek 'ethnos', one can also find a critique of the policy, 'carried out by the Russian Empire and then continued by Soviet authorities, of drawing arbitrary administrative-territorial borders between Central Asian republics'.[26] It transpires from some parts of this book that the Uzbek president would prefer a situation where the different ethnic groups were not divided by national borders but lived in a kind of symbiosis with one another: 'in Turkestan there was a mixture of tribes and peoples ... who were intimately tied with one another through the commonness of their cultures and languages. This mosaic-like ethnic map of the region was made possible by the ethno-cultural and religious closeness of the different peoples who inhabited it'.[27] This approach, at the heart of which lie assimilationist and hegemonic ambitions, in effect questions ethnicity itself as the main principle for the construction of a national state.

The Kazakh leader Nursultan Nazarbaev went even further when, in one of his speeches in 2007, he announced the existence of a 'Kazakhstani nation'.[28] This essentially signified a rejection of the notion of the 'titular nation' and replaced the ethnic interpretation of the nation with a civic one. Whether this idea will be able to overcome the inertia of the past and to attract larger numbers of supporters from among the various different strata of Central Asian society remains to be seen.

CONCLUSION

The process of nation-building in Central Asia, which began in the late Russian Empire and continued with renewed effort in the USSR, reached a whole new level in 1991. At that point, Russo-Soviet patronage ceased and the local elites were forced to choose their own path of development, having to overcome all the problems and difficulties that their choices might bring about. The various nationalisms in Central Asia preserve the 'Soviet matrix' which was part of the original project of their construction in the 1920s, and they retain a variety of common 'Soviet' features.[29] Despite many similarities between the different Central Asian nationalisms, their responses to contem-porary challenges of nation-building are actually quite varied. Each Central

Asian nationalism creates its own representation of its past and its future, trying to work out its own distinct recipe for development.

Translated by Andy Byford and Mark Bassin

NOTES

1. B. Anderson, *Imagined Communities: Reflections on the Origin and Spread of Nationalism*, rev. edn (London, 2006), xiv.
2. A. Haugen, *The Establishment of National Republics in Soviet Central Asia* (New York, 2003); F. Hirsch, *Empire of Nations: Ethnographic Knowledge and the Making of the Soviet Union* (Ithaca, NY, 2005); T. Martin, *The Affirmative Action Empire: Nation and Nationalism in the Soviet Union, 1923–1939* (Ithaca, NY, 2001).
3. G. Smith, 'Post-colonialism and Borderland Identities', in *Nation-Building in the Post-Soviet Borderlands: The Politics of National Identities*, ed. G. Smith, V. Law, A. Wilson, A. Bohr and E. Allworth (Cambridge, 1998), 15–16.
4. Y. Slezkine, 'The USSR as a Communal Apartment, or, How a Socialist State Promoted Ethnic Particularism', *Slavic Review* 53:2 (1994), 414–52. Also see, on the problem of forgetting and recollection of earlier local categorizations in Central Asia, S. Abashin, 'Vozvrashchenie sartov? Metodologiia i ideologiia v postsovetskikh nauchnykh diskussiakh', *Antropologicheskii forum* 10 (2009), 252–78.
5. S. Timchenko, 'Problemy prisoedinenia Kazakhstana k Rossii v sovremennoi kazakhstanskoi istoriografii', in *Tsentral'naia Aziia v sostave Rossiiskoi imperii*, ed. S. Abashin, D. Arapov and N. Bekmakhanova (Moscow, 2008), 338–59.
6. E. Rakhmonov, *Tadzhiki v zerkale istorii* (London, [no date]), 128, 210.
7. Cf. R. Masov, *Istoriia topornogo razdeleniia* (Dushanbe, 1991); R. Masov, *Tadzhiki: pod grifom 'sekretno'* (Dushanbe, 1995); R. Masov, *Tadzhiki: vytesnenie i assimiliatsiia* (Dushanbe, 2004).
8. Rakhmonov, *Tadzhiki v zerkale istorii*, 218.
9. For a more detailed examination, see S. Abashin, 'Mustakillik i pamiat' ob imperskom proshlom: prokhodia po zalam tashkentskogo Muzeia pamiati zhertv repressii', *Neprikosnovennyi zapas* 66 (2009), 37–54.
10. E. Siever, 'Uzbekistan's Mahalla: From Soviet to Absolutist Residential Community Associations', *Journal of International and Comparative Law at Chicago-Kent* 2 (2002), 91–158; V. Koroteyeva and E. Makarova, 'The Assertion of Uzbek National Identity: Nativization or State-Building Process', in *Post-Soviet Central Asia*, ed. T. Atabaki and J. O'Kane (London, 1998), 137–43.
11. A. March, 'The Use and Abuse of History: "National Ideology" as Transcendental Object in Islam Karimov's "Ideology of National Independence"', *Central Asian Survey* 21:4 (2002), 371–84.
12. This idea was actively supported by the former Kyrgyz president Askar Akaev. A. Akaev, *Kyrgyzskaia gosudarstvennost'i narodnyi epos 'Manas'* (Bishkek, 2002).

168 SERGEI ABASHIN

13. M. Laruelle, 'The Return of the Aryan Myth: Tajikistan in the Search of the Secularized National Ideology', *Nationalities Papers* 35:1 (2007), 51–70. For an account of the discussion among historians of Central Asia about the 'Aryan legacy', see V. Shnirelman, 'Aryans or Proto-Turks? Contested Ancestors in Contemporary Central Asia', *Nationalities Papers* 37:5 (2009), 557–87.
14. P. Shozimov, *Tadzhikskaia identichnost' i gosudarstvennoe stroitel'stvo v Tadzhikistane* (Dushanbe, 2003), 172–3.
15. B. Dave, *Kazakhstan: Ethnicity, Language and Power* (London, 2007), 159.
16. A. Kuru, 'Between the State and Cultural Zones: Nation Building in Turkmenistan', *Central Asian Survey* 1:21 (2002), 71–90; M. Denison, 'The Art of the Impossible: Political Symbolism, and the Creation of National Identity and Collective Memory in Turkmenistan', *Europe-Asia Studies* 61:7 (2009), 1167–87. The new president of Turkmenistan, Gurbanguly Berdymukhammedov, continues to support the ideological narrative of his predecessor, if in a more moderate version and without its highly personalized aspects.
17. A. Kosmarskii, 'Smysly latinizatsii v Uzbekistane (konets XX – nachalo XXI veka)', *Vestnik Evrazii* 3 (2003), 66–71.
18. A. Khalid, *Islam after Communism: Religion and Politics in Central Asia* (Berkeley, CA, 2007).
19. L. Monogarova, 'Assimiliatsiia i konsolidatsiia pamirskikh narodov', in *Sredneaziatskii etnograficheskii sbornik* (Moscow, 2001), 47–52; T. Kalandarov, 'Etnokonfessional'nye transformatsii na Pamire v XX – nachale XXI v.', in *Iazyki i etnografiia 'Kryshi mira'* (St Petersburg, 2005), 51–63.
20. N. Negmatov, *Tadzhikskii fenomen: teoriia i istoriia* (Dushanbe, 1997), 21–2.
21. For a discussion on this topic see S. Tabarov, *Spor 'derevenskogo intelligenta's gorodskim intelligentom'* (Dushanbe, 2004).
22. Negmatov, *Tadzhikskii fenomen*, 106.
23. I. Karimov, *Uzbekistan na poroge XXI veka: ugrozy bezopasnosti, usloviia i garantii progressa* (Tashkent, 1997), 99.
24. O. Ferrando, 'Manipulating the Census: Ethnic Minorities in the Nationalizing States of Central Asia', *Nationalities Papers* 36:3 (2002), 489–520.
25. A. Djumaev, 'Nation-Building, Culture, and Problems of Ethnocultural Identity in Central Asia: The Case of Uzbekistan', in *Can Liberal Pluralism Be Exported? Western Political Theory and Ethnic Relations in Eastern Europe*, ed. W. Kymlicka and M. Opalska (Oxford, 2001), 328–30.
26. Karimov, *Uzbekistan na poroge*, 72–3.
27. Ibid., 73.
28. E. Iazeva, 'Natsional'naia ideia sovremennogo Kazakhstana: problemy, poiski, resheniia', *Vseobshchaia istoriia* 4 (2009), 3–14.
29. O. Roy, *The New Central Asia: The Creation of Nations* (London, 2000), 166; L. Adams, *The Spectacular State: Culture and National Identity in Uzbekistan* (Durham, NC, 2010), 151–2.

PART IV

Spaces of national identity

CHAPTER 9

Soviet and post-Soviet Moscow: literary reality or nightmare?

Dina Khapaeva

Moscow sprawling below, all lit up, bright, with a holiday look, as usual: it may be a feast in time of plague, but at least it's a resplendent one.

Sergei Luk'ianenko[1]

Moscow salami, where the life is so balmy.

Viktor Pelevin[2]

Anyone who has taken even a passing interest in Soviet culture knows that descriptions of Moscow abounded in official literature and journalism, with depictions of the architecture of the 'workers' and peasants' capital' acting as direct visual legitimation of propaganda claims. In praising this architecturally perfect city, this storehouse of ancient cultural values and masterpieces of the Soviet builder's art, the values of socialism were asserted and underpinned. Such celebrations of the city became inventories of 'monuments of history and culture', of selected famous buildings, streets and avenues. Red Square, the Kremlin and Red Porch, the Red Gates, the Kremlin Chimes on Spasskaia Gate, the Bolshoi Theatre, Tverskoi Boulevard, the Garden Ring ... It is notable that even Bolshevik cult sites, the Lenin Mausoleum for example, had the primary function of architectural attractions, despite the apparently overwhelming importance of the political symbolism attached to them.

Soviet Moscow was the nation's capital in a particularly active sense. Not only was it the centre in every practical respect (administrative, financial, cultural), but the symbolic centre – the place that every socialist city was supposed to emulate, and the city that every citizen was supposed to love and cherish more than his or her own birthplace. Moscow stood for all Soviet achievements, and for the country in general, as in the famous song 'Moscow in May' by Vasilii Lebedev-Kumach (1938):

The morning beautifies with tender light
The walls of the ancient Kremlin,
The entire Soviet nation
Wakens with the dawn.
Beyond the gates streams cool air,
The noise on the streets is stronger,
Good morning, dear city,
Heart of my motherland![3]

Attachment to one's *malaia rodina* was (at least until the late 1960s) considered suspect, but taking patriotic pride in Moscow was completely proper and appropriate. Schoolchildren all over the country wrote essays and poems about their love of Moscow, as in the case of sixteen-year-old Aleksandr Kobelianskii's 'Parade', published in 1939:

Red Square is festively joyous,
The grey walls of the Kremlin rise up,
With the bright flame of red banners
The flags glimmer, burning in the sun.
With gold the stars on the towers shine,
A loud cry of greeting is heard.
It is our leaders taking their places
On the tribune. Everyone greets them.
And there, rising in his grey greatcoat,
Near, dear, familiar, down-to-earth . . .
Louder the ovations instantly thundered:
'Long live Stalin – the helmsman of the country!'[4]

The uniqueness of Moscow as a focal point of communist ideology and propaganda is best reflected in a passage produced by a canonical Soviet writer, the 'Red Count', Alexei Tolstoy, in his article 'Rodina' ('Motherland'):

Moscow is more than a strategic point, more than the capital of a state. Moscow is an idea that embraces our culture in its national dynamism. Through Moscow lies our path into the future.[5]

'Motherland' evokes a vision of the communist mission which was widely shared by pro-communist left-wing Western intellectuals in the mid-1930s. In the context of the rise of fascism in Europe, Soviet Russia and Soviet Moscow, its 'heart', were imagined as the 'future of humanity', as 'humanity's only hope', to quote a famous phrase by Romain Rolland from the late 1930s.[6] Tolstoy's text also reflects the new turn of Stalinist historical propaganda in the late 1930s. The radical rejection of Russian pre-revolutionary history and the values of the 'dark tsarist age' characterizing

Figure 9.1 Yuri Pimenov, *New Moscow* (1937).

the first twenty years of Soviet power was gone. Now the task was to stimulate the patriotic feelings of Soviet citizens by incorporating Russian imperial history into the Soviet historical narrative.[7]

In actual fact, Moscow was, in the course of the 1930s, transformed into a (*the*) model socialist city – which resulted in the almost complete devastation of the pre-revolutionary urban environment. This 'modernized' city was reflected in the visual arts and literature. For example, Iurii Pimenov's painting *Novaia Moskva* ('New Moscow', 1937) shows the attractive back of a woman driver as she sails down the bright, bustling spaces of the newly constructed Garden Ring (Figure 9.1).

This sunlit, colourful image – full of optimism and joy, like many other pictures and novels of the Soviet *belle époque* – should not hide the fact that the transformation of Moscow's architectural design was explicitly conceived as a monument for the Stalinist terror, serving to represent this artistically and to legitimate it politically. One of the most famous

representations of Moscow as an urban utopia come to life was created by
Lion Feuchtwanger in his *Moscow, 1937* (the print run of his book, translated into Russian and published the same year, shortly after the writer's
visit to Moscow, was 200,000 copies):

One stands on a small raised platform before the gigantic model which represents
the Moscow of 1945 – a Moscow which bears the same relationship to the present-
day Moscow as the latter does to that of the Tsars, which was little more than a large
village ... The vast diagonals which divide up the city, the circular roads which
intersect them, the boulevards, the radial streets, the primary and secondary roads,
blocks of offices and flats, industrial buildings and parks, schools, government
offices, hospitals, educational and recreational centers – all are laid out with geo-
metrical precision. Never before has a city of millions of inhabitants been completely rebuilt with such scrupulous regard for the laws of suitableness and hence
beauty as this new Moscow.[8]

Providing an 'objective' and 'disinterested' viewpoint from a non-
communist foreign writer 'loyal' to the Soviet cause, *Moscow, 1937* fed
directly into the mainstream of Stalinist propaganda.[9] Composed of two
parts, one on the reconstruction of Moscow, another on the show trials,
Feuchtwanger's book – like many other texts by Soviet writers and journalists of the time – openly linked the Terror with the vision of new life
exemplified by Moscow in its transformed state. This intimate link between
Moscow's architectural beauty and political terror was also supported by the
claim that terror was always an integral part of Russian political life.
Turning Ivan the Terrible into Stalin's predecessor,[10] Soviet propaganda
presented the *oprichnina*, the campaign of terror which Ivan the Terrible
established in 1565–72, as a kind of peculiar 'social contract' between the tsar
and the people against the rich, as much a habitual part of Russian culture as
was Moscow's urban landscape. In the words of Alexei Tolstoy:

Viewed from the Poklonnaia gora, she [Moscow] seemed a city out of a fairy tale –
embowered in gardens and groves. The centre of the life of the people was Red
Square; here trading took place, here the people congregated at times of trouble
and unrest, from here the tsars ... addressed their people, here executions took
place, here the famous scene, the scene of Shakespearian force, the scene expressing the planning of a genius took place between Ivan the Terrible and his people –
the *oprichnina* coup ... [Moscow] continues to be the heart of the power of the
people, a treasure of the Russian language and culture, a source of enlightenment
and free thinking.[11]

At one and the same time, as we see from this quotation, political terror was
presented as a pure expression of 'the power of the people' (*narodovlastie*)
and of free thinking (*svobodomyslie*).

Figure 9.2 'Glory to You, Invincible Moscow', poster for the 800th anniversary
of the founding of Moscow, 1947.

The main colours in the imaginary Soviet capital were red and gold. The
city was depicted as a kind of enormous Khokhloma lacquer box, as seen
through the eyes of a naive visitor (Figure 9.2):

> Moscow is the red porch of Russia,
> Moscow is the red gates of Russia.
> Tverskoi Boulevard, the Garden Ring,
> And the poured gold of domes.[12]

Moscow was a symbol of Bolshevik strength and might, a place where the
'songs of Dunaevskii soaked straight into your blood'. One such song,
which became the official hymn of Moscow in 1995, was the hugely popular

'My Dear Moscow' (1942), whose chorus is still universally known today, and which began with the words:

> I've knocked about the world a bit,
> I've lived in mud huts, trenches, the taiga,
> *I've been buried alive twice over,*
> I've known partings. I've loved in anguish.[13]

The oblique association that rose up under the pen of the Stalinist poet will act for us here as Ariadne's thread, guiding us through the labyrinth of changes that Moscow has endured in the post-Soviet era. Leaving aside the issue of whether the city actually does have qualities that might turn it into a lair for monsters, I shall consider here how it has played such a role in the post-Soviet mind. I shall trace how the image of the city has shifted and into which aesthetic conventions it has been inscribed. I shall also reflect on the connections of this image with the current state of historical memory and recollections of the USSR.

I am not primarily concerned here with the actual transformation of Moscow's fabric, though that has been highly significant in the post-Soviet era. Entire historic districts were totally remodelled – Arbat in the 1990s, followed by Zamoskvorech'e in the 2000s – and the city acquired a series of eye-widening trophy buildings and monuments. Iurii Luzhkov, who was mayor of the city for nearly two decades until his summary deposition in September 2010, was a supremely enthusiastic patron of architects and monument-builders, notably of the Georgian sculptor Zurab Tsereteli, whose notorious statue of Peter I counterpoints the rebuilt Cathedral of Christ the Redeemer at the heart of the city. Rather than concentrate on the reworking of the city's fabric (which has been much discussed elsewhere),[14] I shall look at the place of Moscow in the post-Soviet imaginary.

At the centre of my discussion will be two writers – Sergei Luk'ianenko and Viktor Pelevin – who might be considered to represent the two antipodes of contemporary Russian culture. If Luk'ianenko is the author of bestsellers and has no special pretensions to a philosophical understanding of today's reality, Pelevin might be described as one of the most vivid intellectual writers of today. Luk'ianenko's prose could be seen as a *symptom* of cultural change, while Pelevin, who is extraordinarily sensitive to aesthetic change, is an acute and observant *analyst* of the changes affecting culture and society. This does not, however, stop him experimenting with new trends in aesthetics, parodying them and indeed including them directly in his work.

So what has the post-Soviet era in fact added to the literary image of Moscow? In order to answer this question, let us turn to the texts themselves, since they make clear which features of the city have attracted post-Soviet writers and turned it into an essential background for their narratives.

It is striking that, for all the lack of resemblance between the two writers in many other ways, the descriptions of the corners of the city where their novels are set should be so similar. The unfailing attributes of fictional post-Soviet Moscow are kiosks selling vodka, spit-spattered tram-stops, main-line stations pullulating with people.[15] Almost always, refuse is at the centre of the *mise en scène*. Even if a 'prestigious' Stalin-era block should happen to figure – 'a top-level Soviet apartment block with Volgas outside, high-rise, and with a kind of Western look to it'[16] – it is still emphasized that the stairwell is thick with cigarette ends. A favourite place for encounters and denouements and for the hero's first appearance and so on is these filthy stairwells with 'graffiti and the traces of heavy boot-soles on the walls, smashed bulbs and cacky lifts'.[17] If the hero walks through Moscow, then he certainly won't avoid the entrances to courtyards – grimy, stinking, eerie[18] – the favourite places for murderers to strike in Moscow (and not just Moscow – other Russian cities as well). Such details are used like children's building blocks to construct Moscow's urban landscape:

Reaching the end of the building [a huge Stalin-era block], Schwarzneger [*sic*] walked through a courtyard entrance as big as a triumphal arch . . . They walked round a little playground with swings and dived into a labyrinth of narrow passages between rusty garages made of metal sheeting . . . Then suddenly the entrances opened up into empty space surrounded by metal panels in different colours and heights . . . Underfoot, as you'd expect, there were empty bottles lying round and also the usual garage trash: old tyres, the crushed side door of a Lada and a huge quantity of metallic refuse of unknown mechanical origin.[19]

So what about the 'monuments of history and culture'? What does the architectural image of the city look like in the prose of post-Soviet writers? To begin with, there are remarkably few descriptions of such monuments; for instance, on Tverskoi Boulevard the eye may be caught by the stone urns standing on the edges of staircases and (invariably) filled with rubbish and empty bottles,[20] and 'Pushkin wilting in a fug of exhaust fumes'.[21]

The enigmatic disappearance of Moscow monuments, historical sites and 'places of interest' from the Moscow text was pioneered in Venedikt Erofeev's famous novel *Moskva-Petushki* (first published in Israel in 1973 and in Russia in 1989). The influence of this novel on post-Soviet prose could hardly be overestimated. The central symbols of Soviet pride, places of the most important political rituals[22] such as Red Square, simply disappeared without a trace, and become inaccessible for the inhabitants. The traditional Soviet Moscow celebrated by Alexei Tolstoy and others vanished as completely as Kitezh, the legendary drowned city:

> Everyone says, 'The Kremlin, the Kremlin.' I hear about it from everybody, but I have never seen it myself. How many times (thousands) I've walked, drunk or hung over, across Moscow from north to south, east to west, from one end to the other, one way or another, and never did I see the Kremlin.
>
> Take yesterday. Again I didn't see it, and I spent the whole evening wandering around those parts, and I wasn't even so drunk . . . Then I headed for the center of town, since it always works out that when I'm looking for the Kremlin I end up at the Kursk Station. In fact, I really did have to go to the Kursk Station and not the center of town, but I set out for the center all the same in order to see the Kremlin at least once, meanwhile thinking, 'I won't see any Kremlin anyway and I'll end up right at the Kursk Station.'
>
> Now I'm almost in tears, feeling so sorry for myself. Not because I didn't get to the Kursk Station yesterday, of course. (That's nonsense – if not yesterday, then today I'll get there.)[23]

Erofeev portrayed the critical moment when the official propaganda image of Moscow, created to veil the nightmares of Soviet existence, gave way to the new image of Moscow. The architectural splendour of Moscow, its 'hauts lieux de mémoire' (high places of memory) had turned into 'non-lieux', into 'blank spots' of memory (*belye piatna*, a euphemism for the Soviet repressions invented during perestroika). Yet even in its elided state, the Soviet image of Moscow remained critically important for the understanding of post-Soviet texts. The official image of the city as a Khokhloma lacquer box had been reduced to the level of a kitsch tourist souvenir, yet it acted as 'literary reality' in the post-Soviet texts about Moscow, a background against which true nightmares could rise high.

By 'literary reality' I mean the portrayal of a realm free of supernatural phenomena such as monsters, the delineation of what is taken to be the habitual course of events in texts whose major goal is to communicate the feeling of a nightmare. Nightmare has to be opposed to literary reality, otherwise it loses its persuasive power over minds. Literary reality is a *sine qua non* condition of nightmare's existence; it hides the nightmare domain and at the same time points to it; it veils the nightmare domain, yet empowers its representation in a given text.[24] Just so, Soviet texts on Moscow create the background against which the post-Soviet texts emerge;

they are manifestations of a literary reality that disguises and unmasks the nightmares of the Soviet experience. They produce the hidden settings which condition the nightmares of post-Soviet historical memory.

It is worth noting that the viewpoint adopted by post-Soviet writers when looking at Moscow is utterly different from that of Soviet writers. It is now the ordinary inhabitant of the capital, rather than the privileged tourist gazing from the windows of the Hotel Rossiia, whose viewpoint we share, and this person sees Moscow from the inside, and hence quite differently. Usually, the action is set in some dormitory suburb and not on Red Square or in 'the House on the Embankment'.[25] Yet these areas are certainly not represented in a realistic way: 'I stopped on a street down which a tram was crawling . . . The block was monstrous. Flat, with the juice sucked out of it, stuck up on kind of twiggy legs. At first glance it looked like a gigantic pagan memorial to a matchbox. Later, the embodiment of morbid gigantomania.'[26] Such nightmare buildings are a highly effective backdrop, conveying a sense of suffocation and claustrophobia, the inhabitants' incapacity to influence their own lives and fates:

It was quiet. Kind of extraordinarily quiet, even for a Moscow dormitory suburb at this late hour. As though everyone was packed into their flats and lying soundless under their duvets, wrapped up to the top of their heads. 'Lying soundless' – not sleeping. The only movement was the flickering, purplish patches of light – TVs on everywhere. People had got used to living like this – turning on the TV and just watching whatever was on, from the shopping channel to the news. People can't see the world of shadows. But they can feel it closing in.[27]

These high-rise districts don't just generate lifeless despair and apathy, willingness to submit to anything. They also create an urban milieu where the main mood is the sense of being abandoned, of being excluded among people dragging out their dreary existence, of 'being sucked out', of being cut off from civilization (Figure 9.3): 'The Soviet skyscraper provoked an insidious sense of despair, an apparently unfounded but extremely vivid sensation. I've sometimes had this sense when I've been travelling on a train through ruined villages or half-wrecked grain elevators. It's so out of place, it's over the top, it feels like a slap in the face.'[28] Even the protagonists find it hard to believe in the ugliness of the urban environment:

Coming out of Nagornaia metro station onto the surface . . . Serdiuk immediately saw the steel-encased fence, but he couldn't believe this was the one Mr Nobunaga had meant: it was just too ugly and too filthy . . . The places around

Figure 9.3 Contrasting faces of post-Soviet Moscow.

were really wild, they looked like bomb sites, overgrown with weed, in an
industrial area ... From out of the weeds bits of scrap iron stuck out, there
was lots of space and open sky, and black stripes of forest showed on the
horizon.[29]

Not surprisingly, even when it comes to descriptions of warm summer
days, it is emphasized that nothing becomes Moscow like the leaving of it.
The promise of a faint chance of getting out is the only thing that makes the
city bearable. Here the two writers speak as one:

It was cold in the flat, the radiators were hardly warm at all. The only thing that makes me like the winter is that it gets dark early and there aren't many people about. Otherwise I'd have got the hell out to Yalta or Sochi ages ago.[30]

Or again,

What's good about Moscow in the summer isn't the houses or the streets, but the sense of mysterious possibility – the places you could go to beyond Moscow. The hint of this hung everywhere: in the breeze, the bright clouds, the fluff off the poplars.[31]

The Moscow climate seems to underline the inhuman dimension of the narratives. The settings are not just unpleasant, they are close to unbearable. Usually bitter frost or heavy snow is the backdrop; an exception is made only for savage heatwaves. In Moscow it is either damp or freezing, either burning hot or stifling.

Now to the colours: dirt is the main shade in which Moscow is painted. The dominant colour is grey, or at best off-white, the hue of soiled snow or snow mixed with mud. Above all, Moscow is a grey city.[32] The passers-by and cars are all mired in filth: 'Almost immediately a car shaped like a rain-drop shuddered to a halt, it was plastered all over with filthy snow.'[33] The gamut of colours is made up by filthy tramps standing against grey high-rise. Only occasionally does a flash of lightning or the deathly glow of a TV break through: cf. above, 'flickering, purplish patches of light – TVs on everywhere'. Or: 'Mr Nobunaga's description – "you'll see a block of flats" – suited several dozen buildings in his field of view. Serdiuk decided, for whatever reason, that the one he wanted was the grey eight-storey block with the picture-window deli on the ground floor.'[34] The grey, dirty city has its own particular reeks: 'It stank of rotting food out of the refuse chute. Beyond the window was the roar of a main road vanishing into the gloom. The street lights were already beginning to fade.'[35]

But greyness in itself is not the point. The main feature of the Moscow air and atmosphere is the grey *gloom* that hangs over everything. Certainly, this gloom, in Luk'ianenko's books, has a special symbolic role: it is where the unclean spirits live (the shapeshifters, vampires or *Others*), and these beings' capacity to seep into this special medium is what constitutes their onto-logical difference from humans.[36] Pelevin too never stops referring in his books to this grey gloom.[37]

Sometimes strange sparks fly up in the gloom of the grey city: an odd spinning sensation makes itself felt and the big city is simply swallowed up. And although it is not necessarily unclean spirits that emerge, the gloom still has far from pleasant associations: '"It's getting cold," Serdiuk observed, looking round and instinctively feeling that any minute now, a police patrol would emerge from the damp Moscow air.'[38] A sharp sense of danger is the main feeling the gloom induces.

But the main characteristic of the Moscow setting is nevertheless not this gloom and dirt as witnessed by the Muscovites themselves. Both in Luk'ianenko's novels and in Pelevin's, the main action takes place somewhere else – in the city's underground maw. Metro stations and the underpasses near them are the most important settings for the unclean spirits to have their set-tos and attack human beings.[39] The main elevators often live underground or in buildings that closely resemble bunkers, or indeed actually are bunkers. Could one imagine a better setting than this city for communicating a sense of a nightmare?

What is more, both these immensely popular authors – like many of their less successful competitors in the profession – select non-humans (neliudi) as their central characters. The inhabitants of Moscow's sprawling suburbs are their victims, prey or inferior allies. Whether these non-humans hunt humans or even sometimes try to protect them, whether they see them as beef cattle or milch cows makes no odds – they always despise them. Vampires, shapeshifters such as werewolves and witches are the heroes of Pelevin's novels, as they are of Luk'ianenko's. They throng the post-Soviet capital, whose image is an exact aesthetic replication of their own.

In my book *Gothic Society: The Morphology of a Nightmare* (2007)[40] I used the concept of 'Gothic aesthetics' to explain a powerful trend in contemporary culture, where non-humans – a specific kind of monsters – become the protagonists of novels, movies and computer games, and where the main content of these cultural products, their form and their ultimate goal are the representation of a nightmare.

Certainly, the history of literary monsters is not limited to contemporary culture. However, in other eras their role – be it Hamlet's father's ghost, Mephistopheles or Bulgakov's Woland – was to second the plot's main hero, a human; the non-human's function was to fight against him/her, to represent his/her alter ego and so on.

The reason for focusing on non-humans and not supermen stems once more from the deep disillusion in humankind, their world and their capacities. For instance, the very title of Pelevin's novel *Empire 'V': A Tale of a Real Superman* shows how it is now the vampire, not Zarathustra, who has become the real 'superman'.

As I argued in *Gothic Society*, it is not the mere presence of monsters in post-Soviet literature that is at issue, but the direct link between these monsters and suppressed memory. Post-Soviet fiction, despite its predilection for the genre of fantasy, can therefore be used as a source for understanding the mechanisms of historical memory in post-Soviet Russia. The specifics of post-Soviet literature lie in the question of how monsters behave and what they do, or, more accurately, how they reflect the changes occurring in Russian society. If the Gothic aesthetics have succeeded in becoming the symbol of such changes, the aesthetic matrix for the conceptualization of special social relations, that is because a not-worked-through past lies at the root of Gothic society, a lack of desire to consider and to recognize the issue of responsibility for the crimes committed in the Soviet years, and above all for the political repressions of the Lenin and Stalin eras.

Post-Soviet fiction differs from its Western counterpart because it reflects the emergence of a new moral order and social relations which are profoundly influenced by the distorted memory of Stalinism and current historical amnesia. It reflects how Gothic morality and Gothic society have emerged out of the experience of a criminal past and an abortive project of repentance, out of efforts to present Stalinism as a part of 'our glorious history'.

A monster – a vampire, a dragon – cannot be assessed by ordinary human criteria. Disappointment with hypocritical Soviet morality and its travesty of basic humanistic values is widespread, yet the Orthodox Church has also failed to convince society of its right to lay the foundations for moral consensus in the multinational and multi-confessional society. This has resulted in a moral vacuum. Under these conditions, the non-human monster has become the catalysing point for the emergence of a new moral order and of new social relations in post-Soviet society.

An element in Gothic morality that is absolutely central is that good and evil are totally symmetrical and not to be distinguished from each other in any way. It follows that discrimination between good and evil becomes a matter of subjective judgement alone, resting on no norms of any kind, and that such judgement is the sole basis for the identification of categories and criteria. Gothic morality is situational: the essence of prohibitions and the degree of what is permitted are totally determined by the tastes of those in power – most often by the heads of clans, a term which I use to embrace not only mafia organizations but 'legitimate' companies, corporations, and educational and cultural institutions. In turn, such morality cannot pretend to impose obligations upon outsiders. What any such authority figure today terms 'morality' will not have any meaning for those beyond his or her circle. Universalizing morality has been replaced by morality as a deictic gesture,[41] invoking one particular concrete situation that is to be decided here and now – but which, for this very reason, does not need to be described in abstract and universal terms.

If one says that post-Soviet Moscow is full of memories of the Soviet era, one has essentially said nothing. Rather, the city is *made* of memories of Soviet terror, just as post-Soviet prose itself is. Pelevin is a writer who has made an invaluable contribution to the criticism and destruction of Soviet discourse, and he is especially sensitive to memories of everything Soviet. He denounces and mocks such memories unmercifully. And of course, his protagonists do not ignore such memories either. Luk'ianenko's heroes, on the other hand, are as unselfconscious about remembering the Soviet period as most of Luk'ianenko's fellow citizens (and this is typical of other authors too). This is a world where Dzerzhinsky remains a central cultural and historical symbol, and the 'Great Patriotic [War]' the apotheosis of radiant heroism.[42] In Luk'ianenko's work the shapeshifters and vampires in their FSB-agent and banker masks are embodiments of the 'conscience of our age'. For them, the derring-do of the Red Army in the Civil War and 'Stalin's Falcons' in the Great Patriotic War preserve the power of exemplary heroism, valour and courage: they have the force of a moral example. The author and his millions of readers are searching for confirmation of their own moral judgements in the record of barbarism and terror that Luk'ianenko's novels set out, because the history of post-Soviet forgetting has left them no other option. 'We were taught one thing: to give and to take nothing in return. To sacrifice ourselves on behalf of others. To make every step as if walking into a hail of machine-gun fire, to make our gaze noble and wise, not a single empty thought or sinful desire. For we are the Others,' says the shapeshifter, the hero of *Night Watch*:

We've had enough! Our hearts are burning, our hands are clean, our minds are cold as ice . . . Can it be chance that in the Revolution and the Civil War, the Shining Ones almost all joined the Cheka? And if they didn't, they mostly went to the bad. From the hands of the Dark Ones, but even more from the hands of those they were defending. From human hands. From human stupidity, baseness, cowardice, hypocrisy, envy. Our hearts are burning, our hands are clean. Our heads remain cold as ice. Or it cannot be done. But I don't agree with the rest. Let my heart be clean, and my hands burn. That's how I like it![43]

This is Luk'ianenko's entire 'treasure house of metaphors', his 'myth kitty', his complete set of strategies for 'working through the past'. In these reflections by the vampire-raisonneur, the Cheka remains a completely romantic and elevated image; the bloody language of the secret police is the sole point of moral orientation that follows the hero through the novel. It sits sweetly alongside the hero's conviction that communism and fascism amount to the same thing,[44] and his renunciation of belief in any collective project. The 'motto of Dzerzhinsky' – 'Our hearts are burning, our hands are clean, our minds are cold as ice!' – cannot give the hero any support in discriminating good from evil, and this leads to a radical denial of the right of human nature to exist, as expressed in the question 'Am I to live for your sake?' which the vampire addresses to humanity.[45] The real nightmare in Luk'ianenko's novel expresses itself not only through vampires and the otherworldly forces of evil. Rather, it lies in the collapse of the distinction between good and evil and the preaching of the message of trivial egotism that has rushed in to fill the vacuum. Witches, vampires, unclean spirits – here they are, the real heroes of the national nightmare, born in the gloom, spawned by the psychoses of suppressed memory and rising up to realize themselves in post-Soviet literature.[46]

If one thinks about what most resembles this image of Moscow that we have sketched here, then what comes to mind is Joseph Brodsky's lines: 'The Kremlin darkens like a "zone". They say, in miniature.'[47] A prison camp of high-rise blocks, settled by people who have no rights, who are defenceless before the all-powerful non-humans – this is how the symbolic capital of Gothic society is portrayed.

Moscow is an ideal backdrop for Gothic aesthetics turning into Gothic society: it is a city that emerges as an eminently suitable space for nightmares, or for admixtures of these and reality. The nature of modern Moscow facilitates the aesthetic expression of the nightmare owing to its architectural design built to glorify terror.

Let me turn now to the work of Pelevin in order to illustrate how these qualities may be combined. The way that Pelevin's creative principles have developed over time also acts as a demonstration of how the Gothic aesthetic itself has evolved in post-Soviet fiction.

The upsurge of the Gothic aesthetic in contemporary culture goes back to the late 1990s, when several important tendencies acted simultaneously to underpin and to strengthen its development.[48] At this point Pelevin uses as a fulcrum the reflections on the borders of the human and on the boundaries of the transformation of the literary character into a non-human that had been set out in his early novel *Wizard Ignat and People* (1989), where humans and non-humans are opposed already in its title. In *The Zombification of Soviet Man* (1990), reflections on the key points of Soviet history and experiments in the creation of the 'new Soviet man' are directly linked by the writer with reflections on the borders of the human and the non-human. After that he wrote *A Werewolf's Problems in the Central Belt* (1991). In this bold experiment the protagonist's transformation into a werewolf becomes the central subject of the narrative. Simultaneously,

Pelevin becomes interested in the nature of dream and writes a short story 'Fall Asleep'. In *Chapaev and Emptiness* (1996) it is the fusion and elision of the borders between reality, literary reality and the nightmare that are at the centre of his attention. In his next novel, *The Life of Insects*, Pelevin continues his search for a non-human hero, for the boundaries of the human and the non-human. But in his two other novels, *The Sacred Book of the Werewolf* (2004) and *Empire 'V'* (2006), werewolves and vampires once and for all turn into the main characters, indeed more or less the only characters, since now humans practically do not feature, even in minor roles.

As numerous critics have noted, *Empire 'V'* falls neatly into the genre of the *Bildungsroman*, 'maturation narrative', and it is no accident that the book is often compared with classics of the genre. But there is one significant difference between these novels and Pelevin's, which oddly enough seems to have gone unnoticed: the main character and role model for young people is another specimen of non-humans – in this case, a vampire.

It is worth noting that Gothic allusions are widespread in Pelevin's prose, just as they are in the prose of other post-Soviet authors. An example is when Pelevin comments, with reference to the tendency in post-Soviet state symbolism to hark back to the Russian imperial symbolism of the nineteenth century, that in fact it would make more sense to revive the symbolism of the feudal era, given that this era is in every way more similar to the present than the culture of the last but one century.[49]

Equally, in his prose, fences, checkpoints, camouflage scrim are vital details of the Moscow landscape: features symbolizing not just militarism, but atomization behind proliferating ugly walls, and recalling feudal decay, the rise of clans. Behind the concealing fences is the secret world of the non-humans, unknown to mere humans.

In an interview Pelevin has directly linked the characteristic features of the Gothic aesthetic – the fact that non-humans, monsters, act as the central characters, and that the nightmare becomes the main expressive means – and the city as the ideal place for realizing the potential of these features. In response to the question 'Why vampires all of a sudden?' he replies:

OK, I just wrote a book about them. But they've interested me for a long time. I had this instinctive feeling that in Russia, a vampire's more than just a vampire. And I tried to show just how much . . .

I think my vampires are much scarier. Horrible things aren't all the same. We've got used to some of them – they've been around since we were kids, and we've just stopped noticing. I think it's hard to imagine anything scarier than modern cities. What is a city? Somewhere people live because in the past lots of them died there . . .

A city is loads and loads of stories like that, multiplied together. When the crushing lack of meaning in such lives overcomes fear of death, you get wars starting. When fear of death is uppermost, peace rules. So the swings and round-abouts go on, that's our daily life. We watch Bram Stoker's *Dracula* to escape, to relax and give ourselves a breather.[50]

Here Pelevin gives a clear statement of the peculiar relevance of the new Gothic aesthetic to post-Soviet reality, an aesthetic that has found partic-ularly important expression in the transformation of the image of Soviet Moscow, formerly a shrine of red and gold sweetness and harmony. At the same time, the Gothic visions of Pelevin and Luk'ianenko represent not so much the 'return of the repressed' as realizations of a violent potential always inherent in the original Stalinist vision of Moscow, where terror and architectural triumph were intertwined.

Translated by Catriona Kelly

NOTES

I would like to express my deep gratitude to Catriona Kelly for many valuable suggestions that greatly improved this text, as well as for her elegant translation.
1. S. Luk'ianenko, *Nochnoi dozor* (Moscow, 2006), 239.
2. V. Pelevin, *Empire 'V'* (Moscow, 2006), 315.
3. V. Lebedev-Kumach, 'Moskva maiskaia', music by Pokrass brothers (1938), http://rutube.ru/tracks/655523.html?v=9dd4a729ffbfbe43f3dd75bdeaa1cce5.
4. 'Rodina i Stalin v tvorchestve detei', *Literatura v shkole* 6 (1939), 14. On Soviet ideological indoctrination and attitudes to Soviet upbringing, and the complex-ity and compromises of this, see C. Kelly, *Children's World: Growing Up in Russia, 1890–1991* (New Haven, CT, 2008), esp. ch. 3.
5. A. Tolstoy, 'Rodina' (1941), *Sobranie sochinenii*, ed. V. P. Szerbyi (Moscow, 1972), vol. VI, 449. On Stalinism's political culture, see J. Brooks, *Thank You, Comrade Stalin! Soviet Public Culture from Revolution to Cold War* (Princeton, NJ, 1999).
6. On the importance of the opposition fascism/communism and its impact on the Western Left, see F. Furet, *Le Passé d'une illusion: essais sur l'idée du communisme au XX siècle* (Paris, 1997).
7. E. Dobrenko, *Muzei revoliutsii: sovetskoe kino i stalinskii istoricheskii narrativ* (Moscow, 2008); N. Koposov, *Pamiat' strogogo rezhima: istoriia i politika v Rossii* (Moscow, 2011).
8. L. Feuchtwanger, *Moscow, 1937: My Visit Described for My Friends*, trans. I. Josephy (New York, 1937), ch. 1, 'Work and Leisure', www.revolutionaryde-mocracy.org/archive/feucht.htm#1). For a discussion of this text, and of Moscow in the Stalin era, see also K. Schlögel, *Moskau 1937: Terror und Traum* (Munich, 2007).

9. On the fellow travellers and their contribution to the success of Stalinist prop- aganda, see D. Cote, *The Fellow-Travelers* (New York, 1973); P. Hollander, *Political Pilgrims: Travels of Western Intellectuals to the Soviet Union, China, and Cuba, 1928–1978* (Oxford, 1981); C. Prochasson, *Les Intellectuels, le socialisme et la guerre, 1900–1938* (Paris, 1993).

10. M. Perrie, *The Cult of Ivan the Terrible in Stalin's Russia* (Basingstoke, 2001); K. M. F. Platt and D. Brandenberger, 'Terribly Romantic, Terribly Progressive, or Terribly Tragic: Rehabilitating Ivan IV under I. V. Stalin', *Russian Review* 58:4 (1999), 635–54; K. M. F. Platt, *Terror and Greatness: Ivan and Peter as Russian Myths* (Ithaca, NY, 2011).

11. Tolstoy, 'Rodina', 449.

12. Nikolai Nikishin, 'Moskva Rossii krasnoe kryl'tso' (1985), http://moscow. gramota.ru/poetoo.shtml.

13. M. Lisianskii, 'Gimn goroda Moskvy', music by I. Dunaevskii, www.mos.ru/ documents/index.php?id_4=126923. Emphasis added.

14. Studies of the transformation of Moscow in the Soviet and post-Soviet period include T. Colton, *Moscow: Governing the Socialist Metropolis* (Cambridge, MA, 1998); K. Schlögel, *Moscow* (London, 2005); S. Bittner, *The Many Lives of Khrushchev's Thaw: Experience and Memory in Moscow's Arbat* (Ithaca, NY, 2008); A. Bronovitskaya, C. Cecil and E. Harris, *Moscow Heritage at Crisis Point*, rev. and expanded edn (Moscow, 2009); G. Basilico, *Vertiginous Moscow: Stalin's City Today* (London, 2009).

15. Cf. Luk'ianenko, *Nochnoi dozor*, 9, 16, 20.

16. Pelevin, *Empire 'V'*, 14.

17. Luk'ianenko, *Nochnoi dozor*, 70, 107.

18. V. Pelevin, *Chapaev i pustota* (Moscow, 2004), 31. Cf. Luk'ianenko, *Nochnoi dozor*, 70.

19. Pelevin, *Chapaev*, 81.

20. V. Pelevin, *Sviashchennaia kniga oborotnia* (Moscow, 2005), 184.

21. Cf. also Pelevin's description of a monument to Griboedov (Pelevin, *Chapaev*, 239).

22. On political rituals, see C. Lane, *The Rites of Rulers: Ritual in Industrial Society. The Soviet Case* (Cambridge, 1981); N. Tumarkin, *Lenin Lives! The Lenin Cult in Soviet Russia* (Cambridge, MA, 1983), and also Albert Baiburin's contribu- tion in this volume.

23. V. Erofeev, *Moscow to the End of the Line*, trans. H. W. Tjalsma (Evanston, IL, 1994), 13–14.

24. The concept 'literary reality' is developed in detail in my book *Koshmar: literatura i zhizn'* (Moscow, 2010), 86–92. As a brief illustration of how it functions here, let me give two contrasting examples. For instance, one of Luk'ianenko's characters denies that unclean spirits exist, insists that they are unreal, only to have his utterance instantly disproved by another kind of 'reality' – the appearance of unclean spirits, who duly proceed to attack him. Pelevin, on the other hand, uses exactly the opposite strategy in his *Sacred Book of the Werewolf*: a were-fox, speaking in the first person, categorically rejects the concept of 'positive reality' with reference to the transformation

of a shape-changer, something that has just 'really' taken place in the narrative itself ('Can we describe a transformation like this as real? I've never really understood the meaning of that term, particularly as every era assigns its own meaning to it': Pelevin, *Sviashchennaia kniga*, 263). Pelevin follows his great predecessors – Gogol and Dostoevsky – who were equally concerned with the problem of the threshold separating nightmare, reality and literary reality, and for whom the experiments with the nightmare and with readers' perceptions lay at the heart of their literary projects. For detailed analysis of this see: Khapaeva, *Koshmar*, chapters 'Neokonchennye oputy nad chitatelem' and 'Nemota koshmara'.

25. The elite party apartment block opposite the Kremlin, the setting for a famous novel by Iurii Trifonov, *Dom na naberezhnoi* (1976); for an English version, see *Another Life: The House on the Embankment*, trans. M. Glenny (London, 1986).

26. Luk'ianenko, *Nochnoi dozor*, 65.

27. Ibid., 42.

28. Ibid., 259.

29. Pelevin, *Chapaev*, 229.

30. Luk'ianenko, *Nochnoi dozor*, 11.

31. Pelevin, *Empire 'V'*, 24.

32. Luk'ianenko, *Nochnoi dozor*, passim.

33. Pelevin, *Chapaev*, 464.

34. Ibid., 230.

35. Luk'ianenko, *Nochnoi dozor*, 88.

36. Ibid., 40, 51, 126, 246, 371.

37. Pelevin, *Sviashchennaia kniga*, 26.

38. Pelevin, *Chapaev*, 256.

39. Luk'ianenko, *Nochnoi dozor*, 7.

40. D. Khapaeva, *Goticheskoe obshchestvo: morfologiia koshmara* (Moscow, 2007; 2nd edn, 2008). A French translation by N. Kehayan, *La Société gothique* (Paris), is forthcoming.

41. On deictic gesture, see further in N. Koposov, *De l'imagination historique* (Paris, 2009).

42. Luk'ianenko, *Nochnoi dozor*, 364.

43. Ibid., 321–2.

44. Ibid., 343.

45. Ibid., 322.

46. Khapaeva, *Goticheskoe obshchestvo*, 35–41, esp. 37.

47. I. Brodskii, 'Predstavlenie', *Osennii krik iastreba* (Leningrad, 1990), 101.

48. Khapaeva, *Goticheskoe obshchestvo*, 57–77; Khapaeva, *Koshmar*, 261–90.

49. 'Some time ago, I noted the Russian government's kitschy tendency to identify itself constantly with the magnificent shade of imperial history and culture, to assign itself a patent of nobility, a certificate of noble origins, despite the fact that it has about as much in common with pre-revolutionary Russia as a Langobard grazing his goats among the ruins of the Forum with the Flavian dynasty ... But perhaps the problem is less

their invocation of the past as such, than their unfortunate choice of era. They should have gone back to the chronicles of feudal times, not to imperial eagles, where they would have found fellow spirits in plenty.' Pelevin, *Sviashchennaia kniga*, 87.

50. N. Kochetkova, 'Pisatel' Viktor Pelevin: "Vampir v Rossii bol'she, chem vampire"', 3 November 2006, www.izvestia.ru/reading/article3098114.

CHAPTER 10

From the USSR to the Orient: national and ethnic symbols in the city text of Elista

Elza-Bair Guchinova

Elista, the capital of Kalmykia, is also the only city in the republic. In 2008 its population stood at 102,000, or one-third of the population of Kalmykia overall. In the post-Soviet years, Elista underwent a crucial process of transformation, which affected toponyms, monuments and major public buildings. This process was at once highly specific – being related to perceptions of the Kalmyks' history and political role – and typical for Soviet urban centres. In what follows, I shall analyse it and set it in context.

HISTORICAL BACKGROUND

Elista's name comes from the Kalmyk word meaning 'sandy'. The first reference to the existence of a settlement on this site goes back to 1865. However, at the start of the twentieth century, the Kalmyks were still a nomadic people, and their steppe territory included no urban settlements. Prior to 1917, Elista had a low administrative status. Between 1888 and 1907 it was a canton (*volost'*) town; from 1907, the centre of the Manychsk *ulus*. After the Revolution the centre of the Kalmyk Autonomous Province (set up in 1920) was at first located in Astrakhan, since there was no settlement in the Kalmyk steppes that was capable of fulfilling the role of an administrative centre. However, in 1927 the Council of People's Commissars of the RSFSR moved the centre of the province from Astrakhan to Elista. In 1930 a decree of the Presidium of the VTsIK (All-Russian Central Executive Committee) of the RSFSR assigned Elista the status of a city (as opposed to 'settlement' or other such 'populated point'),[1] and in 1935 it became the official capital of the Kalmyk Autonomous Soviet Socialist Republic (ASSR). In the conditions of the totalitarian Stalinist state, the primary function of the capital of an autonomous republic was to act as the centre for regional administration, a function that was also central to planning. Not

191

surprisingly, the only building in the city with any pretensions to architectural merit was the House of Soviets, built in 1932 to designs by Il'ya Golosov.

As is well known, the Kalmyks were one of the peoples to suffer deportation en masse in the Stalin years, in retribution for their supposed collaboration with the Nazis during the period of occupation and their disloyalty to Soviet power. On 28 December 1943 the entire Kalmyk population was loaded onto cattle trucks and taken by rail to the Novosibirsk, Omsk, Tomsk and Krasnoyarsk provinces of Siberia. By the summer of 1944 the total of those deported, which now included Kalmyks from the provinces bordering the ASSR and military personnel from the front, had reached 120,000. The ASSR ceased to exist; its territory was partly assigned to the newly formed Astrakhan province, and partly to other provinces in the region.[2] Elista was occupied by the Germans for five months, and thereafter the city (like the Kalmyks themselves) was subjected to political repression. Its name was changed to Stepnoi (the City of the Steppe), and after the Kalmyks were forcibly exiled it was inhabited exclusively by Slavs (Russians, Ukrainians etc.). The Kalmyk Republic ceased to exist, and its former capital lost its administrative function. Nothing was done even to repair war damage.

The process of restoration of Kalmyk autonomy began in 1956. When the Kalmyks came back to their republic in 1957–8, the town was still in ruins. Though Elista had regained its name and status as capital, the task of reconstruction in a material sense took longer, as fewer than ten public buildings were left. However, the population grew rapidly, and had risen to 23,000 by 1959.[3] The return of the Kalmyks from deportation to their original homeland was a process of great significance. Their supposed war guilt was annulled; not only was their capital restored to them, but so were their rights in the broadest sense. The republic was recreated from scratch, along with its capital city. The building boom of the period offered tangible proof that a new life had begun, and it is notable that informants tend to recall the developments in exactly this light: there was no Elista left when they arrived from their banishment, and everything had to be rebuilt from the bottom up: 'When I first came to Elista in 1958, there was nothing here. The Red House was there, that's it';[4] 'I came here in 1957, there was nothing here then. Not even a sapling, just sand. And the wind – you could hardly open your eyes.'[5]

Many old people remember these years, the late 1950s and early 1960s, as the happiest time in their life, although those who came back to the city had nowhere to live, no jobs and not even enough to eat. Those who had returned from Siberia – whither they had been exiled 'in perpetuity' – and who had now been declared not guilty of the charges of collaboration, felt a sense of joy that overcame any conflicts in the process of ethnic and civic identity; there was a sense of shared fate in a positive sense. It was easy to create what Benedict Anderson famously described as an 'imagined community'. The community administration revived the old tradition of constructing *saman* (wattle and daub) houses collectively. One weekend people would build somewhere to live for one family, and the next weekend for another. In the early 1960s Aleksei Balakaev's 'Elista Waltz' – a song from an operetta of the same name about the young people building the city – became quite a hit:[6] 'Enkr Elst zurknd oor, en balgsn – mini zoor' ('My native Elista is in my heart, it seems – this is the city of my dreams'). The ethnic dream about returning home and the lifting of the accusations of treachery had indeed been fulfilled, the myth of freedom and dignity restored. Girls started to be given a new name, Elistina, pointing to the centrality of the city to the restoration of Kalmykia's identity.

In the present day Elista's standing among Kalmyks rests not just on the fact that it is the capital, but also on the fact that it is the only centre of culture and education. Religion returned to the social life of Kalmykia at the end of the 1980s: Buddhist temples and stupas began to be built, regular services were conducted, the *tsam* mystery plays were performed and special ritual objects such as the mandala were brought into use. Along with this, Buddhist clerics of the highest rank – including His Holiness the fourteenth Dalai Lama – made visits in order to lead prayers. All of this has turned Kalmykia (the westernmost centre of Buddhism in the world) into a centre of pilgrimage for Buddhists all over Europe. At the same time the severe economic hardship and high levels of unemployment in the Kalmyk Republic have provoked outmigration by Kalmyks to Moscow and St Petersburg, along with a population drift into Elista from outlying regions. Natives of Elista now complain that they sometimes do not meet anyone they know out walking the streets.[7] Yet this kind of complaint about a 'deluge' of incomers from the countryside also points to the fact that Elista is acquiring a genuine urban culture.

ARCHITECTURE

The years when Elista started to be built followed the Decree on Architectural Excesses of 1955, which ushered in the drably functional *khrushchoby* (Khrushchev slums), alongside the traditional *saman* houses. The new Elista accordingly mainly consisted of pattern-book new districts and areas of private building. Micro-districts 1, 3 and 4 were all filled with the nondescript five-storey blocks typical of the day. It was in this period that the general city plan was evolved. Ulitsa Lenina (Lenin Street) was laid down as the main thoroughfare, abutting a square of the same name with the inevitable Lenin statue. In the so-called 'years of stagnation' under Leonid Brezhnev, building continued unabated. The tallest building in the city was constructed at this point – the Party Regional Committee, rising to six storeys. This building was also from a standard pattern-book, as was the city's central hotel (the three-star Rossiia). Elista still had no face of its own and looked as anonymous as any Soviet small town.

In post-Soviet Kalmykia, by contrast, important changes in self-perception have taken place. These were precipitated by the introduction of new forms of governance and the institution of the office of president of the Republic of Kalmykia, by the search for a new post-Soviet national image and for new ways of representing this to the outside world, and also by efforts to rethink local history. The fact that Kalmykia was now a republic with its own president was crucial to this new image. The Mongoloid appearance of the Kalmyks, their traditional songs and dances, and their Buddhist heritage all gained a new prominence and led to a search for new architectural forms. It was essential that the *samobytnost'*, or national specificity, of the Kalmyks be paraded before visitors and investors, and that it be reflected in the fabric of the city. The result was that Elista began to undergo a transformation, and Central Asian and Chinese architectural motifs started to proliferate. For example, Lenin Square was now closed off on two sides by golden gates and by an archway reminiscent of those in 'China Towns' the world over. In fact, structures of this kind had never been traditional in Kalmyk culture, and it was hard even to find a translation for the term 'golden gate', since the word 'gate' itself does not exist in Kalmyk. In the end, the phrase 'Altn Boskh' (Golden Structure) was decided on (Figure 10.1).

Buildings of this kind, which had never existed before but which now had been grafted onto 'Kalmyk culture', also needed an interpretive rationale. In the following example of the official interpretation of the new cultural phenomena, the analytical level recalls less a piece of academic anthropology than the kind of weak play on words of the sort you might expect in a school essay:

The archway is the main entrance to the residence, a symbol of the sacred threshold, a symbol of goodness and prosperity, the creative principle, energy, and power. Anyone who passes through the Golden Gates will be spiritually cleansed and will

Figure 10.1 Golden Gates, Elista.

enter a new path, the path of virtue – the white path. Here, as the bells chime, one's most heartfelt wishes will be realized.[8]

An archaic word from the nomadic era, *stavka* (khan's residence), is used to refer to the presidential residence, transforming it thereby into the residence of the great khan himself. The process of spiritual purification is represented just as superficially: it comes about not as the result of moral struggle, but as the automatic consequence of passing through the Archway. Buddhism is adopted simply in terms of outward behaviour.

Here we have a flourishing Kalmyk example of an invented tradition. Elista was witnessing the wholesale development of architectural forms that mix the 'classical Orient' with a sense of self-presentation that is aimed at the outside world. For this reason, a type of explicitly Western, exoticizing rationale is given – you enter through the gates not just because there is no alternative, but because you can purify your karma. The ruling elite in the city manufactured their own 'cultural brands' from a mixture of well-known Buddhist symbols and key elements of 'classical Oriental' culture, thus creating 'a corner of the Orient in the Occident', and legitimating their power. The republic's first president, Kirsan Ilyumzhinov, raising his boyish love of chess to the level of a central affair of state, initiated the building in

Elista of a 'Chess City' ('Siti Chess'),[9] creating yet another analogy to the serai of the khans. Here the main building, the Chess Palace, is constructed as a modern imitation of the traditional yurt.

However, developments inspired by cultural traditions do not in fact dominate the cityscape of modern Elista. Foremost on the post-Soviet architectural agenda is in fact the resurrection of pre-Soviet traditions. Over the years of the Soviet period, every single Buddhist temple on the current territory of the Republic of Kalmykia was destroyed. The only remaining temple, Khosheut *khurul*, was located in an area that was ceded to Astrakhan province in 1943, and never returned to the Kalmyk Republic.

Kalmykia was one of three Soviet republics whose 'titular nationalities' were by tradition Buddhists. But in Buryatia and Tuva, monasteries were allowed to remain open, and the training of monks continued. Thus, for post-Soviet Kalmykia, the building of a new Buddhist temple was considered a project of the first importance. Accordingly, in 1996, Siakiusn-siume (Holy Refuge) temple was erected, in fulfilment of one of Ilyumzhinov's central promises as part of his election campaign in 1993. The building of what was described as 'the largest Buddhist monastic complex in Europe' was one of the most important symbolic gifts presented by the new regime to the Kalmyk people. Constructed in the severe style of a Tibetan monastery, it lies not far away from Elista, but, as befits a monastery, in a tranquil area (chosen by the Dalai Lama himself). While the temple contains an apartment for His Holiness the fourteenth Dalai Lama, and also an apartment for the first president of the Republic of Kalmykia, it is 'beyond the purview' of Elista, and its distance from the urban hustle of the capital also puts it, so to speak, outside 'political space'.

These considerations led to the initiation of a project to build a Buddhist temple right in the middle of Elista, one that would also be larger and more beautiful than the one previously built. The temple, the Golden Hermitage of Buddha Shakyamuni, was constructed in record time (nine months), and duly became the most imposing structure in the Kalmyk capital (Figure 10.2).

The appearance of this gilded temple, raised above the city on an artificial mound, underlined the 'real presence' of political power in the city. Both the temples, but especially this second one, acted as a visual embodiment of Ilyumzhinov's claims to the role of national leader. At the same time, there are simply not enough priests and monks to staff all the temples that have been built in Kalmykia in recent years; a genuine revival of religious practices in the republic would have had to begin precisely with a dynamic ministry. Buildings are not enough: as the Russian Old Believer saying suggests, 'it's bods not logs that make a church' (i.e. the human factor is

Figure 10.2 The Golden Hermitage of Buddha Shakyamuni, Elista.

more important than the fabric).[10] In the present day, precisely this 'human factor' represents the biggest problem. At the same time, the Golden Temple has an especially favourable position, occupying an entire city block and facing onto two of the city's main streets, so that wherever you go, you end up passing by. It has now become the city's most famous building, appearing on calendars and advertisements everywhere. For example, the Elista–Moscow bus is shown against the background of the temple and the Kremlin. The underdevelopment of city planning in Elista makes Buddhist religious architecture the chief 'brand' of the city by default.

MEMORY AND MONUMENTS

In the Soviet period, collective memory in Kalmykia elided pre-revolutionary names, which were linked in one way or another with the 'reactionary' classes (clergy and landowners), and focused on the supposed fact of Kalmykia's 'voluntary absorption into Russia'. As was generally the case in the Soviet Union, the pre-revolutionary figures who were remembered were those who could be presented as revolutionary or 'forward thinking' (for example, the writers Pushkin and Lermontov, after whom streets were named). Lenin dismissed the entirety of Kalmyk history as 'an uninterrupted chain of suffering' ('Brother Kalmyks! The fate of your nation is an uninterrupted chain of suffering! Join the Red Army').[11] It was not worth being remembered; life was supposed to start afresh.

The selection of monuments in Elista during the Soviet period confirms this principle. There were only four of them: statues of Lenin and of Pushkin, the Memorial to the Heroes of the Civil and Great Patriotic Wars, and the equestrian monument to the Civil War hero Oka Gorodovikov. The pre-eminence of Lenin in the symbolic hierarchy is clear from the central position that his monument was assigned when it was constructed in 1970 (to commemorate the centenary of the leader's birth). Although credited to named artists (the sculptors M. and O. Manizer), it had an identikit look to it, and the positioning was also entirely conventional – as dictated by the norms of the cult in any Soviet town.

One of the most notable places in Elista constructed during the immediate post-Stalin years was the memorial with its communal grave, 'Eternal Flame' and sculptural group in the centre set up to honour the Great Patriotic War and the part played by Kalmyks in the victory (Figure 10.3). Erected in 1965, this structure would have had a central place in any Soviet city, but given the accusations of collaboration made against the Kalmyks in the Stalin era, it was especially important here. It was vital to emphasize the Kalmyks' contribution

Figure 10.3 Great Patriotic War memorial ('To the Fallen Heroes'), Elista.

and thus lay to rest the use of the actions of one group of Kalmyks to blacken the entire ethnic group, who had been deported en masse to Siberia. Accordingly, the task of constructing the monument was assigned to the leading sculptor in the republic – People's Artist of the USSR Nikita Sandzhiev. The gallery of figures included was supposed to symbolize the Kalmyks' place in the Russian Federation and their fidelity to Soviet ideals. The memorial turned out a success, and the citizens of Elista quickly came to love it. They paid visits not just on such official holidays as Victory Day, with its collective wreath-laying, but at other times as well: for example, wedding parties would almost always stop there so the bride and groom could pose for photographs in front of the Eternal Flame. In the 1970s private individuals would often lay flowers there.

In 1976 Nikita Sandzhiev designed another memorial, this time to the Civil War hero Oka Gorodovikov, but as this stood on the outskirts of the city and was hard to reach on foot, it did not make its way into the lives of locals. The choice of Pushkin as the subject of the fourth monument – apart from his *primus inter pares* status in the Soviet literary canon – was motivated by the fact that he had actually mentioned the Kalmyks in his writings. In *The Captain's Daughter* the rebel Pugachev narrates the Kalmyk tale of the raven, while in Pushkin's famous late poem 'I Have Built Myself a Monument', the poet anticipates a time when even 'the friend of the steppes, the Kalmyk' will know and love his work. These images in turn pioneered the Orientalist images of the Kalmyks that were current in Russian culture before and after 1917. Thus we can see that during the final decades of the Soviet Union Elista was being turned into the capital of an autonomous republic, but also into a standard-issue small Soviet town; the ethnic markers in the city text were pared to the minimum at this period.

In post-Soviet Elista, on the other hand, the number of monuments soared, from four to over a hundred. The association in the authorities' minds between the problematics of memory and social power meant that tribute was paid to the most varied events, and a huge range of figures – historical, folkloric, Buddhist, pagan etc. – were commemorated in bronze. This created a historical kaleidoscope, a fusion of different narrative strategies and discourses that could not be simply streamlined into a single, linear 'master text'.[12] As a recent guidebook to Russia has pointed out:

In terms of the number of monuments to the square foot, Elista now appears to top the list right across the Russian Federation. Moreover, these are not works of art in the style of Tsereteli,[13] they are perfectly tasteful, ranging from quite small objects in side streets right up to huge monuments. You can find them all over the city centre; the biggest concentration is along Lenin Street.[14]

One of Kirsan Ilyumzhinov's first acts upon coming to power was to have a statue of Buddha Shakyamuni placed next to Government House (the White House). The sculptor, Vladimir Vas'kin, used white marble and worked in a severe classical style – to the general approval of the Elista population. However, when the sculpture was finished, some activists from the Buddhist community (none of whom had ever seen an actual sculpture of the Buddha, since they had all grown up under Soviet power), began to object: how could the great Teacher be shown sitting stark naked in the middle of a public place? They insisted that the Buddha be masked in marble draperies, which was duly done. This spot has now become one of the most honoured places in Elista, and tourists and locals love to have their picture taken there. The preferred pose is to stand with one's back to the statue (despite the fact that, by tradition, turning one's back on the divinity is an act of disrespect).

In the Soviet period the ideological centre of Elista was the Lenin monument not far away from where the Buddha now is. Lenin faced the building housing the regional committee of the Communist Party, as befitted the statue of the Communist 'God' with reference to the 'cathedral' of his 'server-priests'. After 1991 Lenin of course lost his symbolic power, as did the other tokens of socialism. At the same time, his statue was not dismantled or vandalized, as happened in many other Soviet cities. The reason for this was not Kalmyk fidelity to Communism as such, but the leader's own personal links with the nation (his grandmother Anna Smirnova was a Kalmyk). In 1993, when there was talk of removing Lenin's body from its mausoleum on Red Square, Kirsan Ilyumzhinov proposed giving the mausoleum a home in Elista.

In 1994, after the statue of the Buddha was erected – it stands in an avenue next to Government House – an embarrassing contingency arose: the creation of the new sacred space had ended up making the Buddha face Lenin's back, as though he were walking behind him. Another problem was that Lenin also had his back to the Presidential Administration, which had moved in 1993 into the new building of the regional committee of the Communist Party. Accordingly, the statue of Lenin was rotated by 180 degrees, to reflect the new perceptions of necessary spatial hierarchy. Then, in the autumn of 2004, Lenin was moved 100 metres north, and the site where he had stood used for the Pagoda of Seven Days. The statue of Lenin now faces this pagoda, but the displacement from the symbolic centre of the square has made his role considerably less important.

Alongside Lenin and the Buddha, there is another important monument in central Elista, *The Boy Helping the Dragon to Fly*. Again, this was one of the earliest commissions made after Kirsan Ilyumzhinov's rise to power, and it has direct associations with him also. This is not just because of its location next to Government House (on the opposite side to Lenin), but because the youth of the figure alludes to Ilyumzhinov's own tender age when he was first elected president (he was only thirty-one at the time), as does the monument's implicit allusion to the Merkit tribe, to which Ilyumzhinov's ancestors belonged. This is one of many different portraits of President Ilyumzhinov (or the head of the Republic of Kalmykia, as his official title was) in the city. For instance, there are billboards all over Elista showing double portraits of Ilyumzhinov with Patriarch Alexy II, the Pope, and indeed portraits of Ilyumzhinov playing football, or, on the other hand, wearing the traditional dress of the khans and surrounded by his suite.

There is, however, another and quite different symbolic portrait of the former president in the capital city – Il'ia Il'f and Evgenii Petrov's trickster hero, Ostap Bender. Ilyumzhinov's political opponents commonly referred to Chess City as 'New Vasiuki', thus identifying the Kalmyk head of state with the picaro 'son of a Turkish national'.[15] Ilyumzhinov's government responded to the challenge in monumental terms, creating a statue to honour Ostap Bender, and thus humorously neutralizing an accusation that might otherwise have had subversive force. Once again, the subject of commemoration has been reassessed as a result of the process of commemoration: in the Soviet period, Bender's entrepreneurial instincts were officially regarded as reprehensible, but now the statue to him is a gesture of respect for go-getters and for the possibility of business projects that might even seem risky.

In the Soviet years Lenin Square was always empty on ordinary days. Only on state holidays did this change, with the construction of a tribune on which the leadership of the Kalmyk regional committee of the Communist Party would stand and review the parade. These parades vanished into oblivion after 1991, but the square – still always empty during the daytime – became, from 1993, a popular gathering place for Elista's young people, who would throng there from spring to autumn to listen to concerts and take part in discos. However, the construction of the Pagoda of Seven Days was accompanied by a complete remodelling of the square. The boundaries of this are now marked by kerbstones and benches, and a children's playground and giant chessboard for adults have been constructed alongside. A ceremonial place that was usually empty is now always crowded.

Monuments were also raised to different figures from the Kalmyk past. This was also quite a patchy process, given that 'Soviet history' embraced

not only party leaders and Civil War heroes, but also scholars who had
undergone political repression, victims of the wartime deportation to
Siberia, and ambiguous figures such as the first president of Kalmykia's
eponymous grandfather, Kirsan Ilyumzhinov. The latter had imposed
Soviet power on his homeland, but later shot himself, disillusioned by the
political system he had so fervently supported.

A special place in Elista's complex 'politics of memory' is occupied by the
monument *Exodus and Return* by the world-famous sculptor and former
Soviet dissident Ernst Neizvestnyi. The monument is dedicated to the
memory of the victims of the repressions of the Stalin years, and its
unveiling in 1996 was an event of major importance in Kalmykia. It stands
on an ancient burial mound in which, according to local legend, all the
secrets and memories in the universe are hidden. *Exodus and Return* lies to
the east of the city, and thus the return from the east – the direction of
banishment – is also commemorated here. A 'railway', a road of mourning,
approaches the monument, and is carried on in the footway that leads
directly up to it. The main idea is a synthesis of past and present and a
reflection of the spirit of the Kalmyk people, a spirit that should be
honoured and celebrated. A monstrous iron social and technocratic
machine tries to destroy all life, belief and culture, sucking everyone into
its maw, but the Great Spirit gives people the chance to pull down the walls
of the system and return to their native land. The monument is well
integrated into the surrounding landscape. Its peripheral position relative
to the city reflects the marginal status of the deportation, which is commemorated only on one specific day, 28 December. While the monument is
emphatically placed on an artificial mound, the path up to it leads from a
suitably abject place – one of the cattle wagons in which the Kalmyks were
deported along the railway line to Siberia in 1943.

Another important new monument is the figure of Zaya Pandita, the
creator of the written Kalmyk language. Sculpted by R. Rokchinskii in 1999,
the monument was unveiled on the 400th anniversary of Zaya Pandita's
birth, and on the 350th anniversary of his creation of the Oirat script *Todo
bichig* ('Clear Script'). In Soviet times a monument could not possibly have
been erected to Zaya Pandita, given that he was a priest and thus the
representative of a 'reactionary class', in terms of Kalmyk ideology. His
achievements were considered irrelevant, particularly since the alphabet he
created was rejected by the new regime. The sculpture stands by a building
belonging to the Kalmyk State University, and located on the fringes of the
city. The inscription is in Zaya Pandita's own Clear Script, but with a
Russian translation, because the script is readable only by specialists. This

paradox – that Kalmyks today are proud of having their own alphabet, but cannot read it[16] – is also reflected in the monument itself. While Zaya Pandita is portrayed in the prestigious medium of bronze, the statue is located right on the edge of Elista, in a marginal position.

There is also a bizarre flavour to a statue of the famous early twentieth-century *jangarchi* or singer of epics Eélyan Ovla, who is shown sitting at the edge of the park, holding his *dombra* (a traditional stringed instrument). His pose is that traditionally adopted by a social inferior or junior in the presence of social superiors or seniors, even though everyone knows that the *jangarchi* enjoyed extremely high status, and became the most important person in the auditorium when he took up his instrument to play.

A large number of monuments are devoted to figures from folklore. These include the epic heroes Jangar (the protagonist of the most famous Kalmyk epic, a cycle of stories about warriors performing stirring feats of bravery) and Hongor (one of the warriors in Jangar's train and the second most important figure in Kalmyk legend, credited with saving his land and people from enemies on many occasions). The two sculptures are on a formidable scale (the figure of Jangar is 3 metres high), and are placed on vast pedestals (10 metres high in the case of Jangar, and 7 metres high in the case of Hongor). Originally, they were both located on approach roads into the city from the northern and southern sides, but in 2009 Jangar was moved into the city itself.

One of the favourite sculptural figures in Elista is *Echo*, by the sculptor Nina Evseeva. The figure is seated in the lotus position and holds his *dombra* before him, as he listens to its silence and vacancy. The fact that he is clutching this hollow instrument to his heart points to the cultural losses of the Kalmyk people over history, and also to the scrupulous attitude of those who listen across the vacancy of history to dim resonances and echoes. Interestingly, this statue very quickly found its way into the hearts of the locals and even has a nickname, 'Dotr uga' ('No Insides').

As O. V. Riabov has observed, nations evoke emotions, and are the subject of love and of passionate feeling. Nationalism is an aesthetic as well as a political phenomenon: allegorical representations allow communities not merely to be 'imagined', but to be visualized as well.[17] Representations of the Motherland can be seen all over the former Soviet Union, particularly in the capitals of the various republics. In Kalmykia, however, there is no sculpture of this kind. It is not impossible that this absence is traceable to the ethnically mixed character of Elista's population: a 'Motherland' statue with Russian features would annoy the Kalmyk population, and vice versa. The 400th anniversary of the absorption of Kalmykia into Russia was marked by the construction of what a local press report described as 'the largest gilded monument in Russia'.[18] It was rather unimaginatively assigned the title of the 'Golden Rider', as a reflection of material and subject matter, though in fact the subject is once more Jangar. Despite the importance of the historical event commemorated by the statue, it was also placed at the city limits – and, what is more, on the southern approach road, the site of the other Jangar statue. As a result, when you drive into Elista from the south, you can now see a double image of the epic hero: first riding a winged horse, and then, a bit further on, standing lost in thought.

The post-Soviet years witnessed not just a bewildering expansion of the number of monuments in Elista, but also a complete breakdown of the tight control over planning which obtained in the Soviet period. As in other Soviet cities, the construction of monuments was a long, slow process accompanied by much bureaucratic fuss and committee work. The rare, lucrative commissions were assigned only to the best-regarded official artists, including nationally renowned figures. Since 1991, commissioning has taken place haphazardly, and no general aesthetic or technical standards have been imposed. Not surprisingly, the results have sometimes been haphazard as well. At the same time, some of the monuments are genuinely popular, including a statue of an old man in central Elista around which a full-scale cult has grown up. The tree and the bush next to him are decorated with hundreds of the multicoloured scraps of rag traditionally used to mark sacred places.

TOPONYMS

In the Soviet period the streets in the centre were assigned revolutionary names – ulitsa (in Kalmyk, *uul'ntse*) Lenina, Pionerskaia, Komsomol'skaia, Revoliutsionnaia, Kommunisticheskaia, Rosa Luxemburg, Valerian Kuibyshev – or alternatively named after Russian writers of 'progressive' credentials (Pushkin, Lermontov). There was also a whole group of streets named after the famous Soviet aviators Leonid Vinogradov, Polina Osipenko and Anatolii Serov. The last case, ulitsa Serova, was to provoke misunderstandings in the post-war era, since the NKVD general who had organized the deportation of the Kalmyks in 1943, I. A. Serov, bore the same surname, and people indignantly assumed that the street had been named in his honour. Alongside these generic dedications, local heroes were also honoured, for example, heroes of the Kalmyk resistance against the Germans such as Iurii Klykov, Tamara Khakhlynova and Volodia Kosiev. In the entire city, there was only one street with a Kalmyk name, commemorating the epic hero Jangar.

The post-Soviet toponyms of Elista, like the monuments, manifest a variety of diverse tendencies. To begin with, streets have been named after Kalmyk poets, writers and scholars (for example, the poets Aksen Suseev, Mikhail Khoninov and David Kugul'tinov). But alongside such manifestations of nationalism pure and simple, there is nostalgic reference to certain Soviet leaders and writers who performed services to the Kalmyk nation. Thus, one of the squares is now 'Khrushchev Square' because Khrushchev annulled the supposed guilt of the Kalmyks for collaboration, and restored Kalmyk statehood. In other words, he is commemorated for returning Elista to the Kalmyks and for returning them to Elista. Elsewhere a street in the city was named after B. B. Gorodovikov, who served for seventeen years as first secretary of the regional committee of the Communist Party, and was the first Kalmyk to hold this position. It was during his tenure of the post that the Kalmyk Republic was revived, and that the station, airport and university were built.

The case of Kirsan Ilyumzhinov Street is particularly interesting. This street was named not after the current head of state, but after his grandfather, who in the Soviet period counted as an unambiguously heroic figure. The documents indicating that he had killed himself out of disgust at the atrocities committed by the Red Army against the Kalmyk civilian population came to light only under perestroika. But, in contrast to some other Soviet heroes, the revelation of the truth actually enhanced Ilyumzhinov's standing in the new social circumstances: now he came to seem a hero of wounded national consciousness. The street accordingly retained its name, becoming a rare case of a politically motivated dedication that seemed just as appropriate in the post-Soviet era as it had before 1991.

One of the new streets in Elista was named in honour of Iuliia Neiman, who translated the Kalmyk poet David Kugul'tinov into Russian. This dedication to a non-Kalmyk figure stands alongside the retention of other non-Kalmyk names for various streets, for example, ulitsa Knakisa, named after Udlis Knakis, a ranger who was shot in the 1980s by poachers while trying to defend a herd of antelopes, or ulitsa Vetkalovoi, named after a nurse of the 28th Army, which liberated Elista from the Germans, as well as St Sergius of Radonezh Street, and streets named after the ethnographers and specialists in Eurasian culture Lev Gumilev and Galina Starovoitova. Moreover, not all the dedications commemorate people. A number of street names also honour the places where the Kalmyks were forcibly resettled in the years after 1943: Novosibirsk, Krasnoyarsk, Kemerovo, Altai. And a few now have Kalmyk, rather than

Russian, names, for example Zulturgan (Chasteberry), Bagchudyn gerl (Light of Youth), Al'mna Tsetsg (Apple Blossom), Urldan (Struggle).

CONCLUSION

Kalmykia's location between Europe and Asia determines the values and priorities of the local population. The post-Soviet period has seen increasing orientation to European cultural values (whether represented by Russian or Western Europe), manifested, for example, in the rise of individualism and the decline of the traditional values of the extended family. The unrivalled dominance of the Russian language, both spoken and written, is one factor in this; even at home, Russian is usually preferred, with many Kalmyks now having a weak or non-existent grasp of their ancestral tongue. In some provincial areas Kalmyk has held out, but you have to make an effort to hear it in the capital. In schools, pupils are often reluctant to study Kalmyk to graduation level because of fears that they will end up with a lower grade average, and this is generally regarded as completely normal and acceptable. Most Elista schoolchildren speak English much better than they do Kalmyk.

It would be fair to say that the current Elista lifestyle is a fusion of traditional and modern, Kalmyk and Russian, Eastern and Western values. The use of the calendar is a good illustration of this. Kalmyks are perfectly at home with the Gregorian calendar, as used internationally, but at the same time major life events, such as courting rituals, marriages and funerals, are organized according to the astrological Buddhist calendar. The high rates of ethnically mixed marriages, local notions that ethnically mixed features are the most attractive and best-looking, and the wide use of Russian first names (or names understood to be Russian, such as David instead of Dava, Bella instead of Kermen)[19] are all symptoms of progressive westernization. At the same time, the Kalmyk physical appearance, with its unbreakable links to the Orient, is reflected in the competing, and constantly developing, local mythology of 'Asian civilization': the Kalmyks are seen as a people with their own sense of statehood and their own version of Buddhist culture. Image and reality interact: people make increasing efforts to live up to the new behaviour ideals, but concepts of tradition also change as values become more Western.

Elista is currently the site of a contest between a variety of different local narratives, all of which together turn the city into an intertextual phenomenon. As in other Russian towns and cities, images and plot motifs from myth act as ways of binding together these motley and diverse fragments, these sense-defining events, into a larger whole, the contemporary identity of the modern city.[20] Pagodas, Buddhist temples, monuments, proliferating memorials to folk heroes and others are all elements in the search for a new national and local identity. At the same time, emphasis on historical figures and events from the period since the Kalmyks became subjects of the Russian Empire is a consistent feature.

One key style that results is what might be termed 'reactive Orientalism' – an eclectic phenomenon that essentially derives from European Orientalism. During the Soviet period the citizens of Elista were forcibly cut off from their religion, their traditional script and the written texts composed in this script. They were educated in the Russian language and trained to adopt Soviet values. As a result they essentially turned into bearers of westernized and 'orientalizing' views. Like the Orient itself, as described by Edward Said, Elista was subjected to the orientalizing gaze not just because its 'Oriental nature' was laid bare, but because it was possible to *make it* Oriental.[21] At the same time, however, the Kalmyks have also long had a tradition of considering themselves 'European'. It is notable that Kalmyk émigrés traditionally went West rather than East – to the USA, following the path of many Russian émigrés. They see themselves as a people that is 'Asiatic' only in terms of its origins (as with the Finns and the Hungarians).[22]

Despite this, orientalization at the local level continues to be important. The obsession with primordial explications of ethnic identity that characterized Soviet culture has made Kalmyks, like other post-Soviet citizens, see a direct link between their culture and physical appearance. The impact of intermarriage on Kalmykia notwithstanding, most people locally still look 'Asiatic'. Yet Soviet culture, while certainly 'socialist in content', was in no real sense 'national in form'. It had little or nothing to do with the pre-Soviet cultures of non-Russian 'nationalities' such as the Kalmyks. Specialists in the visual arts, such as sculpture, architecture and painting, were given no training in local traditions of representation; they studied in Russian institutions according to the canons of neoclassical art. They acquired no expertise whatever in Kalmyk art, for Buddhist architecture, which was both 'Asiatic' and religious, was under a double taboo.

Orientalization at the local level should thus be seen as a reaction to the standardization of Soviet times: to forcible Russification and to the monotonous drabness of town planning and daily life. The emphasis on cultural exclusivity also addresses another, more purely local, problem. In many republics of Russia (for example, Yakutia-Sakha, or Khanty-Mansy) the so-called 'titular nationality' (which provided the state language etc. during Soviet times) could also present itself as the 'original' nationality. But the Kalmyks – whose national history rested, after all, on the idea of their voluntary absorption into Russia – could not trumpet their 'aboriginal' status. Stressing the unique features of their culture hence became a particularly important form of self-definition. Invoking 'the East' provided the most obvious answer to questions about what a new post-Soviet identity should involve.

This did not, however, mean that it was the simplest answer. A striking example of the tension is a new theatre in Kalmykia, set up to stage classic plays by Kalmyk, Russian and foreign writers. The fusion of European costumes and Kalmyk faces, European names and Kalmyk intonation, has bizarre effects; in traditional realist terms, these stagings are simply not plausible. The undoubted talents of directors and actors notwithstanding, the effect is uncomfortably close to parody.

'Reactive Orientalism' had complex effects in other ways as well, as with the billboard images showing President Ilyumzhinov in the traditional dress of a Kalmyk khan. On the one hand, such images – allied to Ilyumzhinov's style of highly personalized leadership – appeared to endorse the traditional Western image of 'the Orient' as a place of despotic rule and institutionalized corruption. Yet they also offered protection against reprisals on the part of the government of the Russian Federation, by appearing to represent the undemocratic elements in Ilyumzhinov's rule as an expression of 'national tradition'. Even Western experts – who tend to shrug their shoulders over 'Oriental' peccadilloes where they see these as an ineradicable part of local tradition – were likely to find this kind of self-presentation disarming.

Yet Kalmykia's lack of significant natural resources and the small size of its population – which deprives the Kalmyks of the ability to present themselves as a powerful voting lobby at federal level – and the republic's depressed economy empty the sonorous phrases about independence and autonomy (as heard in other autonomous republics of the Russian Federation as well) of real meaning. The Republic of Kalmykia remains 'Oriental' in its 'feminine' dependence, its near-parasitic status with reference to the Russian Federation as a whole. Hence the conservative representation of Kalmykia's relations with Russia, and the emphasis on the inalienable ties with the larger nation. One of the two biggest memorial complexes in the city commemorates the comradeship of Kalmyks and Russians in the Civil War and Great Patriotic War. The other represents the forced exile of the Kalmyks – an episode which in some cultures might form the basis of a national separatist drive seeking to right 'injustice' – as the source of sorrowing and regret, not of reproach. Renaming in the post-Soviet period has found room for new Russian names, as well as Kalmyk ones.

The emphasis on Russian-Kalmyk links naturally reached its high point during the celebrations in 2009 of the 400th anniversary of the voluntary absorption of the Kalmyks into Russia. The official slogan was 'Kalmykia is my Motherland, Russia is my soul'. The selection of such a text – in which Russia was presented as the point of spiritual orientation, and a formerly nomadic people was associated with a fixed 'Motherland' – was typical of current attitudes.

Loyalty to Russia may also be the reason why the Kalmyks make no efforts to commemorate Genghis Khan, a cult figure for other ethnic groups in the Mongol world. At the grass-roots level Genghis does enjoy popularity in Kalmykia – almost every school class has a Genghis or two. The trilogy *To the Final Ocean*, by the Soviet writer Vasily Yan, and the study *Genghis Khan As a Military Leader and His Heritage*, by the Eurasianist Erendzhen Khara-Davan, are found in almost every home library in Elista. As soon as private commercial activity was legalized under perestroika, badges and pennants with Genghis Khan's portrait went on sale. In 1996 the Kalmyk Theatre put on a grandiose production, *Under the Yellow Flag of Genghis Khan*; everyone in Elista knows Sergei Bobrov's film *Mongol* (2007), which includes Kalmyk songs and snatches of Kalmyk dialogue. But making Genghis a hero runs contrary to the dominant understanding of the rise of the Russian state, according to which the overthrow of the 'Tatar-Mongol Yoke' is seen as a vital step in the creation of Russian national identity. Genghis Khan and his grandson Baty Khan are firmly in the enemy camp. Genghis is clearly not going to become a hero of Kalmyk monumental propaganda anytime soon.

All in all, the dominant image of Elista is shaped first and foremost by the political and intellectual elite of Kalmykia, who see ethnic identity primarily as a support of their hegemony. The exoticization of Kalmykia and of Elista as its capital acts as legitimation of the region's claims to special status and underlines the importance of these. They shore up hopes that Kalmykia can project itself as, and remain, not just a specific region of the North Caucasus, but also a politically autonomous area of the Russian Federation.

Translated by Catriona Kelly

NOTES

1. The word *gorod* is used for both 'town' and 'city', the next category down being *poselok* ('settlement').

2. On the deportation, see N. F. Bugai, *Operatsiia 'Ulusy'* (Elista, 1991);
V. B. Ubushaev, *Vyselenie i vozvrashchenie* (Elista, 1991); E.-B. Guchinova, *Pomnit'
nelzia zabyt': antropologiia deportatsionnoi travmy kalmykov* (Stuttgart, 2005).
3. www.mccme.ru/putevod/08/Elista/elista.html [accessed 1 February 2007].
4. V. I. Badmaev, interviewed by E. Guchinova, Elista, 2004.
5. M. Ad'ianova, interviewed by E. Guchinova, Elista, 2004.
6. At the start of the twenty-first century, the 'Elista Waltz' made a comeback too,
but with the words discarded, and in a jazz cover version. In many social
situations Kalmyk has completely fallen out of use, so the words were essentially superfluous. Another very popular song of the post-Soviet period was 'My
Little Elista', a song written by local man Viktor Khaptakhanov. Elista is
represented here as the town of one's childhood, of personal associations, as
one's own little homeland in the wider world.
7. Author's field notes, interview with R. Ivanov, Elista, 2009.
8. Here and below the descriptions of the sculptures and symbols of Elista are
taken from the official site of the mayor of Elista, www.gorod-elista.ru: 'The
Sights of Elista'.
9. This term is, needless to say, native neither to Kalmyk nor Russian.
10. Iu. M. Lotman, 'Arkhitektura v kontekste kul'tury', *Semiosfera* (St Petersburg,
2001), 680.
11. *K istorii obrazovaniia avtomnoi oblasti kalmytskogo naroda (oktiabr' 1917 –
noiabr' 1920): sbornik dokumentov i materialov* (Elista, 1960), 60.
12. See L. Piskunova and I. Iankov, 'Mifologema "stroitel'noi zhertvy" kak mekha-
nizm perekodirovki sovetskogo opyta v formirovanii sovremennoi gorodskoi
identichnosti', *Miasta nowych ludzi*, vol. II (Warsaw, 2007), 61.
13. Zurab Tsereteli is the sculptor responsible for various monuments in Moscow
erected in the Luzhkov era that might politely be described as controversial.
For many commentators, his work is the epitome of 'flash trash'.
14. 'Putevoditel' po Rossii: Respublika Kalmykiia', www.mccme.ru/putevod/08/
Elista/elista.html.
15. Ostap Bender liked to describe himself as 'the son of the Turkish Ambassador'.
'New Vasiuki' is a double joke. Vasiuki was the small town where
Bender attempted to pass himself off as an unbeatable chess champion,
taking on two-dozen masters simultaneously (after numerous elementary
mistakes put him in check all over the place, he was forced to flee the wrath
of the paying spectators). A popular Moscow joke of the late 1970s was that
after the 1980 Olympics the place would be named New Vasiuki.
16. The classic Kalmyk script was replaced by Latin script in the 1920s; in the
1930s this was then replaced by Cyrillic. The classic script would now be
expensive and difficult to reproduce as it follows a vertical sequence.
17. http://cens.ivanovo.ac.ru/olegria/gendernoe-izmerenie.natsionalizma.htm
[accessed 1 February 2007]. See also Ronald Grigor Suny's article in this
collection.
18. K. Shulepov, 'Zolotoi vsadnik vzletel nad Elistoi', *Vesti*, 14 April 2007, www.
vesti.ru/doc.html?id=115780.

19. The name Kermen means 'squirrel'. During the deportation, girls with this name were renamed Bella (from the Russian *belka*, squirrel).
20. Piskunova and Iankov, 'Mifologema', 61.
21. Edward Said, *Orientalism* (New York, 1979).
22. E.-B. Guchinova, *Ulitsa 'Kalmyk Road': istoriia, kul'tura i identichnosti kalmytskoi obshchiny SShA* (St Petersburg, 2004), 147.

CHAPTER 11

The place(s) of Islam in Soviet and post-Soviet Russia

Victoria Arnold

INTRODUCTION

Moscow, 1997: on Poklonnaia Hill, a mosque has just been completed. Its location is symbolic – the hill has for centuries been a place of tribute to the city, and, since the 1980s, the home of a vast memorial to the Great Patriotic War – and, through physical association with the history of Moscow and the defence of the Motherland, binds both the place of worship and the faith it represents to a core element of Russia's national identity. The mosque's position, shoulder to shoulder in commemoration with a Russian Orthodox Church, a Jewish synagogue and a statue of St George slaying the dragon, is suggestive both of the importance and equality of Russia's 'traditional religions' in the post-Soviet era, and of their essential place in Russian culture.

Sergiev Posad, 2005: several youths break into the town's mosque during a service and assault the small congregation, declaring as they do so that 'This is not a place for Muslims!' Though treated by the police as ordinary hooliganism, the incident appears to be a violent expression of growing feelings of opposition to the presence of an Islamic place of worship in the city regarded as the most important site in Russian Orthodoxy. Bishop Feognost of the Holy Trinity–St Sergius Lavra Monastery has distanced himself from the dispute, but the head of the district administration has called Sergiev Posad 'Orthodox territory', and the Union of Orthodox Believers decries the existence of a mosque 'in the heart of Holy Russia' as just as nonsensical as building an Orthodox church in Mecca.[1]

These examples of opposing attitudes to Islamic space in Russia encapsulate the somewhat contradictory attitude that the country has towards its Muslim population, and the different images of the religion which may be projected by views and events on different scales. This chapter takes a geographical approach to the question of the identity of Islam in Russia. Places of worship may be both symbols of a faith and sites at which and

Figure 11.1 The Blue Cathedral Mosque in Kazan (1815–19), undergoing restoration in 2010. The minaret was rebuilt in 2009.

through which that faith's role and identity may be articulated and contested, both by adherents and by other parties with a vested interest in the presence of Islam in the landscape (Figure 11.1). I use examples from both fieldwork in the Perm region and Russian media from across the country to demonstrate the complex position of Islam in the post-Soviet societal and material environment.

For centuries the traditional Russian image of the 'other' was that of a Muslim warrior, a mindset born of a long history of contact with Muslim peoples, much of which was marked by conflict. Despite the fact that much peaceful coexistence has also taken place, and though Soviet policy went

some way towards suppressing religious and cultural differences, Islam is
still regarded by some in Russia as a 'foreign' culture. The size and indigenous nature of the country's Muslim population, as well as the relevance of
Islam to several important strategic priorities (not least the maintenance
of territorial integrity and political control in the Caucasus), have obliged
the Russian government to make a conscious effort to integrate the faith and
its adherents into the Russian state (*rossiiskii islam*) and even into Russian
culture and the idea of the nation itself (*russkii islam*) – a tricky proposition,
given the endless debates, especially since the collapse of the USSR, over
what it means to be Russian – in order to be able to exercise some degree
of control over Islamic practices and attitudes.[2]

Several layers of identity come into play here, most notably the identity of
Islam as a religious culture – that is, its image (or self-image) as constructed by
its adherents, by non-Muslims and by the Russian secular authorities. Islam
may be presented as a natural and accepted part of the heritage of the Russian
state, or as an alien interloper, depending on whose portrayal we see and,
often, the specific history of their part of the country. Another aspect of
identity relevant here is that of particular towns or regions. Their conceptions
of themselves are sometimes challenged by the presence of Islam as materially
manifested in religious spaces – alternatively, as we shall see in the case of
Perm, self-image may be closely connected to a history of tolerance and
integration. Much of the case material here represents a degree of discontinuity with the Soviet period. During times in which mosques, like churches,
were destroyed or converted to secular use, and mosque construction
and most religious education were prohibited, arguments in the media and
between religious groups over the appropriateness or ownership of mosque
sites were unlikely to arise. Nevertheless, despite the differing official attitudes
of the Soviet and post-Soviet Russian governments, sacred place has been seen
by both as symbol and propagator of religious identity and values, and hence
as a site of conflict over the relevance of those values in wider society. What
was a one-way 'argument' in the 1930s and 1940s has become a multifaceted
debate today.

CONCEPTUAL BACKGROUND

I draw on aspects of both the older, Berkeley-style cultural geography and
the more fluid form developed in recent years, with its focus on, for
instance, the religious practices of the everyday.[3] The reasons for this are
simple: in studying mosques as (largely) contested spaces, I combine the
more traditional (i.e. a focus on the 'officially sacred' and on religious

buildings as a standard manifestation of religious expression) with the 'new' tendency towards investigation of different, potentially conflicting meanings of space and the wider consequences this may have. Use has also been made of Winchester et al.'s list of 'rules' for landscape study, several of which are particularly pertinent to the current case.[4] The first involves their exhortation to know the *past* of a place, which is clearly borne out by the Russian history of mosque closures, conversions and rebuilding, as well as the history of interfaith and interethnic relations. Secondly, they emphasize the importance of *geographical* context, as individual landscape features can only be understood in relation to the whole, a notion which lies at the core of work on contested spaces. Finally, they indicate that the 'silences' of a landscape can be as meaningful as its 'text' (which may be seen and 'read'), another significant point in the Russian historical context.

Ceri Peach distinguishes between the 'old' and 'new' cultural geographies by means of a series of dichotomies: the former 'reified culture' was based on observation of the physical and concerned itself mainly with 'control of territory' and 'people and place', while the latter concentrates on the 'contested nature of meaning', 'observes the observers' rather than the observed, and focuses on 'ownership of the gaze' and 'sex and shopping'.[5] Notwithstanding the slightly dismissive tone of these last comments, they nevertheless provide a useful, if crude, illustration of the point. Culture itself – in this case religion, and specifically Islam – is indeed considered an active force, as it is the religious, socio-religious and politico-religious attitudes and practices of various parties which determine much to do with mosque construction and the power relations which emerge in connection with religious sites.[6] Equally, however, the *meaning* of these sites – to Muslim congregations, other local residents, secular authorities and the Russian Orthodox Church – is central to the questions of how and why conflict may arise and of what wider issues (related, perhaps, to local politics or to matters of Russian national identity) such conflict may be reflective. Clearly, observation of both the 'physical' (here, sacred places themselves and the environment in which they are situated) and the 'observers' (those for whom the sites have meaning) is also paramount.

'Control of territory' is crucial. Roger W. Stump's work on religious fundamentalism, which informs the notion of territoriality in this study, employs several concepts applicable to the spatial study of religion as a whole, including the desire to exert control over the meaning and use of space in order to assert identity and define interactions with others.[7] This desire may be manifested in concern over: (a) the creation, preservation or reclamation of sacred space – for example, the regaining of a confiscated

pre-revolutionary mosque; (b) secular space – control of 'activity space'
of populations, such as the imposition of sharia law in several villages in
Dagestan in 1998; and (c) ideological space, as manifested, for instance, in
the idea of a pan-Caucasian Islamic state, or of Russia as the 'canonical
territory' of the Russian Orthodox Church. Peach's remark that the 'new'
cultural geography is concerned with 'ownership of the gaze' is a reference to
the significance afforded to the means, control and influence of representation in current studies in the field – that is, how depictions of space and
landscape in various media affect and are affected by cultural and political
attitudes.[8] This too can be of relevance when examining contested Islamic
spaces in Russia, given the different ways Islam and by extension its spatial
manifestations are represented at different levels – for example, as a traditional, indigenous religion in the 1997 law 'On Freedom of Conscience and
on Religious Association', and as a threat (culturally, politically and territorially) in its so-called Wahhabist form in the North Caucasus.[9]

    Such unashamed borrowing from both the 'old' and the 'new' in cultural
geography does, however, have its limits: the 'cultural determinism' of the
Berkeley school is rejected in favour of an approach which acknowledges
the role of the landscape itself in influencing the nature of its development,
through the physical environment (built and, sometimes, natural) and its far
from unidirectional relationship with human agency. Equally, despite Lily
Kong's exhortations for the geography of religion to move beyond the
'officially sacred' and explore 'different sensuous sacred geographies', this
research stays firmly within Peach's more traditional realm of 'people and
place', with an emphasis on how Islamic sacred places are constructed and
conceived of as spiritual, cultural, social and political sites.[10]

FEDERAL ATTITUDES

About 6 per cent of Russian citizens are Muslim,[11] concentrated for the most
part in two fairly distinct (but not too far distant) regions. This situation
would add weight to any concerted effort to claim full independence from
the Federation, an idea raised by Vladimir Putin as early as 2000, when he
warned that, if Islamic radicalism took a firm hold in the North Caucasian
republics and spread from there to the Volga, either the Islamization or
disintegration of the Russian state would occur.[12] Whether or not one
believes this to be plausible, it is easy to understand why the Russian federal
authorities think it important to cultivate good relations with the Muslim
population. They are too numerous to be ignored, of too long a heritage
in Russia to be dismissed as outsiders, and too closely connected to events in

the Caucasus for them or their faith to be entirely marginalized. With a higher birth-rate among Muslims than among ethnic Slavs, some regions are becoming more Muslim-dominated – Uzzell likens the Russian government's challenge of ruling these areas from Moscow to that of governing colonial India from London.[13] Nevertheless, too liberal an approach would not be accepted, either in government or by the population at large. Perceived extremist elements of Islam must continue to be criticized and resisted if the state is to retain any legitimacy in Chechnya, for example, and Russia's security interests and territorial integrity are naturally of importance. This 'balancing act' is enacted within the context of Russia's experiences in the field of democratization over the two decades. The pluralism embraced in the 1990s has since been curtailed, but a degree of cultural tolerance remains necessary for Russia's acceptance as a major player on an international level and, indeed, in the Islamic world, with which Russia cultivates strategically important ties. This is, however, set against the government's desire to cast the Chechen conflict in the mould of antifundamentalist struggle.

Official federal policy towards what the government sees as moderate forms of Islam has been characterized by its integrative approach; its aim has been to ensure that Muslim citizens' first allegiance is to the Russian state, to counter any negative feeling generated by events in Chechnya, and hence to retain a degree of control over the development of the religion. By and large the authorities have been aided in this by the official Muslim hierarchy – the Spiritual Directorates and the Council of Muftis – which have tended to be run by those whose spiritual goal is the creation of an original and distinctly Russian form of Islam. It is also the case, however, that many of these leaders are not trusted or even held to be legitimate by a large part of the Muslim population, a situation indicative of the lack of cohesion between the federal and local levels.[14]

The government's position has been informed by the 'Russification' policy of Sergei Kirienko, the president's plenipotentiary representative in the Volga region (2000–5), which included the imposition of the Russian language for all Islamic publications, teaching and mosque sermons.[15] The public face of this was aptly portrayed by the statement of former prime minister Yevgeny Primakov (sometime adviser to Vladimir Putin) that 'no other country whose native population is [composed] of a Christian majority and a Muslim minority can better serve as a model of peaceful cohabitation, mutual assistance and enrichment of cultures [than Russia]'.[16] He attributed this to the country's 'bridge' position between Europe and Asia, an interesting nod to the 'Eurasianist' idea that it is in this role, and not in 'the West', that Russia's identity and destiny lie. This perhaps points up the other balancing act that Russia must perform – that of cooperating with Western partners on the one hand (through the medium, for example, of the G8 group) and maintaining Russian independence and influence on the world stage on the other. Such influence, incidentally, may well be wielded by means of ties with Muslim states. In 2003 Russia was invited to join, as an observer, the Organisation of Islamic Cooperation (OIC), and in March 2006 the first meeting of the forum 'Strategic Vision: Russia – The Islamic World' was held in Moscow – and here, again, the incorporation of Russia's own Muslims into the life and identity of the Russian nation (or at least the impression of this) was no doubt seen as highly advisable.

It seems appropriate at this point to acknowledge the difference between the Russian words *russkii* (an ethnic marker) and *rossiiskii* (referring to the Russian state); logically, it would be the second of these concepts into which Islam is to be integrated, but the official language used sometimes comes tantalizingly close to attempting to stimulate cultural as well as political allegiance. With most articles used here coming from translated archive sources (the Russian versions now being mostly inaccessible), it is difficult to gauge the frequency with which each adjective is applied to Islam, but it appears that the general rule is to use *rossiiskii*. In a public lecture at Kazan State University in June 2003, however, Sergei Gradirovskii, Kirienko's chief adviser, attempted to explain why *russkii islam* would be an acceptable term, asserting that the adjective was as much to do with language and culture as it was to do with ethnicity, and arguing that the form of Islam at present developing in Russia had been enriched by elements of Russian culture and had enriched them in its turn.[17] This is a particularly potent indicator of the vehemence of the policy of integration, particularly given the attitude of the influential Russian Orthodox Church, which objects to the very idea of 'Russian Islam' on the grounds that Russianness and Orthodoxy are inextricably linked.

Efforts to bring Islam into the Russian public sphere have been made on both symbolic and practical levels, and in both, significant use has been made of Islamic religious space. Since 2000, for instance, 'Islamic spaces' have appeared in Russians' living rooms, as government policy to pay greater media attention to Islamic holidays resulted in the broadcasting of services at Kurban Bairam (Eid ul-Adha) from the Moscow Cathedral Mosque on the RTR channel.[18] Deliberate association with national media institutions, and, indeed, with Moscow as the heart of the Russian state, is highly suggestive of a 'normalized' Islam which is fully part of Russian life. In the first broadcast in 2000, this impression was heightened by the mufti's reading of a message from then President Putin, the language of which encapsulates the drive towards integration: Muslims are called 'fellow citizens' and their religious traditions 'an important part of the moral foundation of society'. Significantly for the year after the start of Russia's second military operation in Chechnya, Putin also thanked Muslims 'for their support of those efforts of our state aimed at strengthening the territorial integrity of Russia, at the consistent defence of its national interests, and the establishment of law and order in *our common land*'.[19] The expression of such views by the country's highest political figure, inside a mosque, during a service broadcast all over Russia, is an example of the shrewd use of religious space both to illustrate and to legitimize a political position. Although Putin's message was not given in person, it could be argued that its delivery by a Muslim cleric added to its symbolic impact.

The president voiced similar sentiments in 2003, using the occasion of Russia's accession to the OIC as an opportunity to praise Russian Islam's 'spiritual revival', and thank OIC member states for their assistance in the restoration of mosques and the provision of educational facilities.[20] At the same time as acknowledging international support and hence the place of Russian Muslims in the worldwide *umma* (Islamic community), Putin also managed to stress, yet again, the idea of a close and natural connection between Islam and Russia, calling the latter 'an historic fatherland for millions of Muslims' and Muslims themselves 'a full-fledged part of the nation'. An examination of examples at a local level indicates the extent to which constitutional religious pluralism and the federal government's policy of integration have been embraced by secular authorities and Muslim and non-Muslim citizens in various parts of the country.

ISLAM IN PERM

Perm is a large industrial city in the western Urals. Its population is largely Russian and Orthodox Christian, but Muslims (mainly Tatar and Bashkir, but now increasingly Central Asian and Caucasian) account for some 6 per cent in the region of which it is the capital (Perm krai/Prikamye).[21] Since the mid-1990s the Muslim population and its religious leadership have been divided in what is at first glance an administrative schism, but which has involved complex matters of identity. These have focused on which organization has the right to represent the Muslims of Prikamye. Places of worship have

Figure 11.2 The Cathedral Mosque in Perm (1902–3).

been closely implicated, especially the Cathedral Mosque, built in 1902–3 and the only pre-revolutionary mosque in Perm city (Figure 11.2).

The story of the rift is a complex and ongoing one, with new twists emerging every few months even now, long after the first cracks started to appear in 1997. Each side inevitably blames the other, and the matter has been complicated further by the Perm Muftiat's decision to become an independent institution.[22] Somewhat unusually for Perm, the split has attracted the attention of Western scholars of Russia's internal geopolitics and religious politics, who mostly assert that Mukhammedgali Khuzin, leader of the Perm Muftiat, was at least its catalyst, if not entirely responsible.[23]

In 1989 Perm's Cathedral Mosque was returned to Muslim believers by the city soviet.[24] In the early 1990s the mosque's leaders were independent of any administrative authority, but maintained good relations with the newly established Muftiat. The Muftiat comprised around eighty communities (*makhallas*), and was affiliated with the Central Spiritual Administration of Muslims (TsDUM). This authority, based in Ufa, was the *de jure* successor to the Soviet-era Spiritual Board of Muslims of European Russia and Siberia, and has been led by Talgat Tadzhuddin, Russia's supreme mufti.

In the turbulent religious freedom of the early 1990s, a new movement emerged – the Spiritual Administration of Muslims of European Russia (DUMER). This group broke off from TsDUM, and by 1996 had become a direct and powerful competitor for the allegiance of Russian Muslim leaders. DUMER accused Talgat Tadzhuddin of being a 'despot' in his role of supreme mufti, and maintained that TsDUM engaged in 'excessive appease-ment' of the Russian Orthodox Church.[25] TsDUM, for its part, attributed the rise of DUMER to careerism and financial greed of its leader Ravil Gainutdin and his followers, and hinted darkly that they had courted fundamentalist sponsors from Arab nations to bankroll the new organization. Given the lack of a strict Muslim hierarchy, either spiritually or administra-tively, this division took some time to make itself felt in the everyday lives and places of worship of ordinary believers. Indeed, to this day, the high-level authorities are often accused of being out of touch with the interests and problems prevalent 'on the ground'. In Perm, however, the national-level row between the country's two principal Islamic administrative bodies combined with particular conditions in the local *umma* to create a serious conflict over sources of authority and the right to represent local Muslims, which was most dramatically expressed in events at the Cathedral Mosque.

By the mid-1990s, discontent was growing over the alleged corrupt practices of the Perm Muftiat's leader, Khalim Kharisov. In response, in 1997, the Muftiat brought in a new mufti, Mukhammedgali Khuzin, then imam of a mosque in neighbouring Bashkortostan. Khuzin, in his advocacy of liberal Islamic practices and the importance of local Tatar and Bashkir cultural traditions, soon came into conflict with the leaders of the Cathedral Mosque, who favoured a more orthodox approach and saw Khuzin as lacking in both religious rigour and social responsibility. As a result, the mosque's congregation and fourteen other communities formally associated themselves with DUMER, believing this organization espoused religious views close to their own. Hunter attributes the ensuing division to three main issues.[26] These include, firstly, ethnic tensions between the Cathedral

Mosque congregation (by this time, mainly immigrants from Central Asia and the Caucasus) and the unchanged Tatar and Bashkir leadership of the Muftiat – Khuzin, in particular, was accused of extremely rigid attitudes towards foreigners, and was asserted to have fired the mosque imam simply because he was Azerbaijani.[27] Secondly, Hunter points to related tensions between the more orthodox immigrants and the more liberal locals – the core congregation of the mosque, which consisted of the most observant and active individuals (with, nevertheless, some locals among them, including their self-proclaimed mufti), chose to join DUMER explicitly because they considered it more orthodox than TsDUM.[28] Thirdly, the secular authorities' long indecisiveness (what Hunter terms a 'deliberately ambiguous position') hindered a swift resolution – for nearly four years they neither allowed the mosque's congregation to reregister as a separate DUMER-affiliated community nor supported the Muftiat in its legal efforts to retain control of the mosque. When, however, the reregistration eventually went through, the significance of the mosque came to the fore.

The Cathedral Mosque, as the Perm *umma*'s historic spiritual home, a material link with their pre-revolutionary heritage and the only distinctively Islamic building in the city centre, now became the site of the conflict, where wider disagreements over Islamic orthodoxy and administrative authority took physical form. As it became apparent that the Muftiat stood to lose control of the mosque, Khuzin attempted to discredit its leaders (principally Mufti Khamit Galiautdinov) by making accusations of 'Wahhabism' in the local press and on the radio. The DUMER group promptly accused him of the same thing. This sort of claim has become fairly common in disputes between Muslim leaders in Russia; given Russia's bloody campaigns in the North Caucasus, Chechen terrorist attacks (foremost at the time of the Perm conflict were the Moscow apartment bombings of 1999) and the stories of hard-line Islamists from Arab countries aiding the Chechen rebels, the word has emotional resonance. The Perm municipal authorities, however, did not rise to the bait, and maintained their position of non-interference over three years of accusation and counter-accusation. This culminated, in March 2001, in the forcible seizure of the Cathedral Mosque by Khuzin's supporters, who declared that it would now be under the jurisdiction of the Muftiat, and barricaded the doors against the congregation. After some days, however, the congregants themselves persuaded the secular authorities to put pressure on Khuzin, and control was ultimately returned to the DUMER-affiliated leadership.

The Perm Muftiat remained affiliated with TsDUM until early 2006, when Khuzin, who had risen by this time to be Tadzhuddin's deputy and hence vice supreme mufti of Russia, was summarily dismissed by the authorities in Ufa. This took place during a period of reconciliatory measures between TsDUM and DUMER at a national level, and may well have been part of the process, since Khuzin had been a thorn in DUMER's side for some time. Magomedov also speculates, however, that TsDUM would have wished to distance itself from Khuzin after he proposed a zero-tolerance approach to 'Wahhabism' which included the removal of pensions and benefits from convicted terrorists' relatives, and praised the security forces' response (which reportedly included the torture of suspects) to the raids on their premises in Nal'chik in 2005.[29]

PERM'S NEW CATHEDRAL MOSQUE?

The first and most obvious spatial and physical manifestation of the schism was the conflict over the Cathedral Mosque, which resulted in its return to its own congregation's control; in September 2009, ownership was formally transferred to it by the city duma.[30] This has meant that, for more than a decade, the most prominent symbol of Islam's presence in the city has no longer been under the control – administratively or spiritually – of the organization which sees itself as Perm's principal Islamic body (and which indeed is the one which conducts most dealings with the secular authorities). The Muftiat has felt its loss deeply; the mosque, with its pre-revolutionary history and distinctive appearance, is symbolic of Tatar history in the city and the integration of the Muslim community in nineteenth- and early twentieth-century mercantile society. It is also the largest and most central space for congregational worship in Perm, the loss of which made difficult one of the most fundamental elements of Muslim worship: communal prayer. The Muftiat was granted the use of a two-storey wooden house on Bolshevistskaia Street, which has been turned into a combination of mosque, offices and educational centre. A network of prayer houses is also maintained across the city, and purpose-built mosques have been established at Zakamsk, Gaiva and Kondratovo, also under the Muftiat's jurisdiction. Nevertheless, there is still a pressing need for space to accommodate the large Friday congregations who gather for the fulfilment of the mandatory act of collective worship.[31]

In 1999, therefore, when control of the Cathedral Mosque was returned to the DUMER group and regaining it seemed increasingly unlikely, plans were put in place for the foundation of a new Cathedral Mosque, which would become the spiritual and cultural centre for the Muslims of Prikamye. Land on Gagarin Boulevard was granted to the Muftiat by then mayor Iurii

Trutnev; the plot sits high on the edge of the valley dividing Perm from
Motovilikha, overlooking the Southern cemetery, one of the main modern
burial grounds in the city. Over the following ten years the Muftiat worked to
raise funds for construction while also developing the cultural and educational
infrastructure which will eventually move to the new location. Matters have
been delayed, however, by more than fund-raising and preparation; competing claims to the site from commercial users have caused the planning process
to drag on over a number of years, something which has also dogged the
Russian Orthodox diocese in some of its reclamation cases. By 2009 only
about one-third of the original land allocation was left.[32] In order to stake a
claim to the remainder, a temporary wooden mosque was built, and opened
in September 2009. In addition, there is a specifically and formally religious
motivation, one which is acknowledged by the Muftiat itself and reported in
the secular media. The sacred nature of a mosque is derived from its function
as a place of communal worship, and the presence of a working mosque at the
site of the planned major Islamic centre of the region is intended 'to
consecrate it with prayer, to blaze a road to it for Muslims'.[33] 'By tradition',
reported Vetta TV News, 'before erecting a new mosque, the site on which it
will stand should be prayed upon.'[34]

The new Cathedral Mosque is also to be given a symbolic name: New
Afkula. Afkula was the name of a medieval fortress and trading settlement to
the north of Perm, near the present-day village of Rozhdestvenskoe; it is
believed that, as an outlying part of the trading networks of Islamic Volga
Bulgaria, it was the home of the first Muslims in the region. By giving its
name to the new mosque, the Muftiat is linking the new place of worship to
the site of the thousand-year-old roots of local Islam, thus strengthening its
claim to be the authentic representatives of the Perm *umma* through an
assertion of historical legitimacy and spiritual descent from the area's first
Muslims. Excavations have been going on at Afkula for about twenty years,
and have uncovered the remains of various buildings, including what is
thought to be a mosque; the excavation season of 2010, however, was the
first to be opened with *namaz* (collective prayer), led by Mufti Khuzin. The
spiritual and material connection between the historic site and the new
Cathedral Mosque is to be further strengthened through the display of
artefacts from the ancient settlement in a museum of Muslim life attached
to the mosque, and the running of a special bus service linking the New
Afkula with the old.

Despite the long-drawn-out process of construction of its flagship new
mosque, the Muftiat and its affiliated communities have generally managed
to establish places of worship with relative ease in the legal and logistical

spheres.[35] The DUMER administration at the old Cathedral Mosque, meanwhile, has not been able to secure a similar presence in the Islamic landscape, maintaining only fifteen communities in Perm krai to the Muftiat's ninety. While the city duma, in keeping with federal law, formally transferred ownership of the Cathedral Mosque, and it was the secular authorities that forced a truce in the conflict over the building by obliging Khuzin's supporters to hand back control to the DUMER affiliates, there is nevertheless a marked difference in the degree to which each group has managed to articulate its presence and identity through sacred place. The DUMER mufti Khamit Galiautdinov attributes this difference to conscious discrimination on the part of the authorities in the sphere of mosque building.[36] The local government, like the federal government, must maintain harmony in an interconfessional population, and is keen on preserving Perm's liberal and peaceful reputation; it is, therefore, not implausible that it should favour the Muftiat, with its concerted promotion of interfaith tolerance and cooperation, and its construction of itself as the natural successor to a well-integrated Muslim community of long heritage.

ISLAM AS 'DIFFERENCE'

One of the most common problems for religious groups in Russia is that of obtaining space for worship. In those cases in which it involves only the renting of existing property, barriers to the process may be attributed to bureaucratic red tape or individual cases of prejudice on the part of the relevant officials, or indeed a genuine and justifiable interpretation of the law. The majority of cases reported in the Russian press and Western monitoring literature, however, involve objections from a third party, the grounds for which frequently display a spatial or territorial element. This can take a site-specific form, namely opposition to the mosque's visual effect on the landscape or to its location relative to other man-made features, or a more symbolic conception of the mosque as a marker of an interloping culture in the space of the Russian nation or Orthodox Christianity. In some instances the latter argument may be an extension or implication of the former; in others, it is itself the principal basis for opposition. Opposition itself is also manifested in a variety of ways, from the crude and opportunistic, such as vandalism, to the level of formal civil protest by means of petitions and demonstrations, to the public involvement of senior religious and political figures.

    Despite this, the survey results of Karpov and Lisovskaya's analysis of religious tolerance indicate that more than half of Orthodox Russians

Figure 11.3 The Kul Sharif Cathedral Mosque in Kazan, rebuilt in 2005.

(56.6 per cent) would allow the construction of a mosque in their home towns, a proportion noticeably higher than that which would allow the building of a synagogue (47.9 per cent) or a church of a Western denomination (28.9 per cent), but lower than the reciprocal figure for Muslims (72.3 per cent).[37] A clearer picture is revealed by the authors' regional breakdown of these figures, using a scale of tolerance from –8 (maximum intolerance) to 8 (maximum tolerance). The lowest results for Orthodox tolerance of Muslims came from the North Caucasian republics of Dagestan and Kabardino-Balkaria (0.7 and 1.0 respectively), and from the non-Muslim parts of Russia (–0.3).[38] As far as Muslim tolerance of the

Orthodox is concerned, the lowest levels were also found in the North Caucasus (0.9 and 0.6 respectively), but the highest – indeed, the highest tolerance of either group in any region – in 'non-Muslim' Russia (5.3).[39] Apart from this, the greatest tolerance on both sides was to be found in the autonomous Volga region republics of Tatarstan and Bashkortostan, whose secular governments are known for their efforts in maintaining harmony within their multi-confessional populations (Figure 11.3). Karpov and Lisovskaya conclude from these results that two related factors are vital for the development of high mutual tolerance: firstly, direct experience of each other's traditions, leading to a degree of familiarity; and secondly, a history of peaceful coexistence. The Muslim peoples of the Volga republics have lived alongside Russians for over 400 years, and while there have been periods of conflict, it is telling that such high figures for mutual tolerance can be seen here as opposed to the North Caucasus, which the Russian Empire was still engaged in subduing as recently as the nineteenth century. It has been pointed out, meanwhile, that mosques have been and are being built in parts of Russia where there have been none before, bringing local Russian populations into direct contact with distinctive Islamic sacred space, usually for the first time.[40]

Following Karpov and Lisovskaya's argument, it is perhaps unsurprising that conflict should arise. As they suggest, attitudes towards places of worship can be a good (though not all-encompassing) indication of religious tolerance in general, largely because they are such tangible manifestations of presence and identity. Control of space bestows power upon those controlling it, and this is particularly so when the space in question is significant in some way. A place of worship, clearly defined by architecture or positioning, implies ownership and control of space, and a place of worship in an especially prominent location indicates that the religious group in question has a certain amount of social legitimacy.

There have been a number of violent incidents at mosques which have clearly demonstrated a particular view of Islam as alien to Russia and an intruder in its territory. In Roshal, near Moscow, for example, a group of youths attacked an elderly clergyman inside his mosque, declaring, 'This is not your place! This is a Christian place! Stop praying here!'[41] The role of the mosque as religious space and cultural symbol may be more clearly discerned, however, in the cases of opposition to proposed mosque building, in which matters of location and landscape are often paramount.

An attempt in 1994 to construct a mosque on the outskirts of Murmansk, where Muslim Tatars have lived since the 1920s,[42] did not come to fruition because of lack of funds. Another plot of land did not become available until

1999, on a site which aroused the hostility of local residents. Murmansk is a hilly city, and the proposed location for the mosque happened to be at virtually its highest point. If this were not prominent enough, it was also planned that it should have a 24 metre minaret, which, crucially, would rise higher than Murmansk's Great Patriotic War monument, a statue of a soldier, nicknamed Alyosha, which also occupies a prominent hilltop location to the north of the city.[43] This large and distinctive statue, erected in memory of the region's wartime defenders, has become the unofficial emblem of Murmansk; as one protester put it, 'Will the minaret become the symbol of our city?'[44] Other objections raised included the arguments that the mosque would 'block the sun' from many people's homes (if true, perhaps a valid complaint in the short Arctic summer), that residents had been attempting for years to have a children's playground built on the site and that, as the northernmost in the world, the mosque would inevitably attract pilgrims. The 'Alyosha' argument is, however, the most telling: the monument embodies both local and national pride and is a visible link between modern-day Murmansk and the time when it repelled the greatest threat to its existence and identity. It was clearly taken as a great insult to have this overshadowed (figuratively and literally) by a construction which is both the active worship space and the symbol of a religion seen as 'not local'. In this respect, it is somewhat surprising that the city government allocated this site at all.

On being asked what they would do if the building went ahead, local protesters' reactions ranged from 'we shall destroy everything' to 'we shall picket the site and let nobody in'. After a petition to the city authorities failed to halt construction, the partially built mosque was destroyed in a mysterious fire. As one resident remarked, however, 'Nobody is against the mosque, but they want another place for it'; location and presence in the landscape were clearly of significance here, more so than the presence of Muslims in the city. Another site was allocated in 2006, in a less topo-graphically prominent part of town; construction began in 2009.[45]

A similar incident to that in Murmansk occurred in Vladivostok in 1999. The city's 60,000-strong Muslim population had been confined to private homes, gymnasia and social clubs for their services, but after some months of negotiation had finally obtained permission to build a mosque near the centre of Vladivostok. The site had already been prepared and blessed when this permission was withdrawn by the city government, under pressure from the local Russian Orthodox Church. The grounds for this were, again, closely related to territoriality and the significance of location, and were highly suggestive of a view of Islam as an 'outside' faith which should never be permitted to gain ascendancy over Orthodoxy. The mosque's hilltop location and prominent minarets would have allowed it to tower almost 300 m above the Orthodox Cathedral of St Nicholas, itself of symbolic value as the only Vladivostok church to have remained open under Soviet rule. In this instance, too, the opposition was successful, and the Vladivostok Muslims were, moreover, banned from demonstrating at the site. An offer of a different site was rejected as being too far out of town, and stalemate followed for some years until, as in Murmansk, permission to build was again granted, this time in a more outlying residential district and, intriguingly, coinciding with the visit of the president's plenipotentiary representative to the city. This is suggestive of a desire on the part of local authorities to be seen to be following the federal line on the integration of Islam. As of 2010, however, the mosque had still not been built, and local Muslim leaders feared insufficient progress would have been made in time for the 2012 Asia-Pacific summit, when many foreign Muslim dignitaries would be visiting Vladivostok.[46]

In some cases, roles could be reversed and it might be the Muslims of a particular place acting territorially towards an incoming group. One example of this may be seen in Saratov, where the Church of Jesus Christ of Latter-Day Saints has a surprisingly strong presence. In 2003 the Mormons planned to build a church complex in downtown Saratov, having already procured land through a private individual. They were opposed by a united front of local Orthodox and Islamic leaders, whose principal objection was to the close proximity of the proposed church to their own religious buildings; the intended location was described as an insult to Saratov's Muslim and Orthodox residents. After secular authorities did nothing in response to written complaints, a demonstration in nearby Teatral'naia ploshchad' (where Soviet parades were held) was organized and attracted some 3,000 participants. Local Cossack leaders later joined in, pointing out that the Mormon church would be 'dangerously close' to the city's administrative heart.[47]

CONCLUSIONS

Significant use is made of religious space in the pursuit of federal policy on the integration of Islam, from official mosque visits and service broadcasts to state-supported programmes of mosque restoration. As we have seen, however, the ideal of 'Russian Islam' promoted in the official sphere has encountered mixed success on a local scale. An examination of the Russian press and Western religious rights literature has indicated that there have been many instances of conflict over Islamic religious space. In large part these have focused on the specific location and/or landscape presence of mosques – the territorial expression of a view of Islam as something which does not 'belong', either in a particular place or in the space of Russian culture/Orthodoxy as a whole.

Has there been any evidence of success in the 'Russification' of Islam? On an international level, Russia's emphasis on its inclusion of its Muslim population and the apparent success of the 2003 Chechen elections led to its invitation to join the OIC as an observer; this could prove to be a significant advantage in geopolitical terms should Russia ever seriously need to counter US influence in the Middle East. Closer to home, however, the evidence is sparse. There has been some progress in the field of Muslim political representation, with the accession of Refah (a Muslim party linked to United Russia) to seats in the Duma, and the establishment of the Islamic Heritage Association as both a lobbying group and a forum for interconfessional debate. Levels of religious tolerance between Orthodox and Muslims are surprisingly high, but when broken down by region the bias towards the Volga republics is apparent; here, despite some localized tensions, a remarkable level of harmony has been achieved. Given that the cases of conflict over mosques described in this chapter have usually taken place in regions where the Muslim population is largely the result of immigration, it is tempting to suggest a geography of integration, in which areas of greater harmony between Muslims and non-Muslims coincide with those with an indigenous Islamic heritage, such as Tatarstan and the Perm region.

It is easy to overlook the great heterogeneity of Russia's Muslim population when confronted with so many statements about a 'Russian Islam'. We must remember that, among so many different ethnic groups, it will be difficult to find a completely common voice. The situation in Perm, where the conflict over a sacred place has been between two Muslim organizations, suggests that, in some regions, there is a clear division in identity between Muslim groups of Tatar and Bashkir origin and those of an immigrant background; places of worship, both ancient and modern, have been used in the Perm Muftiat's construction of its image as the rightful successor to the region's Islamic heritage and have aided in its promotion of itself as the legitimate representative of the Perm *umma*. While attempting to maintain a degree of balance in its dealings with Muslim congregations, the Perm regional government has tended to conduct most dialogue with the Muftiat.

It is important to ensure that such a large, significant and often indigenous minority as Russia's Muslims has a place in the nation, but to achieve this without alienating large parts of the rest of the population is no easy matter, and Putin's recognition of the importance of religious harmony is to be commended. My principal aim here, however, has not been to pass value judgements, but to examine the role of religious space, and we may conclude that, at a local level particularly, it remains of great importance. The tangible nature of places of worship as material expressions of religious presence and identity is unlikely to cease to elicit reactions, and may thus act as an informative indicator of attitudes 'on the ground'. As a final point, the significance of Islam in Russia and vice versa is hard to overestimate. As a vast territory encompassing many different manifestations of the religion, Russia resembles, to put it rather crudely, a laboratory of various versions from militant radicalism to the support of secular nationalism. The old adage 'a bridge between Europe and Asia' still has relevance in a country with an active policy of developing a distinctly Russian Islam from these diverse roots, and its success or otherwise will be of great interest to European states with their own, albeit usually non-indigenous, Muslim populations. For Islam itself, Russia has proved and will continue to prove to be a challenging but potentially rich homeland. Professor Tariq Ramadan has said that he sees the future of Islam in Western Europe rather than in the old Islamic world;[48] Russia, as ever perhaps, has tended to fall between the two in such discussions, but it will be of immense interest to see how the future of Russian Islam is shaped and how its place in Russian culture is eventually found.

NOTES

1. A. Soldatov, 'Orthodox Monastery Casts Long Shadow over Embattled Mosque', *Moscow News*, 2 November 2005.
2. The situation is complicated further by the fact that Muslims in Russia belong to hundreds of different ethnic groups, including the Turkic Tatars, various Caucasian ethnicities and Slavic converts.
3. K. Knott, *The Location of Religion: A Spatial Analysis* (London, 2005); P. Nynäs, 'From Sacred Place to an Existential Dimension of Mobility', in *The Ethics of Mobilities: Rethinking Place, Exclusion, Freedom and Environment*, ed. S. Bergmann and Tore Sager (Aldershot, 2008), 157ff.
4. H. Winchester, L. Kong and K. Dunn, *Landscapes: Ways of Imagining the World* (Harlow, 2003).
5. C. Peach, 'Social Geography: New Religions and Ethnoburbs', *Progress in Human Geography* 26 (2002), 252–60.
6. These parties may include municipal planning authorities, the Russian Orthodox Church, Muslim congregations, and both Muslim and non-Muslim residents.

7. R. W. Stump, *Boundaries of Faith: Geographical Perspectives on Religious Fundamentalism* (Lanham, MD, 2000).

8. Peach, 'Social Geography'.

9. 'Keston Institute's Translation of New Russian Law on Religion', www.cesnur. org/testi/Russia.htm.

10. L. Kong, 'Mapping "New" Geographies of Religion: Politics and Poetics in Modernity', *Progress in Human Geography* 25 (2001), 211–33.

11. Russian Public Opinion Research Centre poll, 2007. Results: 'Opublikovana podrobnaia sravnitel'naia statistika religioznosti v Rossii i Pol'she', 6 June 2007, www.religare.ru/2_42432.html.

12. Vladimir Putin, interview with television channel ORT, 7 February 2000, reported by Dadan Upadhyay, 'Putin Warns against Islamisation, Disintegration of Russia', 9 February 2000, www.expressindia.com/ie/daily/ 20000209/iin09029.html.

13. L. Uzzell, 'Bringing Muslims in from the Cold', *Moscow Times*, issue 3254, 16 September 2005.

14. Prof. Tariq Ramadan, personal communication, May 2006.

15. S. Hunter et al., *Islam in Russia: The Politics of Identity and Security* (London, 2004).

16. Y. Primakov, 'Politics: A New Threat', *Moscow News*, 7 April 2006.

17. V. Solomatina, 'V Kazani proidet diskussiia o "russkom islame"', 9 June 2003, www.tataroved.ru/news/2003/12/17/rislam/.

18. A. Zolotov, 'Kremlin Woos Moslems on Holy Day', *Moscow Times*, 17 March 2000, www.themoscowtimes.com/news/article/kremlin-woos-moslems-on-holy-day/265439.html. A 'cathedral mosque' (in Russian, *sobornaia mechet'*) is one in which Friday prayers, the principal and compulsory act of Muslim worship, are held.

19. Ibid. Emphasis added.

20. V. Romanenkova, 'Putin Points out Russian Moslem Community's "spiritual revival"', *ITAR-TASS Weekly News*, 16 October 2003.

21. M. Pismannik, 'O religioznoi situatsii v Prikam'e', www.perm.ru [accessed 13 December 2009].

22. The Muftiat is an administrative body responsible for liaising with secular authorities, appointing imams, overseeing religious education, and offering guidance on mosque design and construction.

23. Hunter et al., *Islam in Russia*; K. Matsuzato, 'The Regional Context of Islam in Russia: Diversities along the Volga', *Eurasian Geography and Economics* 47 (2006), 447–61.

24. Hunter et al., *Islam in Russia*.

25. Matsuzato, 'Regional Context', 449–61.

26. Hunter et al., *Islam in Russia*.

27. K. Matsuzato, 'Muslim Leaders in Russia's Volga-Urals: Self-Perceptions and Relationship with Regional Authorities', *Europe-Asia Studies* 59 (2007), 779–805.

28. Mufti Khamit Galiautdinov, interviewed by the author at Perm Cathedral Mosque, May 2008.

29. A. Magomedov, 'Perm Authorities Back Compliant Mufti', *Russia Regional Report*, 27 March 2006.
30. 'Zdanie sobornoi mecheti Permi peredano v sobstvennost' musul'manam goroda', 23 September 2009, www.islamrf.ru/news/rusnews/russia/9980/.
31. Mufti Mukhammedgali Khuzin, interviewed by the author at Perm Muftiat, June 2008.
32. R. Savukova, 'Novaia mechet': sovmestnyi trud i prazdnik', 22 September 2009, www.moslem.ru/index.php?name=News&op=article&sid=207.
33. Ibid.
34. Vetta TV, 'V Permi postroiat novuiu mechet' i muzei musul'manskoi istorii', 3 December 2009.
35. Mufti Khuzin, interview, June 2008.
36. Mufti Galiautdinov, interview, May 2008.
37. V. Karpov and E. Lisovskaya, 'Religious Intolerance among Orthodox Christians and Muslims in Russia', *Religion, State and Society* 36 (2008), 361–77.
38. Ibid.
39. Ibid.
40. Uzzell, 'Bringing Muslims In'.
41. 'Mullah Beaten in Moscow Region Mosque', 25 November 2002, www.themoscowtimes.com/news/article/mullah-beaten-in-moscow-region-mosque/241967.html.
42. There are about 30,000 Muslims in the Murmansk region. Barents Observer, 'Mosque for Murmansk', 10 March 2009, www.barentsobserver.com/mosque-for-murmansk.4565372-16180.html.
43. Hunter et al., *Islam in Russia*.
44. 'Russia – Religion – Feature', *ITAR-TASS Weekly News*, 24 February 1999.
45. 'Pomogite vozvedeniiu mecheti v Murmanske!', www.islam.ru/pressclub/donate/me4eti/murmansk [accessed 12 January 2011]; Barents Observer, 'Mosque for Murmansk'.
46. 'Vo Vladivostoke mecheti net i ne budet!', 1 December 2010, Ansar, www.ansar.ru/rfsng/2010/12/01/8867.
47. PDS Russia Religion News 2004, www2.stetson.edu/~psteeves/relnews/0407e.html.
48. Tariq Ramadan, personal communication, May 2008.

PART V

Languages of national identity

CHAPTER 12

Language culture and identity in post-Soviet Russia: the economies of mat

Michael Gorham

Dlia otsenki polozheniia v strane net slov! Ostalis' odni vyrazheniia.
There are no words for what's happening in Russia! Only [obscene]
expressions.
Kak poslat' na khui ne ispol'zuia neprilichnykh slov?
How do you send someone to fuck without using bad words?

Anonymous

ECONOMIES OF LANGUAGE

It is not by accident that economic metaphors frequently figure in discourse
on language. Whether touting a language's richness and wealth, or bemoan-
ing its cheapening or devaluation, language mavens and folk linguists alike
almost naturally turn to monetary symbolism to make their point. Jean-
Joseph Goux argues that monetary metaphors are so prevalent in discourse on
language because money and language share fundamental affinities that make
their relationship not just analogically close but, as he calls it, 'isomorphic'.
The congruity, Goux writes, lies in the fact that both are representative sign
systems or systems that are commonly acknowledged as 'general equivalents'
to that which they signify, and thus serve as forms of 'exchange' that account
for their formidable power and authority. Money obtains its value for being
a substitution for material worth or commodities; language, through its role as
substitute for meaning.[1]

   Pierre Bourdieu adopts economic metaphors to account for the way
language, like other cultural categories, functions as a domain for the struggle
for, production of and consecration of power and authority. Particularly
useful is his discussion of the 'Economy of Linguistic Exchanges' and the
manner in which discourses (i.e. ideologies) compete for, obtain and perpetuate their control over 'linguistic capital'.[2] Symbolic authority, Bourdieu
argues, is not engrained in the language itself but rather bestowed upon the
speaker or writer by institutions with the power to bestow it by means

of mechanisms of production and reproduction (of legitimate language). Crises in language cultures (and political cultures, for that matter) arise when the relative authority of competing institutions of linguistic production and reproduction are challenged or in flux.

Few periods so invite the application of such economic metaphors for language as the perestroika years, where highly consequential examples abound of both linguistic devaluation (in the decline in authority of the language of the Soviet state) and capital accumulation (in the rise in influence in the language of democratic systems and market-style economies). The value of the spoken word and unscripted public rallies rose markedly and largely at the expense of the more scripted language of party events, pamphlets and decrees, now stigmatized as 'wooden'. While the media had not yet been relieved of state oversight and ownership, the policies and values that dictated the state demands of mass media shifted dramatically, to the extent that the main message coming from the Politburo's media head, Aleksandr Iakovlev, was, quite literally, 'Write anything – just don't lie.'[3]

The more direct, often aggressive style and content of news magazines such as *Ogonek* and television programmes such as *Vzgliad* and *600 sekund* reflected the new premium placed on free speech and open expression of opinion which, along with the relaxation of censorship (of both content and form), helped radically change the style and tone of the language of the mass media. Political and economic factors converged to promote a less censored, more free-wheeling, informal and, at times, crude writing style on the pages of the press. While the old style of speaking and writing had not disappeared entirely, by the final years of Gorbachev's rule the more open, fast-paced, democratic – some would say brash and even vulgar – language of glasnost and *svoboda slova*, or 'freedom of speech', held a majority stake in the market of linguistic capital.

In fact, even the notion of glasnost suffered devaluation in the final year of Gorbachev's presidency. By then it had become clear that the pro-reform 'democrats' had won the rhetorical battle over the term, their broader interpretation of it as a close cousin to 'free speech' eclipsing the narrower notion of 'greater public access to information' espoused by the party appa-ratchiki. But by winning the battle over words they also helped trigger the devaluation of the term itself. In August 1991 Gorbachev escaped captivity but suffered an irreparable blow in legitimacy during the failed coup by the conservative apparatus, which led to the deflation of his own political author-ity and that of glasnost as well. Even prior to the coup it had become a compromised concept, weakened by half measures and the perception of retrenchment. In its place the more uncompromising notion *svoboda slova* (literally, 'freedom of the word') came to the fore to assume a dominant role in the language culture of the early Yeltsin years. As one observer put it, 'The opposition to glasnost had now become not silence' – as was the case in the earlier perestroika years – 'but "freedom of speech". Glasnost itself grew to be seen as a conscious policy of the authorities, as a lie.'[4]

And yet as a newly authoritative language ideology, *svoboda slova* was not lacking in its own symbolic ambiguity. Its mixed, largely non-Russian origins left it open to criticism as a Western import that disregarded more time-honoured Russian attitudes toward the word and allowed it to be associated with metaphors of linguistic, social, economic and moral excess – as encapsulated by the two keywords most central to the attacks on the wild years of the 1990s, *proizvol* ('whim') and *bespredel* (criminal slang for 'lawlessness'). In this chapter I map the rise, and then fall, in symbolic value of Russian obscene language or *mat* – one of the three hallmarks (together with foreign loans and criminal argot) of the language culture of the 1990s – in an attempt to document the mixed linguistic legacy of perestroika and glasnost, and ultimately of the Soviet period more broadly.

THE SYMBOLIC AUTHORITY OF PROFANITY, OLD AND NEW

Profanity has always had its place as a mark of distinction in a variety of settings in everyday life. In some settings its proper use actually functions as a source of linguistic capital.[5] Boris Uspenskii points out that, historically, profane language shares much in common with the sacred language of the Church. Both were prohibited from being pronounced out loud or used in a dismissive or matter-of-fact way: 'Special stress on the unconventionality of the linguistic sign is a phenomenon intrinsic to the sacred sphere, owing to the tabooification of expressions associated with this sphere; thus, in a paradoxical way, the lexicon of the profane is entwined with that of the sacred.'[6] This was, of course, true of Russian *mat* as of profane language in other cultures. In fact, throughout Russian folklore we see examples where the invocation of *mat* and *skvernoslovie* (foul words) actually serves as a more potent means of warding off diabolical forces than prayer.[7]

This being said, *mat* has never been a recognized part of the Russian literary language. Lomonosov's 'lower style' (the bottom of his triad, below 'higher' and 'middle') specifically excluded it as an option.[8] While vulgar speech across most cultures is defined by its taboo status, the gap between sacred and profane was particularly wide in the Soviet context for two reasons. One lies in the traditional Russian linguistic ideology that views the language as a sacred store or marker of national identity.[9] A second reason rests in the emergence in Soviet linguistics of the 'civilized language' (*kul'tura iazyka*) movement – with its primary emphasis on proper usage – as the dominant linguistic ideology, beginning in the 1960s and extending through to the Soviet Union's collapse.[10] Both trends assigned high value to proper, or 'cultured' (*kul'turnoe*), usage of language as opposed to more free-wheeling populist attitudes toward language that valued free speech or individual self-expression.

Once the state loosened its ideological, legal and financial control of the media in the early 1990s, the old attitudes to 'cultured speech' started to be eroded. Papers and programming became not only more democratic, but also more market oriented. A flurry of niche papers, magazines, shows and channels emerged to appeal to more targeted subgroups of the community, each doing its best to cut a linguistic profile that would appeal to its target readers and viewers. Many view the period from August 1991 to the end of 1995 as something of a golden age of the Russian media, in which it served the function of a Fourth Estate truly independent of the state, in terms of both finances and views.[11]

Of course, the new democratic and market orientations came at a price. New dependence on advertising changed both the look and sound of print and electronic media. Increasing pressure to appeal to a mass market led both spheres to think in terms of entertainment rather than education and enlightenment – as had been the case in Soviet times – a dynamic that has been shown globally to lead to a general tabloidization of the media.[12] Newspapers, magazines and publishing houses alike found it hard to resist the allure of pulp fiction and trashy TV (soaps, serials, game shows and sensationalist 'news' exposés), much of which was imported from the West because of the lack of experience, financing and infrastructure to produce home-grown versions.[13] And separate trends of *chernukha* and 'black PR' added further linguistic ambiguity to the mix.[14]

Economically and technologically, many of the linguistic changes that accompanied these radical shifts in the information industries were both natural and essential. A market economy and democratic political system required new terms to describe those processes, many of which did not exist in Russian. Hence the great influx of foreign loans from the West and from English in particular. The new market for freer, more open discourse also inevitably meant more spontaneous language production that tended to be more colloquial in style, a trend exacerbated by the influx of a new generation of journalists and television personalities lacking traditional Soviet training. On one level, this meant a general 'coarsening' of the language of the print and electronic media, but from another perspective, it could also be seen as the price to be paid for democracy – where the people and their language (the 'vernacular' or 'vulgate') held more sway in public discourse.[15] And this inevitably included the rise in prominence in vulgarity, or *mat*.

In addition to these economic and institutional reasons, another reason for the increase in public profanity lies in the notion of catharsis. The vulgarization and (for that matter) criminalization of language in the late 1980s and 1990s reflected social and economic conditions that had, themselves, become vulgar, brutal and criminal. Or, as Viktor Erofeev puts it in his essay 'Dirty Words', 'the syllables blia-blia-blia and yob-yob-yob echo through the air above Russia like the bleeps of a sputnik. Decode these sounds and you have a general distress signal, the SOS of national catastrophe.'[16] Yet *mat* and *blatnaia muzyka* (criminal argot) not only acted as a living, breathing testament to the difficult times, they also provided speakers with a useful outlet for anger and frustration. Such a function is clearly reflected in aphorisms widely circulated at the time (and quoted in the epigraphs to this paper):

Dlia otsenki polozheniia v strane net slov! Ostalis' odni vyrazheniia.
There are no words for what's happening in Russia! Only [obscene] expressions.[17]
Kak poslat' na khui ne ispol'zuia neprilichnykh slov?
How do you send a person to fuck without using bad words?[18]

Evidence was even adduced that *mat* could serve as a form of physical therapy – as in a 2005 clinical study claiming that injured soldiers who were nurtured in a hospital environment of free-flowing *mat* actually healed quicker, because it provided a 'sexual boost of emotion that mobilizes their androgen levels', functioning as what the author called a 'verbal prosthesis':

Our research has shown that wounds scarred over and bones coalesced more quickly in wards where *mat* was audible from morning to night, regardless of whether there were workers or intellectuals there. In the wards 'purified' of *mat*, in contrast, the revitalization process was slow. Historically, during 'transitional' periods there emerges a mass debilitation in society, where it becomes necessary for the most vulnerable layers of society (youth and people with insufficient education) to use the eroticization of their verbal activity as a cultural (anticultural!) defence. Their speech is laden with verbal prostheses – sexually scabrous expressions (as a subconscious protest against social pressure).[19]

Vladimir Zhel'vis, explaining that a large reason for invective's popularity lies in its ability to express emotion that is otherwise difficult to 'transmit with the help of codified resources', likens its force in these instances to

that of the Aristotelian sense of catharsis, 'a purification through experiencing a hero's high tragedy in all its twists and turns' (although in this case, the
'hero' seems to be the *mat*-user him- or herself).[20] Zhel'vis also speaks
of the resulting relief the profanity user receives as a 'defiant harmony'
(*poprannaia garmoniia*) of the sort that breaking rules sometimes brings –
where someone is at once aware of the norms and gratified, however fleet-
ingly, by participation in their violation.[21] In this sense the use of profanity
acts according to the norms of Mikhail Bakhtin's theory of carnival, to
actually sustain the sacredness of the very standards it is, on the surface,
undermining.[22]

INSTITUTIONAL AUTHORIZATION OF *MAT*

The cultural currency of *mat* also increased thanks to 'endorsements'
of various kinds from prominent institutional authorities in the realm of
language – linguists, writers and politicians, in particular. In popular
linguistics we find, from the perestroika era to the mid-1990s, a booming
industry of books on *mat* and *blatnaia muzyka* that effectively enhanced
their linguistic capital and brought them back from beyond the pale
of taboo. They achieved this effect ideologically by anchoring their work
in the long-standing romantic project of identifying and celebrating
ethnic Russian roots, and economically by helping to foster a self-
sustaining market for reference books – however dubious their methodological grounding.

Scholars of Russian profanity and criminal argot have aptly shown that
the history of these speciality dictionaries dates back at least to the nineteenth century and is rooted in the mythology of the outlaw and in
romanticism in general.[23] Even in the midst of high Stalinism, the young
Dmitrii Likhachev, who later became an icon of Russian philology, took on
the subject with a palpable strain of romanticism and mythologization,
writing of the 'magical' and 'incantatory' nature of thieves' argot and
arguing that it only appeared 'substandard' to the outsider; insider thieves
deemed it to be 'heroic and elevated'.[24]

With the emergence of democratic institutions and the collapse of the
Soviet Union, the symbolic capital of this sort of discourse of heroicism
attached to 'substandard' speech styles surged, so starkly contrasted as it was
to the wooden and now discredited language of the Soviet state. Strains
of more or less effusive praise colour the majority of introductions to the
dozens of newly published lexicons devoted to the topic. The editors of one

of the first post-perestroika dictionaries of criminal argot invoked the same discourse of profanity as physical therapy previously mentioned:

[T]he language long ago felt and understood that it had become stock and rubbery and had forgotten that it was Russian, and, tired of being the Soviet-style submissive do-gooder, turned to its roots. Like a sponge, all of those years – without asking permission – it has soaked up the expressive, vivid lexicon of the [prison camp] zone, the thoroughly forgotten, correct, (real!) Russian of the finally permitted Nabokov, Dovlatov, Siniavskii, Aleshkovskii, Platonov . . . And in this manner, it seems, it is healing itself of the metastasis of pharisaism, cliché, official tongue-tiedness, ideologism and mediocrity.[25]

To underscore the legitimate status of this long-suppressed part of the language, compilers even invoked Turgenev to explain how the lexicon of the camp had led the 'great and mighty' (*velikii i moguchii*) Russian language to 'replenish itself' (*popolniat'sia*).[26] Echoing these sentiments from his political rostrum, the nationalist Vladimir Zhirinovskii invoked the discourse of linguistic wealth and 'rehabilitation' when he railed against those of his fellow politicians who called for laws forbidding the use of *mat*: 'Russian is the most expressive language in the world! But we have a hatred of our own tongue. We reject the wealth of the language, and this has led to a rejection of Russian wealth in general. We need to rehabilitate *mat*.'[27]

Even in more serious studies of Russian *mat* and criminal argot we see evidence of aggrandizement if not romanticization of the subject matter. In *Russian Sacred Idioms*, co-editors and Academy of Sciences linguists Anatolii Baranov and Dmitrii Dobrovol'skii deploy an elaborate and creative play on the romantic myth of *mat* as the authentic voice of the people by adopting the device of the 'found manuscript' (in the spirit of Gogol' and Pushkin, among others), inventing and introducing the fictional collector of *mat* Vasilii Bui (rhymes with *khui*, or 'prick'), whom they lionize as an 'elite linguist and Citizen with a capital "C" – a Russian patriot', who roams the Russian provinces in search of new pearls of folk vulgarity:

We tried . . . to contact the author but it turned out that he no longer lives at the address shown. Over the course of four years we received from him from Briansk, Rostov, Saratov, Paris, Ekaterinburg, Gomel' and Baden-Baden short notes with addenda and editorial instructions. All of this material has gone into the 'Vasilii Bui' archive, which we preserve with great care.[28]

The romantic gloss used to highlight Bui's folk authenticity was equalled by the editors' declared amazement over his impressive linguistic pedigree ('The symphonic personality of Vasilii Bui is veiled in mystery. We know nothing about his professional activity, about where he received such an elite linguistic education and what his creative plans [for the future] may be').[29] This device served to increase the value not only of the collection, but also of the legitimacy of the language itself as an object of study. The back cover of the second edition played up these parallel sources of authority by featuring one quote comparing Bui to Koz'ma Prutkov, fictional nineteenth-century author of folk aphorisms, and a second, from the Academy linguist Aleksei Shmelev, praising the dictionary for fulfilling 'the highest demands of linguistic scholarship'.[30]

Of course, above and beyond any romantic or essentialist motivations for producing dictionaries of *mat*, a much simpler and concrete rationale lay in the market appeal of books devoted to these forms of once-taboo discourse. As one reviewer caustically points out, many of the books posing as 'dictionaries' have 'more in common with pornography than lexicography', with even professional philologists (who, he claims, were anyway in the minority) sacrificing their scholarly principles to make a quick buck: 'Thus the helmsmen of great Russian literature make money on Russian *mat*.'[31]

The cultural currency of *mat* also benefited from political endorsements, as the quote from Zhirinovskii suggests. The most notorious example of high-placed invective probably comes in the form of Prime Minister Vladimir Putin's press-conference promise in 1999 to 'flush Chechens down the shithole' ('*Esli my ikh naidem v tualete, to my ikh i v sortire zamochim v kontse kontsov*'), a statement that without doubt cast him as a strong and decisive ruler for many Russians and went far to smooth his path to the presidency.[32] Yeltsin was apparently more of a purist about the use of profanity, although rumours from commentators attributed his distaste for *mat* to the principle that 'only the master should have the right to curse' ('*pravo rugat'sia imeet tol'ko sam khoziain*').[33] Gorbachev had his own *mat* moment at a critical juncture of his presidency, referring to his captors in the aftermath of the coup as *mudaki* (dickheads, jerks) and recounting on television how during captivity he had 'sent them where Russians send people' (i.e. 'to fuck').[34] All three episodes involving profanity at the top not only point to a pattern of political authorization of *mat*: they also underscore its place and role as a discourse of power, reserved for rare instances either to convey anger or threat, or to reiterate the special position of the *mat* user himself.

Writers of the period also turned to *mat* as a mark of distinction. Profanity plays a by now well-known role in works by the 'bad boys' of serious literature such as Erofeev and Vladimir Sorokin, not only by contributing to the texture of their postmodern allure (or revulsion) but also in bringing them publicity through public demonstrations and court cases.[35] In fact, a number of writers and intellectuals are on record as believing that the more *mat* was used by the general public, the more precipitously its cultural capital would actually decline. Hence the curious phenomenon of declarations calling for the actual 'protection' of the sacred status of profanity itself against the overuse and misuse by commoners that would lead to the ultimate defusing of the discourse as a source either of catharsis or of aesthetic innovation. As Viktor Erofeev puts it, 'Opponents fear the degradation of society. Supporters worry that the legalization of profanity will release the tension and weaken the possibilities of Russian.'[36] In a similar manner, Zhel'vis warns of the danger of the 'devaluation' of invective with overuse and the cessation of its 'purifying' function, and the deprivation of society of 'one of its means of realizing negative emotions and forcing it to seek catharsis in other types of activities that are not nearly always safe from a social standpoint'.[37] And Andrei Zorin concludes his essay on profanity by predicting the reduction in the breadth and wealth of *mat* as a result of its 'legalization', its 'change from a special language into just one of the stylistic registers of the literary language'.[38]

Perhaps even more important than the endorsement it received from political and intellectual elites were the allure and coverage of such topics in the mass media, ranging from pulp fiction and cop shows to the plethora of shows and genres imported from abroad, including advertising. Explaining the effect of the media's inundation of the public sphere with this language, Aleksei Plutser-Sarno writes of the 'criminalization of the linguistic self-consciousness':

It only serves to ignite the curiosity of well-intended citizens. Bards sing songs in criminal argot, literati write entire novels. Thousands of films about the criminal world are shot, where noble bandits bump off (*mochit'*) the ignoble right and left, and vice versa. The media commonly circulate the myth about the mafia-like nature of society and the state. And thieves' talk plays a significant part in this circulation process ... In fact, thieves' jargon itself has slowly begun to leave the dictionary of argot and assume the status of widely used colloquial speech ... Thieves' language is becoming the language of the reader, in a kind of criminaliza-tion of the linguistic self-consciousness. Well-intended philistines and everyday law-abiding citizens, we are beginning to see ourselves in the role of noble bandits, offended paupers and fearless slum dwellers.[39]

Drawing similar conclusions, Anatolii Chudinov describes the two-way process of legitimation in terms of 'metaphorical expansion':

It has been clear for a long time that phenomena located at the centre of public consciousness had become a source for metaphorical expansion. Moreover, the active use in speech of criminal metaphor (together with the nearly constant stream in the media of pictures of real crimes) has clearly influenced the public assessment of the situation in the country, engendering the idea that society is actually penetrated by criminal ties and relationships, that in Russia crime is the norm.[40]

As these commentators recognize, language influences perceptions of reality as much as reality influences language. The media projection of shifting norms in everyday language and life may well influence real behaviour, linguistic and otherwise, as was indeed happening from the late 1980s onwards.

FROM 'FREEDOM OF SPEECH' TO 'LINGUISTIC
LAWLESSNESS'

Zhel'vis argues that the rise in profanity was partly a result of a kind of 'testing of the boundaries of freedom, an attempt to . . . see how far one can go in the violation of generally accepted taboos'.[41] If one accepts that argument, then at some point in the middle part of the 1990s that boundary was crossed decisively; in an associated process, the positive discourse on language as free speech, democracy, liberation and westernization ceded cultural authority to the negative language on barbarization, vulgarization and criminalization. Celebration of 'freedom of speech' (*svoboda slova*) ceded authority to laments about 'linguistic lawlessness' or *iazykovoi bespredel*.[42]

Despite the big boost it had received from Boris Yeltsin and peers, the concept of 'freedom of speech' does not really have a long or rich history in Russia. Unlike 'glasnost', *svoboda slova* has never truly occupied a place in the common popular lexicon, and when it has it has largely been restricted to Western-oriented intellectuals and formalistic phrases in national constitutions. One of the hallmarks of liberalism and democracy, the term has its origins in the English Bill of Rights (1689), the French Declaration of Human Rights and Citizenship (1789) and the writings of John Stuart Mill (1806–1873), among others. In Russia, where traditions of liberal democracies were far less developed, the term never really acquired wide circulation in public discourse. In his 1882 dictionary Vladimir Dal' included it under the general headword 'svoboda', but the definition of the latter nicely illustrates the word's perceived potential for doing harm to the moral fabric of society: 'Freedom is a relative term; it can refer to a partial, limited expanse, to a known issue; to various degrees of that expanse; or to full, unbridled whim (*proizvol*) or self-will.'[43] More recently, the linguist Anna Wierzbicka has argued that, while the English 'freedom' is closely linked to notions of individual freedom, the Russian *svoboda* connotes breaking free *from* some greater force and is dependent more on the complicity of others. And while she takes issue with claims that the word is synonymous with 'disorder or the opportunity to indulge with impunity in some kind of anti-social or dangerous behaviour', Wierzbicka notes that it may have undergone 'a semantic turn' during the Soviet period that gave it more '"anarchic" implications'.[44] Although the concept did appear in Soviet constitutions, it did not enjoy much linguistic capital and pragmatically was more likely to be used in a negative context in association with the bourgeois ideologies of the West, which pretended to offer this entity to the masses in order to deprive them of actual freedom.

Though the atmosphere was not so ideologically charged, it is these more ambivalent, if not negative, associations one sees with rising frequency over the latter part of the 1990s. A 1997 commentary on the dire state of public discourse, particularly in the print media, argues that, in spite of hopes that the arrival of freedom of speech would give rise to the drive to speak and write in a truthful and free language, the predominant trend had increasingly become what the author calls 'discursive unruliness' (*slovesnaia raznuzdannost'*) akin to public graffiti.[45] The philologist Vladimir Kolesov likewise interprets the term *svoboda* in a manner that underscores the ethical conditions attached to it, in particular, the link between 'freedom' and 'responsibility'.[46]

So when *svoboda slova* emerged as a dominant keyword of the perestroika and early Yeltsin years, it did so, for all practical purposes, as a calque from the West. This was unproblematic in the peak of perestroika when public opinion was soundly behind more radical interpretations of glasnost. But when the floodgates of freedom – verbal and otherwise – opened wide in the early 1990s, the precarious grounding of the term began to show.

Some critics derided the term for giving rise to 'high-handedness or self-will (*svoevolie*) among journalists' which had led to 'criminalization of public consciousness'.[47] Others mocked it for having grand pretensions that, in reality, boiled down to little more than a licence to swear in public: 'Today *mat* enjoys as much protection as the "White House",' the Russian parliament building that served as the focal point for popular resistance during the failed 1991 coup: 'People have united around it, legalizing its status in literature, armed with golden quills. Barricades have been constructed out of brave and weighty formulas.'[48]

Some dismissed this preoccupation with *mat* as characteristic only of journalists and the marginalized intelligentsia.[49] Still others linked the word in conceptual association with keywords such as 'black PR' or *kompromat* ('compromising evidence') that had come to symbolize the cheapening of the social and ethical fabric of the new Russian society. One of the more interesting of these was the notion of *iazykovoi bespredel*. According to Valerii Mokienko, the word *bespredel* itself was not new, but dated back to the youth slang of the 1960s (where it signified 'lawlessness', '*bezzakonie*'; 'some action carried out beyond all normal limits', '*chto-l., sovershaemoe bez mery*'; 'a crowd of young people', '*bol'shaia tolpa molodezhi*') and before that to thieves' argot where, quite interestingly, it denoted 'lawlessness', but 'not in the official judicial sense – as a violation of legal norms of the state, but rather as the absolute failure to follow the unwritten law, the norms of behaviour, accepted in the thieves' world'.[50] The latter is a point quite interesting in and of itself, given contemporary discussions over Russian attitudes toward the 'rule of law'.

But *bespredel* has deeper associative roots in the notion of *proizvol*, or 'whim', which dates back at least to the era of the Great Reforms. In the context of linguistic debates during political transition, it conveyed a sense of freedom of action dependent solely on the will of the individual and unconstrained by any wider social responsibility.[51] Clearly a negative term, *proizvol* marked a sharp contrast to the more positive 'freedom of speech'. An opinion piece in *Delovye liudi* in 2000 set up the opposition between *svoboda slova* and *volia/proizvol* succinctly:

In general, *svoboda* is somehow not a Russian word. They say it comes naked, they say it is chosen, but few have seen it in the eyes or know what one is supposed to eat it with. *Volia* is more appropriate and comprehensible. When used in reference to the media – *proizvol*. We have no freedom of speech. We have plenty of discursive whim (*proizvol slova*).[52]

The rapid rise of Internet use in the 2000s has provided new impetus for the broad dissemination of profanity and, while the medium may be new, the motivations appear less unique. One of the more notorious sources is *iazyk padonkov* ('skumbag [*sic*] language'), which is a profanity-filled, web-based jargon that uses slang, profanity and orthographic transgression as a brash means of flaunting norm violations.[53] A closer look at the origins and mechanisms of the phenomenon, however, shows it to be rooted in the relatively educated milieu of self-proclaimed 'counter-culture' writers congregated at websites such as fuck.ru and udaff.com beginning in the early 2000s. While the language did ignite into something of a viral trend beginning in 2005 when it first received attention in the popular print media, it originated as the very sort of elite project that reflects the perception of profanity as the special prerogative of intellectuals.[54] And the fact that the language followed relatively strict 'rules' of 'improper usage' suggests that, rather than an expression of anarchic protest, it might better be understood as a form of carnivalesque play – deliberate violations of norms that, by virtue of their rule-governed behaviour, serve in the long term to reinforce the legitimacy of the very norms they violate.[55]

So where does this leave us? How do we account for the different metaphors and symbolic associations linked to vulgarity and criminal argot – from freedom and liberation, to prosthesis and catharsis, to irresponsibility and lawlessness? Although to a certain extent they are discourses that coexist throughout the late- and post-Soviet era, one can clearly detect a shift in the cultural capital proper to each at a point in the mid- to late 1990s, when the language culture, in the eyes and ears of a critical mass, crossed over into the realm of *bespredel*. By 1997 or so, the dynamic had changed and the spectre of the clichéd, wooden discourse of the Soviet state had faded, with new threats, of both foreign origin and internal collapse, coming to the fore. Add to this the nationwide identity crisis embodied in efforts to write new anthems and national ideas and you have a language culture less inclined to celebrate the liberation of discourse and more inclined to seek out root causes of existing pain, and positive forces of stability and pride to counteract it. And it is at this point in the language culture that a more or less free-form celebration of *mat* cedes symbolic authority to discussions of 'linguistic constants' (*iazykovye konstanty*) and 'linguistic mentality' (*iazykovaia mental'nost'* or *mentalitet*) – language-based efforts to identify those more 'organic' and authentic keywords of Russianness that ought to serve as the ethical keywords and guideposts for the speech culture of the new era.

As inevitable as the shifting value and authority of competing discourses on language, however, is the very existence of such debates on proper usage in the first place. From at least the late eighteenth and early nineteenth centuries – a time when national identity itself came to be the focus of political and ideological attention on an unprecedented scale – debates about the Russian language have figured centrally in broader discussions of what it means to be Russian. Two centuries later the link shows little sign of weakening, even though both language 'norms' and technologies of communication continue, stubbornly and unpredictably, to evolve.

NOTES

1. J. J. Goux, *Symbolic Economies: After Marx and Freud*, trans. J. C. Gage (Ithaca, NY, 1990), 2–3. See also Goux, 'Cash, Check, or Charge?', in *The New Economic*

Criticism: Studies at the Intersection of Literature and Economics, ed. M. Woodmansee and M. Osteen (London, 1999), 114–27.

2. P. Bourdieu, *Language and Symbolic Power*, ed. and trans. J. B. Thompson (Cambridge, MA, 1991). In a very different tone and for different ends, Vitalii Kostomarov makes a similar claim in the underlying thesis of his *Iazykovoi vkus epokhi: iz nabliudeniia nad rechevoi praktikoi mass-media* (Moscow, 1994).

3. 'Pishite, chto khotite, tol'ko ne vrite', *Kommersant – Vlast'*, 13 June 2000.

4. A. G. Altunian, *'Politicheskie mneniia' Faddeia Bulgarina: ideino-stilisticheskii analiz zapisok F. V. Bulgarina k Nikolaiu I* (Moscow, 1998), 136.

5. See J. B. Thompson, 'Editor's Introduction', in Bourdieu, *Language and Symbolic Power*, 22.

6. B. Uspenskii, 'Mifologicheskii aspekt russkoi ekspressivnoi frazeologii', in *Anti-mir russkoi kul'tury: iazyk, fol'klor, literatura*, ed. N. Bogomolov (Moscow, 1996), 14.

7. Ibid., 19. At the same time, several other sources note that Russian profanity is only weakly linked to religiously oriented vulgarisms (*bogokhul'stvo*), and dominated, instead, by invectives linked to procreation, presumably due to the prominent influence of pagan culture (where issues of fertility and procreation were dominant) in the emergence of *mat*. V. Zhel'vis, *Pole brani: skvernoslovie kak sotsial'naia problema* (Moscow, 1997), 208–9.

8. A. Zorin, 'Legalizatsiia obstsennoi leksiki i ee kul'turnye posledstviia', in *Anti-mir russkoi kul'tury*, ed. Bogomolov, 135.

9. M. S. Gorham, 'Linguistic Ideologies, Economies, and Technologies in the Language Culture of Contemporary Russia (1987–2008)', *Journal of Slavic Linguistics* 17:1–2 (2009), 163–92.

10. M. S. Gorham, 'Language Ideology and the Evolution of *Kul'tura iazyka* ("Speech Culture") in Soviet Russia', in *Politics and the Theory of Language in the USSR, 1917–1938*, ed. C. Brandist and K. Chown (London, 2010), 137–49.

11. Ia. N. Zasurskii, *Iskushenie svobodoi: rossiiskaia zhurnalistika, 1990–2004* (Moscow, 2004), 27.

12. H. Tumber, 'Democracy in the Information Age: The Role of the Fourth Estate in Cyberspace', in *Culture and Politics in the Information Age: A New Politics?*, ed. F. Webster (London, 2001), 17–31.

13. This period is extensively discussed in A. M. Barker, ed., *Consuming Russia: Popular Culture, Sex, and Society since Gorbachev* (Durham, NC, 1999).

14. *Chernukha*, a derivative from 'black' with derogatory connotations, was a widely recognized trend in the mass media of the 1990s in which negative aspects of Russian history and current Russian reality were depicted in stark, at times exaggerated, tones, sparking public hand-wringing in many intellectual corners over the state of Russian national and cultural identity.

15. Richard D. Anderson argues that closer proximity to the vernacular of public discourse is one key indicator of a successful transition from an authoritarian to a democratic society, as it signals a greater connection between institutions of power and the populace (R. D. Anderson Jr, V. I. Chervyakov and P. B. Parshin, 'Words Matter: Linguistic Conditions for Democracy in Russia', *Slavic Review*

54:1, 1995, 868–95). John Joseph makes a related point but in the opposite direction when he argues that 'standard' language is an imagined ideal that serves the purpose of justifying the use of language as an essential marker of national identity: all class, regional and individual variations to the standard are reduced to 'dialects' ('The Grammatical Being Called a Nation', in *Language and History: Integrationist Perspectives*, ed. N. Love, London, 2006). If this is so, than a logical result of the rejection of such state order (particularly a more authoritarian one) would be a general devaluation of the 'standard' language of that state and celebration of variations, dialects and deviations – a phenomenon we certainly do witness in Russia of the 1990s.

16. V. Erofeev, 'Dirty Words', *New Yorker* 79:26 (15 September 2003), 45 (*'blia'* and *'yob'* derive from common Russian swearwords, 'whore' and 'fuck'). Writing on the verge of the Soviet Union's collapse, another commentator soberly described *mat* as a weapon that enabled speakers to 'most appropriately evaluate the state of a country that is decisively changing its social order' (N. Potapov, 'Mat v pereplete', *Pravda*, 21 November 1991; reprinted in A. D. Dulichenko, ed., *Etnosotsiolingvistika 'perestroiki' v SSSR: antologiia zapechatlennogo vremeni*, Munich, 1999, 240).

17. Unidentified politician, quoted in E. Bernaskoni, 'Language Is Like a Woman: It Needs to Be Loved and Protected', *Ekho planety* no. 8, 16 February 2001.

18. Unattributed aphorism retrieved on 9 April 2008 from *Russkie aforizmy*, www.aphorismos.ru/search/.

19. L. A. Kitaev-Smyk, 'Seksual'no-verbal'nye zashchita i agressiia (maternaia rech' i maternaia rugan')', in *Rechevaia agressiia v sovremennoi kul'ture: sbornik nauchnykh trudov*, ed. M. V. Zagidullina (Cheliabinsk, 2005), 18, 21.

20. Zhel'vis, *Pole brani*, 138, 29–30.

21. Ibid., 32.

22. Ibid., 18. For a more detailed post-Bakhtinian analysis of argot, see V. S. Elistratov, 'Argo i kul'tura', in *Slovar' russkogo argo (materialy 1980–1990-kh gg.)*, ed. V. S. Elistratov (Moscow, 2000), 574–683.

23. A. Plutser-Sarno, 'Russkii vorovskoi slovar' kak kul'turnyi fenomen', *Logos* 2 (2000), 209–17.

24. D. S. Likhachev, 'Cherty pervobytnogo primitivizma vorovskoi rechi' (1935), in *Slovar' tiuremno-lagerno-blatnogo zhargona (rechevoi i graficheskii portret sovetskoi tiur'my)*, ed. D. S. Baldaev, V. K. Belko and I. M. Isupov (Moscow, 1992), 360–5, 369.

25. Baldaev et al., *Slovar' tiuremno-lagerno-blatnogo zhargona*, 6–7.

26. Ibid., 9.

27. Quoted in Erofeev, 'Dirty Words', 48.

28. V. Bui, *Russkaia zavetnaia idiomatika: veselyi slovar' krylatykh vyrazhenii* (Moscow, 1995), vi.

29. Ibid., vii.

30. V. Bui, *Russkaia zavetnaia idiomatika: veselyi slovar' narodnykh vyrazhenii*, 2nd, rev. edn (Moscow, 2005), back cover.

31. A. Plutser-Sarno, 'Maternyi slovar' kak fenomen russkoi kul'tury: russkaia nepristoinaia leksika v slovariakh XIX–XX vv.', in A. Plutser-Sarno, *Bol'shoi slovar' mata*, vol. I (St Petersburg, 2001), 66.

32. This was by no means the last of such violent and vulgar pronouncements uttered by Putin. For a detailed discussion, see M. S. Gorham, 'Vladimir Putin and the Rise of the New Russian Vulgate', *Groniek: Historisch Tijdschrift* 39 (2006), 297–308.

33. A. Korolev, 'Oskorblenie sakral'nogo: matershchina – magiia novogo vremeni', *Literaturnaia gazeta* 15 (11 April 2001), 12.

34. Quoted in G. Guseinov, *D.S.P.: sovetskie ideologemy v russkom diskurse 1990-kh* (Moscow, 2004), 146.

35. For an overview of initiatives taken by the Kremlin-backed youth group 'Walking Together' (*Idushchie vmeste*), against the 'pornographic' works of Vladimir Sorokin, Viktor Erofeev and Viktor Pelevin, see D. Birch, 'In Russia, a New Battle of Morals', *Baltimore Sun*, 9 December 2002, http://articles.baltimoresun.com/2002-12-09/news/0212090265_1_russian-literature-russian-culture-putin.

36. V. Erofeev, 'Tsarstvo mata', *Moskovskie novosti* 27 (23 July 2004), 16. Elistratov talks about the 'complete plebianization of the sanctuary of the thieves' hermetic system' (*Slovar' russkogo argo*, 651).

37. Zhel'vis, *Pole brani*, 135–6.

38. Zorin, 'Legalizatsiia obstsennoi leksiki', 136.

39. Plutser-Sarno, 'Russkii vorovskoi slovar'', 217. Elena Bernaskoni ('Language Is Like a Woman') describes the phenomenon more simply in the now familiar discourse of 'linguistic citizenship', writing that, 'when street cursing is put into circulation, sounding from various tribunals, it acquires something of a right to citizenship'. See also Zhel'vis, *Pole brani*, 196.

40. A. P. Chudinov, *Rossiia v metaforicheskom zerkale: kognitivnoe issledovanie politicheskoi metafory (1991–2000)* (Ekaterinburg, 2001), 103.

41. Zhel'vis, *Pole brani*, 195.

42. V. S. Elistratov makes a similar claim in his delineation of two periods of contemporary Russian language culture ('Natsional'nyi iazyk i natsional'naia ideia', 2 February 2001, www.gramota.ru/biblio/magazines/gramota/28_54). See also L. Ryazanova-Clark, '"The Crystallization of Structures": Linguistic Culture in Putin's Russia', in *Landslide of the Norm: Language Culture in Post-Soviet Russia*, ed. I. Lunde and T. Roesen (Bergen, 2006), 41–6.

43. In the original, 'Svoboda poniatie sravnitel'noe; ona mozhet otnosit'sia do prostora chastnogo, ogranichennogo, k izvestnomu delu otnosiashchemusia, ili k raznym stepeniam etogo prostora, i nakonets k polnomu, neobuzdannomu proizvolu ili samovol'stvu.' V. Dal', *Tolkovyi slovar' zhivogo velikorusskogo iazyka*, vol. IV (1882), 151.

44. A. Vezhbitskaia (Wierzbicka), *Ponimanie kul'tur cherez posredstvo kliuchevykh slov* (Moscow, 2001), 233–41.

45. N. Vainonen, 'Kazhdyi pishet, kak on dyshit', *Zhurnalist* 8 (1997), 38.

46. V. V. Kolesov, *Iazyk i mental'nost'* (St Petersburg, 2004), 108–9.

47. M. A. Grachev, 'V pogone za effektom (blatnye slova na gazetnoi polose)', *Russkaia rech'* 5 (1 September 2001), 67–8.

48. N. Potapov, 'Mat v pereplete', *Pravda* 21 (21 November 1991), 3. Reprinted in Dulichenko, *Etnosotsiolingvistika*, 242.

49. e.g. 'Who, other than the producers of words, seriously wants freedom of speech? The wishy-washy, grumbling and thinking reed – and that's it.' L. Radzikhovskii, 'Led taet, no klimat ne meniaetsia', *Rossiiskaia gazeta* 45 (3 March 2008), www.rg.ru/2008/03/03/radzihovsky.html.

50. V. Mokienko, 'Substandartnaia frazeologiia russkogo iazyka i nekotorye problemy ee lingvisticheskogo izucheniia', in *Dinamika russkogo slova: mezhvuzovskii sbornik statei k 60-letiiu prof. V. V. Kolesova*, ed. V. M. Mokienko et al. (St Petersburg, 1994), 156.

51. Dal' gives the following string of attributes: 'delo otdano na ego proizvol, kak khochet. V postupkakh ego viden polnyi proizvol, samovolie, neobuzdannost' ili despotizm; on ne stesniaet voli svoei nichem' (*Tolkovyi slovar'*, vol. III, 486).

52. 'Perekoshennye khari', *Delovye liudi* 115 (1 October 2000). V. N. Shaposhnikov corroborates the symbolic link between freedom and lawlessness in his own study of the language of the 1990s, where he argues that among the key antonym pairs that have emerged in contemporary discourse are those of *svoboda* versus *ravenstvo, svoboda* versus *poriadok*, and *svoboda* versus *spravedlivost'*, on the one hand, and *bespredel* versus *poriadok* and *zakonnost'*, on the other: *Russkaia rech' 1990-kh: sovremennaia Rossiia v iazykovom otobrazhenii* (Moscow, 1998), 160–209.

53. Some of the more common examples include terms such as превед (*preved*, from '*privet*', or 'hello'), кросафчег (*krosafcheg*, from '*krasavchik*', or 'pretty boy') and аффтар выпей йаду (*afftar vypei iadu*, 'drink poison, author' – an expression of displeasure over a post or article).

54. A. Vernidub, 'U iazyka est' aftar,' *Russkii Newsweek* 17 (16–22 May 2005).

55. For an excellent discussion of the history and significance of *iazyk padonkov* as a form of web-based and rule-governed distinction, see V. Zvereva, '"Iazyk padonkaf": diskussii pol'zovatelei Runeta', in *From Poets to Padonki: Linguistic Authority and Norm Negotiation in Modern Russian Culture*, ed. I. Lunde and M. Paulsen (Bergen, 2009), 49–79.

CHAPTER 13

Policies and practices of language education in post-Soviet Central Asia: between ethnic identity and civic consciousness

Olivier Ferrando

In post-Soviet Central Asia the education sector is of particular interest, in the sense that governments have to cope with the legacy both of a multi-ethnic population and of a multilingual education system. In Soviet times, language was considered a key criterion in differentiating ethnic groups and reinforcing their collective consciousness. Most citizens were consequently guaranteed an education in their own native language. However, Russian played the role of an unofficial *lingua franca* in the multilingual society of the USSR. In Central Asia it became the language of education of most non-native peoples.[1]

Perestroika, and the subsequent collapse of the USSR, had a strong impact on education. Each independent state focused on the legitimization of its newly gained sovereignty by promoting its 'titular nationality' – the one after which the state was named – and, as a matter of fact, disregarding other ethnic groups, which were reduced to the status of minorities. In the education sector, new policies encouraged the use of the state language as the sole language of instruction. As a result, during the first decade of independence, the share of schools where education was provided in the Russian language or in any other non-state language appreciably declined. In recent years, however, Russian schools have recovered the attractiveness they had in Soviet times. Notwithstanding the mass departure of Russians from Central Asia and the resulting lack of Russian teachers, many parents press for the (re)opening of Russian schools.

This chapter examines the issue of education language – the primary language in which education is run – in post-Soviet Central Asia, adopting a double comparative perspective. First, the analysis focuses on three neighbouring countries, Uzbekistan, Kyrgyzstan and Tajikistan, and particularly on the Ferghana Valley, a small but densely populated region often considered as a microcosm of Central Asian complexity (see Map 1). My contention here is that ethnic minorities, which used to have a legally equal status under the Soviet regime, are now subject to differentiated treatment in the education sector, which varies from one target state to the other. Second, the paper focuses on indigenous minorities who were present prior to Russian colonization, namely those known today as Uzbeks, Kyrgyz and Tajiks, who were suddenly cut off from their kin-state after the establishment of international borders between the Central Asian states in the early 1990s. My contention here is that parents belonging to these indigenous minorities have developed alternative education strategies since the collapse of the USSR. In Soviet times parents decided either to foster a civic consciousness in their children by educating them in the state language, and thereby facilitating their integration in the surrounding society, or to promote a specifically ethnic identity by educating them in their native language. I assume that this binary frame, which coincides with the well-known civic vs ethnic identity dichotomy – of which more shortly – is of importance in its own right, rather than masking a more complex situation, where other options might play an increasing role in parents' schooling strategy.

I propose to check these two assumptions at different levels, as follows:

• From a state policy perspective, the paper investigates the treatment of ethnic minorities in terms of education languages, and of the production and supply of textbooks, the initial training and the continuing education of schoolteachers.

• From an ethnic community approach, it examines the discourse that activists and minority leaders use to frame the education sector as a means of community mobilization. The paper focuses on non-Russian ethnic groups insofar as Russian represents neither their native language, nor their state language.

• From a grass-roots individual perspective, it seeks to understand whether parents adhere either to the state policy or to the community leaders' discourse, or whether they develop their own assessment of the education issue and adopt alternative decisions. I argue here that Russian, as a third and unexpected choice, embodies a new pattern of *schooling strategy* from parents who seek a quality education for their children and to ensure them future job opportunities in Russia.

This paper is based on published materials on education and language policies, including statistics and data from ministries of education, and on field research undertaken from October 2006 to September 2008 in the

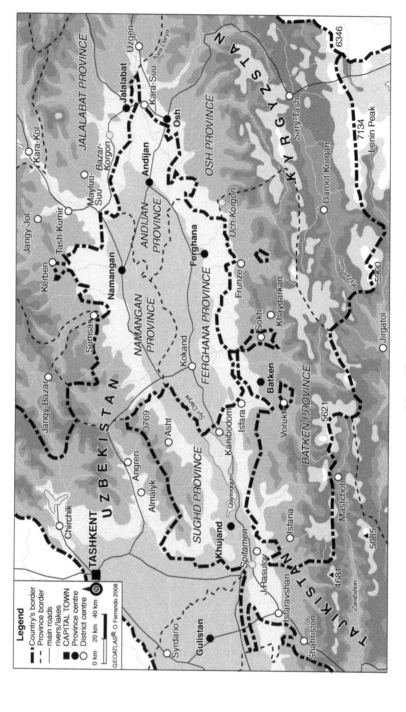

Map 1 The Ferghana Valley

three target countries,[2] where I conducted interviews with state officials, local authorities, community leaders, school directors, teachers and parents.[3]

HISTORICAL AND LEGAL BACKGROUND

As is true throughout post-Soviet space, Central Asian states have largely inherited their educational systems from their Communist past. Between 1924 and 1936, Central Asia became the field for a 'fabrication of nations'.[4] According to Meinecke's well-known dichotomy between civic and ethnic nationalism,[5] the USSR promoted nations on the basis of their own history, culture and language.[6] In the long term, however, the Soviet ideology aimed at building a socialist union of denationalized peoples. As Suny has pointed out,[7] the Soviet Union was the first state to systematically base its political units on ethnicity. Indeed, the Soviet nationalities policy aimed at regrouping and fixing local identities into national categories based on homogeneous criteria (language, religion, cultural practices). This policy consisted of a 'double assimilation': on the one hand, it assimilated peoples into official nationality categories through census, map and other classificatory devices; and on the other hand, it assimilated them into the Soviet state and society through a range of administrative, economic, cultural and political institutions.[8] As a result, the pre-colonial, multilayered political entities of Central Asia were replaced with five national republics, whose borders essentially corresponded with the five newly created nationalities. Even though the rationale of the delimitation was the coincidence of ethnic and political territorial boundaries, there were many cases in which populations from one titular nationality remained outside the republic to which their group gave its name. This was particularly the case of Uzbeks, Tajiks and Kyrgyz who resided outside the borders of their respective national republic.

Under the Soviet regime, constitutions and legal documents guaranteed cultural rights to all nationalities. In the education sector, everyone had the right to 'a schooling in their mother tongue' (article 45 of the USSR Constitution of 1977). In multi-ethnic Central Asian rural societies,[9] a network of native language schools developed on the basis of the ethnic composition of the population. The education system was managed through a double chain of command. The hierarchical chain placed each school under the supervision of a district department of education (*raionnyi otdel obrazovaniia*, abbreviated *raiono*), which in turn was under the control of the provincial department of education (*oblono*), and the whole system was managed by the Ministry of Education (MoE) of each republic. From an operational chain of command, teaching programmes were implemented on a language basis. For instance, all Uzbek-language schools from Central Asia followed the same programme regardless of their location. Curricula, textbooks and teachers' materials were all designed in Tashkent, at the MoE of the Uzbek SSR, in line with Soviet ideology, and distributed all around the region. It followed that an Uzbek-language school located, say, in the Tajik SSR was managed by the MoE of its host republic, Tajikistan, but received operational support from the MoE of its kin-republic,[10] Uzbekistan.

With regard to Russian-language schools, they were attended mostly by Russians, but also by various non-indigenous groups who had reached the region more or less voluntarily (Slavs, Uralian Tatars) or as the result of forced settlement (Koreans, Germans, Caucasians, Crimean Tatars, Greeks, Poles etc.). Such groups generally lived in mixed urban or rural areas and could not therefore manage to arrange separate schooling in their respective native languages. Parents accordingly had a choice for the education of their children, between Russian and any of the local languages available. As they overwhelmingly chose Russian, these ethnic groups were eventually assimilated to the Russian-speaking population. Regarding higher education, state universities used to offer courses in separate language groups. Students were able to enter their native language group in continuation with their primary and secondary education and to take the entry exam in their native language as well. It should, however, be mentioned that these tuition languages were developed by the Soviet regime as the instruments for communicating a common content – the communist ideology – that was shared across all the Soviet languages.

After the collapse of the USSR in 1991, the new independent Central Asian states were left having to manage a complex and costly system of education unaided. Table 13.1 presents the language structure of the education sector of the three target countries in 1991. This was, at that time, entirely inherited from the Soviet Union. Uzbekistan inherited an education system with seven tuition languages; Tajikistan, six, and Kyrgyzstan, four. The distribution of schoolchildren per tuition language corresponded more or less to the ethnic composition of the population, as most ethnic groups were educated in their mother tongue. Among the indigenous languages, Uzbek had a significant position not only in Uzbekistan but also in bordering Tajikistan, where one pupil in four was educated in Uzbek (one in three in the province of Sughd), and in Kyrgyzstan, where the rate was one in eight (one in four in the provinces of Osh and Jalalabad). In

Table 13.1. *Ethnic distribution of the population[a] and schoolchildren and university students per tuition language[b] in Uzbekistan, Kyrgyzstan and Tajikistan (per cent).*

	Uzbekistan			Kyrgyzstan			Tajikistan		
	National ethnic group	School tuition language	University tuition language	National ethnic group	School tuition language	University tuition language	National ethnic group	School tuition language	University tuition language
Uzbek	71.4	78.1	65.1	12.9	12.1	0.3	23.5	23.8	7.7
Kyrgyz	0.9	0.2	–	52.4	55.7	23.4	1.3	1.1	–
Tajik	4.7	2.7	0.4	0.8	0.2	–	62.3	67.2	48.2
Russian	8.3	13.1	32.3	21.5	32.0	76.3	7.6	7.6	44.1
Turkmen	0.6	0.4	–	–	–	–	0.4	0.3	–
Kazakh	4.1	3.0	0.3	0.9	–	–	0.2	0.01	–
Karakalpak	2.1	2.5	1.9	–	–	–	–	–	–

[a] 1989. *Source:* USSR, *Itogi vsesoiuznoi perepisi naseleniia 1989 g* (Moscow, 1991–3) [electronic version].
[b] 1990/1. *Source:* USSR, 'Obuchenie v uchebnykh zavedeniiakh na iazykakh narodov SSSR', *Vestnik statistiki* 12 (Moscow, 1991), 47–55.

Uzbekistan itself, however, the distribution of tuition languages did not respect the country's ethnic structure: only half of registered Tajiks and Turkmens were educated in their mother tongue. The rate fell to 22 per cent for the Kyrgyz. The share of Russian-language schools exceeded the mere proportion of Russians within the population (13.1 vs 8.3 per cent for instance in Uzbekistan) because Russian schools were attended by Russians as well as many other Slavic (Ukrainians, Byelorussians, Poles) and non-Slavic (Uralian Tatars, Germans, Koreans etc.) nationalities.

STATE EDUCATION POLICIES: AN INSTRUMENT TO MOULD NEW NATIONAL IDENTITIES

The Soviet legacy: a status quo with different developments in each state

The 'Law on the State Language' adopted by each Central Asian Soviet republic before the collapse of the Soviet Union, in 1989,[11] is of particular interest, in that this legislation remained in force after independence. Each law introduced a legal hierarchy between the state language (that of the titular nation), Russian as the language of 'interethnic communication', and other languages spoken in 'ethnically compact areas'. In terms of education the laws provide all citizens with a 'free choice for their tuition language' (article 6 of the Uzbek law) or 'an education in their mother tongue ... for the ethnic groups living in compact areas' (article 25 of the Kyrgyz law; article 21 of the Tajik law).[12]

After the first years of transition in the early nineties, during which the school system remained mostly unchanged, Uzbekistan, Kyrgyzstan and Tajikistan started to develop their own education policies, as education was considered a key sector in building an independent nation. New curricula were drafted, textbooks and pedagogical materials were revised, and teachers' training modules were adapted. The effectiveness of the reform depended, however, on the funds made available to the MoEs. Lack of funding compelled the state to set priorities among the different subjects and instruction languages. With regard to subjects such as history, geography and national literature, which were considered to be the most sensitive, the old-fashioned Soviet ideology was quickly replaced by nationalist content. As for the languages, the MoEs focused primarily on state language schools attended by the majority of the titular ethnic group. Consequently, minority-language schools faced quick deterioration of their teaching conditions, since Soviet programmes, still in use, were not compatible with the new national curricula, and textbooks were outdated and in bad shape.

Significant changes also affected higher education in the aftermath of independence. In Soviet times students could attend most courses in their native language, but after 1991 state authorities encouraged the use of the state language in universities. Most courses were consequently made available in the sole state language, while courses taught in minority languages were limited to teacher-training courses. Russian-language teaching was continued on an exceptional basis for subjects in the fields of science and technology, since their literature and documentation existed only in Russian. The exams that students had to take to enter the university were set in only two languages – the state language and Russian. This limitation severely reduced the opportunities for graduates of minority-language schools to enter state universities and obtain grants.

At the same time, this general picture does not reveal the specificities of each state. In Kyrgyzstan and Tajikistan, as the authorities could not cope both in financial[13] and logistic terms with the needs of minority language education, school directors were authorized to adopt alternative solutions in the most liberal way. Russian schools could enjoy direct support either from the local Russian embassy, or through twinning programmes between Central Asia and the Russian Federation. This successful sponsorship contributed to the preservation of a quality Russian education. For other minority-language schools, the MoEs agreed to delegate directly to schools the management of the so-called school fund (*shkol'nyi fond*), a legacy from the Soviet period consisting of a monthly cash contribution from parents to cover education expenses. The Uzbeks from Tajikistan and Kyrgyzstan constitute a telling case-study. As the regional provision of textbooks collapsed, school directors, parents and community leaders agreed to use the school fund to purchase and import textbooks in the Uzbek language from Uzbekistan. By doing this, minorities were just replicating – though in a private form – the Soviet model, where kin-republics used to provide education material to their kin-language schools.[14] As a result, the character of education differed significantly between schools. Kyrgyz and Tajik state language schools continued to get sizeable MoE support and enjoyed the first fruits of reform, while minority-language schools were managed in a less centralized, rather more liberal way. This 'privatization' of book supplies through school funds permitted the schools to maintain the main frame of education material and to address parents' grievances.

Unlike its neighbours, Uzbekistan adopted a tougher line and strictly banned the illegal importation of books in order to avoid any external influence on its ongoing nation-building process. In case of infringement of this law, Uzbek officials did not hesitate to seize and destroy the

Table 13.2. *Schools and pupils by language of education in Uzbekistan, 2004.*

Language of education	Number of schools		Pupils		Population's ethnic distribution (%)
	Total	Monolingual	Number (×1000)	%	
Uzbek	8,801	7,807	5,440.8	89.0	77.2
Russian	753	93	277.0	4.5	5.2
Kazakh	544	262	127.4	2.1	4.0
Karakalpak	376	258	134.6	2.2	1.9
Tajik	282	128	101.8	1.7	4.8
Kyrgyz	67	26	14.4	0.2	0.9
Turkmen	56	30	15.0	0.3	0.6

Source: Uzbekistan, *Development of Education System in Uzbekistan, 2000–2004* (Tashkent, 2005).

unauthorized literature.[15] It would be tempting to assume that the lack of active support offered by Tashkent towards its minority-language schools, along with an authoritarian control over imported publications, was part of a deliberate policy to promote the state language among minorities and facilitate the 'Uzbekization' of education. Indeed, between 1998 and 2005 the number of minority-language schools decreased by 256 schools – from 2,335[16] to 2,079.[17] Table 13.2 shows that in 2004 the share of pupils educated in a minority language was 11 per cent, though minorities represented 21 per cent of the country's total population. If the decrease of the Russian-language schools can be explained by the emigration of the Russian-speaking minorities (the numbers of Russians fell from 1.65 million in 1989 to approximately 1 million in 2004), this is not the case for indigenous minorities, whose share in the country's population has remained the same.

   Another specificity in Uzbekistan was the decision adopted in 1995 to shift the Uzbek language from the Cyrillic to the Latin script. This change had two major consequences in the education sector. First, at the state-wide level, the Uzbek MoE had to manage two scripts – Latin for the Uzbek schools, and Cyrillic, as used for Russian and also some other minority-language schools. Second, at the regional level, a linguistic frontier arose between the Uzbeks from Uzbekistan, who shifted to the Latin script, and the Uzbek minorities in other post-Soviet republics, who had no option but to keep on using the Cyrillic script. For political and financial reasons, their host countries would not approve the change to Latin.

Instilling of civic values through a harmonized multilingual education: from national policies to international support

In the early 2000s the Uzbek government addressed the issue of education in minority languages, to avoid an outbreak of resentment and grievances among parents. Perpetuating the Soviet approach, the Uzbek authorities viewed the language of education as an instrument to provide a common content – what used to be Soviet ideology, and now the unity of the nation. However, this ideology did not take the form of an exclusive ethnic nationalism, but rather an inclusive discourse about concepts of territoriality and statehood, where Uzbekness (*O'zbekchilik*) would constitute civic values for all citizens regardless of their ethnic origin.[18] Education was considered as a key sector in the drive to mould a common civic consciousness among ethnic minorities. Presidential Decree No. 3431, 'On the State National School Education Development Programme for 2004–2009', emphasized the need to harmonize and upgrade national education standards, and to develop new textbooks and teaching materials for all schools, with special attention to minority-language schools.[19] As a result, hundreds of new textbook titles were published in 2006, and 90 per cent of these were in the minority languages – 92 titles in Turkmen, 72 in Kyrgyz, 70 in Tajik and 70 in Kazakh. The availability of textbooks conforming to the new national curricula sharply increased in all schools, reaching an impressive average figure of 92.1 per cent of needs coverage.[20] To foster common civic values, the MoE did not develop specific teaching materials for the minority-language schools, but rather kept a common content by translating the original Uzbek textbooks into the country's six minority languages of education. Through this harmonized content, the Uzbek government made sure that minorities would ultimately embrace the country's customs and traditions, and develop a civic national consciousness regardless of their ethnic belonging.

Kyrgyzstan and Tajikistan developed the same approach, but with a significant delay. First, they produced new textbooks on history, geography and national literature, and outlawed the importation of textbooks in these sensitive subjects. Second, they started to translate materials into their respective minority languages. However, the achievement remained limited until international donors intensified their support of the education sector.[21] In 1999–2003 the Asian Development Bank gave a first grant to the Kyrgyz MoE to print 46 textbook titles (1,247,250 copies), including 7 in Russian and 1 in Uzbek. A second grant was scheduled for the period 2006–11 to produce and print complete sets of textbooks on the same pattern as in

Uzbekistan – original textbooks drafted in the state language and translated into Russian, Uzbek and Tajik.[22] Other international actors such as the World Bank,[23] UNICEF, the Open Society Institute and embassies also provided meaningful support, albeit on a smaller scale.

However, international funding was a mixed blessing. Taking for granted the impending supply of textbooks, President Bakiev decided in 2006 to abolish the school fund. The Uzbek minority expressed scepticism about the removal of the only means of securing funds to purchase textbooks from Uzbekistan until the effective provision of Uzbek language materials could begin in Kyrgyzstan,[24] but to no avail. In Tajikistan there were different problems. International organizations were also committed to support the education sector, but the insufficiency of local skills to develop new teaching material compelled the donors to focus first on capacity-building and training.[25] This delayed the production of new textbooks for minority-language schools.[26]

What appears to be meaningful here is the way both the state authorities and the international donors continued to address the issue of minority education in ethnic terms. The former kept designing education in the Soviet mould, and the latter used the discourse on minority rights to justify their grants. At the same time, perhaps surprisingly, both approaches agreed on the solution – ethnic minorities should continue to be educated in their mother tongue, regardless of the changes in society.

EDUCATION IN KYRGYZSTAN AND TAJIKISTAN: A FRAME TO MOBILIZE ETHNIC MINORITIES

Besides the development of state education policies and the support of international donors, ethnic activists and minority leaders endeavoured to mobilize their communities in a collective request for education rights. In Uzbekistan the state did not leave much space for such a mobilization,[27] but in Kyrgyzstan and Tajikistan ethnic claims became a significant phenomenon. One can see here the effect of what Snow has called a 'frame alignment process', working to 'organize experience and guide action' with regard to expressing the grievances of the population.[28] As Gorenburg argues, 'seventy years of Soviet ethnic policy [have] decisively moulded the perceptions, beliefs, and identities of minority ethnic group members'.[29] In independent Kyrgyzstan and Tajikistan, this legacy of the Soviet policy of nationalities continued to influence the speech of ethnic minorities, at least in their analysis of education needs. According to statements made by such groups, all minority members should have access to a quality education *in their mother tongue.* In the mid-nineties, the deterioration of education conditions in minority-language schools constituted a breeding ground for activists to mobilize their communities.

In Kyrgyzstan, Uzbek cultural organizations played an increasing role in framing the issue of education to mobilize their community. Although this type of association was initially intended to promote cultural events rather than providing assistance to schools, two Uzbek organizations openly addressed the education sector in their agenda. The Uzbek National Cultural Centre (UNCC) branch in Jalalabad province set up, in 1996, a Social Fund on Support of Education, which started to finance the publication of textbooks and literature in the Uzbek language.[30] The impact was, however, limited as textbooks were printed in insufficient numbers, and the initiative had to stop in 2000 owing to a lack of funds. In a second attempt the UNCC branch along with the Osh-based Society of Uzbeks asked the Kyrgyz government to adopt a Latin script for the education of its Uzbek minority. Although this claim sought to erase the script difference with Uzbek as used in Uzbekistan, and accordingly maintain the benefit of imported education material, most Uzbeks were opposed to the measure.[31] When Tashkent stopped producing textbooks in Cyrillic Uzbek, the UNCC set up the Centre for the Publication of Uzbek Language Textbooks (*Tsentr po sozdaniiu uchebnikov dlia shkol s uzbekskim iazykom obucheniia*). Since 1998 the centre has edited dozens of textbooks in various subjects, albeit with a limited print run. Because of a lack of state subsidies, all production expenses had to be covered by the selling price. Consequently Uzbek language textbooks edited in Kyrgyzstan cost twice as much as their Kyrgyz language equivalent, and the majority of parents could not afford them.[32]

Let us focus briefly here on the development of mutual requests from Kyrgyz in Tajikistan, and Tajiks in Kyrgyzstan. In 1992 the Tajiks of Kyrgyzstan, a reported 42,636 people, founded the Association of Tajiks (*Assotsiatsiia tadzhikov*) in the southern province of Batken, where most of them reside. Similarly, in 1995 the Kyrgyz minority of Tajikistan, a reported 65,515 people, established the Society of Kyrgyz (*Obshchestvo kyrgyzov*), with the objective of promoting the rights of the Kyrgyz minority, most particularly in the sector of education and culture. In both cases, minority leaders addressed the issue of education as a framework for mobilizing their respective communities.[33] These claims contributed to the signing in early 2000 of a bilateral agreement between Kyrgyzstan and Tajikistan in the education sector (*mezhdugosudarstvennoe soglashchenie po linii obrazovaniia*). This agreement provided for exchanges at the level of supply of

textbooks and training of teachers, and facilitated access of minority students to the universities of their kin-state.[34] The discrepancies between state
curricula and imported textbooks were considered to be 'marginal in
comparison with the overall benefits of such an agreement'.[35] All parents
and teachers whom we interviewed acknowledged that the cooperation
greatly improved the quality of education in their schools. As we could
observe, minority-language schools were often enjoying a better supply of
textbooks than were state language ones.[36]

In Kyrgyzstan the Association of Tajiks also addressed the issue of higher
education because the Tajik community of Uch-Korgon, located more than
100 km from the closest Tajik border, experienced relative isolation. As
parents were no longer willing to send their children to a distant university,
Tajik leaders seized the new opportunity to frame their claims towards the
Kyrgyz government, and successfully pressed for the opening in 1999 of a
Tajik language section in the Pedagogical Faculty of the neighbouring
Kyrgyz town of Kyzyl Kiya, which started working with four groups of
Tajik language students.[37]

THE EMERGENCE OF INDIVIDUAL STRATEGIES OF EDUCATION (SINCE 2001)

Meanwhile, some parents started to develop a new understanding of their
rights to education, and tried to abandon the frames predefined either by
the Soviet legacy, as used by the states in their nation-building process, or by
the Western human rights approach, used by activists and international
donors to promote the education rights of ethnic minorities. This individual dissent is visible in Tajikistan among the Uzbek minority, particularly in
Spitamen, known as Tajikistan's most Uzbek district, with Uzbeks account-
ing for 84.7 per cent of the total population. In 1994, out of thirty-one
schools, twenty-five taught in the Uzbek language, two in Tajik and four
had mixed language groups, including two with Russian groups. As
Table 13.3 shows, between 1994 and 2006 the number of monolingual
Uzbek schools decreased, while new Tajik groups opened in eight schools
(formerly monolingual). This evolution was the result not of a forced
decision from the education authorities but rather of demands from
Uzbek families that they should have the chance to offer education to
their children in the state language, in other words Tajik.[38] This dissent
can be easily explained by the evidence that the state had still not succeeded
in implementing the education reform within minority-language schools.
Consequently, Uzbek parents demanded education for their children in the

Table 13.3. *Schools and pupils of Spitamen district according to language of education, 1994–2006.*

	1994		2002		2006	
	Number	%	Number	%	Number	%
Number of schools						
Uzbek	25	80.5	20	64.5	16	51.5
Tajik	2	6.5	2	6.5	2	6.5
Uzbek/Tajik	2	6.5	7	22.5	10	32.3
Uzbek/Tajik/Russian	2	6.5	2	6.5	3	9.7
Total	31	100.0	31	100.0	31	100.0
Number of pupils						
Uzbek language	n.a.	n.a.	22,155	89.5	19,996	84.3
Tajik language	n.a.	n.a.	2,322	9.4	3,014	12.7
Russian language	n.a.	n.a.	279	1.1	698	2.9
Total	n.a.	n.a.	24,756	100.0	23,708	100.0

Source: Sughd province education department.

state language schools. Here are some of the reasons parents formulated to explain their choice:

'Being an Uzbek, I never had the chance to learn the Tajik language properly. I want my children to be more fluent than I am.'

'In Soviet times we were motivated to learn Russian. Now we are living in Tajikistan, so our children are better off learning Tajik, so they have the chance to get a job in government administration.'

'Since independence, universities have been closing down all their Uzbek language groups. If my son wants to study, he first needs to know Tajik. It makes no sense to send him to an Uzbek-language school.'[39]

The decision of the Uzbek parents clearly goes against the ethnic model of education, and seems to follow a well-thought-out strategy, one that differs from framing in many respects. First, it appears to be the individual decision-making process which remains limited, while framing is motivated by community leaders to foster a collective response. Second, framing is a tool that seeks to mobilize minorities in a way of thinking that is familiar to them. Indeed, both the state education policy and the nationalistic discourse of the minority activists draw on the same Soviet essence, chiefly on the policy of nationalities. The choice of the tuition language is therefore predetermined by this common doctrine. On the other hand, however, the strategy appears to be a deliberate choice that takes an alternative view. Here the decision is not the result of a collective instilment but is rather driven by individual common sense. It embodies the parents' opportunistic or strategic view, their aim to give the best chances to their children in their future social and professional life.

The opening of a third Russian group and the rapid increase from 279 to 698 Russian-language pupils between 2002 and 2006 reveals a new interest in the Russian language. This cannot be explained by demographic figures, since the number of native Russian-speakers (including not just Slavs, but ethnic Germans and Koreans as well) in the district population has sharply decreased from 2,155 people (2.7 per cent) in 1989 to 421 people (0.4 per cent) in 2000,[40] those remaining being mostly pensioners. Here again the recent opening of a new group was a request from both Uzbek and Tajik parents. It was motivated by their desire to provide their children with the necessary language skills to work abroad.[41]

The Uzbek minority of Kyrgyzstan is experiencing a different situation. For its part, the Kyrgyz MoE launched a large-scale programme to provide minority-language schools with translated textbooks, and Uzbek leaders succeeded in mobilizing members of their ethnic community around the frame of education. For these reasons, individual strategies are not given as much visibility as in Tajikistan. But different patterns can be analysed according to the ethnic environment. In mixed Kyrgyz-Uzbek areas, education used to be provided either in both languages (most commonly) or in one single language, depending on the ethnic distribution of the population. The example of Oogon-Talaa, a village of Bazar-Korgon district in the province of Jalalabad, is indicative. Until 1990 its 2,500 inhabitants were Kyrgyz (60 per cent), Uzbeks (30 per cent) and Russian-speakers (10 per cent), and had at their disposal a single school where education was organized in separate Kyrgyz- and Russian-language groups. Uzbek children who were not being educated in their mother tongue were therefore always educated in one or the other existing tuition language. In 1990, following a landslide, about a hundred Uzbek families from the neighbouring mountainous hamlet of Buokol were resettled in Oogon-Talaa. As Uzbek was the sole tuition language of their former school, they started to press for the opening of an Uzbek language group within the school of Oogon-Talaa. The group was launched in the following year, and is still active today. Following the departure of Russians, and the eventual closure of the Russian-language group in the mid-nineties, the division between Kyrgyz and Uzbeks moved to 50/50. However, in 2006, the distribution of tuition languages remained largely in favour of the Kyrgyz language (77 per cent), with a limited extension of Uzbek (23 per cent).[42] Pupils attending the

Uzbek group came mostly from Buokol families. The Uzbeks from Oogon-Talaa continued to send their children mainly to the Kyrgyz group. It appears clear that the Uzbeks from Buokol, who used to live in a mono-ethnic environment, had not adapted to their host multi-ethnic society. As an Uzbek native of Oogon-Talaa commented:

I completed school in the Kyrgyz language, as did all my relatives. We speak Uzbek at home but when we go to the town, we speak Kyrgyz. Nobody there can tell whether we are Uzbek or Kyrgyz [laughter]. Those from Buokol are just backward (*bezkul'turnyi*). They don't even think about the future of their children. They want everything to be done for them as in Soviet times. Are they aware that we are now living in Kyrgyzstan?[43]

As this case study shows,[44] villagers living in a multi-ethnic environment generally develop a civic understanding of their identity. Being bilingual in their mother tongue and the state language, and with a fair knowledge of Russian, they are tolerant toward other language groups. The schooling strategy appears therefore as the expression of their civic consciousness. On the flip side, villagers living in an ethnically homogeneous isolated community keep thinking in terms of ethnicity. They are usually not as fluent in languages as the former group of villagers, and, above all, they have limited opportunities to mix with other ethnic groups and therefore to get to know about their culture and habits. Tension and disrespect often develop across this virtual but powerful border of the social environment.

Besides this Kyrgyz–Uzbek language issue, it should be noted that interest in Russian-language education has recently re-emerged in Oogon-Talaa. Despite the lack of experienced staff, a new group instructing in Russian had to be created in 2006, to answer the demands of Kyrgyz and Uzbek parents. As in Spitamen, the Russian language is becoming more attractive, even in remote rural areas. A major difference between Tajikistan and Kyrgyzstan, however, is that, in the latter, Russian enjoys the status of official language alongside Kyrgyz. The choice to send one's child to a Russian-language group can therefore be understood not just as something pragmatic, but as the expression of a form of civic consciousness, to help integrating in the new national society.

The influence of the geographical and social environment on education strategies is even more pronounced for the Tajiks of Kyrgyzstan. Although they constitute a small ethnic group at national level (0.9 per cent in 2000), the Tajiks live in compact settlements, where interethnic relations are of paramount importance. In the Andarak municipality at the extreme south-western mountainous part of Kyrgyzstan, Tajiks and Kyrgyz share a small remote valley, but they live in distinct neighbourhoods. Schooling, social life and even religious practices are organized separately. Table 13.4 shows that the ethnic breakdown is mirrored in the breakdown of languages of instruction: Tajiks amount to 44.4 per cent of the population and 48.2 per cent of the pupils are educated in the Tajik language, while for Kyrgyz the figures are respectively 54.8 and 50.2 per cent. (The minor discrepancy between overall profile and educational status may be explained by differing birth rates, or other demographic differences between the two groups.)

In recent years interethnic tensions have broken out about access to land, and also the sharing of water resources and building of common infra-structures. The potential for clashes was considered critical enough to attract the attention of conflict mediators such as the OSCE, the UNDP and the Swiss Agency for Development and Cooperation (SDC).[45]

In Uch-Korgon municipality, located in a more populated plain, a Tajik majority (58 per cent) live along with Kyrgyz (21 per cent) and Uzbeks (17 per cent). Owing to the proximity of dynamic Uzbek towns, Uch-Korgon developed close cultural and economic relations with the Uzbek part of the Ferghana Valley before, during and after the Soviet period. Despite the predominance of the Tajiks in the municipality's population, Tajik is the

Table 13.4. *Population ethnic distribution and school languages in Andarak (Leylek district) and Uch-Korgon (Kadamzhai district).*

	Andarak municipality		Uch-Korgon municipality	
	Number	%	Number	%
Ethnic distribution (1999)[a]				
Kyrgyz	5,944	54.8	5,352	21.3
Tajiks	4,816	44.4	14,523	57.8
Uzbeks	86	0.8	4,271	17.0
Others	0	0.0	980	3.9
Total	10,846	100.0	25,126	100.0
Pupils per tuition language (2006)[b]				
Kyrgyz language	1,559	50.2	1,166	18.6
Tajik language	1,497	48.2	598	9.5
Uzbek language	51	1.6	3,464	55.2
Russian language	0	0.0	1,046	16.7
Total	3,107	100.0	6,274	100.0

[a] Source: Kyrgyzstan, *Naselenie Kyrgyzstana: itogi pervoi natsional'noi perepisi naseleniia Kyrgyzskoi respubliki 1999 g. v tablitsakh*, publication 11/1 (Bishkek, 2000).
[b] Source: Leylek and Kadamzhai district education departments.

language of instruction for less than one in ten pupils, while 55 per cent are educated in Uzbek, 19 per cent in Kyrgyz and 17 per cent in Russian. Among the municipality's eleven schools, there are three exclusively Uzbek-language schools, two Kyrgyz, two Uzbek–Kyrgyz, two Uzbek–Tajik, one Uzbek–Russian and one Uzbek–Russian–Tajik, but no single Tajik-language school. Despite the efforts of the Association of Tajiks to orient parents to Tajik language education, Uzbek schools keep attracting the majority of the pupils.[46] This lack of interest in the Tajik language is also obvious in higher education. Although the association's initiatives in launching Tajik language groups in Kyzyl-Kiya Pedagogical Faculty were at first received positively, the community's mobilization did not last for long. Over the years, candidates became scarce and the Kyzyl-Kiya Tajik section was compelled to close in 2004.

This comparison between Andarak and Uch-Korgon shows that, despite a comparable ethnic composition, the practices of Tajiks in the education sector can differ radically. In the former case, the harsh geographical environment and the competition for scarce resources have moulded the population into a plural mono-ethnic society rather than an inclusive multi-ethnic one,[47] as both groups live in completely separate circles. In such conditions the ethnic frame continues to resonate successfully among both communities, including in the education sector, where no Tajik would enter a Kyrgyz language group and vice versa. In the latter case, Tajiks, Kyrgyz and Uzbeks are living in a more hospitable environment and have developed historical ties with the multi-ethnic society of the Ferghana Valley. If the Soviet policy of nationalities succeeded in framing an ethnic education among Uch-Korgon's inhabitants, the collapse of the USSR and the emergence of economic liberal practices led to a growing interest towards Uzbekistan and the Uzbek language, as well as towards the Russian language. The parents dissociate from the established education system, embodied in the agreement between Tajikistan and Kyrgyzstan to support their respective kin-minority. Parents also oppose the association's active ethnic framing.

As a result, most Tajik parents decide to educate their children in what they consider to be the region's most widely spoken and therefore profitable language, which means primarily the Uzbek language and to a lesser extent Russian. From this individual perspective, the Tajiks of Kyrgyzstan have developed a deliberate education strategy, in the sense that they manage to distinguish clearly between the private sphere, where the Tajik identity prevails at home in language and cultural practices, and the public sphere, where other language proficiencies, mainly Uzbek but also Russian and

Kyrgyz, are fostered to contribute actively to the multi-ethnic and multi-lingual society they live in. This language strategy has neither an ethnic motivation nor a grounding in civic consciousness. Rather, it addresses the issue of education in a broader regional framework, where the opportunistic choice of the Uzbek or Russian language prevails over the Tajik ethnic origin and the assumed civic acceptance of the Kyrgyz state language. If anything, Russian seems to appear as a second alternative choice at school. Here, however, strategic perspectives meet with civic consciousness. If education in Russian will help develop the necessary language skills to emigrate to Russia, a fluent command of Russian would also facilitate the integration of the Tajik minority into Kyrgyzstan's national society, where Russian has maintained a chief position in its administration and public life.

CONCLUSION

The chapter shows that the issue of education of ethnic minorities is complex and can be examined from different perspectives. At the state level, the education policies of the three target countries appear to be similar, albeit at different implementation stages because of lack of funds and/or capacity. At the ethnic community level, aside from Uzbekistan, activists play a major role in framing the issue of education to mobilize their respective minority groups. However, these frames resonate diversely among the population, and are challenged by parents' alternative strategies. This individual level of analysis proves to be the most enlightening, in the sense that parents' choices appear to be very flexible, shifting from ethnic identity to civic consciousness, either by force or deliberately.

By contrasting state policies and the mobilizing speeches of activists to the actual strategies developed by parents, this chapter demonstrates that stakeholders compete in terms of their ways of addressing the education issue and working out solutions. Government officials have made no effort, in the post-Soviet era, to consider the schooling practices of ethnic minorities or include them in their policies. But minority leaders pay no attention to the alternative strategies developed by their community members either. Both the MoEs and the leaders stick to their Soviet-rooted understanding of the right to an education in the mother tongue. If such a right is guaranteed, the key issue in education then becomes how to instil a civic consciousness in ethnic groups that are being educated in separate education systems. The solution that Uzbekistan worked out, and which inspires its neighbours, is to translate textbooks and teaching material into the various tuition languages of the country's education system. As was the case in Soviet times, language is considered as the vehicle of a common ideology. The limits of this approach are obvious, but no alternative policy has been developed yet. The renewed interest in the Russian language that all three target countries have been experiencing in recent years is traceable to geopolitical changes in the region, as well as to the marked, albeit recent, rise of rates of emigration to Russia, and also to Kazakhstan, among the inhabitants of Central Asia.[48] The renewal of the influence of Russia in Central Asia, and the vital role of the provision of remittances by the growing communities of Central Asian émigrés,[49] seems to have had a major impact on the attractiveness of Russian as a tuition language among both the 'titular nations' and the ethnic minorities of the three countries. The primary purpose of Russian-language schools is seen as being to train students fluent in Russian. This fluency will, it is assumed, help future émigrés to settle in better conditions in their new country of destination and gain a higher position in the *Gastarbeiter*'s tough hierarchy.

NOTES

1. By 'non-native' I mean those ethnic groups that moved to the region during the colonial and Soviet period, either voluntarily or forcibly.
2. This research was funded by the French Ministry of Education and Research (three months), the French Ministry of Foreign Affairs (five months) and the French Institute of Studies on Central Asia (IFEAC) in Tashkent.
3. This paper is part of research for a larger project in the field of political sociology, which explores the process of ethnic mobilization in post-Soviet Central Asia in various sectors, such as counting and categorization (census), language practices, cultural and religious identity, political and economic life, and of course education.
4. Expression borrowed from O. Roy, *The New Central Asia: the Creation of Nations* (London, 2000), 8–10.
5. This dichotomy can be traced back to Meinecke's typology of nationalisms, distinguishing the *Staatsnation* from the *Kulturnation*. Meinecke argued that there is a difference between nations that are based primarily on some joint experience of cultural heritage and nations that are based primarily on the unifying force of a common political history and constitution. Therefore the *Staatsnation* is based on a form of social contract, while the *Kulturnation* is described as an ethnic community in which inclusion is based on descent. T. Reeskens and M. Hooghe, 'Beyond the Civic-Ethnic Dichotomy: Investigating the Structure of Citizenship across Thirty-Three Countries', *Nations and Nationalism* 16:4 (2010), 581.
6. H. Kohn, *Nationalism in the Soviet Union* (London, 1933), 86–91.
7. R. Suny, 'State, Civil Society, and Ethnic Cultural Consolidation in the USSR: Roots of the National Question', in *From Union to Commonwealth: Nationalism*

and Separatism in the Soviet Republics, ed. G. W. Lapidus and V. Zaslavsky (Cambridge, 1992), 28. See also Ronald Grigor Suny's chapter in the present volume.

8. This process of ethnic homogenization was intended by Moscow to 'modernize backward peoples'. F. Hirsch, 'Toward an Empire of Nations: Border-Making and the Formation of Soviet National Identities', *Russian Review* 59:2 (2000), 225.

9. In urban areas – particularly in post-Soviet capitals, where the Russian-speaking communities concentrated – the picture is different, and the influence of the Russian language is more marked.

10. For a citizen belonging to an ethnic minority, 'kin-state' means a state where fellow members of this ethnic group make up the 'titular nation', while the 'host-state' is the country where the citizen actually resides.

11. These language reforms go back to the perestroika period, when each Soviet republic adopted a law on the state language which established a hierarchy between languages within that republic. Each titular nation's language became the state language of the republic, and Russian was acknowledged the status of interethnic language. In addition, the laws often recognized the importance of third languages in the areas of homogeneous ethnic settlement. J. M. Landau and B. Kellner-Heinkele, *Politics of Language in the Ex-Soviet Muslim States* (London, 2001), 109–23.

12. This right to an education in the mother tongue was actually never called into question. The 1997 Uzbek Law on Education (article 4), the 2004 Tajik Law on Education (article 7), the 2003 Kyrgyz Law on Education (article 6) and the 2004 Kyrgyz Law on the State Language (article 1), as well as the project for a new Kyrgyz Constitution (article 5), all confirmed the guarantee of education in the mother tongue.

13. In Kyrgyzstan, public expenditure on education decreased from 7.4% of GDP in 1990 to 4.2% in 1993 and 3.7% in 2000. Tajikistan allocated a limited 2.2% of its GDP to education in 1997. M. Mertaugh, 'Education in Central Asia, with Particular Reference to the Kyrgyz Republic', in *The Challenges of Education in Central Asia*, ed. S. P. Heyneman and A. J. De Young (Greenwich, CT, 2004), 153–80.

14. As confirmed by directors and parents from various Uzbek language schools of Tajikistan and Kyrgyzstan, the Uzbek government did not facilitate the provision of teaching material to its kin-minorities abroad either by entering into formal agreement with the Kyrgyz or Tajik authorities or by providing them on a free or subsidized basis, despite the historical link between Tashkent and Uzbek language schools and the fact that Uzbekistan was proceeding to the substitution of all Cyrillic textbooks with new Latin script and had therefore millions of useless books. The purchase was arranged through the intermediary of Uzbek businessmen or by parents or teachers who crossed the border at their own risk to buy books in the bazaars.

15. In July 2001 some 16,000 books given by the Tajik government to Tajik language schools in Uzbekistan were burnt, by order of the Uzbek government.

In Bukhara another 10,000 brochures, books and other items of literature in Tajik were pulped, and given to a local poultry factory for packing eggs. International Crisis Group, *Tajikistan: An Uncertain Peace* (Osh/Brussels, 2001), Asia Report 30, www.crisisgroup.org/en/regions/asia/central-asia/tajikistan/030-tajikistan-an-uncertain-peace.aspx.

16. UNESCO, 'Uzbekistan', *The EFA 2000 Assessment Report* (Paris, 2000).
17. Uzbekistan, *Development of Education System in Uzbekistan, 2000–2004* (Tashkent, 2005).
18. On this analysis of Uzbek civic nation-building, cf. M. Fumagalli, 'Ethnicity, State Formation and Foreign Policy: Uzbekistan and "Uzbeks abroad"', *Central Asian Survey* 26:1 (2007), 105–22.
19. From material published at the international conference 'Tasks of the Education Reform in the Context of Multinational Central Asia', organized by the OSCE and the Uzbek MoE in Tashkent, 28 November 2006.
20. MoE data as reported in UNHCHR, *State Party Report to the UN Committee on the Elimination of Racial Discrimination*, CERD/C/UZB/CO/5/Add.1, Geneva, 21 June 2006, 11–12 www.unhchr.ch/tbs/doc.nsf.
21. The 9/11 turning point in world politics has shed new light on Central Asia, as Western countries were seeking local support for military operations in Afghanistan.
22. Timur Oruskulov, education project manager, Asian Development Bank office, Bishkek, Kyrgyzstan, interview, 4 May 2007. All interviews conducted by the author.
23. Under a rural education grant there are plans to produce and print eight textbooks (760,000 copies), including six in minority languages (information from the World Bank education department, Bishkek).
24. A. Mamaraimov, '"Uzbekskaia obshchestvennost'" Kirgizii pytaetsia samostoiatel'no reshit' problemy shkol'nogo obrazovaniia', Ferghana.ru information agency, *Central Asia News*, 16 March 2007, www.fergananews.com/article.php?id=4983.
25. As an example, the USAid-funded Community Connections Program organized a visit to the USA in October 2007 for education policy makers and textbook authors in order for them to gain experience and skills (Nisso Rakhmonova, programme manager, USAid, Dushanbe, Tajikistan, interview, 11 November 2007).
26. *Vatan Adabiyoti* (native literature), 5th grade (Dushanbe, 2002), was the only new Uzbek language textbook that I saw during my field visit in 2006. Owing to a limited print run and a high price, teachers had only one issue per class (personal observation in Uzbek language schools; Sanat Raupova, deputy director, Sughd Province Teachers' Training and Recycling Centre, Khujand, Tajikistan, interview, 1 November 2006).
27. In Uzbekistan there was restricted space for ethnic claims. The Constitution expressly banned the establishment of 'ethnically based political parties' (article 57) and the government strictly controlled the activities of ethnic cultural organizations.

276 OLIVIER FERRANDO

28. D. A. Snow, E. B. Rochford, S. Worden and R. Benford, 'Frame Alignment Processes, Micromobilization and Movement Participation', *American Sociological Review* 51 (1986), 464–81.
29. D. P. Gorenburg, *Minority Ethnic Mobilization in the Russian Federation* (Cambridge, 2003), 12.
30. D. Khamidova, 'Uncertain Status: Challenges and Opportunities Facing Kyrgyzstani Uzbeks in the Educational Sphere', unpublished Master's dissertation, OSCE Academy in Bishkek, June 2005, 40.
31. M. Fumagalli, 'Framing Ethnic Minority Mobilisation in Central Asia: The Cases of Uzbeks in Kyrgyzstan and Tajikistan', *Europe-Asia Studies* 59:4 (2007), 577–86.
32. Tursunboy Kamilov, deputy director of the Centre for the Publication of Uzbek Language Textbooks, Osh, Kyrgyzstan, interview, 12 December 2006.
33. Abdukhalim Raimzhanov, president of the Association of Tajiks, Bishkek, Kyrgyzstan, interview, 4 May 2007, and Zourakan Davlatlieva, head of the Society of Kyrgyz, Dushanbe, Tajikistan, interview, 15 November 2006.
34. Muhammad Melikov, head of the MoE department of international relations, Dushanbe, Tajikistan, interview, 13 November 2006, and field visits to Kyrgyz language schools in Dzhabbor-Rasulov and Isfara districts (Tajikistan) and Tajik language schools in Isfana and Kadamzhai districts (Kyrgyzstan), autumn 2006.
35. Merinsa Aydzhigutova, head of Batken province education department, Batken, Kyrgyzstan, interview, 25 October 2006.
36. This was observed in the Tajik language schools of Andarak and Uch-Korgon (Kyrgyzstan) and the Kyrgyz language school of Matpari (Tajikistan) in autumn 2006.
37. Saidaziz Pulatov, initiator of the project, Uch-Korgon, Kyrgyzstan, interview, 16 December 2006.
38. Head of the education department (*raiono*) of Spitamen district, Nov, Tajikistan, interview, 6 November 2006.
39. Interviews with Uzbek parents in the villages of Taghoyak, Saidqurghon and Kushtegirmon (Spitamen district, Tajikistan), autumn 2006.
40. Data from the national population censuses of 1989 and 2000.
41. Interviews with Uzbek and Tajik parents of Spitamen district, Tajikistan, autumn 2006.
42. Raya Abdurakhimova, school director, Oogon-Talaa, Kyrgyzstan, interview, 11 December 2006.
43. Interview conducted in Oogon-Talaa, Kyrgyzstan, 11 December 2006.
44. The conclusions that I drew from Spitamen district and Oogon-Talaa village case studies were confirmed by field research in Dzhabbor-Rasulov and Kanibadam districts (Tajikistan) and Aravan, Kara-Suu, Bazar-Korgon and Nooken districts (Kyrgyzstan) during several trips between 1999 and 2007.
45. Foundation for Tolerance International, 'Case Study on Successful Conflict Resolution Efforts: Andarak Conflict Cluster', unpublished paper, Bishkek, 2000.

46. Indeed existing Tajik–Uzbek schools have failed in collecting enough requests to open Tajik first-grade classes since 2000. When older pupils (from grade 7 to 11) complete their Tajik language education, Uzbek will become the sole tuition language in both schools.

47. I borrow the expression 'plural mono-ethnic' from A. Sen, *Identity and Violence: The Illusion of Destiny* (New York, 2006).

48. Although exact figures are difficult to obtain, the number of Central Asian émigrés in Russia is estimated at 2.3 million, including 1 million Uzbeks, 800,000 Tajiks and 500,000 Kyrgyz. M. Laruelle, 'Central Asian Labour Migrants in Russia: the "Diasporization" of the Central Asian States?', *China and Eurasia Forum Quarterly* 5:3 (2007), 104–5.

49. According to unofficial data, in 2006, remittances from Russia amounted to 50% of Tajikistan's and Kyrgyzstan's GDP. Ibid., 116.

CHAPTER 14

Surviving in the time of deficit: the narrative construction of a 'Soviet identity'

Anna Kushkova

'When did you first hear the word "deficit"?'
'Well, we lived with it ... We were born with this word. For 70 years we ate only mayonnaise. It always tasted the same, and it was as familiar as the hammer and sickle.'[1]

The German tragicomedy *Goodbye, Lenin* (director Wolfgang Becker, 2003) is set in 1989, several months after the reunification of Germany. A woman who all of her life has lived in East Germany and who used to be a very devout Communist wakes up from a long coma, not knowing that the opposition of 'us' and 'them' does not exist any more, nor the Communist Party itself, and that capitalist consumerism has won a complete and irreversible victory in the former socialist Germany. Since any agitation may kill the woman, her son Alex decides to conceal the fact of reunification from his mother, and takes it upon himself to 'revive socialism in one room' where he transports his mother after she is released from hospital. In this arduous task, food is probably the most difficult matter: old socialist brands are not sold or produced any more, including his mother's favourite Spreewald pickles. In an attempt to conceal the potentially lethal news of the recent political change, Alex collects empty jars, boxes and bottles with old 'socialist' labels, puts new 'capitalist' foodstuffs in them and gives them to his mother. His trick works, and the fake Spreewald pickles in particular perform the role of a signifier for the radically displaced social order, while at the same time helping his mother maintain a corporeal connection with it.

This 'cultural mnemonics' not only allows this food item to serve as a vehicle for restoring the context of the past for the sick woman, but also – in conjunction with other attributes of the socialist 'habitus' such as clothes, television programmes, family celebrations – 'fosters historically validated forms of [personal] identity'[2] that she possessed in this past. After a couple of months the woman dies without ever learning about the deception performed out of kindness.

The symbolic potential of food to stand for the whole context of social relations of which it is a part, and thus to restore the continuity with this context if it does not exist any more, is of primary importance to the understanding of Soviet and post-Soviet identity. The internal structure of the socialist society was organized around access to food, which has been described by a social historian as 'the key indicator of societal stratification, not on the basis of class, but through the power of the "trough"' (*kormushka*, approximately 'gravy train'). The system of food distribution at workplaces organized 'from above' embodied the traditional model of 'feeding' (*korm-lenie*), within which 'masters' would 'feed' 'their people' in exchange for their work and personal loyalty.[3] This principle should not be exaggerated, yet one may argue that the 'patrimonial' type of relations was clearly present in this segment of relations in Soviet society.

An abiding characteristic of Soviet supply was thus the phenomenon of the so-called 'food orders' (*prodovol'stvennye zakazy*), centrally organized supplies of household provisions via the workplace or residence-based 'supply offices'.[4] However, this phenomenon cannot be viewed independently from the larger context whence it emerged, i.e. the pervasive food deficit in Soviet society at large. This food deficit was a complex situation that brought forth a large number of practices of food procurement, consumption, exchange and so on, as well as a wide array of individual and collective subjectivities associated with them. If 'political regimes . . . to this or that degree are understood through the prism of their dominating styles of consumption',[5] then it was precisely deficit that determined the nature of '(fully) developed socialism' in the Soviet Union (stretching from the early 1970s to late 1980s).[6] Starvation had vanished as a phenomenon (the last really significant bread shortages took place in the early 1960s), but *scarcity* remained an abiding characteristic of Soviet society, generating the infamous queues in state shops, as well as a lively black market.[7] What is more, in the 1990s and 2000s, 'deficit' became an abiding topic in memories of the past. Trying to stress the inseparability of the late Soviet social order and the availability of consumer goods, one informant said: 'Well, this [deficit] was a part of that system . . . and what could one expect of this system? This was completely obvious, so to speak, that everything was abnormal, and it was clear what it was connected with. Here . . . we did not have any illusions whatsoever. What-so-ever.'[8]

The role of scarcity in the Soviet economy at the time was highly significant. People had to find ways of trying to turn goods that had been wished on them into appetizing meals (food packages offloaded unpopular goods as well as distributing desired ones), and they also had to track down

supplies of essential items. Oral history records all this, which is almost
completely absent from official sources. But remembrance of the past is also
an activity that has meaning in the present: informants constantly describe what
it is like to discuss shortages with other people from their generation or talk
about it to those who never experienced shortages: 'and when I talk about this
[standing in queues, fighting for scarce food items in stores etc.] to my grand-
daughter, she bursts out laughing'; or: 'there were pie-shops [*pirozhkovye*] there.
With very tasty pies. And we could afford them. So, during work we used to go
to these shops with a friend of mine. And we always recall this time. Because
coffee was cheap, and the pies were good, whereas now all this "hurts".'[9]

Interviews thus not only record the past, but create a 'memory community'. In some respects, this is heterogeneous (people remember different
things about their survival strategies, and the emotional palette of recollections varies), but narrative strategies (for instance, the assumption that
younger interviewers do not really understand deficit) may be held in
common; one can also single out a number of recurrent themes common
to the majority of interviews. One such theme was that 'There was nothing
in the stores.'[10] Often people reminiscing about food shortages resort to
what may be called 'horror stories' (*strashilki*),[11] which constitute a regular
type of narrative about deficit. For example:

they'd stand [in line], for instance, starting at 5 a.m. . . . You could bring a nursing
baby, but you still had to check in every hour. It wasn't enough to come with the
nursing baby just once, you had to bring it every hour . . . But by the time the store
opened, it was too dangerous to bring babies. Because they could be crushed [by
the crowd]. Everybody understood that, so small children weren't brought along
when the store actually opened.[12]

Another person described how products had to be literally snatched off the
tray when they were brought out to customers in a store: 'we would send
Lionia for curd cheese (*tvorog*) . . . All those elderly women were standing
there [waiting] . . . Lionia was tall, and with his hand . . . he could reach
above everybody's head . . . and grab four packs . . . you weren't supposed to
take more than four.'[13] One person had two recurrent dreams about deficit:
in one of them she finds herself in an empty food store, discovers a lot of
'longed-for' sausage there, and may not be able to decide whether to take it
or not, though no one can see her; in the second dream a similar situation
repeats in relation to sugar during the time when it was rationed: all
attempts to approach the sugar basin on the table at home without being
noticed and to tuck into the sugar are thwarted by some external circumstance. Both dreams made the informant 'very tired'.[14]

Every single informant has his or her horror stories about endless standing in lines: 'We queued 24 hours a day! You see, there were all these
queues . . . people had to check in regularly, wrote [numbers] on their
palms . . . Somehow . . . we got used to it, see?'[15] Many mentioned the
drastically limited variety of foodstuffs ('We had only "cheese" and "sausage"'; 'Cheese was cheese. Under one name –"cheese"') and the 'inedibility'
of some products: 'sprat paté – totally inedible', '[imported] coffee was a
scarce product, and Soviet coffee was undrinkable', 'We used to go to the
brewery "Red Bavaria" for smoked sausage . . . then once we cut into some,
and saw chicken feathers inside!'[16]

Deficit was seen not only as degrading, but also as heroic. In numerous
cases people employed war metaphors or used military terminology to stress
the precariousness of existence under 'deficit', and the extremity of their
deprivation: '[19]88 . . . here we didn't have anything at all . . . every winter
we were prepared to die. Well, as if we were in a city under siege!'[17] People
described how they would 'fight hand to hand' (*bilis'*) for a number of
desired products, give each other 'dry rations' of food after celebrations
(*sukhoi paek*, usually given to soldiers) and make 'strategic reserves' of
products.[18] In this situation the system of food packages was described as
a counter-strategy by the powers that be, a way 'to let out steam' and 'not let
Novorossiisk be repeated' (i.e. a way of preventing people from open
expression of discontent, as in the strikes and riots of 1962), 'to pacify
people, to put a stop to the idea that there is nothing to eat in the country'.[19]

A second common interview theme was 'We visited all the stores.' As well
as remembering the stresses of food deficit, people also liked to remember
how they coped with this; they recall the specific rhythms of food procurement and consumption in times of deficit:

we visited all the stores . . . we knew that here, on the corner of Vosstaniia and
Kirochnaia streets . . . at 4 or 5 p.m. they sold meat. So, Lionia would run there
from his department. And I knew at what time and when there was milk. And oil,
too . . . Washing powder was in Sestroretsk[20] . . . We knew everything precisely,
everything was according to the schedule.[21]

The exchange of information was not just a passive response to shortages, it
also helped create horizontal ties among people sharing vital information
about 'where and when'. Sometimes people directly cooperated in procur-
ing food: 'to exchange coupons for food (*otovarivat' talony*), one had to
know, where! . . . For instance, a neighbour would call me up: "Something's
being given out ['sold', *daiut*] there and there! Lena, can you get some for
me as well?"'[22]

Another way of coping was buying as much as possible of whatever was available: 'I usually procured several whole cheeses at one go'; 'you'd go to Repino[23] in a car, and buy 20 crates of canned peas at once'; 'you couldn't calculate, as they do abroad, to spend so much money per week. You just couldn't! For instance, a certain product would be brought to a certain store ... and people would start grabbing as much as they could (po maksimumu).'[24] This 'maximum' was determined not only by how much money a person had; often the store administration or people queuing themselves spontaneously established a norm limiting the number of identical food items or their weight 'per person' (v odni ruki): 'So, it was decided ... the crowd shouted: "3 dozen [eggs] per person!!! 3 dozen per person!!!"'[25]

People would also reserve scarce products for special occasions. 'And this can of sprats, for instance, it was kept till some ... [special event], it was kind of shameful and preposterous to eat it just like that. Senseless! Nonsensical! You cook your everyday soup – what's the sense of putting green peas in it? Are you crazy? ... You need it for the festive table.' Or again: 'it's not consumed right away! Those dry cakes, for instance, get hidden! For six months, till New Year, let's say, or a birthday.' This 'natural' logic was clear even to children – even if they might try to find and eat foods hidden 'for a special occasion'.[26]

The main purpose of reserving food was to celebrate events in the family life cycle (e.g. birthdays) and 'universal' holidays such as New Year: 'Sometime at the beginning of October we would start collecting food for the winter holiday period, because in winter there were many birthdays, the New Year etc. In other words ... we always tried to hold back certain products, for instance, anything canned or bottled, till the holidays came round.'[27] Scarce ingredients were reserved for the ritual Soviet salat Oliv'e ('Russian salad') which was made 'for the days of festive gatherings ... birthdays, and, I'm ashamed to confess, for the "red dates of the calendar", New Year, and, excuse me for saying so, November 7'.[28] Nobody wanted to 'risk going without Olivier'.[29] This association of holidays and scarce products distributed through the system of 'food packages' (mayonnaise, green peas, sausage, sprats etc.) was reinforced also by official practices: the packages were themselves selected so as to meet 'traditional' expectations with regard to the Soviet holiday menu (with green peas appearing in December and so on). Supply was designed to match demand.[30]

Another abiding element of the shortage economy was a radical distinction between 'seasonal' and 'non-seasonal' foods, especially in relation to fruit and vegetables:

One time I had stomach problems, and here in spring there was nothing but macaroni, and even that was not always available . . . this was terrible, there was nothing to eat. And I literally . . . I was not hungry, but this food, it emaciated me completely . . . I couldn't eat what was sold . . . I needed vegetables, at least something . . . but there was not even a carrot in spring.[31]

At the same time, even those who were not very keen on preserving food knew how to put by basic vegetables for spring and summer 'till the new harvest comes, because new stuff appears late in this country'.[32] However, only those foods could be preserved that were locally produced and abundant at some times of year (e.g. cabbage, mushrooms). Oranges, tangerines and bananas were considered to be special treats in the winter (tangerines in particular were associated with New Year presents for children).[33] Many people went to the market, where products were more expensive, only when certain fruit were 'in season'.[34] The notion of 'seasonal' products persisted into the post-Soviet period as well,[35] but did not have such an imperative character as under 'developed socialism'.

As well as emphasizing resourcefulness, people sometimes refer to instances of 'sharp practice', for instance, grabbing children who were playing around and passing them off as one's own in order to get twice as much 'per person': 'women hired us, children, for ice-cream . . . they would take a boy along: "There are two of us!". . . This way I would sometimes "make" several ice creams.'[36] People would arrange things so that they could keep their place in more than one queue at the same time, and get several times more than what they were 'entitled' to: 'I figured out that there were two shop assistants, one at one end [of the store], and one at the other. So I . . . I got my stuff in the first line, and then I went to the second line, and – lo and behold! – I got a whole kilogram!!! [of red caviar].'[37] People would use all kinds of (semi)legitimate means to obtain something not-obtainable otherwise:

a guy from a milk factory used to come to us [our work place] at nights. And he would bring to us – must have been stolen – curd cheese, milk, and sour cream . . . he brought all this wrapped in a plastic sheet, which we had to give back to him the next night. And we washed this plastic sheet in the toilet . . . in a sink, under the cold tap! Greasy plastic!!! And this curd cheese . . . we packed it ourselves, into small plastic bags . . . at night. And next morning everything would be sold out . . . since I participated in the process, I helped myself to extra curd cheese [*laughs*].[38]

Trickster stories once again remind us that memories of food shortages take account of the present, as well as the past. Informants are trying – consciously or not – to create an ironic distance in relation to their not always pleasant Soviet food experience. People often present their food predicaments in a comic mode, as a kind of narrative joke (*anekdot*). They laugh at themselves and expect laughter on the part of the interviewer: 'I did not have enough years of party service to be entitled to a bottle of corn oil [*laughs*]. They would give you a bottle of corn oil only if you'd been in the party for at least 50 years.'[39] Also:

Once I delivered a lecture in a party district committee, and the first secretary liked it a lot, and he ordered . . . I was given, or sold, 5 kilograms of hake at the state price. And when I brought this to my mother-in-law . . . for the first time she seemed to have got the idea that our marriage [with her daughter] was not a complete misalliance [*laughs*]. That there was some use in it.[40]

Frequently jokes would be introduced with some obvious verbal marker: 'Let me tell you something even funnier'; 'This was terribly funny'; 'now it's funny to think about'.[41]

Even this brief sketch of recurrent themes related to food deficit (the general insufficiency of food, its low quality and lack of variety, the extremely high input of effort and extraordinary resourcefulness necessary for its procurement, the special rhythms of food consumption etc.), and of the emotional involvement on the part of the informants, clearly shows the importance of 'deficit experience' both in Soviet identity itself and in people's memories of late socialism:

and so Lionia pops by a store across from his department, and sees that they are bringing out a tray with ham. And for all those coupons he got a kilogram of ham! . . . And all the members of the department got a sandwich, and [his wife's] father said that even 300 years after his death he would remember this, and that this event was much more important than the battle of Stalingrad . . . than [the capture] of Berlin.[42]

At times the symbolic role of this experience was expressed in the narrative construction of the 'us-group' as possessing a special, almost cryptic knowledge inaccessible to those who did not share various food practices of the time: 'Those who did not live through it cannot understand it.' This was a frequent motif in many interviews: 'and when you tell this . . . even to people your age . . . they don't understand, see? This is . . . so far away from them!'; 'Well, sure, you're too young, you don't remember.' 'Not understanding' is equated with 'not remembering'.[43] While food (in the variety of practices related to it) indeed 'serves both to solidify group membership and to set groups apart',[44] age plays a crucial role in establishing the borders between 'us' and 'them'. Other parameters are of far less significance: even though nowadays our informants may belong to very different social groups (e.g. those who are still working in state organizations, those who have already retired, those who may be counted among the so-called 'new Russians', those who live permanently or semi-permanently in a Western 'consumer society'), they share similar recollections about food deficit in the time of 'developed socialism'.

However, this *confluence of food and memory* does not yet answer the question whether 'experience of deficit' may be seen as a part of people's individual and/or collective identity. Two possible takes on this question are: first, whether this experience was important for constructing 'Soviet identity' in late Soviet time itself, and secondly, whether it helps maintain this 'Soviet identity' now, whatever form this might take.

The evidence with reference to both issues is mixed. At times, our informants used the pronoun 'we' in the sense of 'We, the Soviet people' in general. But in some cases this naming referred to all those living in the country; in others, to one group as victims of the food situation in that country. So, on the one hand, informants might say: 'with the deficit that existed, since *our* economy was the way it was', or compare the Soviet Union and the West: 'Yes, we knew that beyond the border ... not even that everything was better there, it's just that they simply had what we didn't ... We didn't have this, they did.'[45] But on the other hand, they might see themselves as part of a downtrodden, non-elite group within Soviet society: '*we* wrote numbers [indicating our place in a queue] everywhere – when you were buying a pair of trousers, a bar of soap, a piece of fabric! ... people [were expected to be] grateful for what they were tossing *us*!'[46]

Whichever way, in these and other similar cases when people referred to themselves as 'the Soviet people', they were not so much making statements about identity in an absolute sense as giving an indication of their ascribed collective nationality during the time discussed. There seemed to be only one conception of what might be called an overall 'Soviet identity' as far as food practices are concerned. This was the identity of a 'procurer' or 'breadwinner' (*dobytchik, kormilets*), which was seen as a shared feature of all those who lived under 'developed socialism'. Not only was the ability to procure (scarce) foodstuffs seen as a measure of individual 'value' (cf. 'you procure food packets ... and you may be asked, what are you worth in life?'[47]), but it was also transferred to Soviet society as a whole. All Soviet people were seen primarily as 'food procurers'. The common stereotype about empty stores and full refrigerators[48] may serve as an illustration of this notion.

If an identity is taken for granted, it may, of course, not necessarily be named and narrated. But all the same, it does seem that a number of more particular distinctions were much more relevant to our informants than the general notion of a 'Soviet person'.

The majority of our informants belonged to the so-called 'middle Soviet intelligentsia', a group that 'talked a lot but didn't work much'.[49] They perceived themselves as distinct from the following.

Industrial workers. These were supplied better, in the informants' view, mainly because they were feared by the government: 'workers were top of the list for food products – to keep them quiet'.[50] As compared to industrial enterprises, informants argued, 'institutions of culture' were 'poor organizations',[51] and often did not get any 'food support' at all.

Leaders (*nachal'stvo*), e.g. the directors of enterprises, as compared to 'ordinary employees'. This was perhaps the most pervasive juxtaposition in our interviews. 'Leaders' were those who 'decided on our behalf what we'd like to eat'.[52] It was generally believed that 'leaders' got better food packages and in general were much better off in terms of food supply.[53] This, however, was seen as the 'natural order of things'. According to a specific 'Soviet logic' the 'higher' the person stood, the more benefits he was entitled to.[54]

Party officials as a specific category among the 'leaders', from party functionaries at lower levels to 'lesser gods' such as secretaries of district, city and regional party committees. It was often said that 'Central Committee *nomenklatura* workers' and 'Old Bolsheviks' were 'eating from a special trough'.[55] This category was, one hears, getting food packages with unheard-of delights in them ('pressed and unpressed caviar, chicken, smoked tongue, wine, cognac ... real crabs ... cold-smoked sausage – everything!')[56] They had the right to buy food in special 'supply bureaus' (*stoly zakazov*): 'There were food supply bureaus for the chosen – for party members, for the leading party authorities ... You could come inside such a store and see what they ate – if you were allowed to – but those foods were not for you.'[57] Such places were 'annexes' of top quality department stores, which delivered food straight to the homes of the privileged.[58] Even rank-and-file party members were believed to be in a privileged position: the party membership card was also sometimes called a 'bread card' (*khlebnaia kartochka*), again with direct reference to the war: 'This was a pass to get anywhere! Food and everything! ... You could go to the regional committee, to their cafeteria, and get everything you wanted. For mere kopecks. Sandwiches with caviar, salmon – here you go, 11 kopecks. I still remember.'[59]

Salespeople and people responsible for the system of food distribution. These people 'lived luxuriously. Deficit was an advantage for them ... And they hated this abundance of goods [that came later on], because previously they had deficit right in the palms of their hands. Maybe it was in their interests to create deficit in the country.'[60] In connection with this category of people, many informants recall a well-known humorous monologue by the famous Soviet comedian Arkadii Raikin, which portrayed directors of large department stores and food supply facilities as the most 'respected people', sitting in the first rows in the best theatres for all the top shows.[61] Any service personnel working in stores, whether big or small, were allegedly 'providing' food for 'their own people': 'even some cleaning woman who happens to work in a store, of course she gets herself three cans of green peas when there's a delivery' (Figure 14.1).[62] 'To be friends with a butcher' (*imet' znakomogo miasnika*) was a common Soviet cliché describing someone's access to (better) meat.[63] As a rule, 'knowing the right people' presupposed exchange of services; usually a person had to be 'useful' him- or herself in order to maintain these relations.[64] Food exchanges were thus a crucial part of the Soviet 'economy of favours'.[65]

Figure 14.1 An instant meal of tinned braised meat and tinned peas.

'Special' groups, such as war veterans, newly-weds, diabetics, donors etc., who were officially entitled to additional and/or special products. In most cases our informants saw this entitlement as quite 'natural' in the sense of being justified by special circumstances, although certain 'extremely scarce' (*ostrodefitsitnye*) products such as buckwheat could often be obtained only if one had diabetes.[66]

Alongside these distinctions according to social strata, a very important distinction with regard to 'access to food' is deduced from geography. Informants clearly differentiate between those who lived in Moscow and Leningrad and the rest of the country's population: 'there was nothing beyond the precincts of Sadovoe kol'tso';[67] everybody else 'was supposed to live on their own resources'.[68] One often hears that food rationing was introduced in the provinces 'as early as the 1970s' (something that is objectively true only of some provincial cities).[69] The commonest cliché of all is that 'all Russia used to come to Moscow for sausage'.[70] The only comparison in favour of localities other than the two main cities emerged in a story about an extremely rich market in Groznyi at the end of the 1960s, where the informant saw 'absolutely stunning poultry . . . piles of fruit and vegetables' that she 'had never ever seen in Petersburg [*sic*]'.[71] Yet generally the two capitals counted as the prime locations where food could be got, and many stories related precisely to the 'shopping tours' undertaken by people from the provinces to these two cities.[72]

The sets of distinctions listed above may be seen as much more significant in terms of identity formation than are the shared memories of 'experienced deficit'. The reason for this is not so much the fact that some of these memories may potentially be unpleasant or even traumatic to our present-day informants – after all, identity may be composed of a 'set of attributes, beliefs, desires, or principles of action . . . the person takes no special pride in'.[73] The point is that practices under 'food deficit' varied so much, depending on the niche people occupied in late Soviet society and their subjective preferences, that people find it difficult to see any overall imaginary affinity with others who shared them.[74]

Importantly, people themselves do not generally see the 'deficit experience' as something that separates them into a special social group: 'In principle . . . a kind of common remembrance may emerge, yes, but it does not unite . . . certainly, people lived at the same time and had largely similar experiences.'[75] If 'identity' is understood in the broadest sense as 'experience of commonality',[76] we may assume that in the late Soviet period groups of Soviet citizens as classified according to their consumer capacities and practices might indeed have formed 'identity groups'. However, at present, the Soviet 'deficit heritage' does not seem to play any significant role in people's understanding of who they are. Rather, people take pride in *transcending* this heritage.

The notion of what a 'Soviet person' might be, and whether interviewees themselves thought they could be counted as one, was brought up in a number of our interviews. Some people would refer to the common public rhetoric that 'we are Soviet people, and we can't get rid of this . . . all our behaviour, some reactions to some things . . . these are the reactions of a Soviet person'.[77] Some people defined 'Sovietness' as the 'perception that we are together, that we are doing something important', and yet on the other hand as 'social mediocrity', as a syndrome of 'forced collective existence' that entailed 'personal irresponsibility', and 'unending serfdom', in the sense of forced dependence upon somebody or something.[78] Another conversation added 'a manipulative mentality', sensitivity as to where power was located, 'a very hierarchical cast of mind', 'respectfulness of authority in all its forms', 'incredible adaptability, based on inventiveness and imagination', 'not much respect for other people's space' (both in the direct and the metaphorical senses) and the 'underlying anxiety about deficits of material goods'.[79] But again, even this last may hardly be seen as a heritage of the late Soviet period unless it is expressed in specific common practices or some kind of 'collective agency' based on collective acknowledgement of this trait.[80] Even in its 'softest' constructivist version identity requires 'affiliative forms of self-understanding'.[81] If these forms existed in the past, nowadays they seem to be rather questionable. If shared deficit was once a social glue, there is no sign that it now acts as such. The impression is that people now see social solidarity as something they were *forced* into by repressive politics – hence the frequent emphasis on *individual* resourcefulness when describing the past.

All of this created a situation that was rather different from the image from *Goodbye, Lenin* with which we started. Several years ago one of my colleagues organized a celebration to commemorate his deceased father's hundredth birthday. The table was loaded with rich delicacies, among which two dishes stood out clearly: exquisite gefilte fish on the one hand, and modest cans of sprats on the other (Figure 14.2). While the first dish was a tribute to the Jewish background of the family, the second one seemed to embody the connection with the Soviet past, where sprats, like Salad Olivier, signified a special occasion, distinguishing between 'common' and 'festive' days. These sprats – just like the Spreewald pickles mentioned at the beginning – fulfilled the role of a cultural signifier, referring to the

Figure 14.2 Tins of sprats and pike-perch.

epoch when the host's father lived, yet unlike these pickles they did not seem to contain any relevant present-day identity-marking significance for those who were invited, although the majority of them had lived during the time of 'developed socialism'. When the meal ended, the sprats had been left by the guests more or less untouched.

NOTES

1. Oxf/AHRC-SPb-08, PF49-ANK (female informant b. 1955). The research on which this chapter draws was sponsored by the Arts and Humanities Research Council as part of the project 'National Identity in Russia from 1961'. It draws particularly on my own interviews with informants in St Petersburg, coded as follows: project identifier (Oxf/AHRC), place (SPb), date of interview, recording number, and interviewer's initials. The informants, in the age range thirty to ninety when interviewed, all had personal memories of Soviet food deficits.
2. J. Holtzman, 'Food and Memory', *Annual Review of Anthropology* 35 (2006), 367.
3. T. Kondrat'eva, *Kormit' i pravit': o vlasti v Rossii, XVI–XX vv.* (Moscow, 2006).
4. The system of 'food packages' started at the end of the 1960s/beginning of the 1970s, when the principle of economic accountability (*khozraschet*) was introduced, and directors of enterprises, 'in order to attract labour and managerial personnel . . . began to advertise their rules for distributing goods' (Kondrat'eva,

Kormit, 154). Usually organizations would establish relatively independent ties with food stores, vegetable storage facilities (*ovoshchebaza*) and collective farms, where 'food packages' would be parcelled up before being delivered to an organization. As a rule, these packs consisted of two parts: scarce (*defitsitnye*) products and the so-called 'load' (*nagruzka*). The former were very hard or impossible to get in stores, while the latter usually included items that were easily available and often not essential. As a result, 'in order to get a can of caviar to put on the table for guests, you had to buy a lot of junk along with it' (Oxf/ AHRC-Spb-07, PF13-ANK). The content of food packs, their quantity and the frequency of their delivery varied from one organization to another; often the number of food packs was (considerably) less than the number of employees, which produced internal competition and a number of practices aimed at regularizing distribution.

5. S. Ushakin, 'Kolichestvennyi stil': potreblenie v usloviiakh simvolicheskogo defitsita', *Sotsiologicheskii zhurnal* no. 3–4 (1999), www.socjournal.ru/article/ 266.

   Almost every episode of Leonid Parfenov's documentary series *Namedni* ('Lately'), a popular history programme about the Soviet and post-Soviet period, opened with the words: 'Events, people and phenomena that determined the way of life; something without which we cannot be imagined, even less – understood', and contained something related to food and/or consumption, e.g. pressure-cooker (1965); broiler chicken (1969); '6 *sotkas*', small plots of land in large community gardens given to members of Soviet institutions and organizations as a means of self-support (1970); self-service stores (1971); scarcity of sausage (1972); rotgut or *bormotukha*, low quality fortified wine (1976); 'potato trips', to help collective farmers in harvesting potatoes (1977); electric samovar (1981); 'Andropovka' vodka, the introduction of pollack as a mass-market fish (1983); the lowering of prices on Pacific sardines (1984); the arrival of McDonald's in Moscow (1990); Turkish tea (1990); 'tobacco riots' (1990); the food crisis and 'humanitarian aid' (1991); marketization, the abolition of the state vodka monopoly, Rasputin vodka (1992); Snickers, Bounty and Mars chocolate bars (1993); supermarkets (1994); small wholesale markets, illegal vodka, certified labels (1995); Baltika beer, cheap caviar (1998) etc.

6. The introduction, in 1971, of the new concept of 'developed socialism', a 'central ideological contribution of the Brezhnev leadership', was supposed 'to excuse the failure of present-day Soviet institutions to match the standards of full communism' (See: A. B. Evans Jr, 'Developed Socialism in Soviet Ideology', *Soviet Studies* 29:3 (1977), 412–14).

7. Shortages were often referred to obliquely in the Soviet press – in stories along the lines that supplies of potatoes/cabbages/meat were about to improve – and were an abiding topic in reportage by Western journalists: see, for example, Hedrick Smith's *The Russians* (New York, 1976).

8. Oxf/AHRC-Spb-08, PF17-ANK. In this chapter I focus solely on the issue of food, but deficit was indigenous to virtually every sphere of late Soviet consumption: 'the uniform quality of all kinds of resources – their insufficiency . . .

There was not enough living space, food, clothes, footwear, books and journals, furniture, paper, land, materials, fuel, wood, transportation means – not enough of anything!' (O. Kuratov, *Khroniki byta*, Moscow, 2004, 15).

9. Oxf/AHRC-SPb-08, PF31-ANK; Oxf/AHRC-SPb-07, PF13-ANK. See also: Oxf/AHRC-SPb-07, PF7-ANK; Oxf/AHRC-SPb-08, PF17-ANK.

10. Oxf/AHRC-SPb-07, PF25-ANK. See also: ibid., PF10-ANK; Oxf/AHRC-SPb-08, PF31-ANK; Oxf/AHRC-SPb-07, PF25-ANK; Oxf/AHRC-SPb-08, PF41-ANK; ibid., PF44-ANK etc.

11. A particular genre of Russian folklore that highlights bizarre, grotesque and sometimes bloodthirsty occurrences, for instance, the emergence of a strangling hand from wallpaper etc. Also used more loosely to mean hair-raising narratives, shockers.

12. Oxf/AHRC-SPb-07, PF10-ANK.

13. Oxf/AHRC-SPb-08, PF31-ANK.

14. Oxf/AHRC-SPb-07, PF8-ANK.

15. Oxf/AHRC-SPb-08, PF31-ANK. On queues as the 'focal point' of Soviet culture, see e.g.: V. Nikolaev, 'Sovetskaia ochered'': proshloe kak nastoiashchee', *Neprikosnovennyi zapas* 43:5 (2005), http://magazines.russ.ru/nz/2005/43/ni11. html; E. Osokina, 'Proshchal'naia oda sovetskoi ocheredi', *Neprikosnovennyi zapas* 43:5 (2005), http://magazines.russ.ru/nz/2005/43/oso10.html.

16. Oxf/AHRC-SPb-07, PF25-ANK; Oxf/AHRC-SPb-08, PF48-ANK; Oxf/AHRC-SPb-07, PF25-ANK. For his part, my own father was absolutely sure that pollack was suitable only for cats and inedible by human beings, and only in the middle of the 'hungry 90s' did he grudgingly agree to eat it himself.

17. Oxf/AHRC-SPb-07, PF25-ANK.

18. Ibid., PF10-ANK; Oxf/AHRC-SPb-08, PF23-ANK etc. Cf., on war realities as a 'precedent text' in people's stories of food deprivation under socialism: 'Food coupons introduced on 1 December [1990] were supposed to guarantee that every city inhabitant would be able to purchase the minimal set of foodstuffs ... It was especially emphasized that bread cards had not been introduced. Yet it was precisely the word "cards" that people started using for the coupons, with clear reference to memories about the siege of Leningrad' (S. Karnaukhov, 'Pokhorony edy: zametki o prodovol'stvennoi korzine 1990 goda', *Novoe literaturnoe obozrenie* 84 (2007), http://magazines.russ.ru/nlo/2007/84/ka25.html [accessed 10 October 2010].

19. Oxf/AHRC-SPb-08, PF49-ANK; ibid., PF46-ANK.

20. An outlying city suburb that takes about 50 minutes to reach from the centre.

21. Oxf/AHRC-SPb-08, PF31-ANK.

22. Ibid., PF44-ANK.

23. Another suburb, also at a distance of *c.*50 minutes from central Leningrad.

24. Oxf/AHRC-SPb-08, PF48-ANK; ibid., PF31-ANK; ibid., PF41-ANK. There is a joke about this – it is the Soviet era, and a man is trying to fetch something from the overhead cupboard in his apartment (*antresoli*). He makes a wrong move, and an avalanche of products starts falling down: jars with Hungarian

green peas, fruit preserves, packets with various types of grain, sugar, pickles. The man swears and exclaims: 'For God's sake, will this famine never be over?!'

25. Oxf/AHRC-SPb-07, PF25-ANK. See also: Oxf/AHRC-SPb-08, PF31-ANK; Oxf/AHRC-SPb-07, PF10-ANK.

26. Oxf/AHRC-SPb-07, PF10-ANK; ibid., PF8-ANK.

27. Ibid., PF6-ANK.

28. Woman b. 1953, interviewed by A. Kushkova, 1 August 2000. Note her embarrassment about admitting to celebrating a state holiday.

29. Oxf/AHRC-SPb-07, PF10-ANK.

30. One memoirist, who used to be a well-paid and 'well-connected' state official during the time under discussion, observed that Soviet cuisine was rather monotonous, even if people had access to scarce products: 'in spite of the abundance of dishes, we and people of our circle were pretty conservative as far as the festive menu was concerned' (Kuratov, *Khroniki byta*, 136).

31. Oxf/AHRC-SPb-07, PF25-ANK.

32. Ibid.

33. Ibid., PF13-ANK.

34. Oxf/AHRC-SPb-08, PF46-ANK; ibid., PF28-ANK.

35. e.g. ibid., PF23-ANK.

36. Oxf/AHRC-SPb-07, PF25-ANK. Many people recollect standing in interminable lines 'as the second pair of hands', since goods were often sold 'per person' (ibid., PF6-ANK), and even 'growing up in lines' (Oxf/AHRC-SPb-08, PF17-ANK), or being allocated a certain amount of money 'in case you see something being sold', and being expected to inform their parents about such occasions (ibid., PF28-ANK), or else instructed about various aspects of the 'queuing code' in order not to be reproved by the crowd of customers (Oxf/AHRC-SPb-07, PF8-ANK).

37. Oxf/AHRC-SPb-07, PF3-ANK. This informant also recollected the precise day when this 'caviar miracle' happened – 27 January, the anniversary of the day when the siege of Leningrad was lifted. She directly connected the two events, and stressed that she was very proud of her achievement. The example nicely points up the difference between food shortages in the actual war and those in the era of deficit.

38. Ibid., PF25-ANK.

39. Oxf/AHRC-SPb-08, PF31-ANK.

40. Ibid.

41. Oxf/AHRC-SPb-07, PF25-ANK; ibid., PF10-ANK; Oxf/AHRC-SPb-08, PF41-ANK etc. Describing deficit experience by means of jokes started when deficit was an everyday reality; among the most popular ones were jokes about a person who comes to a store and asks for 'half a kilo of food', a riddle about 'something long, green and smelling of sausage' (a train transporting people from the provinces on their regular trips for food to the big cities) or a joke about a man who returns home, sees his wife with a lover, and shouts: 'While you're wasting time on that nonsense, you could have been over the road buying buckwheat!'

42. Oxf/AHRC-SPb-08, PF31-ANK.

43. Oxf/AHRC-SPb-07, PF7-ANK; Oxf/AHRC-SPb-08, PF41-ANK etc. One might suggest that the 'anecdotal' way of presentation, apart from the ability to take off the potentially traumatic psychological edge, is seen as the most suitable means of presenting material for the comprehension of those who did not understand because they don't remember.

44. S. W. Mintz and C. M. Du Bois, 'The Anthropology of Food and Eating', *Annual Review of Anthropology* 31 (2002), 109.

45. Oxf/AHRC-SPb-08, PF46-ANK.

46. Oxf/AHRC-SPb-07, PF13-ANK; Oxf/AHRC-SPb-08, PF29-ANK. Emphasis added.

47. Oxf/AHRC-SPb-07, PF11-ANK.

48. Ibid., PF13-ANK.

49. Ibid., PF25-ANK; cf. ibid., PF10-ANK.

50. Ibid., PFA13-ANK; cf. ibid., PF25-ANK.

51. Oxf/AHRC-SPb-08, PF29-ANK.

52. Oxf/AHRC-SPb-07, PF1-ANK.

53. Ibid., PF10-ANK; ibid., PF3-ANK; ibid., PF13-ANK.

54. There is only one example in the whole body of our interviews where a person recalls a public statement against the privileged position of the enterprise leader, but even this took place during the family celebration at home and did not have any results/consequences: 'I remember saying ... how is it the case that bones without flesh are being thrown to us? Thrown to the people?' (ibid., PF13-ANK).

55. e.g. ibid., PF5-ANK.

56. Oxf/AHRC-SPb-08, PF31-ANK.

57. Oxf/AHRC-SPb-07, PF13-ANK.

58. Oxf/AHRC-SPb-08, PF31-ANK. Even during the siege of Leningrad these people were commonly believed to have everything they wanted, so that 'those living in no. 26–28 Kirovskii prospekt [a building inhabited by party high-ups], when they were hungry, they could get extraordinary things out of the refuse pits' (ibid.). This address was where the Leningrad party leader Sergei Kirov had lived up to his death in 1934.

59. Ibid., PF48-ANK.

60. Oxf/AHRC-SPb-07, PF13-ANK.

61. Ibid., PF1-ANK; ibid., PF13-ANK.

62. Ibid., PF13-ANK.

63. e.g. ibid., PF13-ANK; Oxf/AHRC-SPb-08, PF17-ANK; ibid., PF46-ANK; ibid., PF48-ANK.

64. Cf.: 'Dentists never stood in lines ... I had my patients – butchers, directors of food stores or departments. I would call: "I need this, this and this. When shall I come?" Problem solved' (Oxf/AHRC-SPb-08, PF48-ANK).

65. See e.g. A. Ledeneva, S. Lovell and A. Rogachevskii, eds., *Bribery and Blat in Russia* (Basingstoke, 2000); A. Ledeneva, *How Russia Really Works: The Informal Practices that Shaped Soviet Politics and Business* (Ithaca, NY, 2006).

66. Oxf/AHRC-SPb-07, PF6-ANK.

67. The central part of Moscow, as bounded by the inner ring road.
68. Oxf/AHRC-SPb-08, PF17-ANK.
69. Oxf/AHRC-SPb-07, PF1-ANK.
70. Oxf/AHRC-SPb-08, PF29-ANK; cf. ibid., PF46-ANK; ibid., PF49-ANK etc., etc.
71. Ibid., PF41-ANK.
72. Here is just one example of such stories, which again contains references to the Second World War (ibid., PF17-ANK):

> the most difficult thing was to transport meat [in this case, from Moscow to Ul'ianovsk]. And here the mighty weight of popular experience . . . had it not been for that, I would have been lost. Somebody . . . recollected . . . I think this was rooted in folklore [that] during the war, when they had to preserve meat in a partisan detachment . . . it was necessary not just to put it in the ground, but wrap it in nettle leaves . . . So we had to go out and search for nettles in the middle of Piter [*laughs*].

73. J. D. Fearon, 'What Is Identity (As We Now Use the Word)?', 3 November 1999, www.scribd.com/doc/7260022/Fearon-What-is-Identity. L. Gudkov, in his book with the characteristic title 'Negative Identity' (*Negativnaia identichnost'*, Moscow, 2004), suggests that at present the character of Russian society is defined by those 'who did not get enough', and that this negative identity presupposes an essential 'experience of failure', which he derives from the repressive and restrictive character of the institutional regulation of life in Soviet and post-Soviet society, especially in relation to practices existing beyond the borderlines of the state distribution system.
74. Cf.: 'It is somehow difficult to say that "all Soviet people did so . . .". No, not all of them did so . . . there was an individual aspect to it' (Oxf/AHRC-SPb-08, PF46-ANK).
75. Ibid.
76. R. Brubaker and F. Cooper, 'Beyond "Identity"', *Theory and Society* 29:1 (2000), 2.
77. Oxf/AHRC-SPb-07, PF10-ANK.
78. Oxf/AHRC-SPb-08, PF41-ANK; ibid., PF46-ANK; ibid., PF41-ANK.
79. Man b. 1938, personal communication.
80. K. A. Cerulo, 'Identity Construction: New Issues, New Directions', *Annual Review of Sociology* 23 (1997), 385–409.
81. Brubaker and Cooper, 'Beyond "Identity"', 20.

PART VI

Creeds of national identity

CHAPTER 15

Competing orthodoxies: identity and religious belief in Soviet and post-Soviet Russia

Catriona Kelly

It was hard for citizens of imperial Russia, including the majority Orthodox population, to avoid seeing attachment to a confession as part of their identity. Births were registered by ministers of religion, as were marriages; 'divine law' (*zakon Bozhii*), or religious education, was taught in all schools; the First General Census of 1897 collected data on confession, rather than nationality. The standing of the Holy Synod as equal to the highest secular organ of administration, the Senate, was underlined by their occupation of two identical wings of one building in the capital. Religious rites – in the Orthodox Church, *treby*, such as baptism, marriages, and funerals – were an essential part of the ceremonial life of town and country.[1]

Religion – or rather, lack of this – was also central to self-definition among opponents of the established political order. In the words of Ariadna Tyrkova-Williams: 'It was not just the Marxists who considered religion a survival of former superstitions, the opium of the people.' The intelligentsia in general 'had stepped away from the Church, mocked it in secret, denigrated it. The only reason why no-one stormed the Church was that police control made this impossible.'[2] Among those vehemently opposed to the Church, even so bland a custom as decorating a Christmas tree was seen as a tribute to the forces of reaction. Many other Russians went through the motions of religious observance when this was essential, but without letting official Orthodoxy affect their conscious lives. Alternative religions such as Tolstoyanism or spiritualism were all the rage.[3]

Between February and October 1917 the Provisional Government edged uneasily round this inherited situation. Discrimination against the non-Orthodox was ended by the Decree on the Abolition of Confessional and National Restrictions of 20 March 1917 and the Decree on the Freedom of Conscience of 14 July 1917. On 5 August 1917 the Synod was abolished. But efforts were also made not to alienate the Orthodox hierarchy. In a draft bill put before the Pre-synodal Council on 5 July 1917, Orthodoxy was given the role of the 'premier confession' in the new state.[4]

Once the Bolsheviks took power, reform was far more radical. The Decree on the Freedom of Conscience, the Church and Religious Societies of 20 January 1918 disestablished the Orthodox Church, nationalized its property and that of the other confessions, and made membership of a 'religious society' a strictly private matter. These 'societies' had no status as juridical subjects (which stopped them, for example, from acquiring property by purchase or donation). The seizures of church valuables in 1922 had a pragmatic motivation – aid to the starving in the Volga regions – but also enforced the message that religious societies held all moveable and immoveable property on sufferance (Figure 15.1). Opposition on the part of believers was ruthlessly crushed. In Soviet propaganda, faith was represented as a sign of 'backward' attitudes, an attribute of the 'uncultured'. In the words of doggerel verse published in *Young Proletarian* magazine in 1925:

> Not going to the church today,
> You won't get me there, no way.
> To the Komsomol I'll go,
> And listen to the rad-i-o.[5]

The fight against religion was seen as an inalienable part of the creation of a new Soviet consciousness: 'Only then will the revolution be fully established, when it *enters the flesh and blood* of every citizen, when no one *is able to think any differently* than as the resident of the country of the victorious revolution.'[6]

Once the first five-year plan got under way, attitudes hardened still further. The Decree on Religious Organizations of 5 April 1929 prohibited religious education and all such organizations' work with children, charitable initiatives and 'religious propaganda'. 'Cultic buildings' could now be removed from believers if they were needed for 'state and social needs'. A wave of closures followed. The demolition in 1929–30 of some of the most famous medieval Orthodox buildings in Moscow (the Chudov Monastery and the Iberian Gate) signalled that heritage protection now took second place to the struggle with religion, and that major Soviet public spaces should not be decorated with 'relics of the past'.

Between 1929 and 1936 local authorities across the country tore down and blew up 'cult buildings' that were impeding the progress of 'socialist construction' (Figure 15.2). In Leningrad, prominent victims of the new policy included the Church of St Paul the Apostle, built by A. M. Zakharov, the architect of the Admiralty (destroyed in 1929, despite a campaign by the Old Petersburg Society to save it), the early eighteenth-century Trinity

Figure 15.1 Still life from a closed church: an icon and smashed window-frame
in the Smol'nyi Cathedral (1748–64).

Cathedral on what was now Revolution Square (which was elaborately restored in the 1920s, but demolished in 1934), and the Church of the Annunciation on Labour Square (dismantled in 1929 to facilitate a tram junction). In later years churches were often replaced by metro stations. Soviet city planning required that a city square should have a dominating feature appropriate to a socialist city (by contrast, tsarist planning legislation had decreed that churches must have prominent sites).[7]

Split by internal conflicts that the Soviet authorities encouraged on a 'divide and rule' basis,[8] the Orthodox Church was transformed from one of the Russian Empire's most powerful political institutions to a beleaguered

0

302 CATRIONA KELLY

Figure 15.2 Church of the Trinity (1785–90), known from its shape as 'Kulich and Paskha', or 'Easter Loaf and Easter Pudding', photographed *c*.1937. The church was at this point scheduled for demolition (hence the photograph, meant to show it impeding free movement of transport), though it in fact survived, and reopened for worship in 1946.

minority group. Harassment by party and government organs and by the secret police was rife. The situation in Leningrad provides a snapshot of what was happening nationwide. Priests and nuns were arrested and imprisoned or exiled, and in 1937–8 many were executed. Large numbers went underground, or renounced their faith out of fear, expediency or a genuine change of heart. By 1 July 1938 there were ten priests and two deacons officiating across Leningrad.[9] If a church had no priest, this provided an excuse for declaring it redundant, and closing it for good.

Economic forces also contributed to closures. A condition of using a 'cultic building' was that repairs should be carried out as demanded by the authorities. If not, the religious society could be expelled. Members of the *dvadtsatka*, the group of twenty or more believers required in order to constitute a viable religious society (in the Orthodox Church, a 'parish'), were personally as well as collectively responsible for the condition of the building and its contents. Yet they also had no legal means – other than appealing to their dwindling congregations – by which they could raise funding to carry out repairs, or to pay local taxes and ground rents. While some *dvadtsatki* protested against closure (it was possible to appeal against a local decision to close a religious building by lobbying the Central Executive Committee of the Communist Party), some backed down in the face of practical difficulties.[10] The authorities acted to hasten closures: in 1938 a leading official in the department of Leningrad city soviet deputed to manage 'religious societies' reported that a colleague 'had expressed aston-ishment that no one's whacking a whole load of taxes on them and generally putting the squeeze on. I took the hint and I'm going to do over the Greek Orthodox as soon as I can, both on grounds of obeying Soviet law and on grounds of doing repairs and paying the lease fees.'[11]

Once 'cultic buildings' had closed, their fate was in the hands of local authorities. Under the conditions of forced industrialization, the demand for scrap metal and building materials such as brick was acute, which often brought pressure for demolition. Obviously, an ideologically embarrassing building, even if historic, would be high up the list for recycling.[12] If they survived, religious buildings were converted, sometimes to 'cultural and educational ends', but often for use as workshops or warehouses. Removal of obvious ecclesiastical features (crosses, inscriptions, sometimes also domes and bell towers) was a normal procedure.[13] Only working churches actually looked like churches, to the untrained eye, and only a few of these were left in each city (Leningrad, with its population of 2.5 million, had eight in 1940, only three of which were in prominent places).[14] It was possible to forget that Russia had ever been a majority Orthodox country. As early as 1923 the writer A. Men'shoi reported that, riding down Comrade Nakhimson prospekt (once named after the Church of the Vladimir Icon of the Mother of God), he had heard the tram conductor shout out the next stop as 'Comrade Nakhimson Church!'[15]

The destruction of churches and devotional objects, in particular icons, deprived Orthodoxy of the major symbols and tokens of belief. A 'prayed over' church or icon (*namolennaia*) was the focus of special affection.[16] This quality of 'being prayed over' had zero or negative value in the new society. Where churches and devotional objects were conserved, this was on the basis of historical or aesthetic value, not religious significance, and monument status did not necessarily offer protection. In 1932 officials in Lensovet drily observed that the Church of the Protecting Veil in Kolomna, though a monument of the third class, 'does not have much historical value'.[17]

The Russian Orthodox Church (ROC), like other 'religious societies', was in the paradoxical position of a blatantly non-Soviet organization in a nation that was officially supposed to espouse a uniform socialist belief system. The concordat with the Church brokered by Stalin in 1943 eased pressure on the hierarchy and believers, and a few churches were reopened – for example, in Leningrad the Church of the Trinity started working in 1946. Charges levied for the performance of weddings, christenings and other *treby*, and profits from the sale of candles, provided a regular income (though one that the secular authorities also did their best to milk). But the full weight of the Soviet bureaucracy continued to fall on 'religious societies'. Alongside the specialist Council on the Affairs of the Russian Orthodox Church (absorbed into the Council for Religious Affairs in 1965), whose chiefs were traditionally members of the secret police, believers had to negotiate with the tax inspectorate, with state insurance companies, with health and safety legislation, and with the inspectorate of architectural monuments (GIOP). Dealing with the last was a formidable task, since the inspectorate was very demanding, and believers and professional conservationists did not necessarily see eye to eye on priorities.[18]

The assault on the Church, not to speak of its role as a source of consolation during the Second World War, had improved its standing with some intellectuals. By 1942 the art historian Nikolai Punin found that attending a service held out the prospect of solace: 'If only the churches were open and thousands were at prayer, probably weeping too, in the glimmering gloom, how much less we would feel the dry metallic milieu in which we are now living.'[19] But church life continued to be at variance with Soviet society, even in linguistic terms. When writing to other churchmen, priests used pre-revolutionary formulas such as 'your humble servant'; they called a report a *rapport*, not an *otchet*. They often had difficulty accommodating to new values. In 1948 the senior officiating priest (*nastoiatel′*) at the St Nicholas Naval Cathedral in Leningrad contacted Metropolitan Grigorii (see below) to express anxiety about a police campaign to remove beggars from the church grounds: 'The Word of the Lord says: "Blessed is he that understandeth concerning the needy and the poor".'[20] As Anatoly Krasnov-Levitin remembered, churchgoers were, in the 1920s, a group with little cultural capital: 'It was mostly the small fry of Petersburg: postmen, janitors, watchmen, petty officials. A few intellectuals.' There was a marked gender imbalance: 'Mostly women in kerchiefs, young and old.'[21] This description remained accurate in later decades as well.[22]

The Soviet religious reforms severed the links between congregations and the broader communities in which they lived. With only one church per administrative district, the 'parish' was a bureaucratic term, rather than a social reality. Worshippers often had to travel long distances, and attend services in places with which they had no other connection. In cities, people usually picked a church whose atmosphere they liked, and attended it occasionally, rather than going regularly to somewhere along the street. For example, the poet Anna Akhmatova felt an emotional connection to St Nicholas Naval Cathedral, about fifty minutes' walk from her home, rather than the Transfiguration Cathedral, which could be reached in nearer to fifteen minutes.[23] Residents of a given district felt no special attachment to their local church: for Joseph Brodsky, growing up in 1940s Leningrad, it was the fence outside the Transfiguration Cathedral, made of Turkish cannons, not the church, that drew him.[24]

This story of religious persecution and marginalization has been told many times.[25] In recent Orthodox histories the term used for the Soviet period is *likholet'e*, 'years of savagery', which emphasizes the gulf between sacred and secular authorities.[26] Yet everyday relations between the Church and the authorities were messier than would be suggested by the Soviet heroic narrative about the victorious war against superstition, or the religious narrative of martyrdom.[27] This process became especially obvious during the 1960s, both because the revival of hard-line attitudes to religious societies under Khrushchev had intimidating effects on churchmen, but also because clergy who had trained in the seminaries that were reopened on Soviet soil from 1943 were a different breed from the pre-revolutionary clergy who had presided in the 1920s and 1930s, or the returning members of the Russian Orthodox Church Abroad who had held leading positions after the war.[28]

Metropolitan Grigorii (Chukov) of Leningrad had warmly supported believers' efforts to get churches reopened in the late 1940s and early 1950s (though he also sanctioned services of prayer when Stalin died).[29] His successors were more circumspect. Metropolitan Pimen (Izvekov, who held office in 1961–3), in particular, was regarded by Grigorii Zharinov, the hard-line plenipotentiary of the Council on the Affairs of the ROC, as a man the authorities could do business with: 'It is quite easy to decide questions of rational transfers of clergy, and of the pointlessness of appointing priests to economically weak parishes, with Pimen. Pimen's correct behaviour and reactions have often facilitated the fact that when various churches were closed, e.g. the Chapel of the Blessed Xenia, there were no undesirable manifestations from clergy and believers.'[30] Pimen's manner in dealing with petitions was abrupt. When the parishioners of the Trinity Church at Lesnovo appealed to him to intervene in order to halt demolition of their church for road-building, he wrote to the patriarch in Moscow, spelling out why the demolition was necessary:

It is correct to suggest that the executive committee of the Vyborg district soviet of the city of Leningrad has approved the demolition of certain buildings and among them the Trinity Church, Lesnovo, in view of the widening of the highway and the planned new construction along the route to the cemetery of victims of the Blockade, where a monument has been erected and an eternal flame lit.

The executive committee of the Vyborg district soviet has informed the community of believers of Lesnovo Church of this decision, giving due notice . . . Regarding the premises of the former large brick church which is on the same site as the building of the Lesnovo Church now scheduled for demolition, this is occupied by an organization of the factory type equipped for that purpose, with machines and lathes in place. The claim that the lease on these premises expires in 1964 is not founded on fact . . . Whether the believers themselves have made representations to the effect that this building should be put at this disposal to any official body, I cannot say.[31]

Metropolitan Nikodim (Rotov, 1929–1978), on the other hand, who held office from 1963 to 1978, put a good deal more effort into representing believers' interests, but was not averse to enjoying the perks that attached to his office as chairman of the Department of External Affairs at the Moscow Patriarchate, such as the right to use the 'deputies' lounge' at Pulkovo airport, or have extra carriages hitched to the Red Arrow train when he needed to organize a business trip to Moscow at short notice.[32]

Believers themselves also developed a modus vivendi with secular authority, in however limited a sense. Petitions invoked the official requirements for the opening of churches (above all, the fact that there were no other working churches in the same district). However, if applying to have a church reopened that was a listed monument, they might also emphasize the historical significance of the building, and the fact that it would be better looked after if returned to use by believers.[33] This line of argument was driven less by the letter of the laws regulating religious building use than by the hope of gaining support from GIOP, which was responsible for allocating the leases of historic buildings.

On the other hand, when under pressure to carry out costly repairs, the executive organs of *dvadtsatki* sometimes lobbied with the local plenipotentiary, hoping he would get GIOP to back down.[34] Like most groups in the Soviet Union, the Orthodox did not so much wage outright or covert war as manoeuvre to the best of their ability within the straits of bureaucratic *force majeure*.

Despite the ranting tone and crude stereotyping of religious propaganda, Soviet officials' views were by no means uniform either. The post-war plenipotentiary in Leningrad, Aleksandr Kushnarev, took a flexible attitude to church relations; Grigorii Zharinov, who held the post in the early 1960s, did not.[35] This was partly in the nature of the times: plenipotentiaries tended to be as accommodating as top-down policy allowed.

Yet relations were often less cosy, at least where ordinary believers were concerned. In August 1966 the chairman of the executive committee of the Vsevolozhskii district soviet responded brusquely to a petition from inhabitants of Murino, a former estate village in the area, requesting the reopening of the Church of St Catherine. 'We don't need that church, we'll tear it down, and as for you lot, I'll have you in one at a time, then we'll see how many of you still want to press ahead with this rubbish.'[36] Churches could also be the target for plain robbery or vandalism on the part of officials, dressed up as iconoclasm. In 1964 the chairman of the local district soviet turned up with cronies at the Church of St George, Lozhgolovo, and simply removed large amounts of church property.[37] But in these cases churchmen sometimes complained to the plenipotentiary, as well as reporting up the ecclesiastical line. Indeed, given that the civil authorities had to be informed about every incident of possible note, the line between the Church and civil authorities was porous.

The Church thus represented an eccentric and particularly disempowered but in some ways recognizably *Soviet* institution. Believers themselves were Soviet citizens too, of course – though this did not always work in predictable ways. Ordinary Soviet citizens had recourse to church rites in large numbers, a situation regularly raised as a problem by the plenipotentiaries.[38] In some places (Leningrad, Moscow, Irkutsk and other major intellectual centres), the revival of interest in early twentieth-century Russian religious philosophy could be a route to rapprochement with Orthodoxy, and from there, even a path to the priesthood.

The Church was not necessarily a comfortable place for such free spirits: in the words of one of them, 'The Church gave off an air of freedom for me, that's what's interesting. But then later that feeling disappeared, you know, it disappeared. I realized that there wasn't any freedom in the church, by and large, you've ended up in particular canons, rules, and so on.'[39] However, rampant atheism was – by the post-Stalin era – unusual. Even official surveys turned up large numbers of people who saw nothing particularly wrong with religion, and who defended it on the grounds that it was a 'Russian tradition' (this being a time when 'customs' and 'traditions' were being celebrated everywhere in the USSR).[40]

The ROC celebrated its millennium in 1988, a year that marked a turning point in Church–state relations. For the first time since the 1940s, churches began opening in large numbers. Initially, the new opportunities were greeted by the Church authorities with caution. Metropolitan Alexy of Leningrad (later to become Patriarch Alexy II) wrote on 21 February 1990 to the chairman of the executive committee of the Leningrad city soviet declining the offer to transfer St Isaac's Cathedral to use by the eparchy. The metropolitan claimed that the pressure to have the church restored came from 'certain informal associations which in many cases have no understanding of the Church's real needs and capacities'.[41]

In the case of another important historic church, the Koniushennaia (Royal Mews), Metropolitan Alexy was still more direct. Taking over responsibility was impossible, 'in view of the great difficulties that will be caused by restoring the interior of the church (since I assume that the interior decoration has not survived). The opening of more than twenty churches in Leningrad and Leningrad province has also created problems about priestly cadres to staff these.'[42]

However, after the collapse of Soviet power, the ROC found itself in a more favourable legal situation. The presidential decree of 23 April 1993 On the Transfer of Cultic Buildings to Religious Organizations formally recognized the rights of such organizations to the restitution of buildings historically used for worship. It was followed by further federal legislation in 1994 and 2001, and also regional and local statutes (for instance, the Law of St Petersburg passed on 9 March 2006, No. 59–12, On the Procedures for the Transfer into the Possession of Religious Organizations of Property Intended for Religious Use Currently in the Possession of the State Organs of St Petersburg).[43] In some respects religious communities were now in a better position than other lessees: for example, a presidential order of 1994 releasing monuments of architecture for privatization did not apply to religious buildings.[44]

At the same time, with state funds drying up across the board, religious societies had to rely entirely on their own resources in order to restore the buildings returned to them. But fund-raising – forbidden before – was now not just permitted, but encouraged. The Law on Freedom of Conscience and Religious Organizations of 1997 offered such societies tax concessions on earnings, which in practice meant the ROC enjoyed tax-free profits not just on charges levied for rites, but on its business concerns, for example, the bottling and sale of 'Sacred Spring' mineral water. In addition, the Church was often successful in finding individual sponsors for restoration, rebuilding and new building projects. One of the leading projects in St Petersburg, the restoration of the Church of the Protection of the Mother of God on Lieutenant Schmidt Embankment, which took nearly two decades and required a team of fifty restorers at a time to work on the badly decayed wall-paintings, was carried out with funding from a businessman living nearby.[45]

State control had not completely disappeared along with the funding, however. Religious societies still leased their buildings according to the principle of 'use without payment' that had operated in Soviet times. The procedure of transfer of use to a religious society was intricate. A central government decree of 30 June 2001, On the Transfer to Religious Organizations of Property with a Religious Function in State Ownership, required such a society to present, along with its application for transfer, a form of agreement with the monuments department, a historical description and inventory of the building and contents ('passport'), a buildings survey and a draft contract.[46]

Previously, religious societies had put up with this kind of bureaucratic regulation because there was no choice. Now that the ROC's position was becoming stronger, grumbling and frustration started to be common. In the words of the *nastoiatel'* of one of the cathedrals in St Petersburg:

See, our Cathedral, it's state property. And the use . . . it's simply handed over to us. At the same time, our contract with them says we have to keep it in order, pay the repairs and so on. And do you think we get a kopeck out of them?! Even though it's state property. And so we're forever looking for sponsors to keep it up, to do this and that, this repair, the next – we're obliged to look for people to help. Because the state says, 'we've got no money' . . . And now they're talking about making over all these churches as Church property. But that raises a really serious issue. Because say they hand over the churches today, and then tomorrow they slap a tax on. And what then? Think we can pay it? There's no way we can. The Russian Church is always in the same position – whatever the tsar says, so to speak. Whether it's the general secretary, or the president, same difference. If they want, they'll make it your property, but then the next minute they'll slap a tax on it.[47]

Against the background of mistrust in state intentions, believers maintained a cult of self-reliance. They took enormous pride in describing how *they themselves*, with God's help, of course, but by dint of unceasing effort, had managed to restore, and in the cases of formerly closed churches, bring back to life, a particular building (Figure 15.3). Interestingly, narratives about this might be not simply religious in character (though of course the description

Figure 15.3 Church of St Anna of Kashino, St Petersburg (1907–9), under restoration.

of how the church was resanctified was of extreme importance, especially since secular lessees in the Soviet period often treated the building in frankly sacrilegious ways, by placing lifts, machinery or even public lavatories in the altar space).[48] In believers' stories, humble everyday details – say, how they managed to make somewhere to worship in a church that was still being used by some secular organization – might be just as important as the strictly liturgical procedures. The elder of a historic St Petersburg church returned to believers in the 1990s lovingly remembered the work:

INTERVIEWER: So did anything get restored here? Did you have any restorers working?
INFORMANT: No. We did it all ourselves ... See this here, it was a toilet [pointing at the west end of the right-hand nave]. And we got the church in order. And the communion vessels, and all that ... It was all smashed and broken. We fixed it and cleaned it ... All of it, all by ourselves.[49]

The informant went on to describe how a sponsor had made a donation of rubber mats of the kind used in trolley buses, which had been used to cover the floor at first. This intimate, even domestic, sense of parishioners' relationship with the church persisted in everyday relations after it was opened for worship, as the description of 'housekeeping' the iconostasis indicated: 'It looks the same as it always did. We just clean it, give it a vacuum now and again.'[50]
A pamphlet by Father Aleksandr Budnikov of the Church of St Elijah the Prophet in northern St Petersburg made the same connection of the sacral and the domestic, the spiritual and the everyday:

There were heaps of earth round the church, rubbish, these wild trees and bushes and a huge ditch from a heating pipe that had never got laid. You had the feeling it would take years before you could hold a service in the church. But something amazing happened – a real miracle! By sheer effort on the part of the believers, with the help of a few seminarians, we were able to clear the entire church and grounds of all that rubbish.[51]

Another priest, this time occupying a junior position at one of the Leningrad cathedrals, was proud that only restorers attached to the cathedral had ever worked there: 'We have never had state restorers here, we don't have now, and we're never going to.' He thought of this as a model for other churches as well. Restoration might be under the control of state organs (particularly the monuments department), but the financing was organized by parishioners, who had funded some major restoration works since 2000.[52]
Again and again, clergy and believers emphasized their own role in restoration: 'Work always was funded, and still is, by voluntary contributions from believers, with almost no help from outside.'[53] Where state agencies were mentioned, they usually appeared in the role of a nuisance. For instance, Father Aleksandr Budnikov, recalling the restoration works in the Church of St Elijah the Prophet, emphasized the lack of interest that state restorers had shown in the 1970s:

The restorers reconstructed the main dome of the church, which had been destroyed in the 1974 fire, and the external columns of the rotunda. But work progressed very slowly, and it is not clear whether the restoration would ever have been completed, or whether the church would have been allowed to fall down. But 1988 altered and transformed things for ever.[54]

Believers' insistence that their absolute right to a church derived not just from their beliefs, but from their hard work and capacity to appreciate architecture, was partly of defensive origin. As the restitution of church property got under way, it inspired resistance not just from many of the lessees who were occupying former churches, but also from large sections of Russian society. Particularly inflammatory, in terms of public opinion among Russian intellectuals, were cases where the church concerned was in use for some cultural purpose. In the words of a contributor to the Scepsis.ru website:

Museums have spent decades doing restoration work and have kept their buildings in good condition. It is not surprising that the ROC has turned its attention to those buildings in the first instance. And unlike big companies, museums do not have the funds to lobby for their interests and defend themselves from attack, and so they have become the first objects of conflict.[55]

This assessment simplified reality. The staffs of a number of Leningrad museums, for example the Museum of Four Cathedrals (in whose care were the St Isaac's, St Sampson, Saviour on the Blood and Smol'nyi cathedrals) and the Museum of the Arctic, were remarkably successful in 'lobbying for their interests'. And the record of museums as lessees, in the Soviet period, was – according to the records of GIOP – rather mixed.[56] Ironically, one of the worst violators of protection of monument legislation in Leningrad was the State Restoration Studio, which occupied the Church of the Elevation of the Cross (begun in 1740). A report of 5 June 1984 carried out by members of the All-Russian Society for the Protection of Historic and Cultural Monuments noted that the church was 'in a dangerous condition', with rusty metal braces hammered into the walls, a metal container for shavings attached to the dome in such a way that it was destroying the plasterwork, illegal sheds in the grounds, and a general air of chaos and dilapidation.[57]

But use by a museum or other cultural institution was certainly less detrimental to the condition, in a physical sense, of church buildings than use by a factory (or, as in the case of the Church of the Protection of the Mother of God on Lieutenant Schmidt Embankment, a skating rink).[58] Intemperate and misleading remarks were not the sole prerogative of the pro-museum lobby. Some believers adopted an equally hard-line position, arguing that any secular use of an ecclesiastical building was sacrilegious:

How many 'monuments of architecture' have still to be returned to the Church all over Russia! And yet it has long been known that culture does nothing to save people and the nation generally from sin and degeneration. What is more, a concert hall, an art gallery and all the more something 'multifunctional' sited in a church building is nothing other than sacrilege.[59]

With restitution the dominant trend, 'jumping the gun' was not unknown – for instance, the local hierarchy in Vologda developed a policy of inviting the governor of Vologda province to services in the St Sophia Cathedral on major feast-days in the winter months, when it was officially closed, so that the museum directorate was forced to open the building after all.[60]

By 2008 – twenty years after the millennium – it looked as though the tide had turned once and for all in favour of restitution. A draft law of that year proposed the return, on terms of absolute property ownership, of all immovable property owned by religious confessions before 1917. This proposed statute also represented an interesting case in terms of legal principle, both because of the absence of any comparable law proposing the return of property to pre-1917 legal owners from the secular world, and because it explicitly recognized pre-1917 legislation as valid (in the Soviet period, tsarist statute had no standing whatever).[61] Increasingly, the Orthodox Church took a leading role in national commemoration, particularly of the victims of war and political terror.[62] With members of the Church's hierarchy prominent at state occasions, and a political leader who was warmly disposed towards the faith in the person of Vladimir Putin, the Church looked well on the way to becoming the established state faith.

But the restoration to the ROC of its pre-1917 role as the most powerful political force in the country was a different matter. The key legislation relating to religious freedom – the Law on Freedom of Conscience and Religious Organizations of 1997 – recognized freedom of belief for all citizens of the Russian Federation. In the 1993 Constitution of the Russian Federation (article 28), the freedom to profess 'any religion or none' was guaranteed.[63] Conversions notwithstanding, the Russian Federation still had a large population of non-believers, not to speak of significant religious minorities (Muslims, Jews, Catholics, Lutherans, Baptists and others). Even efforts to stigmatize apparently soft targets – adherents of 'sects', such as Moonies – were treated with disquiet.[64]

Indeed, the more powerful the ROC became, the more vocal the opposition to it was. Human rights organizations regularly criticized the unconstitutional nature of the ROC's cosy relationships with government organizations.[65] The efforts of some self-nominated Church representatives to impose unilateral ecclesiastical censorship were fiercely resisted.[66] Publications on sites such as Scepsis.ru used an anti-clerical rhetoric discarded by Russian intellectuals who were hostile to Soviet power around the outbreak of the Second World War.[67] There was also disquiet within the Church over, for instance, the *dirigisme* and doctrinaire inflexibility of the upper echelons of the hierarchy, and the involvement of the Church in commercial activity.[68] While most Orthodox were pleased to see the Church taking a leading part in the nation's symbolic life, cooperation with the state also meant cooperation with secular values – something at odds with the religious separatism that many grass-roots believers and priests espoused.[69]

In some ways the status of religion in the post-Soviet period represented an inversion of what obtained under Soviet power. Where the ROC had been the target of satire, it had become the focus of obsequious deference. Where parishes had struggled to pay taxes, they now enjoyed tax concessions. For the new believers who drifted into observance from the late 1980s, the very same outward tokens of religious practice that were condemned in the past – wearing a cross, having your children christened, hanging an icon in your living space, fasting in Lent – became the primary practices signifying 'religious'.[70] But while *not* believing was an essential part of being 'Soviet' in the official sense, governments of the Russian Federation – for all their many concessions to the Orthodox leadership – never attempted to impose the view that Orthodox belief was essential to being Russian (whether in the sense of citizenship, *rossiiskii*, or ethnic belonging, *russkii*). The pragmatic demands of 'managed democracy' in a multinational, multi-faith society simply would not permit such a stance.

NOTES

1. This chapter draws on archival research, interviews and fieldwork for a project on churches that were official monuments of architecture in Soviet Leningrad, sponsored by the Ludwig Fund (New College, Oxford). Work in the Archive of the St Petersburg Eparchy (ASPbE) was carried out by me with the blessing (*blagoslovenie*, the preferred formula for 'permission') of Metropolitan Vladimir of St Petersburg and Ladoga. I am grateful to him and to Ol'ga Khodakovskaia, and also to the staff of the Archive of the Committee of the State Inspectorate for the Preservation of Monuments (NA UGIOP), the Central State Archive of Literature (TsGALI-SPb.), at the State Archive, St Petersburg (TsGA-SPb.), especially Mikhail Shkarovskii, and staff of the other archives and libraries listed in the notes. Some interviews for the project were carried out by Veronika Makarova and Aleksandra Piir, to whom I also offer thanks. Canon Michael Bourdeaux was most helpful with advice, as were A. V. Kobak, A. D. Margolis, Konstantin Erofeev and Vitaly Bezrogov. Above all, I am grateful to the many

conservators, members of the Orthodox Church, and involved and non-involved observers who took time to share their views and memories, on and off the record, and made gifts of materials and advice. I should emphasize that none of the individuals or institutions who helped is responsible for the arguments advanced here.

2. A. Tyrkova-Vil'iams, *Vospominaniia: to, chego bol'she ne budet* (Moscow, 1998), 242.

3. Christmas trees: see 'Anketa o elke', *Svobodnoe vospitanie* no. 10 (1913), 57–68. Outward observance only: V. Nabokov, *Speak, Memory* (Harmondsworth, 1969). On Tolstoyanism, see e.g. W. Edgerton, ed., *Memoirs of Peasant Tolstoyans in Soviet Russia* (Bloomington, IN, 1993); on spiritualism, see e.g. J. Mannherz, 'Mysterious Knocks, Flying Potatoes and Rebellious Servants: Spiritualism and Social Conflict in Late Imperial Russia', in *Four Empires and an Enlargement*, ed. D. Brett, C. Jarvis and I. Marin (London, 2008), 1–15. On the impact of religious imagery upon political discourse, see M. D. Steinberg, *Proletarian Imagination* (Ithaca, NY, 2002).

4. D. Pospelovskii, 'Na puti k sobornosti', *Kontinent* no. 121 (2004). http:// magazines.russ.ru/continent/2004/121/po10.html.

5. 'Paskhal'nye chastushki: stikhi Nikolaia Semenova', *Iunyi proletarii* 7 (1925), 16–17.

6. O. Barabashev, ed., 'Za krasnyi byt', *Iunyi proletarii* 1 (1924), 4. Emphasis added.

7. See C. Kelly, 'Socialist Churches: Preservationism and "Cultic Buildings" in Leningrad, 1924–1940', *Slavic Review* (in press).

8. E. Rosloff, *Red Priests: Renovationism, Russian Orthodoxy, and Revolution, 1905–1946* (Bloomington, IN, 2002), 211; M. V. Shkarovskii and V. Iu. Cherepnina, *Sankt-Peterburgskaia eparkhiia v dvadtsatom veke v svete arkhivnykh materialov, 1917–1941* (St Petersburg, 2000), and the document selection edited by Shkarovskii, 'Iosiflianstvo: techenie v Russkoi Pravoslavnoi Tserkvi', St Petersburg, 1999, www.krotov.info/history/20/1920/shkarov_001.htm; A. Krasnov-Levitin, *Likhie gody, 1925–1941* (Paris, 1977), 75–6.

9. For numbers of priests and working churches in 1938, see TsGA-SPb., f. 7384, op. 33, d. 50, l. 79. See also Father D. Burmistrov, 'Leningradskaia eparkhiia v usloviiakh antitserkovnykh gonenii v 1929–1939 gg.', 1 June 2009, www.religare.ru/2_65553.html. *Bezbozhniki za rabotoi* (Leningrad, 1938) reported that among particularly popular anti-religious lectures at the Ordzhonikidze Factory had been 'the radio-lecture "Spies in Cassocks"' (p. 12) and 'The Church in the Service of Fascism' (p. 18).

10. See e.g. NA UGIOP, f. 150, t. 1919–40, l. 136, document of 19 July 1932 from the *dvadtsatka* disclaiming responsibility for the Co-Religionist Church and contents.

11. TsGA-SPb., f. 7384, op. 33, d. 50, l. 111.

12. e.g. the Pokrovskaia Church, Kolomna, was demolished for building materials in 1932. TsGA-SPb., f. 1000, op. 49, d. 39, l. 99.

13. For example, when the Co-Religionist Church in Leningrad was converted for use as the Museum of the Arctic in 1936, the domes were removed, and the

tablet on the outside with information about the building and its architect made no reference to the fact that the building had ever been a church. See NA UGIOP, f. 150, t. 1919–40, l. 121; f. 150, Nauchnyi pasport b. Edinovercheskoi tserkvi – Muzeia Arktiki, l. 91.

14. 'Spisok deistvuiushchikh tserkvei' [1940], TsGA-SPb., f. 7834, op. 33, d. 74, ll. 1–2. The three churches in the centre were the Cathedral of the Transfiguration, the St Nicholas Cathedral and the Prince Vladimir Cathedral. There were also three churches in cemeteries on the margins of the old centre (the Volkovo, Serafimovskoe, and Georgievskoe cemeteries), and two on the city's outskirts. In addition, three churches in satellite settlements were open (in Pushkin, Kolpino and Peterhof).

15. A. Men'shoi, 'Gorod pyshnyi, gorod bednyi', *Petrograd* 14 (1923), 16.

16. See e.g. M. Petrov, 'Spasti namolennyi sobor', *Molodezh' Estonii*, 24 August 2000, www.moles.ee/00/Aug/24/1-3.html [accessed 7 July 2009].

17. TsGA-SPb., f. 1000, op. 49, d. 39, l. 98.

18. For example, in 1927 the *dvadtsatka* of the Transfiguration Cathedral was criticized by the city department for the preservation of monuments (OOP) for spending effort on restoring the paintings in the dome (NA UGIOP, f. 171, t. 1919–40, l. 119), and in 1936 the paintings were washed over (ibid., ll. 380b.–39).

19. N. Punin, *Mir svetel liubov'iu: dnevniki, pis'ma*, ed. L. A. Zykova (Moscow, 2000), 347.

20. Throughout the Soviet period it was common to find beggars at church gates in Soviet cities – the only place where one regularly saw them.

21. Krasnov-Levitin, *Likhie gody*, 75–6.

22. See e.g. the list of *dvadtsatka* members of the Trinity (Kulich and Paskha) Church in Leningrad, 31 December 1949, ASPbE, f. 1, op. 7, d. 6, ll. 105–6, and 15 April 1961, ibid., d. 73, ll. 8–9.

23. Akhmatova's funeral service was also held at the St Nicholas Naval Cathedral.

24. J. Brodsky, *Less Than One* (London, 1987), 490.

25. There is an enormous literature on Church–state relations in the Soviet period. See e.g. D. Pospielovsky, *The Russian Church under the Soviet Regime, 1917–1982*, 2 vols. (New York, 1984); F. Corley, ed., *Religion in the Soviet Union: An Archival Reader* (Basingstoke, 1996).

26. See e.g. G. Dluzhnevskaia, *Utrachennye khramy Peterburga* (St Petersburg, 2003).

27. For a micro-study of Church–state relations emphasizing their inconsistent nature, see D. Rogers, *The Old Faith and the Russian Land: A Historical Ethnography of Ethics in the Urals* (Ithaca, NY, 2009), ch. 4. It should be said that the Old Believers, as a group persecuted before 1917, were treated more considerately by the Soviet authorities than adherents to Orthodoxy, whose capacity for dissidence is a constant anxiety in the secret files of Lensovet, for example.

28. An excellent study of the different generations of church leader is given in N. Mitrokhin, 'Russkie natsionalisty v Russkoi Pravoslavnoi Tserkvi, 1945–

1985 gg.', paper presented at National Identity in Eurasia I: Identities & Traditions, New College, Oxford, 22–4 March 2009.

29. Metropolitan Grigorii (1870–1955) held office from 1945 to 1955. An example of his responsiveness to believers' petitions was in 1948, when his secretary (certainly with his knowledge) tipped off the *nastoiatel'* (senior priest) of the 'Krylechko' Church in Tikhvin Monastery that a good strategy for having the larger Cathedral of the Dormition opened would be to emphasize that parishioners would care for an ancient monument. ASPbE, f. 1, op. 11a, d. 10, l. 3.

30. Quoted from M. V. Shkarovskii, *Russkaia Pravoslavnaia Tserkov' i sovetskoe gosudarstvo, 1943–1964: ot 'peremiriia' k novoi voine* (St Petersburg, 1995), doc. no. 26, 188. Pimen (1910–1990) was to make his way inexorably up the hierarchy, which culminated in his appointment as patriarch in 1971. See also the spread of documents from his personal file: M. I. Odintsov, ed., 'Kak budto listaesh' zhizni mgnoven'ia', http://rusoir.ru/president/works/249/index.html#_ftn13.

31. Rapport Mitropolita Pimena Patriarkhu Aleksiiu, 24 April 1963, ASPbE, f. 1, op. 7, d. 122, l. 61.

32. Archimandrite Avgustin (Nikitin), *Tserkov' plenennaia* (St Petersburg, 2008), 86–102.

33. See, for example, the petitions from the late 1940s and 1950s on the opening of the Samson Cathedral, ASPbE, f. 1, op. 11, d. 13.

34. For instance, when the administration of the Prince Vladimir Cathedral was put under pressure in 1949 to gild the crosses on the domes in preparation for the 250th anniversary of the founding of St Petersburg in 1953, Metropolitan Grigorii obtained Kushnarev's support in resisting this – though in the end the Church had to back down (ASPbE, f. 1, op. 7, d. 18, ll. 27–34).

35. A useful discussion of the characters of the different plenipotentiaries, and of relations with the Council on the Affairs of the ROC generally, is given in Elena Shun'gina's candidate's dissertation, 'Politika sovetskogo gosudarstva v otnoshenii Russkoi Pravoslavnoi Tserkvi v 1940–1950-kh gg.: vozvrashchenie kul'tovykh zdanii tserkvi (po materialam Leningrada)', St Petersburg, 2009.

36. See the account by one of the petitioners, Georgii Slukhov, sent to the All-Russian Society for the Protection of Historic and Cultural Monuments (VOOPIiK) in 1970: TsGALI-SPb., f. 229, op. 1, d. 224, ll. 10–11.

37. ASPbE, f. 1, op. 24, d. 43, l. 206.

38. In 1961, 38% of children in Leningrad province had undergone christening, and in the city itself, 44%; 26% of funerals in the province were religious, and 28% in the city. The estimate for the number of Leningraders attending church on major holidays was around 200,000 (i.e. more than 10% of the adult population). Russian State Archive of Recent History (RGANI), f. 5, op. 34, d. 100, l. 198.

39. Priest from St Petersburg b. 1946, interviewed by Catriona Kelly, Oxf/AHRC-Spb-09, PF7-CK. (Here and below, project interviews are cited in the form: AHRC identifier; place where interview was conducted; date of interview; recording number; interviewer's initials.)

40. See e.g. the findings in 'O rabote komitetov komsomola Pskovskoi oblasti po ateisticheskomu vospitaniiu iunoshei i devushek, vnedreniiu novykh obriadov v zhizni', Russian State Archive of Political History, Youth Organizations Section (RGASPI-TsKhDMO), f. 1, op. 95, d. 371, ll. 9–10 (24 March – 4 April 1986).

41. ASPbE, f. 1, op. 11, d. 99, l. 43.

42. Ibid., l. 50.

43. For a detailed analysis of the legislation and the gaps and vague formulations in this, see K. Erofeev, 'Kommentarii k zakonu Sankt-Peterburga "O poriadke peredachi v sobstvennost' religioznykh organizatsii imushchestva religioznogo naznacheniia, nakhodiashchegosia v gosudarstvennoi sobstvennosti Sankt-Peterburga"', 28 February 2009, http://finanal.ru/oo2/kommentarii-k-zakonu-sankt-peterburga-o-poryadke-peredachi-v-sobstvennost-religioznykh-organizat.

44. 'O privatizatsii v RF nedvizhimykh pamiatnikov istorii i kul'tury mestnogo znacheniia': the list of buildings to be privatized (26 November 1994) specifically excluded religious ones. *Rossiiskaia gazeta*, 3 December 1994 (Legislation database, Russian State Library).

45. Information from a restorer working on the project. Oxf/AHRC-SPb-09, PF6-CK.

46. Erofeev, 'Kommentarii k zakonu'.

47. Oxf/AHRC-SPb-09, PF2-VM, interviewer Veronika Makarova.

48. For example, lifts were installed in the Church of St Anna of Kashira on prospekt Marksa, now Bol'shoi Samsonievskii (church visit, 2009), and ice-making machinery in the Church of the Protection of the Mother of God on Lieutenant Schmidt Embankment (Oxf/AHRC-SPb-09, PF6-CK).

49. Oxf/AHRC-SPb-08, PF12-AP, interviewer Aleksandra Piir.

50. Oxf/AHRC-SPb-09, PF12-AP.

51. Father A. Budnikov, *Tserkov' Sviatogo proroka Il'i* (St Petersburg, 1998), 5.

52. CK, field notes, St Petersburg, April 2009.

53. Budnikov, *Tserkov'*, 12. Cf. ibid., 6.

54. Ibid., 1–2.

55. D. Verkhoturov, 'Bor'ba tserkvi za imushchestvo, nevziraia ni na chto', 20 September 2007, http://scepsis.ru/library/id_1486.html. Cf. L. Vorontsova, 'Razrushat' li muzei radi tserkovnogo vozrozhdeniia?', in *Religiia i demokratiia* (Moscow, 1993): 'Only a small proportion of cultic monuments were transferred to museums – it goes without saying that precisely those monuments have survived to the present day in the best condition' (http://scepsis.ru/library/id_904.html).

56. For evidence of conflict between GIOP and the directorates of museums, see NA UGIOP, f. 150, t. 1959–86, l. 204, complaint dated 16 September 1960 from GIOP to the Director of the Museum of the Arctic about the unsanctioned appearance of brackets to hold flags on state holidays; l. 193, report of 26 January 1961 that no work was being done on the facade of the Museum etc.

57. TsGALI-SPb., f. 229, op. 1, d. 540, ll. 84–5.

58. As well put by M. E. Kaulen: 'It is naive to suppose that if churches had not been turned into museums they would have been left open. Historical experience suggests they would simply not have survived at all. It was no accident that the Church itself regarded museums as a defence, a refuge, a chance of salvation' (*Muzei-khramy i muzei-monastyri v pervoe desiatiletie sovetskoi vlasti,* Moscow, 2001, 143–4).

59. 'Russkie tserkvi' site: comment signed by Liudmila Il'iunina on the page of the Protection of the Mother of God Church on Rybatskii prospekt, St Petersburg, http://russian-church.ru/viewpage.php?cat=petersburg&page=48.

60. CK, field notes, Vologda, 2008.

61. My thanks to Konstantin Erofeev, a St Petersburg lawyer specializing in restitution cases, for this commentary.

62. For example, the Prince Vladimir Cathedral in St Petersburg has set up a 'Book of Remembrance' for the dead.

63. www.constitution.ru/.

64. For critical observations about Orthodox attempts to marginalize other groups by use of the terms 'sect' and 'cult', see the contribution by Mariia Akhmetova to Forum 8 in *Forum for Anthropology and Culture* 5 (2008), http://anthropologie.kunstkamera.ru/files/pdf/eng005/forum.pdf.

65. See the survey by M. I. Odintsov, 'Konstitutsionno-pravovye garantii svobody sovesti i veroispovedaniia v Rossii', http://rusoir.ru/president/works/163/.

66. An example was the court case in 2010 against Iurii Samodurov and Aleksei Erofeev, the organizers of the 'Forbidden Art' exhibition in 2006. After a campaign by the Popular Synod (*Narodnyi sobor*) and Orthodox Standard-Bearers, they were indicted for 'fomenting hatred' (a criminal offence under article 282 of the Criminal Code of the RF). The prosecutor had demanded a prison sentence, but after a high-profile campaign they received fines of 200,000 and 150,000 roubles (about 6,500 and 5,000 US dollars). As of July 2010 the case was under appeal.

67. In forums the ROC is regularly the target of vulgar abuse, which often focuses on priests *ad hominem* – 'fat bellies', 'greasy beards', 'why doesn't the church pipe down – money coming out of their ears', 'crucifix paunches', 'popes in their Land Cruisers', 'some can grab all they like, so long as they have the blessing' etc. See the survey of such materials by K. Belousov and N. Zelianskaia, 'RPTs MP – goskorporatsiia Dukha', http://smi2.ru/zashibis/c43374 [accessed 2010].

68. A remarkable insider's view of the former is the memoir of Iuliia Sysoeva of life as the wife of a rank-and-file Orthodox priest, *Zapiski popad'i* (Moscow, 2008), which describes with much humorous irony how priests who expend vast efforts to restore a church are likely to find themselves immediately dispatched to another parish to repeat the same magic on another wreck, and how their wives are under pressure (from congregations as well as clergy) to lead thoroughly traditional lives, so that holding a job (except as a choir-leader) or driving is frowned on. On disquiet over the ROC's commercial activity, see M. Edel'shtein and N. Mitrokhin, 'Ekonomicheskaia deiatel'nost' Russkoi

Pravoslavnoi Tserkvi i ee tenevaia sostavliaiushchaia', 2000, http://krotov. info/libr_min/e/edelst.html. Belousov and Zelianskaia, 'RPTs MP', comment that in online discussions 'The ROC's commercial activities are unanimously condemned, both by believers and non-believers.' Before 1917 Orthodox priests were prohibited from engaging in commercial activity of any kind.

69. See the remarks in our interviews cited above.

70. My thanks to Marina Loskutova for this insight.

CHAPTER 16

'Popular Orthodoxy' and identity in Soviet and post-Soviet Russia: ideology, consumption and competition

Alexander Panchenko

INTRODUCTION

During the Soviet years, formal religious observance was subordinated to state regulation. But controlling religious and para-religious practices outside 'cult buildings' was more difficult. Before 1917, such practices had been entrenched, attracting the hostility of church authorities, particularly during the period of intensive modernization that took place under Peter I and Empress Anne.[1] Under Soviet rule, the assault on what was seen as 'super-stition' continued. During the 1920s, relics of saints were exposed (in the most literal sense, i.e. unwrapped from their bindings) and campaigns of militant atheism organized; these peaked during the time of forced collectivization (1929–33). The Khrushchev era witnessed not just a renewed assault on official religion, but also new attacks on unofficial religious practices.[2] Although folk culture as such – *narodnaia kul'tura* – was, particularly from the late 1930s, constantly invoked as a foundation of official national identity, vernacular religious practices were not considered to be a genuine part of 'national heritage'. Soviet ethnographers and folklorists regularly recorded unofficial religious practices in a spirit of relative neutrality, presenting these as signs of *dvoeverie* ('double faith'), i.e. the survival of robust traditions of paganism under a thin veneer of monotheistic veneration. At the same time, Soviet attitudes to 'superstition' were in important ways quite clear-cut; the much more permissive attitudes to non-official religious practices that set in after 1991 transformed the social and political status of these.

The whole topic of 'popular religion' creates difficulties of categorization (for instance, it could include practices such as lighting candles in church), so I will concentrate here on practices that were identified in Soviet sources themselves as belonging to 'popular religion'. Important among these was the veneration of sacred objects and places (springs and wells, 'footprint stones', ancient graves and cemeteries, chapels, tombs of locally venerated saints etc.). Such practices to some extent eluded the control of both parish priests and local authorities, and provided opportunities for 'informal' religious activities and social networks within village communities or groups of villages.[3] Anthropologists have interpreted such local cults in terms of negotiation with sacred agents, and the creation of sacred boundaries within the natural and social environment;[4] as specific practices for the accumulation and distribution of 'crisis information';[5] or as local resources for collective memory.[6] However, the most visible aspect of the veneration of local holy places is the role played by them in what one might call 'religious consumption'. This might be embodied, for instance, in the acquisition of various material media of sacred force (water, sand or pebbles, lamp oil, pieces of bark etc.) that were believed to be curative and helpful in crisis situations; in the redistribution of 'worldly' goods, including money, textile, clothes and food; and in the exchange of information within and among communities, which, as we will see, was not limited to or by 'crisis' topics. These particular forms of consumption and networking were in turn among the principal targets of the official struggle against 'superstitions', thus coming to stand, on both sides of the ideological divide, for particular forms of religious and social identity.

HEALING, HYGIENE AND HOLINESS

The Great Terror of the mid-1930s resulted, in addition to its other dire consequences, in the closure of the majority of Orthodox parish churches in the Russian countryside. In Novgorod province, for example, more than 500 parish priests were either executed or imprisoned between 1933 and 1938.[7] Usually, after the departure of a priest, local believers were forced to agree to the closure of their church. Church buildings were used for the secular needs of collective farms (as clubs, storehouses and so on); icons and other 'objects of veneration' were burnt and destroyed by local authorities, the party and Komsomol activists. This massive sacrilege and destruction of sacred objects was a uniquely traumatic event for vernacular religious culture, as can be seen in the upsurge of oral narratives about sacrilege and divine punishment.[8]

   The closure and desecration of parish churches in the late 1930s meant that the religious practices of the rural population were inevitably forced out of public life and the officially recognized (albeit not approved) domain of existence that they had inhabited in the first twenty years of Soviet power. They retreated to the sphere of private culture and local knowledge. As a result, 'unofficial' religious leaders gained much authority in 'priestless parishes', and local holy places began to be the centre of religious life in the countryside. Not surprisingly, these leaders and places soon became the primary targets of a new campaign of 'militant atheism'.[9]

The first sign of the next wave of persecution of religious life was the decree of the Central Committee of the Communist Party 'On Serious Defects in Scientific-Atheistic Propaganda and on the Measures Required for its Improvement' (7 July 1954). It referred to the 'unsatisfactory' state of scientific-atheistic propaganda, the revival of pilgrimages and the drinking that accompanied religious festivals, which 'seriously damages the national economy, diverts thousands of people from their work and undermines labour discipline', and was inimical to the building of communism.[10] However, four months later, another decree, 'On Mistakes in Carrying Out Scientific-Atheistic Propaganda among the Population', ran in the opposite direction. It stated that atheistic work should not offend believers in any way and that the main focus of propaganda should be the scientific enlightenment of the Soviet people.[11]

A full-scale official campaign against religion in general, and the Russian Orthodox Church in particular, began only four years later, in the spring of 1958. The initiative came from the Department of Propaganda and Agitation for the United Republics of the Central Committee of the Communist Party of the Soviet Union (CPSU), and was led by Mikhail Suslov, secretary of the Central Committee. In May 1958 the department arranged a conference on the problem of atheistic propaganda, which was attended by local party and Komsomol functionaries, journalists and publishers.[12] On 12 September 1958 the department issued a memorandum entitled 'On the Defects of Scientific-Atheistic Propaganda'. The main idea of the paper was that the contemporary rise in influence of the Russian Orthodox Church, Islam, Judaism and the so-called 'sectarians' (i.e. evangelical Protestants) demanded an immediate response on the part of state officials.[13] Three weeks later, on 4 October 1958, the Central Committee adopted a secret decree, 'On the Memorandum of the Department of Propaganda and Agitation of the Central Committee of the CPSU, "On the Defects of Scientific-Atheistic Propaganda"', which put forward a wide range of measures aimed at sharply reducing the public influence and financial power of the Russian Orthodox Church and other confessions and denominations in the USSR. As a matter of fact, just before this decree the Council on the Affairs of the Russian Orthodox Church (the government body regulating the Church's activities) had submitted to the Central Committee its ideas and suggestions specifically related to undermining the position of Russian Orthodoxy. The suggestions included not just levying a heavy tax on candle workshops, and increasing the severity of monastic rule, but initiating 'activities aimed at the liquidation of the so called "holy places" and pilgrimage to them'.[14]

The last point had been discussed in detail in a separate secret memorandum (No. 487/c) submitted to the Central Committee on 24 September 1958.[15] The Council (which, it was stated, had since the late 1940s 'nearly annually' informed the Central Committee about pilgrimages to 'so-called holy and healing springs') claimed that, although the number of such places had decreased, holy places were still very popular among the rural population of Russia, especially in the Kursk, Ul'ianovsk, Gorkii, Kirov, Voronezh and Stalingrad regions. There were some examples given of especially venerated places, including three holy wells on Nikol'skaia (or Nikolina) gora near the Surskoe settlement in Ul'ianovsk region, a holy spring near the Velikaia River in Kirov region and the famous spring at Korennaia Monastery, near Kursk, which attracted about 10,000 pilgrims annually in the mid-1950s. The Council stressed that while these places did not receive support from the official hierarchy (in 1948–9 'the Patriarch ordered that the clergy should neither abet this pilgrimage nor attend it'), such initiatives were supported by 'vagrant clergy and monks', 'charlatan elements that are interested in the spreading of superstition among the population and who succeed in extorting huge amounts of money from believers'.[16]

The Council suggested that local Communist Party committees and state authorities should elaborate both propagandistic and administrative measures to prevent pilgrimage to holy places – for instance, that they should establish series of anti-religious lectures in the regions where popular holy places existed. The aim was 'to use these places, according to local conditions, for purposes that would make pilgrimages impossible', 'to strengthen labour discipline at collective farms on the days of pilgrimages' and:

> to recommend to the Patriarch and to the Synod: (a) to order priests yet once more never to participate in pilgrimages to the 'holy springs', and to explain to their flock that the pilgrimages are organized by individuals who have no relation to the Church and spread the superstition to suit their own selfish ends, (b) to organize a struggle against *klikushestvo* in churches by means of preaching.[17]

The mention of *klikushestvo* (which could mean both hysteria and possession by an evil spirit) is notable.[18] Although this type of demonic possession might be cured by the use of water and other types of sacred objects obtained from a holy place, the image of the *klikusha* was not inseparably linked with the veneration of holy places. Moreover, there existed (and still exists) a belief that the ritual of exorcism could be performed only by priests who had relevant prayer-books at their disposal.[19] At the same time, since the early eighteenth century *klikushestvo* had been considered to be one of the most representative and inflammatory aspects of 'folk religion'. According to imperial decrees of 1715 and 1737, *klikushestvo* was to be persecuted as a superstition and 'pretended possession'. In fact, this campaign against *klikushestvo* drew no distinction between 'women suffering from a certain disease and visionaries or simply those who claimed to be cured with the help of icons or sacred relics'.[20] Representations of *klikushestvo* were also widespread in Russian literature of the nineteenth century, and during the late nineteenth and early twentieth century the physiological and social nature of the condition was extensively discussed.[21] It is likely that these traditions stimulated the use of the term in political discourse, particularly in articles and books written by Lenin, Trotsky and Bukharin, who used such wordings as 'left SR [Socialist Revolutionary, i.e. radical populist] *klikushi*' and so on. Although the author of the memorandum No. 487/c used the word in its more or less ethnographically correct meaning, a subsequent decree of the Central Committee confused its ethnographic and political meanings.

On 28 November 1958 the memorandum was discussed by the members of the Presidium of the Central Committee.[22] The Presidium adopted a secret decree, 'On the Measures to stop Pilgrimage to the So-Called "Holy Places"', which was generally based upon the recommendations made by the Council on the Affairs of the Russian Orthodox Church. In particular, the decree reads:

The Central Committee notes that in a number of districts and regions of the country there exists a tradition of pilgrimage of believers to so-called 'holy places'. Such pilgrimages are organized by various *klikushi, iurodstvuiushchie* (holy fools) and other disreputable persons, who use these 'holy' places for the spread of superstitions, the kindling of religious fanaticism and the extortion of huge amounts of money from the population. The leaders of religious centres and associations, while constantly declaring that the clergy is not involved in pilgrimages, in practice encourage and support in every possible way those venerating nearby 'holy springs' and those performing 'healing', prophecy and sorcery ... Whereas representatives of the church encourage believers to visit 'holy places' and adopt 'healing' rituals, they themselves use the achievements of contemporary medicine to restore their health, and willingly undergo medical treatment in sanatoriums and health resorts with genuine spas.[23]

The guidelines for local party and Soviet officials given in the decree generally repeated the suggestions by the Council, although it was stated that 'work aimed at ending pilgrimage and at the closure of the so-called "holy places" should only be done when it is approved by the local population'. As to Orthodox clergymen, they were to be warned once more that they must help to prevent 'fraudulent activities' on the part of '*klikusha* elements and organizers of pilgrimages', for example, trips 'to so-called "holy places" and springs': 'If they will not do that by themselves, the Soviet authorities will take the strongest measures against *klikushi* who sought to exploit ignorance.' The new campaign against vernacular religion had started.

Although the major amount of practical work was to be done by local authorities and party committees coordinated by regional representatives of the Council on the Affairs of the Russian Orthodox Church, the leaders of the Communist Party thought that atheistic propaganda by means of printed books, mass media and various lecturing activities would nevertheless be helpful. From the start of the 1960s, large numbers of popular anti-religious brochures were issued by central and regional publishing houses. These texts allow us to observe the arguments and rhetoric that, in the judgement of the Soviet elite, would influence public opinion in the countryside.

Besides various stories of 'frauds' committed by 'greedy churchmen', and of unsuccessful healing in holy places, the pamphlet *Secrets of 'Holy Places'*, published in 1961 by journalists Anatolii Belov and Arkadii Pevzner, included a special chapter entitled 'What Harm is Caused by "Holy Places"?'[24] According to the text, pilgrimage to various sacred places and objects was especially harmful to the 'character' and even the mental health of an individual: 'Will a pilgrimage to a certain "holy place" not darken one's consciousness or break one's mentality? In dreams of "healing", one gets away from reality, enters the vicious circle of the mystical world view.'[25] At the same time, the most harmful aspect of the rituals related to local sanctuaries was said to be the violation of hygiene norms: 'Pilgrimage to "holy places" is often the cause of transmission of infectious diseases and the spread of epidemics.'[26] Propagandistic texts of this kind[27] usually employed just one narrative schema: they showed a naive person expecting a miraculous cure from a holy place, but getting a severe infectious disease instead: 'After kissing the "holy" stone, Liubov' Mikhailovna caught diphtheria. Obviously, there had been a person here before who had been ill with this infectious disease. And the sick woman had to spend several weeks in hospital after her pilgrimage.'[28] Bathing in the water of a holy spring could also be harmful to health: 'After undergoing "therapy" at the "holy" spring Nasten'ka K. caught a cold and spent several months in hospital.'[29]

It was constantly repeated that pilgrimage to holy places was especially harmful for children 'brought up in religious families. The result of this upbringing often means that children become infected with religious superstitions and grow into spiritual cripples'.[30] This idea was widespread in propaganda of the time, as in an anti-religious story, 'Miraculous' ('Chudotvornaia') by Vladimir Tendriakov (1923–1984), published in the journal *Znamia* in 1958. It portrayed a peasant boy, Rod'ka Guliaev, who found an old icon on the riverbank. The icon appeared to be the miraculous image of St Nicholas that had mysteriously disappeared from the parish church in 1929, when it was closed by local officials 'as a survival of the past'.[31] In addition, it was the same icon that had once been discovered in a bog by a shepherd boy, Panteleimon, whose mother had then been miraculously healed by the sacred image. The place in the bog where the icon had been discovered was considered to be holy by the local population and a church had been built there.

After the icon was found, the house where Rod'ka lived with his mother and grandmother became the centre of local religious life. Religious activists of the village, including some old women, a drunk and disabled war veteran, and the shifty director of the local store, praised Rod'ka as 'a second Panteleimon' and believed him to be a saint. The boy's grandmother forced him to wear an Orthodox cross and tried to keep him out of school. The only person who attempted to protect the boy from religious 'infection' was his old schoolteacher Paraskov'ia Petrovna. The contradiction between real life and the ugly world of popular religion made Rod'ka hysterical and nearly insane. Finally, he destroyed the icon and tried to commit suicide.

Tendriakov, who was born and spent his childhood in a village in the Vologda region, made good use of rural religious folklore in his story. The narrative of a shepherd boy finding a miraculous icon or meeting a saint in the wilderness is quite typical of East Slavic religious legends about local holy places. The author also cited other widespread motifs from Russian religious folklore in the story. What is especially interesting here, however, is the name of the shepherd who originally found the icon in 'Miraculous'. In Russian popular religious culture, St Panteleimon the Healer is one of the best-known saints believed to heal various diseases. At the same time, he is one of the few Orthodox male saints pictured on icons and frescoes without a beard, i.e. as a young man (or even a teenager). Thus, the motifs of healing and youth that were so important for the official propaganda against holy places are present in the story not only explicitly, but at subtextual or contextual level too.[32] It may also be important that the schoolteacher has a popular saint's name, Paraskov'ia.

Tendriakov's 'Miraculous' was so popular (or at least was considered to be so handy for anti-religious propaganda) that between 1958 and 1987 it was republished at least nine times as a separate text – mainly in the series for children at secondary school issued by the Detskaia literatura ('Literature for Children') publishing house in Moscow – and about ten times in various collections of stories by the author. There was even an abridged version of the story for reading in primary school entitled *Mednyi krestik* ('A Copper Cross'), published for the first time in Moscow in 1963.[33] In 1960 a screen version of 'Miraculous' was released (by Mosfilm studio, directed by Vladimir Skuibin), and in 1963 an adaptation for the stage, *Bez kresta* ('No Cross'), was put on by the Sovremennik (Moscow Contemporary) Theatre, produced by Oleg Efremov and directed by Galina Volchek.

These three themes – mental health, public hygiene and the safety of children – were obsessively repeated in official discourse related to 'holy places'. Another idea that was widely used in this context was of the greed and deception of the 'churchmen' who allegedly used local holy places to get money from believers. This accusation was in fact baseless, and derived from the fact that the idea of the 'exploiter Church' had been a commonplace of democratic propaganda in nineteenth-century Russia. Certainly, voluntary offerings of money or various goods of particular symbolic value were an accepted part of the 'religious economies' in both the Orthodox and the Catholic worlds. But, in the Soviet period, offerings from ordinary believers to the Orthodox Church were almost unheard of, and the 'greedy churchmen' blamed by official propaganda were, in fact, local religious leaders who managed the veneration of local holy places because of the non-availability of parish priests. They did not necessarily have any actual relations to the official Church.

Moreover, at this period, the Russian Orthodox Church was making no effort to protect the vernacular religious practices of its flock. Indeed, in 1959, the patriarch yielded to the pressure of the Soviet officials and issued a special encyclical which stated that habitual pilgrimage to holy places was not related in any way to the Church and should not be supported by diocesans and local clergy.[34] This meant that 'priestless' Orthodox believers in the countryside were left to themselves in the extremely unfriendly context of the official campaign against 'holy places'.

The question of what actually went on in the countryside where various local authorities were supposed 'to stop pilgrimage to the so-called "holy places"' is very interesting. One can get a fairly detailed picture of the campaign from a file preserved in the archive of the plenipotentiary of the Council on the Affairs of the Russian Orthodox Church (known from 1965 as the Council for Religious Affairs) for Novgorod region.[35] It includes materials reflecting practical measures against holy places both in the regional capital and in outlying districts.

The first document in the file is a secret report prepared (on demand of the plenipotentiary or the regional committee of the Communist Party) by the Fourth Department of the KGB in Novgorod province during late August 1959.[36] The main goal of the investigation had been to give a detailed list of 'holy places' and 'holy springs' venerated in the region. According to the author of the report, one Captain Ivanov, at that point there were twenty-seven holy places in the region. (In fact, there could have been many more venerated sites, but the authorities took into account only those which attracted considerable numbers of people on certain religious holidays, usually hundreds or even thousands.) Among the most popular and, consequently, 'harmful' places the report named Seven Springs near the village of Velikusha in Okulovka district, where about 2,000 pilgrims from neighbouring regions and even from Leningrad had converged on the day of St Panteleimon the Healer (9 August); the holy spring near the village Serafimovka in Borovichi district (about 1,000); the holy lake of the boy saints Ioann and Iakov of Meniusha (about 1,000) and the former Rublevskaia Monastery (several thousand).

It was stressed, however, that during the past year both local authorities in a number of districts and the regional KGB department had done their best to reduce the number of pilgrims, if not to stop pilgrimages altogether. The venerated stone with 'the footprints of Jesus Christ' near the village of Kalmykovo (Okulovka district), which had attracted about 800–900 pilgrims in previous years, had been blown up by the order of the district council. But this had not acted as much of a deterrent: 'Some fanatical believers collected the pieces of the stone, stuck them together with clay and cement, and put the stone back in its former place.'[37]

The struggle against the holy spring near Serafimovka was more successful. On the so-called 'Tenth Friday' in July, the KGB undertook a variety of crowd-management measures:

A geological party was dropped off at the location of the spring. Two instructors from the District Committee were sent to neighbouring villages to arrange political work. Bus traffic to the outskirts of Serafimovka was considerably reduced. The regional traffic officers increased control upon cars on the roads to Serafimovka. KGB officers were sent to the place to undertake Chekist assignments [*chekistskie meropriiatiia*, i.e. secret police work]. As a result, only about 150 people visited the spring over 3 days.[38]

At the site of the former Rublevskaia Monastery in Shimsk district, sacred objects were simply destroyed. 'This year, the Fourth Department of the KGB along with the party and Soviet officials undertook a number of actions there. The stone fence around the tomb of St Antony Leokhnovskii was broken down by tractor, crosses were taken down, and the wells were filled up.'[39] The same was done with a chapel and a holy spring near the village of Kerest' in Novgorod district. However, once again, local action subverted the authorities' intentions: 'Fanatical believers restored the chapel and cleared the spring.'[40]

In his secret report to the regional committee of the Communist Party dated May 1960, the plenipotentiary of the Council on the Affairs of the Russian Orthodox Church in Novgorod region, G. E. Kapitsa, added some information about the measures taken against local holy places in 1958 and 1959. He especially noted the active anti-religious work of Okulovka district council, which decided in May 1959 'to abolish all the so-called "holy" springs in the district and to use their sites for economic needs'. In 1958 'the officers of Okulovka police station arrested at the "holy" spring [near Velikusha] one Iakov Zavolokin, who had been providing pilgrims with prayers for pecuniary reward; he was sentenced to imprisonment in a labour camp as the habitual organizer of pilgrimages'. In 1959 'the territory of the "holy" spring was used for a greenhouse and fenced in. An organizer of pilgrimages, local resident Vladimirov S. V., who previously had brought his own icon of St Panteleimon to the spring, was warned that these activities were unacceptable.' To prevent the pilgrimage to the footprint stone near Kalmykovo, the village soviet 'declared an emergency ten-day period (*dekada*) for digging potatoes and other food crops. Consequently, on the day of the pilgrimage (10 October) all the collective farmers were busy with digging potatoes and nobody local came to the "holy" stone.'[41]

In Sol'tsy district there existed a popular sacred spring near the village of Molochkovo, where the parish church still functioned.[42] That may have been the reason behind a special propagandistic campaign organized here by Kapitsa. He suggested that local authorities should 'prepare statements by 2 or 3 local citizens in the district newspaper concerning this nest of church-men and its possible liquidation'.[43] Both the party and the Soviet authorities in Sol'tsy backed the plenipotentiary. According to his report:

The Department of Agitation and Propaganda of the Sol'tsy District Committee of the Communist Party has made the best use of collective farmers themselves, having exploited the pages of the district newspaper to tell the story of the machinations the churchmen had employed in order to deceive those who believed in the 'miracle-working' spring ... Therefore, a meeting of collective farmers agreed with little persuasion to liquidate the chapel at the spring that had been used extensively by the churchmen to extort additional income from the population . . . In order to divert the population from churchgoing, the feast of the Assumption was declared to be the appropriate day to store fodder for private cattle, and the collective farmers were occupied with this work.[44]

The Molochkovo priest (who continued to hold services on the feast of the Assumption) was later moved to another parish.[45]

In general, however, Kapitsa was not too optimistic about the first results of the campaign. Although he stated that 'in some districts, in 1959, there was a considerable decline of pilgrimage, and there were no pilgrimages to a number of so-called "holy" places and springs at all', he pointed to a number of districts where 'the work on unmasking, before the population, of charlatanry by the organizers of pilgrimage, by the *klikusha* elements who spread superstitions around so-called "holy places" and "holy springs", is insufficient. Nothing is being done to suppress activities aimed at the deception of credulous Soviet citizens.'[46] A particularly disturbing situation was observed in Shimsk district, where, 'on 7 July 1959, the churchmen organized a religious procession to the so-called "holy" lake near the village Mokroe Veret'e. Many pilgrims who had come from Novgorod, Leningrad and other regions expecting miracle cures at the lake took part in the procession.'[47] This lake, where, according to legend, the bodies of St Ioann and St Iakov of Meniusha had appeared miraculously, as well as the tomb of these two saints in the abandoned church of the village of Meniusha,[48] remained the main targets of the Novgorod campaign against holy places over the next decade as well.

After their failures in 1959, the local authorities decided to push still harder against these pilgrimages. According to a report by the chair of Shimsk district executive committee,[49] in 1960 they exercised both propagandistic and administrative measures. These included 'two thematic antireligious meetings in Meniusha', 'atheistic lectures aimed at the local population' and 'elucidative and preventive work' with 'the organizers of the pilgrimages':

Shortly before the day of the pilgrimage, the collective farms of Meniusha and Medved' village soviet called meetings of collective farmers, who in turn unanimously supported the measures taken by the Party District Committee and the District Executive Committee, and aimed at stopping the pilgrimage. The feast of 'the boys of Meniusha' was declared to be an urgent day for storing cattle feed. As a result of these measures, all the able-bodied inhabitants of surrounding villages were occupied with haymaking, just as in the previous year. Only 50 or 60 persons who came from other districts tried to come to the spring on the day of pilgrimage;

however, they were not allowed to approach. They were told that visits to the spring were impossible. Meanwhile, the territory near the lake was covered with oil under the pretence of using this as a pesticide against malaria mosquitoes, so access to the lake was made difficult.[50]

The next year, however, the pilgrimage continued.[51] According to another report prepared by Kapitsa's successor A. Gerasimov, both in 1968 and 1969 some 3,000 pilgrims visited Meniusha on 7 July.[52] By now, too, official attitudes to the situation had changed. According to a journalist from a local newspaper whose draft report written in 1968 is also included in the file, nobody from the local authorities tried to prevent the pilgrimage that year. Local believers were prepared to be frank when explaining the reason to a journalist: 'The saint boys had made an appearance to our chairman [of the collective farm] in the church, so he has become more tolerant.'[53]

In 1969, Gerasimov reported to his superiors, 'of the 33 "holy" places and "holy" springs that existed in the region, 31 no longer exist', and that the only two left were the lake near Meniusha and the site of the former Perokomskii Monastery in the Novgorod district.[54] But this statement does not seem to have been true. In fact, the physical destruction of a sacred object did not mean that a community could not create another holy place instead. In 1964 the Soviet and party authorities of Valdai district decided to prevent pilgrimage to a holy spring between the villages Izhitsy and Iazhelbitsy that took place every year on the day of Our Lady of Kazan (21 July). When the members of the district committee and the district executive committee accompanied by a traffic police officer, Comrade Kalin, came to Izhitsy they realized that the pilgrimage was already over. However, they then went to the house of seventy-year-old Nina Irinicheva, who was known as 'the organizer of pilgrimages' and who used to bring her own icon of Our Lady of Kazan to the spring. Here, they seized the icon forcibly and took it outdoors:

At the time, about 10 or 15 believers clustered near Irinicheva's house; they asked that the icon be handed over to the church in Valdai, but Comrade Aleksandrova [the secretary of the district executive committee] would not agree. By her order, comrade Kalin broke the icon into small pieces in the presence of the indignant believers and then burnt it 10 metres away from the house.[55]

Yet aggressive measures of this kind did not stop the activities of local religious leaders. On the same day 'they planted a tree at the place where the icon was burnt and started considering the place to be a "holy" one'.[56]

Despite all the steps that the authorities of Novgorod province could take, the campaign against local holy places had next to no success.

Although certain local sanctuaries were destroyed or used for various secular purposes, pilgrimage to some of them resumed in the 1970s, and, meanwhile, new holy places appeared. In sum, propaganda work and the use of administrative measures on the part of both central and regional authorities (which included not just destruction and prevention, but systematic attempts to introduce 'new Soviet rituals'[57]) did not have any significant impact on the vernacular religious culture of the Russian countryside.

It is interesting to consider how the struggle against local sanctuaries in the 1960s is reflected in local oral tradition. My field research in Meniusha in 2002–4 did not reveal any texts related to the campaign of the 1960s that could be compared with the stories of sacrilege and divine punishment created here in the late 1930s.[58] Although my informants remembered the campaign, their recollections were not particularly dramatic:

It was like this, the militia was there. They wouldn't let us. They wouldn't let us go to the lake. I remember that my brother went to the lake, and the militia was there. 'Where are you going?' one of them asked. And he said, 'To the lake.' 'What for – why do you want to go there?' 'I'm on vacation,' he said, 'I go where I want.'[59]

Various people came here . . . And the bosses carried fuel oil there, and poured it all over the place, so that people wouldn't come there. And . . . crosses used to stand there, all the crosses were taken down, they didn't like all that.[60]

At the same time, there are some pieces of religious folklore that became widespread all over Russia in the 1960s and can be viewed as a form of reaction to the atheistic campaign. One of the most popular texts of this kind is the so-called 'Standing of Zoia' (*Stoianie Zoi*) that tells about a certain girl who did not have a partner at a dancing party and decided to dance with an icon of St Nicholas. At the dance she suddenly became petrified, and stood motionless for 128 days. Then, after a prayer by a certain holy elder, she began to move; soon afterwards, she died, appealing to all the people to repent and pray. The episode allegedly took place in Kuibyshev (Samara) in 1956.[61] Although this plot about a girl dancing with an icon and being punished for the sacrilege was already recorded by folklorists in the late nineteenth century, the fact that this text became immensely popular in the 1960s and circulated both in handwritten and oral forms up to the beginning of the twenty-first century testifies to its contemporary resonance.

CONSUMPTION AND COMPETITION

The fate of cults of local holy places as well as other vernacular religious practices in the post-Soviet decades was closely related to the fate of rural communities in Russia in general. The massive migration to regional centres and big cities that started in the 1970s, and reached a peak in the late 1980s and early 1990s, resulted in the demographic collapse of many rural regions, especially in the northern part of the country. Most rural residents in post-Soviet Russia were elderly people (more often women than men) who preferred to stay in their villages for the rest of their life, rather than moving to an urban environment. Others would spend 'the cold months' in towns and cities, but return to their native villages for summer. From the 1980s onwards, many townspeople purchased summer cottages (dachas[62]) even in remote villages, and these 'summerfolk' often played important economic and social roles in the life of rural communities.

These demographic and social changes inevitably forced vernacular religious culture in the countryside to merge with urban ideologies, beliefs and practices, which in turn often fused Orthodox identity with quasi-scientific and New Age ideas and explanatory modes. Now, the power of a particular sacred place or a miracle-working icon could be alternatively explained in terms of 'cosmic energies' and 'extra-sensory forces'. The 1990s and 2000s witnessed rapid growth of these 'post-secular' forms of popular religious culture in Russia. At the same time, after the collapse of the Soviet Union, large numbers of Russian Orthodox rural parishes had to be re-established; parish priests usually came from the urban environment as well. Some of them were inclined to consider local holy places as manifestations of 'paganism' or 'superstition'. But at the same time they realized that these cults represented the only form of public religious activity they could rely on while trying to revive spiritual life in the villages. They made efforts to integrate the religious practices of the local population with what they considered 'proper' types of worship and spirituality. In addition, many local sacred places rapidly became the objects of spiritual tourism organized by the Orthodox dioceses and various travel agents. As a rule, this tourism was supported by both local priests and secular authorities, since both regarded pilgrimages from urban centres as an opportunity for economic development and the promotion of local places of interest.

The coexistence and competition of different religious cultures or discourses related to a local sacred place was investigated by Jeanne Kormina in a case study of the Pskov region. She argued that 'pilgrims who came from urban centers, local priests and church activists, ordinary locals and migrants, chose different types of stories, or even genres, when they talked about the sacred'.[63] The convergence and competition of at least three religious discourses, 'local', 'clerical' and 'pilgrim', emerged as typical of contemporary cults of local holy places in Russia.

That did not mean, however, that these competing discourses were impermeable and could not influence each other or interact to create new types of religious practices, narratives and identities. The key problem here was related to the idea of authenticity, the way that traditions were used and manipulated by various groups and persons seeking spiritual authority and symbolic control of a particular local cult or cults. Nobody doubted the efficacy of holy places, but the manner in which they should best be consumed could still be the subject of discussion. The recent history of sacred places in Meniusha provides a good illustration of this.

After the collapse of the Soviet Union some Orthodox parishes of the Shimsk district were re-established, but the Meniusha church was left a partial ruin, as before. But from the early 1990s the Novgorod diocese paid special attention to this local shrine. Church services were performed here annually on 7 July and occasionally on some other days. In 1996 the archbishop of Novgorod attended the local festival of saints Ioann and Iakov.[64] The flow of pilgrims coming to Meniusha grew rapidly, so the place became the object of contemporary spiritual tourism. The festival in 2003 was not attended by the archbishop, but the liturgy on the day was performed by three priests: one from the nearby village of Medved', another (an archpriest) from the district centre of Soltsy and a third from a church in Novgorod. Besides local believers and visitors from neighbouring villages, the festival was attended by more than sixty urban pilgrims from Soltsy, Novgorod and St Petersburg.

For local believers, a festival afforded a rare opportunity to attend a liturgy, confess to a priest and receive communion. They regarded it as a link to 'institutionalized religion', and also understood that the reputation of their village was related to the local shrine. Hence, they continued to aspire to be the 'keepers' of the cult. At the same time, their own religious practices were represented mainly by oral narratives and private rituals. Personal or family vows were, to all appearances, much more important for them than liturgies and religious processions. As to the local authorities, they used festivals as a way of constructing local identity in both spiritual and secular terms. Accordingly, they emphasized both the 'holiness' and the 'historical meaning' of the cult of saints Ioann and Iakov.

Unlike local believers, the urban pilgrims who came to Meniusha were predominantly oriented toward collective rituals. At the same time, their activities could equally well be described as 'religious consumption', since they were mostly interested in the acquisition of various material media of sacred force. In fact, obtaining these 'spiritual souvenirs' seemed to be the principal goal of the pilgrimage; the history of a particular shrine was less important for the travellers. In this type of religious culture, authenticity was represented by material objects, rather than by narrative traditions.

CONCLUSION

Students of Russian rural culture have sometimes argued that Soviet anti-religious campaigns in the village resulted in the revival and spread of 'pre-Christian' or 'archaic' and 'irrational' beliefs and rituals.[65] With regard to the material considered here, this statement is not accurate. What one can observe here is the reorganization of religious consumption, and the creation of new informal social networks managed by local religious leaders, without any special relation to imaginary 'pre-Christian' culture. Moreover, the particular and hostile interest in these religious practices on the part of the Soviet authorities can be explained in terms of social discipline rather than of rationalism, modernization and the influence of Enlightenment ideas. The most 'harmful' aspect of this consumption and networking, in Soviet terms, was actually its informal and uncontrolled nature, which could not be tolerated within an authoritarian society. (And this despite the fact that Soviet ideologists were trying to create a set of 'Soviet rituals' both in the 1920s and 1960s, and did not seem to be bothered with the 'irrational' character of these.[66]) The fact that social discipline was a primary goal would also explain the intensive use of medical metaphors in the anti-religious campaigns discussed above, since the idea of hygiene is closely related to metaphorical representations of discipline.

It appears, however, that the 'purity and danger' metaphor was not read correctly by its more or less 'virtual' target group of 'superstitious' mass believers. Religious consumption in fact overcame disciplinary ideology. One can contrast the 1920s, when the anti-religious campaign made genuine inroads among grass-roots believers.[67] The Khrushchev era, for all the emphasis on 'rationalism triumphant' that prevailed in official ideology, can thus be seen as a key stage in the development of the obsession with alternative spiritualities that was to flower so luxuriantly in the 1990s and 2000s.

At this point, disciplinary metaphors gave way to an image of spiritual and historical authenticity that fostered veneration of local sacred places and other forms of 'popular Orthodoxy' in Russia. Out of the welter of competing discourses came new types of religious consumption and identity; local rural culture was eroded by 'postmodern' patterns of urban spirituality.

NOTES

1. G. L. Freeze, 'Institutionalizing Piety: The Church and Popular Religion, 1750–1850', in *Imperial Russia: New Histories for the Empire*, ed. J. Burbank and D. L. Ransel (Bloomington, IN, 1998), 210–49; A. S. Lavrov, *Koldovstvo i religiia v Rossii, 1700–1740 gg.* (Moscow, 2000); E. Smilianskaia, *Volshebniki, bogokhul'niki, eretiki: narodnaia religioznost' i 'dukhovnye prestupleniia' v Rossii XVIII v.* (Moscow, 2003).
2. See S. Fitzpatrick, *Stalin's Peasants: Resistance and Survival in the Russian Village after Collectivization* (New York, 1994); G. Young, *Power and the Sacred in Revolutionary Russia: Religious Activists in the Village* (University Park, PA, 1995); S. Smith, 'Heavenly Letters and Tales of the Forest: "Superstition" against Bolshevism', *Forum for Anthropology and Culture* 2 (2005), 316–39; M. Froggatt, 'Science in Propaganda and Popular Culture in the USSR under Khrushchev', DPhil thesis, University of Oxford, 2006.
3. For ethnographic data related to these cults, see A. A. Panchenko, *Issledovaniia v oblasti narodnogo pravoslaviia: derevenskie sviatyni severo-zapada Rossii* (St Petersburg, 1998).
4. L. Stark, *Peasants, Pilgrims, and Sacred Promises: Ritual and the Supernatural in Orthodox Karelian Folk Religion*, Studia Fennica Folkloristica 11 (Helsinki, 2002).
5. T. B. Shchepanskaia, *Kul'tura dorogi v russkoi miforitual'noi traditsii XIX–XX vv.* (Moscow, 2003), 244–317.
6. J. Kormina, 'Pilgrims, Priest and Local Religion in Contemporary Russia: Contested Religious Discourses', *Folklore* 28 (2004), 31–3, www.folklore.ee/Folklore/vol28/pilgrims.pdf.
7. M. N. Petrov, *Krest nad molotom* (Novgorod, 2000), 324–75.
8. See V. E. Dobrovol'skaia, 'Neskazochnaia proza o razrushenii sviatyn'', *Russkii fol'klor* 30 (1999), 500–12; A. B. Moroz, 'Ustnaia istoriia russkoi tserkvi v sovetskii period (narodnye predaniia o razrusheniia tserkvei)', *Uchenye zapiski pravoslavnogo universiteta apostola Ioanna Bogoslova* 6 (2006), 177–85; S. A. Shtyrkov, 'Rasskazy ob oskvernenii sviatyn'', *Traditsionnoi fol'klor Novgorodskoi oblasti* (St Petersburg, 2006), 208–31.
9. For a general outline of relations between the Soviet state and the Russian Orthodox Church in the 1940s–50s see M. V. Shkarovskii, *Russkaia Pravoslavnaia Tserkov' i sovetskoe gosudarstvo v 1943–1964 gg.: ot 'peremiriia' k novoi voine* (St Petersburg, 1995); T. A. Chumachenko, *Gosudarstvo, pravoslavnaia tserkov', veruiushchie. 1941–1961 gg.* (Moscow, 1999).
10. *Zakonodatel'stvo o religioznykh kul'takh: sbornik materialov i dokumentov*, 2nd rev. edn (Moscow, 1971), 34–5.
11. Ibid., 40–5.
12. Chumachenko, *Gosudarstvo*, 180–2.
13. *Vlast' i tserkov' v SSSR i stranakh Vostochnoi Evropy, 1939–1958 (diskussionnye aspekty)* (Moscow, 2003), 359–66, no. 39, www.rusoir.ru/03print/02/239/index.html.

14. Chumachenko, *Gosudarstvo*, 183; *Vlast' i tserkov'*, 367–70, no. 40, www.rusoir. ru/03print/02/240/index.html.

15. 'Dobit'sia zakrytiia tak nazyvaemykh sviatykh mest', *Istochnik: dokumenty russkoi istorii. Vestnik arkhiva prezidenta RF* 4 (1997), 120–7.

16. Ibid.

17. Ibid.

18. On *klikushestvo* in general, see: C. Worobec, *Possessed: Women, Witches, and Demons in Imperial Russia* (DeKalb, IL, 2001); A. A. Panchenko, *Khristovshchina i skopchestvo: fol'klor i traditsionnaia kul'tura russkikh misticheskikh sekt* (Moscow, 2002), 324–41; E. A. Mel'nikova, 'Otchityvanie besnovatykh: praktiki i diskursy', *Antropologicheskii forum* 4 (2006), 220–63.

19. Ibid., 249–58.

20. Lavrov, *Koldovstvo*, 393.

21. See esp. Worobec, *Possessed*.

22. 'Dobit'sia zakrytiia', 127–8. The recent publication of the archive of the Presidium of the Central Committee of the USSR omits both the stenographic record and the draft protocol (no. 193) of this session: *Prezidium TsK KPSS 1954–1964: chernovye protokol'nye zapisi zasedanii. Stenogrammy. Postanovleniia*, ed. A. A. Fursenko et al., vol. I (Moscow, 2003), 340, and vol. II (Moscow, 2006), 896.

23. 'Dobit'sia zakrytiia', 127.

24. A. Belov and A. Pevzner, *Tainy 'sviatykh mest'* (Moscow, 1961), 67–71.

25. Ibid., 69.

26. Ibid., 71.

27. See also: I. G. Vitkovskii, *Pravda o 'sviatykh' istochnikakh* (Tambov, 1961); A. Belov, *Pravda o 'sviatykh' mestakh* (Moscow, 1964).

28. Belov and Pevzner, *Tainy*, 38.

29. Vitkovskii, *Pravda*, 23.

30. Ibid., 72.

31. V. F. Tendriakov, *Apostol'skaia komandirovka* (Moscow, 1984), 21.

32. An adherent of intertextual methodology would also find allusions to Dostoevsky's *Crime and Punishment*, and to Eduard Bagritskii's 'Death of a Pioneer Girl', but that subject lies outside the present analysis.

33. V. F. Tendriakov, *Mednyi krestik* (extracts from 'Chudotvornaia') (Moscow, 1963).

34. O. Lavinskaia and Iu. Orlova, 'O zakrytii pravoslavnykh monastyrei v SSSR i zapreshchenii palomnichestva k sviatym mestam (1958–1961)', *Pravoslavnyi palomnik* 4 (2002), 61; I. D. Savinova, *Likholet'e: Novgorodskaia eparkhiia i sovetskaia vlast', 1917–1991* (Novgorod, 1998), 84.

35. State Archive of Novgorod Province [GANO], f. P-4110, op. 1, no. 231, 'Spravki i informatsii o "sviatykh mestakh" Novgorodskoi oblasti, 1959–1969'. Some additional materials from the same archive are published in Savinova, *Likholet'e*, 83–5.

36. GANO, f. P-4110, op. 1, no. 231, ll. 1–110b.

37. Ibid., l. 2.

38. Ibid., l. 3.
39. Ibid., l. 5.
40. Ibid., l. 8.
41. Ibid., ll. 14–15.
42. Some information about contemporary veneration of springs can be found in E. V. Platonov, 'Sakral'naia topografiia dereven' v nizhnem techenii r. Shelon'', *Antropologicheskii forum* 7 (2007), 240–2.
43. Savinova, *Likholet'e*, 84.
44. GANO, f. P-4110, op. 1, no. 231, ll. 15–16.
45. Ibid., l. 50.
46. Ibid., l. 16.
47. Ibid., l. 17.
48. On this cult see: A. A. Pančenko, 'Ivan et Iakov: deux saints étranges de la région des marais (Novgorod)', *Archives de Sciences Sociales des Religions* 130 (avril–juin 2005), 55–79; A. A. Panchenko, 'Ivan i Iakov: strannye sviatye iz bolotnogo kraia (religioznye praktiki sovremennoi novgorodskoi derevni)', in *Religioznye praktiki v sovremennoi Rossii: sbornik statei*, ed. K. Russele and A. Agadzhanian (Moscow, 2006), 211–36.
49. GANO, f. P-4110, op. 1, no. 231, l. 24.
50. Ibid., l. 24. This was not the only occasion in the region when a holy place had fuel oil poured over it. The same was done to a spring near the village of Kiul'viia in Pestovo district (Savinova, *Likhoket'e*, 84).
51. GANO, f. P-4110, op. 1, no. 231, l. 25.
52. Ibid., ll. 52–3.
53. Ibid., l. 43.
54. Ibid., l. 48.
55. Ibid., l. 34.
56. Ibid.
57. A. V. Belov, A. M. Pevzner, *O prazdnikakh prestol'nykh* (Moscow, 1960).
58. A. A. Panchenko, 'Religioznyi fol'klor sela Meniusha', *Russkii fol'klor* 33 (2008), 323–65.
59. EU-Shimsk-03-PF-11. Interview recorded 12 July 2003, Meniusha, female informant, b. 1925, lives locally; interviewer E. A. Mel'nikova.
60. EU-Shimsk 02-PF-1. Interview recorded 17 July 2002, Staroe Veret'e, female informant, b. 1920, lives locally; interviewers A. L. L'vov, E. A. Migunova and A. A Panchenko.
61. *Rukopisnaia religioznaia proza Nizhegorodskaia kraia: teksty i kommentarii*, ed. Iu. M. Shevarenkova (Nizhnii Novgorod, 2008), 234–41.
62. On the Russian dacha see S. Lovell, *Summerfolk: A History of the Dacha, 1710–2000* (Ithaca, NY, 2003).
63. Kormina, 'Pilgrims', 25. For general observations on the 'competing discourses' of pilgrimage, see J. Eade and M. J. Sallnow, 'Introduction', *Contesting the Sacred: The Anthropology of Christian Pilgrimage* (London, 1991), 1–29; M. Bowman, 'Procession and Possession in Glastonbury: Continuity,

Change and the Manipulation of Tradition', *Folklore* 115:3 (December 2004), 273–85.
64. S. V. Moiseev, 'Arkiereiskaia sluzhba v Meniushe', *Sofiia* 3 (1996), 3.
65. Fitzpatrick, *Stalin's Peasants*; Smith, 'Heavenly Letters'.
66. See Albert Baiburin's chapter in this collection.
67. See Catriona Kelly's contribution in this volume.

CHAPTER 17

Religious affiliation and the politics of post-Soviet identity: the case of Belarus

Galina Miazhevich

INTRODUCTION

The relationship between ethnicity, language and religion in the expression of national identity is well revealed in post-imperial contexts, where the struggle for solidarity and resistance is accompanied by a quest for beliefs or traditions to hold groups together.[1] Here, the rise of nationalist sentiments, the foregrounding of ethnic solidarity and the reinstatement of the local language, together with the revival of religious practices, which at times gain a more devout following in this process, all signify the dismantlement of traces of the imperial past and the re-establishment of a cohesive societal structure.[2] The post-colonial framework has been successfully applied to numerous situations. However, the unusual status of Belarus as the former periphery to an imperial state, rather than an ex-colony proper, deserves special attention.

This study attempts to uncover the continuity, or more accurately, discontinuity, of Soviet and post-Soviet identities, and to account for tensions underlying the construction of Belarusian nationhood, which is viewed as closely intertwined with the Soviet/Russian imperial legacy. In exploring this, my article also analyses the intersection between religious affiliations and post-Soviet nation-building, where the latter is seen as inclusive of ethnicity and geopolitical components. It proposes that the official religious identity project supported by the mass media (involving the imposition of a *pro-Russian* Orthodox model) has led, among other things, to the revitalization of a hitherto dormant *pro-Belarusian* identity project among religious believers. The latter, I suggest, exhibit a complex and contradictory attitude to the stance of the state, which involves elements of assimilation, (mis)appropriation and disjunction.

341

UNDERSTANDING POST-SOVIET NATIONHOOD

Belarus as a periphery of the former Soviet empire

Belarus, which lies at the very edge of the former Soviet empire,[3] and functions as a borderland (*pogranich'e*) between Europe and Eurasia, remains a blind spot in post-Soviet studies. Given the extent of scholarship on the post-Soviet world generally,[4] and, more specifically, the significant body of work on the Baltic States,[5] Ukraine and Poland,[6] Belarus represents the least studied case among the post-Soviet successor states.

All this provokes reflection on the relationship of this part of the post-Soviet world to other areas. When considering the post-Soviet experience within the framework of post-imperialist studies more generally, one needs to account for (a) the peculiarities of the Soviet-Russian empire, which was based on geographical contiguity rather than overseas conquest; (b) the fact that the Soviet Union was not an empire in the conventional sense but an 'imperial' state; and (c) the fact that policy towards different republics varied considerably. While in the Central Asian region the (post)colonial framework is the most convenient paradigm for analysis,[7] in other parts of the former USSR it is more appropriate to talk about the policies of a 'nationalizing state' (those of Russification, for example), and use a 'centre–periphery', rather than 'colonial', framework.[8]

Ironically, despite the Russian tendency to treat Belarus as part of Russia, it was precisely during tsarist rule that Belarus began to define itself as a nation as a result of the metropolitan centre's ethnographical study of its subordinate periphery.[9] Moreover, inconsistencies in Soviet nationalities policy tended themselves to exacerbate, rather than suppress, nationalist aspirations in the non-Russian republics.[10] In a way, Belarusian patriotism owed much of its 'construction' to the Russian metropolis.[11] At the same time, the Sovietization of the western periphery of the USSR, where 'the erosion of the linguistic and cultural boundaries ... facilitated identification ... with the "Soviet people"',[12] culminated in the emergence of Belarus as a peculiar case of the 'last Soviet republic',[13] with 'a culture that is neither exclusively colonial nor native'.[14]

After passive acceptance by Belarusians of independent statehood in 1991 (in stark contrast, for instance, to the Baltic States),[15] the new republic dropped out of the cohort of post-Soviet 'civic' states, and, until recently, embraced the model of the '*Russian* "nationalising state"',[16] in which Belarusian citizens were denied their political rights and encountered the denationalization of their cultural heritage.[17] This was further complicated by the competing principles according to which Belarusian national identities were being built: the linguistic issue (the Belarusian/Russian language), the geopolitical divide (the pro-European West and the pro-Russian East) and its religious corollary (the Orthodox/Catholic split).[18]

Owing to this political-cultural proximity to the metropolitan centre (and corresponding hybridization), the Belarusian regime needed to forge a new nation from incompatible elements. The official ideological management in Belarus draws on the most easily accessible ideas (anti-globalization) and the most popular ones (Soviet revivalism). At present, official discourse distinguishes Belarus from the metropolis by reaffirming Soviet ideals abandoned by Russia (e.g. the Belarusian partisan narrative), yet undermines the separatist potential of this reaffirmation by appealing to the Slavic trinity (Russia, Ukraine, Belarus). In the light of the deteriorating relations between Russia and Belarus by the start of the 2000s, the state line included pragmatic manipulation by various historical myths and available plausible symbols to revitalize the ethno-cultural community bond.[19] This, however, omitted any references to an alternative path of identification with Europe and its supranational community. Equally, hostility to globalized modernity[20] accompanied modernist reassertions of Soviet *mnogonarodnost'* ('multi-peopled-ness'). These contradictions were matched within unofficial Belarusian revivalism, in which anti-Russianness coexisted alongside Slavic pride, 'Nativists' were at odds with the '*Russian-speaking* anti-Lukashenko-and-pro-Europe group',[21] and Catholicism and Orthodoxy collided.[22] As the meanings of '"self" and "other" were constructed, reproduced and contested for entirely new ends'[23] on an ad hoc basis in the context of recentralizing the Belarusian regime,[24] these contradictions multiplied, fostering multiple hybrid identities of unusual complexity.

RELIGIOUS AFFILIATION IN POST-SOVIET BELARUS

Belarus as a multi-confessional (Christian) state

According to the 1999 census, the Republic of Belarus's population was 9.7 million, including Belarusians (81.2%), Russians (8.2%), Poles (6.3%) and Ukrainians (1.7%). Other ethnic groups included Lithuanians, Jews, Latvians, Armenians and Tatars. Belarus is mostly Orthodox, with Catholicism dominating in the western regions. According to the Office of the Plenipotentiary Representative for Religious and Nationality Affairs, around 50% of Belarusians call themselves religious. Of this group, approximately 80% belong to the Belarusian Orthodox Church (hereafter BOC),

9.9% (or 15–20% according to other sources[25]) profess the Catholic faith, 4% identify themselves as members of eastern religious groups (Muslims, Hare Krishna and Baha'i), and somewhere between 0.7 and 2% are Protestant.[26]

In another survey, more than 85% of the population declared Belarusian to be their native language, but only 41.3% stated that they used it at home. The dominant language was Russian, spoken by nearly 60% of ethnic Belarusians, more than 95% of Russians and around 84% of Ukrainians. Poles were the ethnic group who most frequently used Belarusian at home (58%).[27]

Thus, post-Soviet Belarus emerges as a predominantly Slavic, Russian-speaking and multi-confessional (Christian) country. However, it is important also to consider its peculiar relationship (for instance in comparison to the well-studied case of neighbouring Ukraine) with the multicultural Russian/Soviet imperial state.

Dilemmas of the religious revival in Belarus

Despite the fact that 'the Soviet Union ... went the furthest of any multinational state [and] categorically excluded religion as a criterion of nationality recognition',[28] the rigorous anti-religious drive could not wipe out religiosity, and in many cases this meant that religious practice was preserved as part of cultural tradition, or converted into latent religiousness. Several factors contributed to this phenomenon. To start with, the Soviet policy of imposed atheism fluctuated over time (particularly notable were the easing in policy during the Second World War, and in the late Soviet period).[29] Secondly, this policy was posited on a perceived connection between faith and national identity (as manifested in the hostility towards Judaism, or Belarusian and Ukrainian Greek-Catholicism, the relative tolerance of Roman Catholicism and the gradual co-option of the Orthodox clergy by the state). The situation in Soviet Belarus was quite similar to that in the Ukrainian SSR, where those in rural areas, especially in the western parts, continued to exercise their religious practices (e.g. Roman Catholicism), sometimes without a priest or any other religious authority or available facilities, and were often overlooked. Moreover, the trend in the 1970s to register, rather than prohibit, Baptists and other minority religious groups to ensure their loyalty to authority helped advance religious representation and diversity.[30]

As a result, after the fall of the USSR, Belarus, together with other nations in the former Soviet Union, witnessed an immediate revival of the religious practices suppressed during Soviet times. Along with various symbols, religious beliefs developed into useful markers for determining lines of group 'inclusion' and 'exclusion'. To quote Johnson: 'As the universalistic Soviet identity was openly challenged ... a society-wide search for alternative ethnic and religious identities became both real and necessary.'[31] Alongside the sense of new times as an opportunity to exercise religious freedom, the need for community support in unstable politico-economic conditions made religious affiliation an important identity parameter in this transformational context.[32]

However, over time, Soviet anti-religious policy (involving severe restriction of the activities of religious communities and execution or deportation of religious leaders and believers) had resulted in a contradictory attitude towards religion among the majority of the population. Despite the proliferation of churches and the rapid growth of religious believers registered throughout the former Soviet Union, many questioned whether this was really 'an authentic religious revival'.[33] Many of the respondents knew little about religious practice and had insubstantial and/or superficial beliefs.[34] In some cases this 'fragmented' identification[35] even bordered on heretical views such as belief in karma or rejection of orthodox beliefs, such as the Second Coming of Christ.[36] One of the most prominent illustrations of the post-Soviet phenomenon of a 'secular believer' combined with the traditional 'cultural identification with Orthodoxy'[37] is President Lukashenko's famous claim that he is 'an Orthodox atheist'.[38]

Overall, however, it is fair to say that religion became significant for a large sector of post-Soviet society – despite the fact that only 18% of the population regularly attend religious services.[39] Some would argue that these overall figures give a misleading picture, particularly of Catholics in western Belarus,[40] where 70–80% of the population are practising believers and ethnic Poles retain a strong affinity to the Roman Catholic Church (they account for 41.6% of Catholic believers in Belarus[41]).

While on the surface it seems that religion does not constitute a critical polarization of society or a means of mobilization, belief does prove meaningful in the daily experience of certain sections of Belarusian society.[42] It is particularly important among the growing number of Catholic and Protestant believers. For instance, out of those people who identify themselves as Roman Catholic, 50% overall regularly attend religious service[43] (and an even higher proportion in some places, as we have seen), which represents a dramatic dissimilarity when compared to numbers of passive and practising Orthodox believers. The rapid growth in the number of Protestants,[44] as well as their attempts to mobilize society, are other important features (one case in particular, involving the Minsk-based Protestant Church 'New Life',[45] provoked repressive measures on the part of the state). In turn, this particularly negative attitude towards Protestants makes their religious identity more salient for the followers of this and other confessions, as well as for secular parts of society.[46]

All this is particularly important in light of the state's pro-Orthodox stance.[47] Orthodoxy in Belarus, as in Russia, appears to be useful for official nation-building projects. President Lukashenko has described the BOC as the 'main ideologist in the country', declaring that 'we have never separated ourselves from the Church'.[48] The Orthodox religion is implicitly linked with the state[49] and in turn to the titular nation.[50] Thus, a Russian or Belarusian person is in the eyes of the state, by implication, an Orthodox believer.

However, the situation creates several dilemmas for Belarus's official culture. Firstly, the implication of making Orthodoxy central to Belarusian national identity is that links with Russia are established at the expense of other Orthodox nations (e.g. Bulgaria). In this way Belarus detaches itself from Western and Central Europe and creates confusion about its ethnic (Slavic/non-Slavic) component. Secondly, the regime's attempt to distinguish itself from the imperial centre precisely by its (far from coherent) Soviet revivalism creates an immediate contradiction when it attempts to strengthen its lost, Orthodox-Slavic essence, because of the associations between communism and atheism. Emphasis on Orthodoxy also undermines the (re)Sovietization narrative by challenging nostalgia for the Soviet Union. Last but not least, the recognition of the imperial heritage (and its association with the preference for Orthodoxy) makes it much more difficult to account for the presence of Catholics, Protestants and Uniates within the supposedly harmonious society.

INSIGHT INTO THE 'ALTERNATIVE' RELIGIOUS
IDENTITIES OF BELARUSIANS

Methodology

The remarks that follow are based on fieldwork with informants. Instead of focusing on religious identity as something compartmentalized, and assuming the existence of clear-cut religious affinities, with corresponding ethnic backgrounds and political views, I attempt here to investigate the intersection of various identities via the lens of religious self-identification. My discussion neither assumes that increased religious awareness should necessarily result in nationalist mobilization and vice versa, nor does it imply a predetermined interrelationship between the ethnic and religious elements of identification. As the correlation between religious affiliations and the geopolitical (Slavic/non-Slavic) aspects of post-Soviet subjectivity has yet to be researched, such an approach is timely.

Unlike some of the studies in the region dealing with the official version of national consciousness, such as Wolczuk's study on Ukraine,[51] I will try to go further and complement the official narrative with non-official ones. In order to shed light on the process of the renegotiation of Belarusian identity, I will explore individual narratives of Belarusian Christian believers as they emerge from a set of semi-structured interviews (2008), and try to position them with regard to the state's pro-Orthodox stance. In order to explore 'alternative' religious identities, the 'in-group'/'out-group' categorization framework employed in SIT is used.[52] Deploying the notion of fluidity and instability of identity, I refer to identity markers or attributes (such as speech) and categories (how people define themselves, for instance, 'Russian-speaker', 'Orthodox' etc.) to detect the stance adopted by the respondents. In order to expose identity boundaries I will take into consideration respondents' attitude towards language, religious practices, geopolitics and the image of nationhood involving their stance on patriotism (local/regional/global) and reinterpretation of the past (Russia as the enemy, historicization of the nation etc.). The interview questions also tried to elicit responses reflecting the respondents' attitudes towards official media pronouncements involving religion.

Given the existence of a gap between practice and beliefs in the former Soviet Union, the respondents were selected on the basis of their verbal account of how often they went to church, and the depth of their knowledge about religious practice. The list of believers interviewed is provided in Table 17.1. In total, nine interviews were conducted in 2008, seven of which were held in Minsk and two in Grodno. Two respondents were from the capital; four respondents originated from the Grodno region (the north-western part of Belarus) and two were born in the eastern regions of Belarus before coming to work in the capital, where they eventually had settled down. The final respondent migrated from Russia. There were four females and five males, with the youngest male respondent twenty-one and the oldest female sixty-one years old. The average age was forty-two. The respondents had the following religious identifications: three, Catholic; three, Orthodox; two, Protestant; one, Uniate.

Table 17.1. *Interview sample.*

	Name	Religion	Gender (F/M)	Age	Language of interview/ language the respondent regularly uses	Place of the interview/other comments
1	Natalia	Catholic	F	54	Russian/Russian and Belarusian	Minsk/originally a respondent from Grodno region
2	Sergei	Catholic	M	21	Russian/Polish, Russian, Belarusian[a]	Grodno
3	Nikolai	Catholic	M	33	Russian/Russian and Belarusian	Minsk/originally a respondent from Grodno region
4	Larisa	Orthodox (Belarusian Orthodoxy)	F	61	Belarusian/Russian and Belarusian	Minsk/links with Belarusian Orthodox from Bialystok
5	Svetlana	Orthodox	F	47	Russian	Minsk
6	Ekaterina	Orthodox	F	56	Russian	Minsk
7	Andrei	Protestant	M	37	Russian	Minsk
8	Mikhail	Protestant	M	37	Russian/Russian and Belarusian	Minsk
9	Vladimir	Uniate	M	34	Belarusian/Russian and Belarusian	Grodno

[a] Three languages given in respondent's order of preference for conversation.

The Belarusian media and the promotion of Orthodox religious identity

State restrictions on the freedom of the press have been a significant problem in Belarus since 1995. In combination with suppression of religious freedoms,[53] this constitutes a dilemma. Firstly, bias in reporting is obviously related to the state–BOC symbiosis (reflected in the politically engaged character, *zaangazhirovannost'*, of the media).[54] Further, the absence of a tradition of religious reporting during the Soviet period makes it difficult to meet the criteria of objective coverage. Currently an attempt to reflect religious diversity can be observed: the media report all major religious holidays, provide a balanced account (terminology-wise) and omit negative aspects (religious fanatics or religious zeal). Extra space is granted to Catholics to 'strike a chord in order to translate into mass support',[55] to reflect their important presence (as a main religion with a claim on Belarusian identity) and their loyalty to the state. However, by and large the construction of the category of a 'believer' in the Belarusian media occurs at the expense of other denominations (reflecting the state support for the Orthodox Church).

Moreover, media framing involves the construction of 'acceptable/unacceptable' religious denominations. For example, Protestant denominations are less favoured by the regime 'presumably for their perceived links with the United States'.[56] One could add to this that their rapid expansion is seen as possibly threatening the traditional confessional structure.[57] Another tendency involving other denominations is to silence 'inconvenient issues' such as the unresolved issue of different strands within the BOC (as well as the existence of Uniates within Catholicism). The religious confessions most frequently featured are the BOC and (though to a significantly lesser extent) Catholics. Even then, the voices present (in the direct as well as indirect speech in the articles) are those of representatives of state or high-ranked religious figures. In the case of the BOC, one can often observe political/ideological (re)framing. The identification strategies of religious believers at the grass roots need to be investigated from other material.

Interviews with religious believers: an analysis

Despite the fact that my study specifically targeted religious believers with a strong sense of religious identification (detectable via in-depth knowledge gained in church and/or self-education, regular and devoted service attendance, and so on), the interviews demonstrate that Catholics, Protestants and Uniates tend to be more knowledgeable about their faiths, and more open to cross-confessional dialogue. Orthodox believers at times were uncertain about some aspects of religious practice. In part this might be related to the reasons for religious conversion (such as the serious illness of a husband, which caused one respondent, Svetlana,[58] who originated from a family of perfunctorily observant Catholics, to turn to the Orthodox religion). However, as was frequently mentioned by representatives of different religious confessions, the Orthodox Church appears to be one of the least welcoming (or most 'passive', as labelled by Sergei) in terms of the drive to engage new members or educate existing ones. Its priests are less approachable, the language of its service is difficult to comprehend, and there is little information about Sunday schools or other courses which might help people to learn more about religion. Nevertheless, it should not be assumed that the respondents from other confessions actively seek new knowledge; at times they also have a tendency to rely on a limited number of ingrained attitudes (e.g. a Catholic believer whose acquisition of knowledge relates mostly to the time when she was educated by her grandmother as a child). The respondents' comments highlighted the peculiarity of post-Soviet identities, where the general public often demonstrate religiously coloured, but nonetheless secular, national identities (i.e. an attraction to ritual without understanding the essence of the religion; declaring oneself as a believer might mean attendance at only one or two major annual Church celebrations, unsubstantiated by any knowledge of prayers, the order of service etc.). In most of the cases this routinization of faith was attributed to the significant number of Orthodox believers – so-called believers 'on paper' (*na bumage*), as described by Mikhail. Some of the respondents demonstrated an active exploration of religious affiliation. The joy of 'uncovering' one's religious identity was obvious in a conversion narrative from a 37-year-old successful lawyer who became a devout Protestant follower. Similar experience was described by Nikolai, who converted from Orthodoxy to Protestantism because he did not feel religious (*ne chuvstvoval veru*) in the Orthodox Church, but found his faith in the Protestant Church, where he 'can talk to God'.

Most of the respondents expressed tolerance of 'changes' in religious belonging (e.g. involving their relatives' or friends' conversion) and described others' attitudes (as in the interview with Ekaterina) with relation to their own *prikhod k religii* (choice of religious stance) as generally positive.[59] The believers revealed high tolerance of other confessions, including the Orthodox Church (despite its privileged position in the country). Catholics, for instance, demonstrated a neutral stance, running from a position of ecumenism (as adopted by Sergei) to the positive appreciation articulated by Nikolai: 'Orthodox religion is more difficult, but once you've got it (*poimesh*), then a great depth of religious faith opens up for you (*togda takaia duvnost' otkryvaetsia*).'[60] In many cases a high level of acceptance was associated with 'recognized' Belarusian national features such as tolerance and even indifference (*abyiakavasts*,[61] the term used by Sergei).

Some of the respondents proved to be less ambivalent than others. Quite predictably, pro-Orthodox believers were more inclined to look eastward and/or to look up to 'the big brother' (for instance, Ekaterina in her narrative was continuously stressing the activity and importance of the Moscow Patriarchate), speak the Russian language and erase links with other Slavic European nations. Here Russia stood for the most accessible re-translator of Orthodoxy (the meanings are transferred between the centre and its periphery). So, according to Svetlana, 'Orthodoxy is inherently (*iskonno*) our religion … starting from Vladimir's conversion of Rus in

988 . . . it suits us – Slavic people – better.' In turn, Catholics tended to be more pro-European, more often Polish- (rather than Russian- or Belarusian-) speaking and had the themes of 'Slavic/Russian/Belarusian' as well as 'nationalism' or 'ethnicity' virtually omitted from their narrative. The fuzziness of their identities was, above all, related to immediate localism (with the importance of the geographical place of their birth and permanent location), which at the same time involved other localities (the Vatican or special places of worship in Western Europe, Belarus etc.).

Uniates, on the other hand, emerged as pro-Belarusian in terms of language and history. Their geographical references were not confined solely to the current Belarus's borders: they included an interspatial dimension (the Uniate Church abroad involving both close neighbours such as Ukraine and more distant Uniate centres in France, the US or the UK etc.) and an inter-temporal one (the reference to a more or less distant past when Belarus was a part of other imperial states). As Vladimir put it: 'We have a certain focus on Belarusianness (patriotism) . . . we turn to Belarusian history, literature . . . language plays an important role in our services . . . ordinary "Soviet" people come here . . . then they start to identify themselves with Belarus(ianness).' At the same time, Uniates demonstrated the highest level of tolerance of other confessions: 'We are not interested in converting somebody who has already found his/her place in other confessions . . . we are more interested in those who haven't found faith yet . . . we are not interested in numbers' (Vladimir). Protestants, in turn, were even more universalist (a case in point was Andrei, when speaking about freedom of expression) and less territory-bounded.

However, even these generalizations should be treated cautiously. Religious affiliation and geopolitical vectors can coexist in an ambivalent fashion. The historical importance of Poland for Catholics in Belarus could potentially be undermined by the declining importance of religious affiliation in contemporary Poland, where a new type of religious believer is emerging, under the influence of globalization processes. For instance, Polish Catholics, according to Nikolai, are 'used to routine and tradition' (*vse derzhitsia na traditsii*), have a more formal, less emotional attitude, which they 'have in their blood or acquired subconsciously' (*s kroviu, na podsoznatel'nom urovne*). Their churches are 'turning into museums, where the service resembles a theatrical show' and their understanding of religion is based on imitation, which only later on in life is accompanied by understanding. Belarusian Catholics (in comparison to Polish ones), according to him, are more religious, i.e. more devoted to their faith and feel it at a 'deeper level'.

In addition to these findings, there are indicators of a multiplicity of national identity projects, as cultural elements (language, history, traditions) are appropriated differently between and within confessions. For instance, the importance of services in the Belarusian language is different for various communities within the BOC.[62] This might also have shifting importance for the believers within the same confession: for two Protestant believers I interviewed, it ranged from irrelevant to extremely important. Moreover, a lack of collaboration between confessions results in a multiplicity of faiths calling themselves 'Belarusian Churches', e.g. the Uniates and the BOC, and appealing to different historical periods. The three cases below explicate the complex configuration of the identity components in the post-Soviet Belarusian context further.

Natalia, a Catholic believer (fifty-four years old) from the Grodno region, is fluent in both Russian and Belarusian, but speaks in the language dictated by the people with whom she is communicating. She does not distinguish any of the languages she speaks as her 'native' one (in a way, her conversational partner's language of convenience is selected as this). She is a devout Catholic; her faith originates from her childhood, when she attended church services in the Grodno region, which were and still are predominantly held in Polish. At the same time, she defines her nation as Slavic (the unity between three nations: Russia, Ukraine and Belarus) without any explicit links with Poland, and displays high support for the regime and the president. In her narrative, devoid of available links to the pre-revolutionary past, there is a reliance on the 'Soviet' experience to describe current nation-building in Belarus. Thus, Natalia's narrative presents her *civic* post-Soviet identity as something *given* and causes her identification strategy to take the post-Soviet/Slavic path.

Larisa is an Orthodox believer (sixty-one years old). She is an active member of the BOC and speaks only Belarusian. She supports the movement for the establishment of the Belarusian Autocephalous Orthodox Church (BAOC), which she expects to be a slow but manageable process, happening in collaboration with the state and people (who, she thinks, need to become ready for it). As was the case with the others, this respondent's religious path also started in the USSR. However, in comparison to a previous case, the initial religious transformation started after contact with the BOC in Poland, and her identification can be defined in terms of a nativist/pro-European project. Currently, she is an active member of a religious Orthodox brotherhood (*bratstvo*), which promotes services in Belarusian, and is centred on 'Three Vilna (*Vilenskiia*) Saints' (who were 'Belarusian' during the time of the Grand Duchy of Lithuania), thus rejecting the Russian historiographic interpretation of key historical events and figures. She describes the nation in its current state as post-Soviet, and demonstrates an ambivalent attitude towards the regime. Alongside, her narrative suggests fragmentation of the nation as she draws an opposition between the intelligentsia and *narod* ('the People').

Mikhail is a Protestant believer (aged thirty-seven) from Minsk, whose 'conversion narrative' exposes an immediacy of the faith's confirmation: 'I saw ... I realized' (*ia uvidel ... pochuvstvoval*). He speaks both Russian and Belarusian, but appears to be more pro-Belarusian. He links the Protestant religion with the US or Western Europe in the first instance, but also uses references to the Belarusian past (such as to Francysk Skaryna, who was the first publisher in Eastern Europe to print the translated Bible in the sixteenth century). He also claims that other prominent figures of that time were Protestants. In his narrative he goes further, suggesting that Belarus was originally Protestant, and closely affiliated with Europe. According to him, Russian imperialism is endangering Belarus. The respondent is critical of the regime. However, his 'European'-style liberal views at times coexist with critiques of Western 'political correctness'. While acknowledging the importance of European heritage ('Europe was the cradle of reformation'), he expresses dissatisfaction with the ambitions of European politicians who 'do not seem to care about people dying from hunger in the twenty-first century'.

Despite the above-mentioned confessional differences, there are points of unity among the respondents. Firstly, they adhere to Christian values and belief in one God for everybody. However, their consolidation is triggered by a hostile 'other'. In this case there are several 'enemies' constituting a potential threat: Muslims and members of various occult sects. While the 'othering' of a sect's activity is self-explanatory, the displayed (implicit) vigilance towards Islam deserves more attention. On the one hand, it can be seen as constructed around the existence of 'anti-Soviet' attitudes, which in turn are linked to anti-multicultural and, by implication, anti-Semitic and/ or anti-Muslim sentiment. On the other hand, it can be attributed to the anti-Semitic and anti-Caucasian sentiments internalized within the metropolitan mentality (displaying the after-effects of the USSR's multiculturalism policy, which was riddled with confusion). But, as such points were mentioned predominantly by Orthodox believers, they primarily expose the tension between Orthodoxy and Islam. Secondly, however, these statements rested on a common narrative about universal religious values, which were held to unify everyone, transcend all boundaries and stand above the power of the state (the latter was particularly true in the case of Protestant believers).

Here a comment about the intersection between religious and ethnic identity would be in order. As the second and third cases demonstrate, there was a tendency, which Smith has seen as generally characteristic of the post-Soviet world, to essentialize ethnic identity through the emphasis on 'some intrinsic and essential context to any identity . . . in terms of oppositions', drawing on 'either a common origin (our homeland, language, community) or a common structure of experience (colonized/colonizers, immigrants/ indigenous) or both'.[63] Among several indicators of this process were (a) the prevalence of attempts to 'historicize'[64] ethnic components by singling out particular historical periods or figures, such as the Grand Duchy of Lithuania and saints from its capital, Vilna; (b) the expression of a belief in the linear progression of the primordial nation, where a narrative of lost purity (the Grand Duchy of Lithuania heritage) may prove incompatible with another narrative relating to the 'repression' of the 'historically' Protestant nature of the first Belarusian public figures, for instance, the printer Francysk Skaryna; (c) the exclusion from historical accounts of 'inconvenient' elements, including historical religious shifts (for instance, the widespread conversions to Catholicism during the Polish-Lithuanian Commonwealth).

At the same time, one can claim that the (re)negotiation of Belarusian identity by religious believers does not have a clear-cut ethnic–civic division. This can be cross-referenced with the phenomenon of 'a fusion between ethnic and civic identities' established in recent research by Polese and Wylegala in Ukraine.[65] It is related above all to the localism displayed by the respondents when discussing national identification, as well as their appeal to universal/internationalist values, which often came up while religious faith was discussed. The situation is complicated further by the ongoing re-Sovietization of Belarus: often the narratives bridged the Soviet and post-Soviet identity through an essentialization of Soviet revivalism.

All the above-mentioned cases can be also analysed in terms of a more or less bottom-up 'religious conversion' approach. Although the official ideo-logical line (supported by the media) could be detected in the narratives (as, for example, in the references to the theme of Slavic unity) the hybridization of identities goes well beyond the symbols and mythologies disseminated by the state. As is evident from the cases of Catholic and Protestant believers, the (re)negotiation of Belarusian religious identity has been influenced by religious authority rather than by the pro-governmental elites (as shown by the fact that cases of conversion to non-Orthodox confessions were more frequent than conversions to Orthodoxy, despite the dominant official narrative). Thus, the configuration of Belarusian identity components proves highly complex, even in a small-scale study of this kind, which did not attempt to account for the influence of other complicating factors such as age, gender,[66] education, marital status, work affiliation and so on.

CONCLUSION

The discussion here has uncovered numerous tensions in Belarusian subjects as they struggled to figure out a path between the multiple components of their post-Soviet identities. In the context of the state's pro-Orthodox stance, the differences between Orthodoxy and other religious confessions were, I have argued, accentuated, which strengthened ties between non-Orthodox believers. In many cases this appeared to be linked with the revitalization of a hitherto dormant pro-Belarusian identity project. In respect to religious affiliation, this identity project was evident in the revival of Belarusian cultural elements (language, history) and their selective appropriation by various confessions. This led to: (a) the emergence of a multiplicity of 'Belarusian Churches', among them, the Uniate Church, but also the BOC; (b) fragmentation within one confession: consider the different streams within the BOC, including campaigners for the BAOC; and (c) divisions among individual believers (which was observable above all in the case of Protestant respondents).

Some of the dilemmas of alternative nation-building projects were prompted by the pro-Russian Orthodox stance, as broadcast through the official media. Elements of this kind included, for instance, the representation of Belarusian/Russian as Slavic, to the exclusion of other Slavic Orthodox countries. Yet such projects also evoked resistance to the suggested separation from Western Europe. At times believers tended to stress the link between Catholicism and an orientation towards Poland, at the expense of excluding the Orthodox East. Confusion was also shown in the fact that European-liberal views coexisted with hostility towards leftist 'political correctness'.

In sum, no single alternative Belarusian identity project could be identified. Different faiths appropriated Belarusianness in quite different ways, sometimes in support of, and sometimes in opposition to, the state's nation-building narratives, and sometimes borrowing from those narratives, but using the adopted motifs for different purposes.

The analysis points to one further conclusion. With its re-Sovietization strategy, Belarus provides clear evidence of the fact that classic national identity theory and its distinction between 'civic' (chosen) and 'ethnic' (given) modes[67] needs to be adapted to take account of East European, post-communist peculiarities. As the interview data showed, there is, in Belarus, a tendency to essentialize Soviet revivalism (we witness the conversion of *civic* post-Soviet identity into something *given*). Conversely, there is a trend for 'civilizing' (or 'making civic') what is usually given (religious tradition). Here religious affiliation provides the sense of an alternative identity which can be adopted and changed (as shown by, for example, informants' display of tolerant attitudes towards conversion from one set of beliefs to another, or their positive attitude to the exploration of, and even experimentation with, religious affiliation). Religious practice is associated with flexibility and the active embrace of experience, rather than rigidity and the passive acceptance of inherited tradition.

NOTES

1. The author would like to thank Stephen Hutchings for his comments on several drafts of the paper, as well as the Arts and Humanities Research Council (the paper was written during the AHRC-funded project AH/D001722/1).
2. In many cases these historically rooted interethnic issues are intertwined with struggles between elites over resources and with social disruption. However, this topic goes beyond the scope of this paper.
3. The country is situated in the geographical centre of Europe, bordering Russia, Ukraine, Poland, Lithuania and Latvia.
4. D. C. Moore, 'Is the Post- in Postcolonial the Post- in Post-Soviet? Toward a Global Postcolonial Critique', *PMLA* 116:1 (2001), 111–28; G. Smith, *The Post-Soviet States* (London, 1999); M. K. Beissinger and C. Young, eds., *Beyond State Crisis? Postcolonial Africa and Post-Soviet Eurasia in Comparative Perspective* (Washington, DC, 2002).
5. K. Raevskis, 'Toward a Postcolonial Perspective on the Baltic States', *Journal of Baltic Studies* 33:1 (2002), 37–56.
6. J. Korek, *From Sovietology to Postcoloniality: Poland and Ukraine from a Postcolonial Perspective* (Stockholm, 2007).
7. V. Tolz, *Russia: Inventing the Nation* (London, 2001).
8. For an in-depth exploration of centre–periphery relations and nationalist mobilization among titular nationals in various republics in the RF, see E. Giuliano, 'Theorizing Nationalist Separatism in Russia', in *Rebounding Identities: The Politics of Identity in Russia and Ukraine*, ed. D. Arel and B. A. Ruble (Washington, DC, 2006), 34.
9. V. Bulgakov, *Gistoryia belaruskaga natsyianalizmu* (Vilnius, 2006).
10. R. Suny, *The Soviet Experiment: Russia, the USSR, and the Successor States* (New York, 1998).
11. Cf. Sergei Abashin's discussion in this volume.

12. K. Wolczuk, 'History, Europe and the "National Idea": The Official Narrative of National Identity in Ukraine', *Nationalities Papers* 28:4 (2000), 673.

13. S. Parker, *The Last Soviet Republic: Alexander Lukashenko's Belarus* (Bloomington, IN, 2007).

14. G. Alley-Young, 'Articulating Identity: Refining Postcolonial and Whiteness Perspectives on Race within Communication Studies', *Review of Communication* 8:3 (2008), 307–21.

15. The country has even been referred to as a 'denationalized nation': D. Marples, *Belarus: A Denationalized Nation* (Singapore, 1999).

16. T. Kuzio, '"Nationalising States" or Nation Building? A Critical Review of the Theoretical Literature and Empirical Evidence', *Nations and Nationalism* 7:2 (2001), 135–54, at 148–9.

17. The framing within the model of the 'nationalizing state' is questionable, especially in the light of the critique of the applicability of Brubaker's concept of the 'nationalizing state' (R. Brubaker, *Nationalism Reframed: Nationhood and the National Question in the New Europe*, Cambridge, 1996) to Central and Eastern European countries (A. Polese and A. Wylegala, 'Odessa and Lvov or Odesa and Lviv: How Important is a Letter? Reflections on the "Other" in Two Ukrainian Cities', *Nationalities Papers*, 36:5, 2008, 787–815; Wolczuk, 'History', 671–94), owing to the diversity of these countries, and the possibility of the coexistence of the civic realm together with their ethno-cultural core. In respect of Belarus, the 'nationalizing state' model is disputable in itself – consider the granting of official status to two languages, Belarusian and Russian (Constitution, article 17), or the concession of rights of other kinds to ethnic minorities etc.

18. This division partly reflects the almost twenty-year-long separation of the country, when western Belarus was part of Poland according to the Riga peace treaty signed between the USSR and Poland in 1921. Western Belarus was annexed to the Belarusian Soviet Socialist Republic in 1939, after the Soviet invasion of Poland from the east (with the Axis powers simultaneously occupying Poland from the west, under the terms of the Molotov–Ribbentrop Pact).

19. N. Leshchenko, 'A Fine Instrument: Two Nation-Building Strategies in Post-Soviet Belarus', *Nations and Nationalism* 10:3 (2004), 333–52.

20. A. Pikulik, 'Paternalism, Rurality and Xenophobia as Building Blocks of Ideology: Reflections of Globalization and the West in the State-Official Discourse of Belarus', unpublished MA thesis, Sociology and Social Anthropology Program, Central European University, Budapest, 2005.

21. I. Ioffe, 'Culture Wars, Soul Searching and Belarusian Identity', *East European Politics and Societies* 21:2 (2007), 360.

22. See e.g. 'Kak sovremennye katoliki otnosiatsia k pravoslavnym?' [online discussion], http://community.livejournal.com/ru_catholic/50179.html#comments.

23. C. Young and D. Light, 'Place, National Identity and Post-Socialist Transformations: An Introduction', *Political Geography* 20 (2001), 948.

24. G. Miazhevich, 'Official Media Discourse and the Self-Representation of Entrepreneurs in Belarus', *Europe-Asia Studies* 54:8 (2007), 1331–48.

25. Among other groups, the Catholic Church includes adherents of the Greek
Catholic Church (Uniates), which acknowledges the Pope's authority, but
retains the Eastern Orthodox liturgy. The Uniate Church (which existed
legally in Belarus from 1596 to 1839, during the Polish-Lithuanian
Commonwealth) had around three-quarters of the Belarusian population as
members when it was abolished. After it was re-established in the early 1990s, it
evoked debate both of a theological and a political nature. It is taken by its
adherents, as my interviewing shows (see below), to be a 'national' Belarusian
church. However, though some religiously uncommitted people have turned to
it, resisting the dominance of the Orthodox and Roman Catholic Church, it has
had little success in sustaining this interest (A. Kishtymov, 'Uniatstvo i belo-
russkaia natsionalnaia ideia: ot Kastusia Kalinovskogo do nashikh dnei', *Open
Society / Adkrytae gramadstva* 2:13, 2002, www.data.minsk.by/opensociety/
2.02/5.html). According to Serdiuk, in 1999 the Uniate Church accounted
for approximately 3,000 followers (aged on average twenty-five to thirty), who
were mostly members of the intelligentsia (V. V. Serdiuk, 'Rimo-katoliki
Belarusi, 1991–2001 gg.', in *Postkommunisticheskaia Belarus' v protsesse religioznykh transformatsii*, ed. A. V. Danilov, Minsk, 2002, 32). In 2007 the Uniate
Church had thirteen registered communities, a slight increase on 1994, when it
had nine (see 'Belarus: religiia', http://belarus-china.com.ru/bel/religion.htm;
Russian Club, 'Religiia', www.belarus.russian-club.net/spravka_religion.
html).
26. U.S. Department of State, 'Belarus: International Religious Freedom Report,
2007', www.state.gov/g/drl/rls/irf/2007/90165.htm.
27. Belarusian Institute of Statistics, 'Perepis' naseleniia 1999 g. (osnovnye itogi)',
2008, http://belstat.gov.by/homep/ru/perepic/p6.php.
28. D. Arel, 'Introduction: Theorizing the Politics of Cultural Identities in Russia
and Ukraine', in *Rebounding Identities*, ed. Arel and Ruble, 16.
29. J. Johnson, 'Religion after Communism: Belief, Identity and the Soviet Legacy
in Russia', in *Religion and Identity in Modern Russia: The Revival of Orthodoxy
and Islam*, ed. J. Johnson, M. Stepaniants and B. Forest (Aldershot, 2005), 3.
For instance, during the Great Patriotic War, and for a limited period of time
after that, the Uniate Church effectively functioned on Belarusian territory.
30. N. A. Beliakova, 'Iz istorii registratsii religioznykh ob''edinenii v Ukraine i
Belorussii v 1976–1986 gg.', http://krotov.info/history/20/1980/belyakova.htm.
31. Johnson, 'Religion', 1.
32. C. Wannar, 'Explaining the Appeal of Evangelicalism in Ukraine', in
Rebounding Identities, ed. Arel and Ruble, 241–72.
33. Johnson, 'Religion', 18.
34. I. Borowik, 'Between Orthodoxy and Eclectics: On the Religious
Transformations of Russia, Belarus and Ukraine', *Social Compass* 49:4 (2002),
497–508.
35. This in most cases involves a declaration of a 'believer' status – someone who
respects the church's role in preservation of the cultural heritage, but who is not
observant.

36. D. K. Bezniuk, 'Sostoianie i spetsifika religioznoi situatsii v Belarusi', *Sociological Research* 2 (2006), 129.
37. Ibid., 131.
38. Kishtymov, 'Uniatstvo'.
39. U.S. Department of State, 'Belarus: International Religious Freedom'.
40. A. Sahm, 'Political Culture and National Symbols: Their Impact on the Belarusian Nation-Building Process', *Nationalities Papers* 27:1 (1999), 649–60.
41. A. V. Danilov and V. A. Martinovich, 'Osobennosti konfessional'noi struktury Respubliki Belarus'', in *Postkommunisticheskaia Belarus'*, ed. Danilov, 7–8.
42. While accepting that religion does not constitute a core element of the Belarusian national myth, my discussion here considers religious identification to be an important variable in the overall context of low institutional commitments and political apathy.
43. U.S. Department of State, 'Belarus: International Religious Freedom'.
44. In just over a decade (1994–2005), the number of Protestant communities increased by 5.4 times (from 178 to 955 congregations). At the same period, Orthodoxy's congregation grew by only 1.5 times (N. Sharai, 'Belarus stanet protestantskoi?', *Express novosti*, 22 July 2005, www.expressnews.by/1148.html). According to the latest survey there are twice as many Protestant groups as Catholic ones (V. Miadzvedzeva, 'Kol'kasts' khramau u Belarusi pavialichvaetstsa', *Zviazda*, 11 March 2009, www.zvyazda.minsk.by/ru/issue/article.php?id=30929). Bezniuk ('Sostoianie', 131) claims that Protestants account for 2–5% of all believers (in contrast to the data quoted earlier of 0.7–2.0%).
45. Members and supporters of this church, established in 1992, 'went on a high-profile hunger strike on 5 October 2006 . . . having failed to secure the right to use their own land and building for worship'. The hunger strike lasted for three weeks, with several members being hospitalized during it (G. Fagan, 'Belarus: Faith-Based Political Opposition Emerges', *Forum 18*, 29 November 2006, www.forum18.org/Archive.php?article_id=880).
46. 'Kruglyi stol na saite "Nashe Mnenie", posviashchennyi voprosam svobody sovesti s uchastiem organizatorov Kompanii v zashchity prav na svobody veroispovedaniia Sergeia Lukanina i Alekseia Sheina', 6 August 2007, www.forreligiousfreedom.com/news2007.php?subaction=showfull&id=1186430246&archive=&cnshow=news&start_from=&ucat=3&.
47. In 1990 Belarus became an exarchate of the Russian Orthodox Church, thus creating the Belarusian Orthodox Church (BOC). The BOC is headed by an ethnic Russian, Metropolitan Filaret, who heads an exarchate of the Moscow patriarchy of the Russian Orthodox Church. The Roman Catholic Church in Belarus is headed by an ethnic Pole, Archbishop Kazimir Sviontak, who has close ties to the Church in Poland. Attempts to introduce the Belarusian language into religious life were not successful because of the cultural predominance of Russians and Poles in their respective churches, and the low everyday usage of the Belarusian language. Alongside the revival of the old historical tension between Orthodoxy and Roman Catholicism – partly due to

the pro-Polish activity of the Catholic Church – the Uniates and Protestant confessions are also perceived with suspicion by the Orthodox Church in Belarus (U.S. Department of State, 'Belarus: International Religious Freedom').

48. U.S. Department of State, '2008 Human Rights Report: Belarus', 25 February 2009, www.state.gov/g/drl/rls/hrrpt/2008/eur/119069.htm.

49. Despite the fact that there is no state religion, a 2003 concordat with the BOC, a branch of the Russian Orthodox Church, grants the BOC privileged status (U.S. Department of State, 'Belarus: International Religious Freedom'; *Minskie eparkhial'nye vedomosti* 2, 2003, 33–4).

50. J. B. Dunlop, 'Orthodoxy and National Identity in Russia', in *Identities in Transition: Eastern Europe and Russia after the Collapse of Communism*, ed. V. Bonnell (Berkeley, CA, 1996), 118.

51. Wolczuk, 'History'.

52. M. A. Hogg, D. J. Terry and K. M. White, 'A Tale of Two Theories: A Critical Comparison of Identity Theory with Social Identity Theory', *Social Psychology Quarterly* 58:4 (1995), 255–60; H. Tajfel, ed., *Differentiation between Social Groups: Studies in the Social Psychology of Intergroup Relations* (London, 1978).

53. See, for instance, the monitoring of Forum 18 (www.forum18.org/). The status of religious confessions other than Orthodox has been significantly undermined since 2002, when new legislation on religion was passed in Belarus (it in many ways echoes the Russian 1997 Law on Religion, which was aimed at restricting the influence of Western Protestant denominations, and at strengthening the central role of Orthodoxy in Russian statehood). Although the 2002 law guarantees religious freedom, it increases 'the Government's control of the activities of religious groups' through various means, including governmental approval for literature distribution, prevention of religious visits of foreign missionaries, clergy and humanitarian workers affiliated with churches, denial for religious school establishment for the clergy, and complication of registration requirements (U.S. Department of State, 'Belarus: International Religious Freedom').

54. For instance, there is an agreement between the BOC and the state regulating and legitimizing church media presence ('Soglashenie o sotrudnichestve mezhdu natsional'noi gosudarstvennoi teleradiokompaniei Respubliki Belarus' i Belorusskoi Pravoslavnoi Tserkov'iu', 6 September 2004, www.church.by/resource/Dir0009/Dir0015/Page0028.html).

55. Arel, 'Introduction', 7.

56. U.S. Department of State, 'Belarus: International Religious Freedom'.

57. The several examples of this include an article by N. Janovich ('Belarusi ugrozhaet perspektiva prevratit'sia v protestantskuiu respubliku, ili nas nastoichivo tolkaiut k predatel'stvu very nashikh predkov', *Narodnaia gazeta* 19, 20 April 2000), films such as *Expansion* (*Ekspansiia*) and other biased media representations of Protestant believers (see E. V. Pastukhova, 'Sovremennoe sostoianie piatidesiatnicheskogo dvizheniia v Respublike Belarus' (soiuz khristian very evangel'skoi)', in *Postkommunisticheskaia Belarus'*, ed. Danilov, 67).

58. Full names are not used because of confidentiality agreements.
59. In one case, anticipation of a hostile societal attitude towards religious followers was expressed: 'some think that you have turned to religion, because you
are weak (*slabak*)' (Nikolai). This evokes concerns about the post-Soviet
ambiguous attitude toward religion as well as the USSR's legacy in relation
to stereotypes of masculinity, which should be explored further.
60. This corresponds to Bezniuk's conclusion ('Sostoianie', 130) about the more
positive attitudes of Catholics towards Orthodox believers (which are not
usually reciprocated).
61. In Russian, this term would be translated as *bezrazlichie*.
62. The question of the current divisions within the BOC, including groups with
more pro-Belarusian and pro-Russian sentiments, lies beyond the scope of this
article, as does a detailed exploration of different regional identities.
63. G. Smith, 'Post-colonialism and Borderland Identities', in *Nation-Building in
the Post-Soviet Borderlands: The Politics of National Identity*, ed. G. Smith,
V. Law, A. Wilson, A. Bohr and E. Allworth (Cambridge, 1998), 15.
64. Ibid., 16.
65. Polese and Wylegala, 'Odessa', 808.
66. According to Danilov and Martinovich ('Osobennosti', 8), the younger generation are becoming more religious (25.3%) alongside the older (more than
sixty years old) cohort (44.4%). Protestant followers tend to be more educated
(30.1%). Orthodox and Catholic confessions tend to attract females (64.2%
and 70.5% respectively).
67. A. D. Smith, *National Identity* (Reno, NV, 1993).

Index

Abdrashitov, Vadim, *Magnetic Storms* 67–8, 70
adulthood
    initiation into 96–7, 101–2, 103
    rights and responsibilities of 102
Aivazovskii, Ivan 44–5
alcohol
    and religious festivals 323
    and young people 108
alphabets
    Kalmyk Clear Script 202–3, 207
    in post-Soviet Central Asia 158–9, 262,
        265, 274
Anderson, Benedict 18, 150
    see also imagined communities
antilogy 39–41, 48–9
anti-Semitism 28
architecture
    of Elista 193–7
    Islamic 212–31
    of Moscow 171–5; as represented in literature
        177–82, 185
    post-Soviet church restoration 308–13
    Soviet treatment of churches 300–7
    see also urban environment
Armenia, and Soviet historiography 28
art, visual
    depicting Stalinist construction 173
    and post-Soviet controversy 319
    pre-revolutionary, and ideology 44–5
    Russification of non-Russian artists in
        USSR 207
    in Soviet ethnographic exhibitions 74, 77–81, 85
atheism, Soviet campaigns for 300
    and destruction of religious buildings 300–7
    effect of in Belarus 344–5, 346; effect of in
        Kalmykia 196–7
    and festivals 92–4
    role of museums in 84, 85
    and vernacular religious practices 321–33, 336
    see also Russian Orthodox Church, and Soviet
        rule

Balabanov, Aleksei 47–8
    Cargo 200, 68–9, 70
Baltic States, and Soviet rituals 95
Baranov, Anatolii 243–4
Bashkortostan 227
Bekmambetov, Timur
    Night Watch 69
    Day Watch 69
Belarus
    and attitudes towards Islam 353
    and attitudes towards Poland 351, 352, 355,
        359–60
    and attitudes towards West 353, 355
    demographics 343–4
    and independence 342–3
    and language choice 344, 351, 352, 359–60
    and patriotism 342
    relationship to Russian Federation 341, 343,
        346, 350–1, 353, 355
    re-Sovietization of 346, 354, 355–6; and Russo-
        Soviet rule 341–3
    see also Belarusian Orthodox Church; Greek
        Catholicism; Protestantism; Roman
        Catholicism
Belarusian Orthodox Church 343, 349, 352
    and links with Belarusian state 346, 348–9,
        355
Berkeley school 214, 216
black market 279
    representation in films 67
Bourdieu, Pierre 237–8
Boym, Svetlana 15, 70
Brandenberger, David 25, 27
Brezhnev era
    and construction work in Kalmykia 194
    and food shortages 279
    post-Soviet nostalgia for 58, 69
    representation in post-Soviet films 60, 67, 69
    and toleration of nationalist sentiment
        30, 31
Brudny, Yitzhak 29–30

Buddhism
  and architecture 193, 194–7, 207
  in Buryatia and Tuva 196
  in Kalmykia 193, 195–7, 200, 206
Bukhara 162

Catholicism *see* Greek Catholicism; Roman
  Catholicism
censorship
  under Khrushchev 136
  during perestroika 238
  and Russian Orthodox Church 314; Central
    Asia *see individual countries*
Chechnya and Chechens 217, 219, 222, 230
  and political rhetoric 244
  and post-Soviet film-makers 45–7
chernukha 58, 240
childhood
  and connection to native land 115, 122
  nostalgia for 56, 68–9
  representation in films 55, 69
  see also adulthood, initiation into; children;
    education; family; fatherhood; motherhood
children
  and curfews 300–8
  and 'Gagarin games' 142–3
  patriotic essays by 123, 172
  'red christenings' of 93
  and religion 327–8
  see also adulthood, initiation into; childhood;
    education; family; fatherhood; motherhood;
    naming of children
China, cultural influence of 194
Chudinov, Anatolii 245
Chukhrai, Pavel, *A Driver for Vera* 61–3, 66–7
Church of Jesus Christ of Latter-Day Saints 229
churches *see* Belarusian Orthodox Church;
  Church of Jesus Christ of Latter-Day Saints;
  Greek Catholicism; Protestantism; Roman
  Catholicism; Russian Orthodox Church
cinema *see* film
citizenship
  bestowal of on young people 91–2, 96–103
  and collective identity 101, 104
  obligations conferred by 47, 97, 100–2, 114, 121,
    122, 123
  passport as symbol of 91–2, 96–7,
    98–103
closed shops 286
corruption, political
  after collapse of USSR 32
  representation in post-Soviet films 68–70
crime
  criminal argot 241, 242–3, 245–6,
    248, 249

representation in post-Soviet films 60–1,
  68–9
see also terror, Stalinist; violence

deficit *see* shortage economy
democracy
  corruption of 33
  and language 238–9, 241, 242–4, 246
  and media 240–1
  and post-Soviet Kalmykia 208
  and Russian Federation 32, 33, 217
  see also freedom of speech
de-Stalinization 30, 137–8
diasporas
  Kazakh 163
  Kyrgyz 163
  Tajik 163–4
  Turkmen 164
  Uzbek 164
  see also ethnic minorities; migration
dissidence, lack of in Soviet Central Asia 151, 154
Dobrovol'skii, Dmitrii 243–4
Dunaevskii, I. 174
Dushanbe 156, 162

education
  and Central Asian nation-building 260,
    261–3
  and parental choice in Central Asia 255–7, 258,
    266–72
  purpose of, according to Soviet ideology 113–14
  and Russification of ethnic minorities in USSR
    207, 258
  Soviet administration of 257–8
  see also textbooks
Elista
  architecture 192, 193–7
  early history 191–2; in post-Soviet era 193,
    194–7, 199–209
  post-Stalin restoration 192–3, 198–9
  public monuments 197–204
  toponyms 205
  see also Kalmykia
emotion
  and cathartic value of swearing 241–2, 245
  and Gagarin cult 135
  and imperial rule 21–2
  and nationalism 19–21, 203
  and patriotic education 118–19, 120
  and post-Soviet identities 33, 120
  and Soviet rule 23, 25, 118
Erofeev, Venedikt 177
Erofeev, Viktor 241, 244
ethnic minorities
  in Central Asia 158, 163, 164–6, 254–73

ethnic minorities (cont.)
  and post-Soviet film-makers 48
  in Russian Federation 120, 121–2, 208–9,
    216–17
  see also Chechnya and Chechens; Kalmykia;
    migration
ethnogenesis 5
ethnography
  and Gagarin cult 143
  and Soviet policy on religion 321
  see also State Museum of the Ethnography of
    the Peoples of the USSR
ethno-nationalism 3–4, 5, 22, 24, 26, 28, 31–2
Eurasian Economic Community 161
Eurasianism 32, 217

family
  as institution 123
  as metaphor for national ideologies 46–7,
    139–40
  as modelled by Gagarin cult 137–42, 143–4
  in post-Soviet film 46–7, 62–3, 65, 69
  see also childhood; children; fatherhood;
    marriage; motherhood; rituals, Soviet rites of
    passage
fatherhood
  and Gagarin cult 139, 141–2
  representation in films 55
  see also childhood; children; family; marriage;
    motherhood
Feuchtwanger, Lion 173
film
  adaptations of classic novels 56–7
  and artificial approach to past 63–6, 70
  chernukha genre 58
  concern with everyday life 58, 60, 61
  and criticism of Soviet past 58–71
  and emotion 61, 63
  and imperialist discourse 45–7, 49, 57–8, 70
  and nostalgia 56–7, 58, 60, 69, 70–1
  during perestroika 57, 58
  post-Soviet attitudes to Soviet films 58
  and Russian national identity formation 57
  science fiction 131–2
  and violence 60, 67, 68–9, 70–1
First World War 22
folk culture
  celebration of in post-Soviet Kalmykia 203
  importance in late Soviet period 142–3
  and influence on Soviet rituals 94–5
  and obscenity 239, 243–4
  and Soviet ethnographic museums 79, 80
  see also rituals; Russian Orthodoxy, vernacular
    practices of; tradition
food shortages *see* shortage economy

freedom of speech 238–9, 246–8
Friendship of the Peoples 23, 26

Gagarin, Aleksei (father of Yuri) 141
Gagarin, Boris (brother of Yuri) 141
Gagarin, Yuri
  candid demeanour of 134, 135–6
  charisma 134
  conspiracy theories about 129
  and family life 137–42, 143–4
  as focus of hope for Soviet society 130–3
  media coverage of 133, 134–7
  as object of quasi-religious devotion 133
  post-Soviet views of 144–6
  as quintessential Russian 132, 133–4, 137–9, 140,
    142–3
  reactions to cult of 137
Gagarina, Anna Timofeevna (mother of Yuri)
    140, 144
Gagarina, Elena (daughter of Yuri) 146
Gagarina, Valentina (wife of Yuri) 140–1
Gellner, Ernest 42
Genghis Khan 156, 209
German, Aleksei Iu., *Khrustalev, My Car!* 61
glasnost 238–9, 247
  and film-making 57
Gorbachev, Mikhail
  and collapse of USSR 24, 238
  and invective 244
  and political reforms 32
Gorodovikov, B. B. 205
Gothic aesthetic, in post-Soviet literature 182–7
Goux, Jean-Joseph 237
Gradirovskii, Sergei 218, 221–3
Great Patriotic War
  and Kalmyks 192, 198–9, 204
  in late Soviet culture 135, 139
  memorials to 198–9, 212, 228
  museum responses to 79
  patriotic discourse during 26–8
  and post-Soviet literature 184
  and Russian Orthodox Church 304
  significance for Gagarin cult 143
Greek Catholicism, in Belarus 351, 358
Gudkov, Lev 69, 295

Hastings, Adrian 37–8
health
  as metaphor in Soviet propaganda 336
  and vernacular religion 324–6, 336
  see also physical culture
heroes
  film portrayals of national heroes 27, 57, 60
  Kalmyk commemoration of 197–205, 209
  in post-Soviet Kazakh culture 156

in post-Soviet Tajik culture 156
in post-Soviet Uzbek culture 153–4, 155
Yuri Gagarin as ultimate Soviet hero 129–46
hygiene *see* health

Il'f and Petrov, in Kalmyk culture 201
Ilyumzhinov, Kirsan (first president of Kalmykia) 195, 200, 201, 208
Ilyumzhinov, Kirsan (grandfather of first president of Kalmykia) 202, 205
imagined communities 6, 17, 113
indigenization policy, Soviet 24, 150
intelligentsia
  in Central Asia 154, 158–9
  and collapse of USSR 31, 32, 33
  and defence of non-Russian cultures 31
  as distinct social group 286, 353
  and freedom of speech 246
  and obscene language 244–5, 248
  of post-Soviet Kalmykia 209
  and religion 299, 304, 307, 312
  and Soviet culture 23, 30
interfaith relations
  in Belarus 343–56
  between Christians and Muslims 212–31, 353
  in Russian Federation 212–31, 313–14
internationalism
  in Soviet ideology 23, 116
  late Stalinist rejection of 28
Internet, and obscene language 248
Iran, and Tajik nationalism 162
Islam
  attempts to Russify 214, 217–19
  Belarusian attitudes towards 353
  in Central Asia 159–61, 162
  hostility towards 212, 213–14, 353
  radical interpretations of 160, 216–17
  in Russian Federation 212–31
  television broadcasts of services 218–19
  and Vladimir Putin 216, 219, 231
Ivan the Terrible 173–4

Jewish Autonomous Region 4
jokes
  about post-Soviet life 34
  about shortages 284, 292

Kalmykia
  and Buddhism 193, 195–7, 200, 206
  emigration from 193
  and Genghis Khan 209
  and language 202–3, 206
  and Lenin 197–8, 200
  and Orientalism 207–8
  political life of 194, 196, 200–1, 208–9

and post-Stalin return from exile 192–3, 198–9
and relationship with Russia 203–4, 208–9
and Soviet culture 207–8
and wartime deportations 192, 202
and westernization 206, 207
see also Elista; Ilyumzhinov, Kirsan (first president of Kalmykia); Ilyumzhinov, Kirsan (grandfather of first president of Kalmykia)
Karimov, Islam 161, 164, 165–6
Kazakhstan
  and aspirations to regional leadership 161
  attitudes to Kazakh diaspora 163
  attitudes to Russo-Soviet rule 152
  celebration of national culture 156
  language policy of 158
  policy towards ethnic minorities 164, 166
  religion in 160
  see also virgin lands campaign
KGB
  investigation of religious activities 329
  representation in post-Soviet film 62–3
Khlebnikov, Boris, *Koktebel'* 55
Khrushchev era
  and condemnation of Stalin 30, 136, 137–8
  and emergence of nationalist thought 30, 31
  and impact of first space flight 129–44
  and meta-ethnic Soviet nationality 4
  and religion 305–6, 321, 323–32, 336
  representation of in post-Soviet film 60, 61–7
  and restoration of Kalmyk autonomy 192–3, 198–9
Khuzin, Mukhammedgali 220, 221–3
Kirienko, Sergei 217
Kobelianskii, Aleksandr 172
Korolev, Sergei 133, 141–2
Kyrgyz people, as minority in other Central Asian states 163, 258–60, 265–6
Kyrgyzstan 319
  and attitudes to Russo-Soviet rule 152
  and heritage 155–6
  language policy and ethnic minorities 158, 258–61, 263–6, 268–72
  religion in 160

language
  and Belarusian identities 344, 351, 352, 359–60
  Central Asian policies on 157–61, 254–73
  in Kalmykia 202–3, 206
  see also obscenity; Russian language
Lenin, V. I.
  funeral of 94
  and Kalmykia 197–8, 200
  in late Soviet patriotic education 118–19

Lenin, V. I. (cont.)
  mausoleum 171, 200
  monuments to 197–8, 200
Leningrad
  inhabitants' participation in public rituals 107
  privileged existence in 288
  and Russian Orthodox Church 300–8, 312
  youth curfew 107
  see also St Petersburg
Levitan, Yuri 135
Likhachev, Dmitrii 242
literature
  and anti-religious propaganda for children 327–8
  film adaptations of classic novels 56–7
  and Gothic aesthetic 182–7
  literary reality 177–8, 186
  Moscow; in post-Soviet literature 176–87; in Soviet literature 171–5
  and nostalgia for Soviet past 56–7
  and obscene language 244–5
  and post-Stalin Russian nationalism 30, 38
  Pushkin and Kalmyks 199
Lukashenko, Aleksandr, views on religion 345, 346
Luk'ianenko, Sergei
  and attitude to Soviet past 184–5
  and monsters 182–3, 184–5
  and Moscow 176–7, 178–82, 185, 187
  Night Watch 178, 181, 184–5
Luzhkov, Iurii 175

Maiakovskii, Vladimir, 'Verses on the Soviet Passport' 100
marriage
  between partners of different ethnicities 206
  as modelled by Gagarin family 140–1
  registration of 92, 97, 299
  representation in films 62–3, 65, 69
Martin, Terry 26
Marxism, and national identity 3, 31
Masov, Rakhim 153
media
  in Belarus; and religion 341, 348–9, 355; restrictions on 348–9
  and Islam 218–19
  and nationalism 41
  and perestroika 238–9, 245–6
  in Russian Federation 34, 240–1, 245–6
  and Soviet atheism campaign 326
  Soviet control of 133, 136, 238–9
  and vulgarity 238–9, 240–1, 245–9
  see also film; Internet; newspapers; radio; television
migration
  impact on rural areas 334

of Kalmyks 193, 207
  restrictions on 91
  between Russia and Central Asia 159, 254, 262, 273
  Soviet and post-Soviet attitudes towards 119, 122
  see also diasporas; ethnic minorities
Mikhalkov, Nikita 39, 48–9
military
  and claims about Russian national identity 47
  management of Soviet space programme 133
  representation of; in educational materials and propaganda 121, 122; in post-Soviet films 46–7, 48, 61–3; in Soviet films 27
  and Yuri Gagarin 139
  see also citizenship, obligations conferred by; Great Patriotic War
Miller, Alexei 40
Mokienko, Valerii 248
Mongols
  in Kalmyk culture 209
  in Kazakh historical mythology 156
monuments
  architectural 303, 306, 308, 312–13
  commemorating Great Patriotic War 198–9, 212, 228
  in Elista 197–204
  in Moscow 171, 175, 212
  in post-Soviet Central Asia 154–7
  as represented in post-Soviet literature 177–8
Mormons *see* Church of Jesus Christ of Latter-Day Saints
Morozov, Pavlik, contrast with Gagarin cult 139, 143–4
Moscow
  as heart of homeland 117, 121, 171–3, 212, 218
  places of worship in 212, 218, 300
  post-Soviet development of 175
  in post-Soviet fiction 176–87
  privileged existence in 288
  representation in post-Soviet films 65–6
  in Soviet literature 171–5
  under Stalin 171–5
motherhood
  as modelled through Gagarin cult 140, 144
  representation in films 62–3, 65
  see also childhood; children; family; fatherhood; marriage
motherland
  allegorical representations 114, 203
  citizens' obligations to 25, 27, 97, 98, 100–2, 114, 121, 122, 123
  as focus of common Soviet patriotism 23, 25, 28, 33, 117–19
  Kalmyk attitudes to concept of 203, 209
  with Moscow at centre 117, 121, 171–3, 212, 218

in post-Soviet Russia 34, 114, 119–22
and symbolism of Gagarin cult 139–40
Murmansk, religious activity in 227–8
museums
  and architectural monuments 312–13
  in honour of Yuri Gagarin 137, 140, 141, 142–3
  ideological functions of 73–4
  see also State Museum of the Ethnography of the Peoples of the USSR
music
  in post-Soviet films 63–6
  see also national anthems

naming of children
  in post-Soviet Kalmykia 193, 206
  'red christening' ceremonies 93
  special Soviet names 65, 93
national anthems
  in Russian Federation 34
  Soviet (1944) 29
National Bolshevism 25
nationality, Soviet policy on 3–5, 23–9, 31, 82, 150, 257
  and internal passports 91, 104
  legacy in post-Soviet Central Asia 264–5, 267–8
natural environment
  as focus of patriotism 115, 117, 120, 142, 145, 161
  as feature of Gagarin cult 142, 145
  see also urban environment; village prose
new Soviet man, creation of
  and campaign for atheism 300
  as seen in post-Soviet literature 185
  and Soviet rituals 94
newspapers
  after fall of USSR 240
  and Gagarin cult 134, 136, 140
  and glasnost 238
  readers' letters 95, 134, 140
  role in Soviet atheism campaigns 330–1
  see also media
Niyazov, Saparmurat 153, 157
nostalgia
  challenging of 60, 63, 69–71, 346
  and post-Soviet cinema 56–7, 58, 60, 69, 70–1
  and religion 346
  for Soviet period 8, 23, 34, 55–7, 58, 60, 145, 205
  types of 70
  and village prose 30

obscenity
  cathartic functions of 241–2, 245
  and intellectuals 244–5, 248
  in late and post-Soviet media 238–9, 240–1, 245–9

lexicons of 242–4
use by politicians 244
see also emotion, and cathartic value of swearing
Organisation of Islamic Cooperation (OIC), Russian membership of 218, 219

Parfenov, Leonid 56, 291
passports, internal
  appearance of 96–102
  and discrimination 91
  distribution and entitlement to 91, 96, 98
  functions of 91, 96, 103–4
  and nationality 4, 26, 29, 91, 104
  retention in Russian Federation 103–4
  rituals of presentation 91–2, 96–102
patriotism
  in Belarus 342, 351
  and Great Patriotic War 26–8, 79
  and Stalinist Russocentrism 25, 26–9, 173
  tension between ethnicity and Soviet patriotism 29
Peach, Ceri 215–16
Pelevin, Viktor
  Chapaev and Emptiness 176, 179–80, 181, 186
  and cultural analysis 176, 184, 186
  Empire 'V' 181, 182, 186
  The Life of Insects 186
  and monsters 182–3, 185–7
  and Moscow 176–7, 178–82, 185, 186, 187
  The Sacred Book of the Werewolf 186, 189–90
  A Werewolf's Problems in the Central Belt 185
  Wizard Ignat and People 185
  The Zombification of Soviet Man 185
perestroika
  effect on Russian language 238–9, 242, 247
  and the media 238–9
  representation of in post-Soviet films 67–9
  and status of non-Russian languages 260
Perm 219–25, 230
physical culture 94
pilgrimage
  in post-Soviet Kalmykia 193
  in post-Soviet Russia 334–6
  secular, in connection with Gagarin cult 143
  Soviet measures against 324–33
places of worship
  Buddhist, in post-Soviet Kalmykia 193–7, 207
  Muslim, in Russian Federation 212–31
  post-Soviet Orthodox church restoration 308–13
  Soviet treatment of Orthodox churches 300–7
  see also pilgrimage
Plutser-Sarno, Aleksei 245

Poland, Belarusian attitudes towards 351, 352, 355, 359–60
Popogrebskii, Aleksei, *Koktebel'* 55
Primakov, Yevgeny 217
Protestantism, in Belarus 345–6, 349, 350, 351, 353
public holidays
    commemorating first space flight 135–7
    Memorial Day (Turkmenistan) 153
    Physical Culture Day (USSR) 94
    private preparations for 282
    and scheduling of other rituals 99
    Soviet creation of 92–4, 95
    in Soviet Kalmykia 201
    see also religious festivals
Purges 25
    representation in films 57
Pushkin, Aleksandr, in Kalmyk culture 199
Putin, Vladimir
    characteristics of period of presidency 34, 56, 59, 145
    and invective 244
    and Islam 216, 219, 231
    and Russian Orthodoxy 313

radio
    broadcast of Gagarin space flight 134–5
    significance in Soviet life 135
Rakhmon, Emomali 152, 153, 156, 159
'Ready for Labour and Defence'
    programme 94
religious festivals
    Islamic 218–19
    Orthodox revival of in post-Soviet Russia 335
    under Soviet rule 92–3, 94, 323, 328–30
rituals
    creation of; in early Soviet period 92–4, 336; in late Soviet period 94–6, 98, 336
    performed by Church 299, 307–8
    post-Soviet survival of Soviet rituals 103–4
    Solemn Presentation of the Soviet Passport 91–2, 96–102
    Soviet rites of passage 92–4, 95, 96–104
    see also public holidays; religious festivals; tradition
Roman Catholicism, in Belarus 343, 345, 349, 350, 351, 352, 354
    see also Greek Catholicism, in Belarus
Russian Federation
    internal passports 103–4
    and Islam 212–31
    non-Russian population of 32, 104, 120, 121–2, 208–9, 216–17; *see also* Chechnya and Chechens; Kalmykia

and relations with former Soviet states 86; Belarus 343, 346
and Russian-language education in Central Asia 261
and Russian Orthodox Church 32, 183, 212, 308–14, 334–6
territorial stability of 216–17
Russian language
    in Belarus 344, 350, 352, 353
    criminal argot 241, 242–3, 245–6, 248, 249
    to describe new post-Soviet reality 240–1
    in Kalmykia 206
    and the media 240–1, 245–6
    in post-Soviet Central Asia 157, 254–64, 266, 268–72
    and post-Soviet Russian nationalism 45–7
    Soviet emphasis on proper usage 239–40, 242
    as Soviet *lingua franca* 114, 118
    and vernacular religion 239
    Western influences on 240–1
    see also obscenity
Russian Orthodox Church
    and 1917 revolution 299–300
    and Islam 212, 218
    in pre-revolutionary society 299
    in Russian Federation 32, 183, 212, 308–14, 334, 335
    and Soviet rule 300–8, 322–4, 325, 326, 328
Russian Orthodoxy, vernacular practices of 239, 321–36
    see also Belarusian Orthodox Church; Russian Orthodox Church
Russocentrism
    as propagated by Soviet museums 74, 85
    in Russian Federation 116, 119–22
    under Stalin 24–9, 116, 132

St Petersburg, religious buildings and activity in 308–13
    see also Leningrad
Saratov, religious activity in 229
schools *see* education; textbooks
science *see* science fiction; space exploration
science fiction 131–2
Scriabin, Alexander 130
Second World War *see* Great Patriotic War
Sergiev Posad 212
Seton-Watson, Hugh 40
Shaburova, Ol'ga 66
Shakhnazarov, Karen, *Vanished Empire* 67
shortage economy
    as characteristic of late socialism 279
    efforts to circumvent 283, 289
    jokes about 283–4

post-Soviet memories of 279–86, 288–9
regional variations in 288
and social identity 284–6, 288–9
and Soviet social order 279, 285–8
Slavic culture
and identity in Belarus 343, 346, 350–1,
352, 355
and post-war rhetoric 79–80
and religion 346, 350–1, 355
as represented in Soviet museums 74, 79–81
Smith, Anthony 37, 41–2, 43
Smith, Graham 150, 354
'socialist nations' 3
Sokurov, Aleksandr, *Aleksandra* 46–7
space exploration
conspiracy theories about 129
in early Soviet films 131–2
as herald of communism 132
media coverage of first flight 134–7
secrecy surrounding 133
and utopianism 130–3
see also Gagarin Yuri
sport *see* physical culture
Stalin era
and development of Moscow 171–5
in late and post-Soviet film 57, 60–1
and nationalities policy 4, 24–9
and patriotic education 117
in post-Soviet literature 182–7
and religion 300–5, 321, 322–3
and repression of Kalmyks 192, 198–9, 202
and rituals 94
and technology 132
see also de-Stalinization; terror, Stalinist
State Museum of the Ethnography of the Peoples
of the USSR
'aestheticization' of 80–1
bias towards Slavic nationalities 74, 79–81
after collapse of USSR 86
and colonial perspective on USSR 83–5
and promotion of unified Soviet nationality
82–5
and Soviet Russocentrism 74, 85
state interference in 73–7
visitor responses to 77, 79, 80, 81
stiliagi, representation in films 63–6
swearing *see* obscenity

Tajikistan
attitudes to Russo-Soviet rule 152–3
attitudes to Tajik diaspora 163–4
celebration of national culture 156
educational system 258–61, 263–8
language policy and non-Tajik population 159,
258–61, 263–8

and religion 160–1
territorial ambition 162–3
Tajiks, as minority in other Central Asian states
163–4, 258–60, 265–6, 269–72
Tamerlane 155
Tatarstan 227
television
broadcasting of religious events in Russian
Federation 218–19
and nostalgia for Soviet past 56, 58, 291
role in Gagarin cult 135–6
see also media
terror, Stalinist 173–4
and post-Soviet literature 182–5
and religion 322–3
textbooks
and non-Russians in Russian Federation 121–2
in post-Soviet Central Asia 261–6
in Russian Empire 116, 122–3
in Russian Federation 116, 119–22, 123
and Stalinist propaganda 132
in USSR 116–19, 122, 123
Thaw *see* Khrushchev era
Tlostanova, Madina 39, 41
Todorovskii, Valerii, *Hipsters* 59
Tolstoy, Alexei 172–4
toponyms, alterations to 114, 151–2,
204–6
film discussion of 55
in honour of Yuri Gagarin 137
tourism
and Gagarin cult 143, 145
and religious pilgrimage 334–6
tradition
in Central Asian nation-building 154–7
in post-Soviet Kalmykia 195–6
revival of in post-Stalin era 307–8
as sign of backwardness 76, 84–5
see also public holidays; religious festivals;
rituals; Russian Orthodoxy, vernacular
practices of
Turkmenbashi *see* Niyazov, Saparmurat
Turkmenistan
attitudes to Russo-Soviet rule 153
language policy 158–9
nationalist literature 157
policy towards Turkmen diaspora 164
religion in 160

Uniate Church *see* Greek Catholicism
urban environment
of Elista 192–207
in post-Soviet literature 176–87
in Soviet propaganda 171–5
utopianism

utopianism (cont.)
and heroism 133
and Moscow 173–4
and patriotic education 113–14
and technology 130–2
Uyghur 163
Uzbekistan
alleged aggression against Tajiks
152–3
and aspirations to regional leadership 161
attitudes to Russo-Soviet rule 153–4
attitudes to Uzbek diaspora 164
cultural wealth 154–5
educational system 258–60, 261–3, 272
language policy 158–9, 260, 261–3, 272
and non-Uzbek population 163–4, 165–6, 263,
272
and religion 160
and Tajik territorial ambition 162–3
Uzbeks, as minority in other Central Asian states
164, 258–60, 264, 265, 266–9,
270–1

vampires, in post-Soviet literature 181–7
Veresaev, V. V. 93
village prose 30, 38
violence
against religious believers, in Russian
Federation 212, 227
in post-Soviet film 67–9, 70
see also crime; terror, Stalinist
virgin lands campaign 132
Vladivostok, religious activity in 228–9

war *see* First World War; Great Patriotic War;
military
West
Belarusian attitudes towards 353, 355
influence in Kalmykia 206
influence on Russian-language culture 239,
240–1, 246–7
and post-Soviet film-makers 47–9
and post-Soviet media 240
Stalinist hostility to 28
Wierzbicka, Anna 246
women
role of according to Soviet propaganda 140–1
see also family; marriage; motherhood

xenophobia
and post-Soviet film-makers 38
under Stalin 28

Yeltsin, Boris 34, 244
and freedom of speech 246–7
Yevtushenko, Yevgenii 23
young people
and age-restricted activities 96
and physical culture 94
and sectarian violence 212, 227
see also adulthood, initiation into; childhood;
children; youth culture
youth culture, film representations of 63–6

Zaya Pandita 202–3
Zhel'vis, Vladimir 241–2, 245, 246
Zhirinovskii, Vladimir 243

Lightning Source UK Ltd.
Milton Keynes UK
UKHW021233040321
379692UK00021B/396